GW01508018

POSTMODERN INSURGENCIES

Also by Ronaldo Munck

ARGENTINA: From Anarchism to Peronism

BELFAST IN THE THIRTIES: An Oral History (*with B. Rolston*)

CRITICAL DEVELOPMENT THEORY: Contributions to a New Paradigm (*co-editor*)

IRELAND: Nation, State and Class Conflict

LABOUR WORLDWIDE IN THE ERA OF GLOBALIZATION (*co-editor*)

LATIN AMERICA: The Transition to Democracy

MARX @ 2000: Late Marxist Perspectives

POLITICS AND DEPENDENCY IN THE THIRD WORLD: The Case of Latin America

POLITICS, CULTURE AND POSTMODERNISM IN LATIN AMERICA (*co-editor*)

REVOLUTIONARY TRENDS IN LATIN AMERICA

THE DIFFICULT DIALOGUE: Marxism and Nationalism

THE IRISH ECONOMY: Results and Prospects

THE NEW INTERNATIONAL LABOUR STUDIES: An Introduction

Also by Purnaka L. de Silva

POLITICAL VIOLENCE AND ITS CULTURAL CONSTRUCTIONS Representational and Narrative 'Realities' in Times of War (*forthcoming*)

Postmodern Insurgencies

Political Violence, Identity Formation and Peacemaking in Comparative Perspective

Edited by

Ronaldo Munck
Reader in Political Sociology
University of Liverpool

and

Purnaka L. de Silva
Lecturer in Politics
Queen's University of Belfast
Northern Ireland

Foreword by Adama Dieng

First published in Great Britain 2000 by
MACMILLAN PRESS LTD
Houndmills, Basingstoke, Hampshire RG21 6XS and London
Companies and representatives throughout the world

A catalogue record for this book is available from the British Library.

ISBN 0-333-71997-2

 First published in the United States of America 2000 by
ST. MARTIN'S PRESS, INC.,
Scholarly and Reference Division,
175 Fifth Avenue, New York, N.Y. 10010

ISBN 0-312-22692-2

Library of Congress Cataloging-in-Publication Data
Postmodern insurgencies : political violence, identity formation and
peacemaking in comparative perspective / edited by Ronaldo Munck and
Purnaka L. de Silva
p. cm.
Includes bibliographical references and index.
ISBN 0-312-22692-2 (cloth)
1. Insurgency. 2. Political violence. 3. Conflict management.
4. Reconciliation. 5. Group identity. 6. Post-communism.
I. Munck, Ronaldo. II. De Silva, Purnaka L.
JC328.5.P65 1999
303.6'09'049–DC21   99–15423
                                                                        CIP

Selection and editorial matter © Ronaldo Munck and Purnaka L. de Silva 2000
Foreword © Adama Dieng 2000
Chapters 1 and 5 © Ronaldo Munck 2000
Chapters 9 and 12 © Purnaka L. de Silva 2000
Chapters 2–4, 6–8, 10, 11 © Macmillan Press Ltd 2000

All rights reserved. No reproduction, copy or transmission of this publication may be made without written permission.

No paragraph of this publication may be reproduced, copied or transmitted save with written permission or in accordance with the provisions of the Copyright, Designs and Patents Act 1988, or under the terms of any licence permitting limited copying issued by the Copyright Licensing Agency, 90 Tottenham Court Road, London W1P 0LP.

Any person who does any unauthorised act in relation to this publication may be liable to criminal prosecution and civil claims for damages.

The authors have asserted their rights to be identified as the authors of this work in accordance with the Copyright, Designs and Patents Act 1988.

This book is printed on paper suitable for recycling and made from fully managed and sustained forest sources.

10 9 8 7 6 5 4 3 2 1
09 08 07 06 05 04 03 02 01 00

Printed and bound in Great Britain by
Antony Rowe Ltd, Chippenham, Wiltshire

*For our friends, past and present,
who made this book
possible and worthwhile*

Contents

Foreword by Adama Dieng	ix
Preface	xi
Notes on the Contributors	xiv
List of Abbreviations and Acronyms	xvii

1. Deconstructing Terror: Insurgency, Repression and Peace
   Ronaldo Munck — 1

2. Private, Public and Political: Learning Processes of the Revolutionary Left in Argentina
   María Matilde Ollier — 14

3. Political Processes and Identity Formation in El Salvador: From Armed Left to Democratic Left
   Gerardo L. Munck and Dexter Boniface — 38

4. South Africa: From 'Racial Conflict' to Democratic Settlement?
   Alan Emery and Rupert Taylor — 54

5. Northern Ireland: From Long War to Difficult Peace?
   Ronaldo Munck — 71

6. Ethiopia: Success Story or State of Chaos?
   Aregawi Berhe — 96

7. Palestinian Authority, Israeli Rule: From Transitional to Permanent Arrangement?
   Mouin Rabbani — 125

8. Somalia After the Cold War: Anarchic Factionalism, Intervention or Peacemaking?
   Abdullah A. Mohamoud — 148

9. Sri Lankan Futures: Conflicts, Alternatives and Twenty-First Century Possibilities
   Purnaka L. de Silva — 167

10. Women, War and Peace: Engendering Conflict in Post-Structuralist Perspective
    Honor Fagan — 201

11 Islamisms: Globalisation, Religion and Power
   Azza M. Karam 217

12 Post-Cold War Futures: Peacemaking, Conflict Management and Humanitarian Action
   Purnaka L. de Silva 237

Index 271

Foreword

I take great pleasure in writing the foreword to this timely collection of essays, which examine present-day realities from an illuminating comparative perspective, within the broader framework of a global approach to questions of conflict, peacemaking and humanitarian action. And at a time when the international community and multilateral agencies are grappling with problems related to peacemaking, conflict resolution, democracy, human rights and transitional justice, this publication will prove to be of critical importance.

Ideologically-based insurgencies, political violence and armed conflicts, have been part and parcel of the Cold War in various regions of the world. The Cold War was a phenomenon characterised by massive violations of human rights and the rule of law, by all sides, and the existence of undemocratic and repressive rule by despots. Furthermore, the zeal of combating real or perceived enemies overcame any attempts at accountability. In addition, due to the dynamics of geopolitical and economic considerations, the international community did not act cohesively or consistently to promote peace, democracy and global good governance. The time for a sea change arrived with the end of the Cold War, which also brought with it a new set of problems, such as violent conflicts along ethno-political and politico-religious lines.

The new possibilities of transition to democratic rule in the twenty-first century have therefore been accompanied by tremendous challenges, as well as hopes and aspirations. And in order to overcome these challenges, and fulfil the hopes and aspirations of many, it is imperative that a thorough understanding of conflicts and peacemaking is combined with genuine efforts at a radical overhaul of the global system of humanitarian action and justice.

As a response, the International Commission of Jurists (ICJ), for its part, has been concerned with the fact that major violations of human rights occurring in all parts of the world take place during periods of 'emergency' rule – which has been defined as 'the suspension of or departure from legal normality in response to political, economic or social crises'. The ICJ has, therefore, conducted in-depth research into the effects of states of emergency on human rights during situations of ethnic conflict and political violence in Sri Lanka, Rwanda, Liberia and Congo, to name but a few of the countries studied.

Needless to say, the comparative essays in this volume are a definite step in the right direction. And whatever the past and present politics of the contributors, one thing is very clear and that is their unity *vis-à-vis* the importance of democratic dialogue, human dignity and justice. There is no doubt that the variety as well as the richness of experiences contained in this book will certainly be a useful guide and tool for practitioners, diplomats, academics, NGO leaders and students, who are concerned with issues of political violence, identity formation, peacemaking and global reform. It will also provide food for thought for all those engaged in more popular endeavours which are aimed at a reorganisation of civil society along democratic lines and trying to achieve peace and justice throughout the world. This book will also assist jurists and other members of the legal profession to reach a shared vision and new ideas for strengthening their role in society at the dawn of a new century.

ADAMA DIENG
Secretary-General
International Commission of Jurists
Geneva
Switzerland

Preface

As we settle into a post-Cold War, post-nationalist and postmodern era, there is a danger of slipping into complacency with regard to the conflicts that remain active across the globe. In the warm glow projected by the imperial heartlands, many have become anaesthetised in relation to conflict, war and human suffering. Perhaps the most (in)famous case is Baudrillard's attempt to assert that the Persian Gulf War did not really happen, that it was just a media event, a CNN spectacular as it were. This book brings together a number of political thinkers who, directly or indirectly, have been close enough to the 'front-line' to know that war is still real and that a just peace is worth struggling for. Apart from this closeness to their subject matter, the authors are bound by their acute sense of self-critical realism. If nothing else, the post-everything era has made us all a little less sanguine about our expectations of social transformation and the arrival of the political 'promised land' in a new world order.

Ronaldo Munck (Chapter 1) opens this collection with some general methodological reflections on how best to understand the interlinked processes of insurgency, repression and peacemaking. In deconstructing conventional approaches to 'terrorism', Munck advances a radical post-structuralist alternative, where the formation and reconstruction of political identities is seen as crucial to our understanding of insurgency, in this ostensibly postmodern era we are living in. Subsequent chapters seek to 'flesh out' this novel perspective.

María Matilde Ollier (Chapter 2) continues developing the theme of political identities in a meticulous account of the changes which the Revolutionary Left underwent in Argentina, following the military coup of 1976. Based on testimony gathered from survivors of the 'dirty war' waged by the generals, Ollier allows us to glimpse the painful interface between the private and the public in the making of post-insurgent political identities.

Gerardo L. Munck and Dexter Boniface (Chapter 3) also focus on identity formation and political processes, in this case examining events in El Salvador – where an armed left gradually became committed to the democratic political process in a complex shift of identities. This is a transformation that exemplifies in many ways the position of the left in Latin America, which shifted from an insurrectional to a constitutional mode of operation during the course of the 1980s – a process which Munck and Boniface's case study helps illuminate.

Alan Emery and Rupert Taylor (Chapter 4) deal with a paradigmatic former insurgent movement in the African continent, namely, the African National Congress (ANC), which also became wedded to political compromise and constitutional legality. Emery and Taylor approach the recent transition to democracy in South Africa through a critical examination of the 'race war' theories, which for a long time dominated political debate and fashioned deeply polarised identities.

Ronaldo Munck (Chapter 5) examines the long-running conflict in Northern Ireland via a discourse-analytic approach to Irish Republican ideology. He examines in detail how the 'peace process' in Ireland emerged and the tensions it is now subject to in the late 1990s. This is one insurgent movement which many (if not most) observers thought could not be amenable to a democratic settlement and is thus an exemplary case study of the difficulties but also possibilities for conflict resolution.

Aregawi Berhe (Chapter 6), in a key insider's account of the Tigray People's Liberation Front (TPLF), provides readers with a critical review of war and peace in contemporary Ethiopia. Taking us behind the political rhetoric and apparent success story of the TPLF-led Ethiopian People's Revolutionary Democratic Front (EPRDF) regime in Addis Ababa, Aregawi paints a stark picture of an old-style liberation movement's track record in a new era – which must provide food for thought for its supporters and for other uncritical followers of insurgent movements who claim to be struggling for 'liberation.' He also discusses the root causes underlying the current border war between Eritrea and Ethiopia.

Mouin Rabbani (Chapter 7) develops a parallel theme in relation to the long struggle of the Palestinian people to establish their own homeland. The saga of the Palestinian Authority and the Oslo peace agreements is fraught with controversy. Rabbani provides a close-up view of what Arafat's transitional arrangements have actually meant for people on the ground and current events in the region are greatly clarified. His analysis includes a critical evaluation of the future prospects of the 'peace process', and the role of the US government and State Department as 'honest brokers'.

Abdullah A. Mohamoud (Chapter 8) examines the background to the fragmentation of the Somali state and presents a critical account of future possibilities for peace and stability. Mohamoud's recent interviews with key 'warlords' give credence to his argument, which also examines their role in the light of peacemaking and traditional structures of consensus-building. Somalia is an important comparative case study and has many lessons for the international community and multilateral agencies, in the event of future interventions in similar situations of armed conflict and humanitarian disaster.

Purnaka L. de Silva (Chapter 9) examines the roots of ethnonationalist conflict in Sri Lanka and explores alternative prospects for a future settlement. In a dense narrative, with much first-hand testimony, de Silva takes us closer to an understanding of Tamil separatist-nationalist paramilitaries and other participants in this bitter and deeply divisive conflict. This chapter is also a contribution to the process of establishing a peaceful multicultural and multiracial society in Sri Lanka.

Honor Fagan (Chapter 10) demonstrates how the twin processes of war and peace are always gendered. She argues that a gendered analysis is a prerequisite for a critical understanding of insurgency and the formation of political identities. In opposition to more common gender-blind accounts, Fagan illustrates through various case studies how cultural formations of gender and war intersect at all levels. This chapter can be seen as an implicit critique of some of the other accounts of insurgency in this book which ignore or overlook the gender dimension.

Azza M. Karam (Chapter 11) also broadens our analysis through a measured consideration of the international political discourse of Islamisms. Going beyond the stereotypical portrayals of 'Islamism' in the Western media and the dire forecasts of defence strategists, Karam sets the topic in the context of globalisation and postmodern dynamics. She provides a critical but well-informed account of a heterogeneous and rather diverse 'movement' – which has often been a byword for 'international terrorism' and even posited as a big enough problem to be an alternative post-Cold War enemy to the now defunct Soviet bloc.

Purnaka L. de Silva (Chapter 12) rounds off the volume with a wide-ranging consideration of the future of peacemaking and conflict management in the late twentieth century. His discussion touches on the moral, ethical and legal responsibilities of the international community, multilateral agencies and NGOs – arguing that double standards, lack of political will and mismanagement are not uncommon in the history of such engagement. De Silva goes on to argue that the international justice system is cumbersome, lacks proper financing and will not have the capacity to handle the tasks at hand (as illustrated by the Bosnian and Rwandan examples) unless radical reform is initiated to ensure that transitional justice is swift, legally binding, exacting and oblivious to the position of perpetrators.

Notes on the Contributors

Aregawi Berhe is former head of the Tigrayan People's Liberation Front (TPLF), during the decade and a half-long liberation struggle against the Derg military regime that was led by the now exiled dictator Colonel Mengistu Haile Mariam. Having resigned from the TPLF shortly before the capture of state power, he is currently engaged in the democratic opposition politics of Ethiopia and is also working in applied research on democratisation in Africa.

Dexter Boniface is a Doctoral Candidate in the Department of Political Science at the University of Urbana-Champaign. In his dissertation he examines the relationships between processes of economic reform, labour migration and democratic consolidation in Brazil.

Purnaka L. de Silva is a Lecturer in Politics at Queen's University, Belfast, and also Director of Finance and Planning at the University's Centre for the Study of Ethnic Conflict. He was previously at the University of Amsterdam. He is also attached to the International War-related Trauma and Humanitarian Intervention Trust (IWTHI), a North–South/South–South collaborative initiative aimed at human capacity-building and policy-making in divided societies. He is author of *Political Violence and its Cultural Constructions: Representational and Narrative 'Realities' in Times of War* (forthcoming) and a number of specialist books and journal articles on Tamil paramilitary nationalisms. He is Series Editor of *Ethnic Conflict Studies* (Pluto Press).

Alan Emery is a Doctoral Candidate in the Department of Sociology at the University of California, Los Angeles. In his writings he focuses on the South African transition from apartheid to democracy.

Honor Fagan is Lecturer in Sociology at the National University of Ireland, Maynooth. She has carried out research and published in the subject areas of gender and development, and cultural politics and identity formation. She is author of *Culture, Politics and Irish School Dropouts: Constructing Political Identities* (Bergin and Garvey) and is currently working on a book on globalisation and culture.

Azza M. Karam is Lecturer in Politics at the School of Politics and Programme Manager at the Centre for the Study of Ethnic Conflict, Queen's University, Belfast. She previously held the post of Senior Programme Officer at the International Institute for Democracy and Electoral Assistance (International IDEA) in Stockholm. She is author of *Women, Islamisms and the State: Contemporary Feminisms in Egypt* (Macmillan) and editor of *Women in Parliaments: Beyond Numbers* (International IDEA 1998), as well as contributing a number of other articles in books, journals and newspapers on political Islam, comparative politics and gender-related issues. She is Series Editor of *Critical Studies on Islam* (Pluto Press).

Abdullah A. Mohamoud is attached to the Department of International Relations, University of Amsterdam. His doctoral research and numerous contributions to journals and newspapers, focus on the fragmentation of the Somali nation and related issues. He is also a regular contributor to the magazine *West Africa*.

Gerardo L. Munck is Associate Professor of Political Science at the University of Illinois at Urbana-Champaign. He is author of *Authoritarianism and Democratization: Soldiers and Workers in Argentina 1976–83* (Pennsylvania University Press) and numerous articles in *Comparative Politics, Journal of InterAmerican Studies and World Affairs, Latin American Research Review, Sociology* and *Third World Quarterly* among others. He is currently working on a book on regime dynamics in Latin America during the twentieth century.

Ronaldo Munck is Reader in Political Sociology at the University of Liverpool, having previously held appointments at the University of Ulster and the University of Durban – Westville, South Africa. His work on Ireland includes *The Irish Economy: Results and Prospects* (Pluto Press) and *Ireland: Nation, State and Class Struggle* (Westview Press), and, with Bill Rolston, *Belfast in the Thirties: An Oral History* (Blackstaff Press). His wider interests include Latin American and Third World politics and contemporary social theory. His current research focuses on the impact of globalisation on labour.

María Matilde Ollier obtained her PhD at the University of Notre Dame and is author of *Dimensions of the Political Learning Process: The Private, the Public and the Political. The Survivors of the Argentinian Revolutionary Left, 1966–1996* (University of Notre Dame) as well as several books in Spanish. She is currently advisor to Graciela Fernandez Meijide, the leader of the left coalition in Argentina.

Mouin Rabbani is a Palestinian researcher based both in the West Bank, Palestine and The Hague, the Netherlands. He is the author of numerous articles on the Israeli–Palestinian conflict, which have appeared in *Al-Ahram Weekly, Arab Studies Quarterly, Encyclopaedia of the Modern Middle East, Journal of Palestine Studies, le Monde Diplomatique,* and *Third World Quarterly*.

Rupert Taylor is Senior Lecturer in Political Studies at the University of the Witwatersrand, Johannesburg. He has written widely on South African politics in books and journals, including *Telos, Race and Class, Transformation, South African Sociological Review* and *Critical Arts*. Currently he is editor of *Politikon: South African Journal of Political Studies*.

List of Abbreviations and Acronyms

APPO	All Amhara People's Organisation
ALF	After Liberation Front
ANC	African National Congress
ANDM	Amhara National Democratic Movement
ARDF	Afar Revolutionary Democratic Front
ARDU	Afar Revolutionary Democratic Union
ARENA	National Republican Alliance
CAFPDE	Coalition of Alternative Forces for Peace and Democracy in Ethiopia
CD	Democratic Convergence
CEDES	Centre of Studies on Society and State
CEO	Chief Executive Officer
CISEA	Centre for Social and Economic Research
CLASCSO	Social Science Latin American Council
COEDF	Coalition of Ethiopian Democratic Forces
COSATU	Congress of South African Trade Unions
CP	Conservative Party
CPJ	Committee to Protect Journalists
CR	Council of Representatives
CRM	Revolutionary Coordinating Committee of the Masses
CTT	General Workers' Confederation
DEPDU	Southern Ethiopian People's Democratic Coalition
DMLE	Democratic Movement for the Liberation of Eritea
DOP	Israeli–Palestinian Declaration of Principles on Interim Self Government Arrangements
EDU	Ethiopian Democratic Union
EHRCO	Ethiopian Human Rights Council
ELF	Eritrean Liberation Front
ELF-RC	Eritrean Liberation Front – Revolutionary Council
EPDP	Eelam People's Democratic Party
EPDM	Ethiopian People's Democratic Movement
EPLF	Eritrean People's Liberation Front
EPRDF	Ethiopian People's Revolutionary Democratic Front
EPRLF	Eelam People's Revolutionary Liberation Front
EPRP	Ethiopian People's Revolutionary Party
ERP	People's Revolutionary Army

ETA	Basque Homeland and Liberty
FALANGE	Anti-Communist Armed Forces of Liberation by Wars of Elimination
FATEH	Military Wing of the PLO
FDR	Democratic Revolutionary Front
FIS	Front Islamique du Salut
FLACSO	Latin American School of Social Science
FMLN	Farabundo Martí Front for National Liberation
FOM	Free Officers Movement
FPL	Popular Liberation Front
FSNL	Frente Sandinista de Liberación Nacional
GIA	Armed Islamic Group
HAMAS	Islamic Resistance Movement
IFJ	International Federation of Journalists
IFP	Inkatha Freedom Party
IGAD	Inter-Government Authority and Development
IISS	International Institute for Strategic Studies
INLA	Irish National Liberation Army
IPKE	Indian Peace Keeping Force
IRA	Irish Republican Army
IRP	Islamic Renaissance Party
ISI	Inter-Services Intelligence Agency (Pakistan)
JVP	People's Libration Front
LTTE	Liberation Tigers of Tamil Eelam
MEDHINE	Ethiopian Medhine Democratic Front
MEISON	All Ethiopian Socialust Movement
MK	Umkhonto we Sizwe
MLLT	Marxist Leninist League of Tigray
MNCPE	Multi-National Congress Party of Ethiopia
MNO	Movimento Nacional de Opinión
MNR	National Revolutionary Movement
MPLA	Movimento Popular de Liberação Angolana
MPSC	Popular Social Christian Movement
NATO	North Atlantic Treaty Organisation
NP	National Party
NSC	National Salvation Council
OAU	Organisation of African Unity
OLF	Oromo Liberation Front
ONC	Oromo National Congress
ONLF	Ogadeni National Liberation Front
OPDO	Oromo People's Democratic Organisation

ORDEN	National Democratic Organisation
OSCE	Organisation for Security and Cooperation in Europe
PA	People's Alliance
PAC	Pan-Africanist Congress
PCS	Communist Party of El Salvador
PD	Democratic Party
PFLP	Popular Front for the Liberation of Palestine
PFP	Progressive Federal Party
PKK	Kurdish Workers' Party
PLO	Palestinian Liberation Organisation
PLOTE	People's Liberation Organisation of Tamil Eelam
PRT/ERR	Partido Revolucionario de los Trabajadores Ejército Revolucionario del Pueblo
PRTC	Central American Worker's Revolutionary Party
PWG	People's War Group
RUC	Royal Ulster Constabulary
RN	National Resistance
SACP	South African Communist Party
SADF	South African Defence Force
SDLP	Catholic Social Democratic Labour Party
SEPDC	Southern Ethiopia People's Democratic Coalition
SLPF	Sri Lanka Freedom Party
STF	Special Task Force (Sri Lanka)
TAND	Tigrian Alliance for National Democracy
TELO	Tamil Eelam Liberation Organisation
TGE	Transitional Government of Ethiopia
TLF	Tigray Liberation Front
TNO	Tigrayan National Organisation
TNRT	Tamil National Retrieval Troops
TPDM	Tigray People's Democratic Movement
TPLF	Tigray People's Liberation Front
TRC	Truth and Reconciliation Commission
TTE	Tigray Tigrigni Ethiopia
UDF	United Democratic Front
ULFA	United Liberation Front of Assam
UNITA	National Union for the Total Independence of Angola
UNP	United National Party
ZANU	Zimbabwe African National Movement

1
Deconstructing Terror: Insurgency, Repression and Peace

Ronaldo Munck

To situate the various narratives of political violence and identity formation which follow, this introduction examines some guiding concepts. The objective is to guide the reader and interested parties through the conceptual minefields associated with studies on 'terrorism', insurgency and the search for peace. Theoretical abstractions may seem like a diversion from practice, but given the confusion in this area introduced by various agendas, clarification may be seen as a necessary prerequisite to intervention. There is now considerable attention paid to the phenomenon of 'postmodern' war and according to the widely respected work of Van Creveld (1991), *On Future War*, this new form of warfare would have certain defining characteristics:

- it will not be conducted by formal armies, with various irregular formations prevailing;
- there are few time constraints on the insurgents who can afford to fight a 'long war';
- the insurgents will usually operate below the level of sophistication of the state's weapon systems;
- postmodern conflicts will not be focused on territory.

In a sense, what is happening is that the old distinction between low-intensity (guerrilla) warfare and high-intensity (regular) war has faded. Conventional military theory and diplomatic practice are a poor guide to understanding the new postmodern forms of conflict. The new wars are informal rather than formal, open-ended rather than punctual engagements and community- rather than army-based. That they are crude and cruel probably makes them no different from any other war, but there is no pretence that war is based on science or rationality in these cases. If the big industrial era land-based wars are probably over – with only India and China probably remaining in the running given their vast and disciplined armies, high degree of nationalistic fervour and having the stamina to sustain the necessarily high casualty rates of old fashioned warfare – the new conflicts, called 'postmodern' for want of a better word, are coming into their own. Postmodern wars call for postmodern peace and here again, the old ways are superseded, I think. Cultural and identity factors come to the fore, and war strategies are more flexible and open-ended. My own emphasis here will, however, be less on the phenomena of postmodern war and more on post-structuralist forms of analysis which I believe are essential for understanding the new forms of identity formation, conflict and conflict resolution that exist in this era of globalised postmodernism which we live in.

Discourse and terror

For discourse theory, language can no longer be viewed as a simple instrument of communication. Following Pêcheux (1982) I would argue, rather, that words take on meaning in conflicting discourses and not in common language. More specifically, language takes on meaning and discourses are constructed through struggle. Thus a word such as 'terrorism' can only be seen as part of a wider discourse. It must, furthermore, be seen as the site of a struggle and it is not just an innocent, value-free word, but one invested with considerable political charge. Moreover, all discourses are ideologically positioned and none are neutral (Macdonell 1986:59).

For raw material to pursue this line of enquiry, I turn to the prolific literature on 'political terrorism' (for example, Wardlaw 1982). As an example, chosen for its liberal setting and overall discourse, I focus on a 1980 Council of Europe conference report titled *Defence of Democracy Against Terrorism* (Council of Europe 1981). We are told by the delegate from the Spanish state that 'terrorism' is not only 'a general threat to the stability of democratic institutions' but represents 'a war declared against Western civilisation' (Fanjul 1981:2). Insurgency is thus equated with barbarism, Satanism or whatever we humans fear most. Citizens everywhere are in danger as 'the blows it strikes grow in savagery' and 'become ever more treacherous and bloodthirsty' (ibid.:3). When captured, the 'terrorist' should not be afforded too many legal niceties, but 'dealt with energetically, in keeping with his dangerous cunning and indeed malevolence' (ibid.:8). Society must deal with this creature in terms of 'his criminal and psychic characteristics ... his fanaticism and his pathological desperation' (ibid.:9).

The British delegate to the Council of Europe conference on 'terrorism', Paul Wilkinson, an academic specialist on the matter, developed the same theme. Using Ireland as his example, he declared confidently that the terrorists 'represent nothing but their own hate-filled and criminal mentalities', with their only 'objective' being 'to impose their own petty tyranny of the gun and the bomb' (Wilkinson 1981:4). Ironically, in view of the subsequent peace process, he argued that 'a democratic government which negotiates with [these] murderers loses ... its moral right to govern' (ibid.:6). The 'terrorist' is thus clearly anathema, stigmatised and placed beyond the pale of civilised society. This discourse is brought up to date by the latest offering by Walter Laqueur (1996) on 'Postmodern Terrorism'. Apart from the threat to society from the likes of the 'Unabomber' and the 'Restoration Ecologists', Laqueur believes that the likes of the *Partia Karkaris Kurdistan* (Kurdish Workers' Party or PKK), the Irish Republican Army (IRA), Basque separatists of *Euskadi ta Askatasuna* (Basque Homeland and Liberty or ETA) and separatist 'Tamil Tigers' of Sri Lanka (Liberation Tigers of Tamil Eelam or LTTE) 'on the verge of defeat or acting on apocalyptic visions may not hesitate to apply all destructive means at their disposal' (ibid.:36). Needless to say, this cryptic statement conjures up dark images of nuclear destruction, chemical and biological warfare, not to mention cyber-guerrillas. It is all a seamless web of threatening, irrational, millenarian behaviour that we are presented with. And all the 'right-minded' reader comes away with, or is intended to come away with, is fear.

Michel Foucault's history of 'madness' (Foucault 1965) is probably the best guide towards deconstructing the 'terrorist' discourse and its concomitant political enterprise (cf. Herman and O'Sullivan 1989). Neither discourse can detach itself from the conditions of its own emergence and, as Visker puts it, 'having arisen as a moral practice ... [psychology] can only lay claim to being a science by forgetting the stigma of its own conditions of emergence, a stigma which has never disappeared' (Visker 1995:21). Often, as at the European Council of Ministers, the academic experts do not pretend scientific certainty, but don instead the mantle of witch-finders (or exorcists), reminiscent of the Spanish Inquisition of a bygone era. The discourse of 'terrorism' becomes itself a disseminator of terror as with the Argentinian general, who infamously declared in 1976 that 'First we are going to kill all of the subversives; then their collaborators; then their sympathisers; then the indifferent; and finally the timid.' Discourses can now be seen to be closely related to systems or modalities of power. In this Foucaldian conception of power, discourse and language are of central importance to the social processes of modern society and the controlled management of populations. Conversely, we also need to pay more attention to the question of power in discourse analysis. What I have begun to do in this section has been to sketch out the 'regime of materiality' of the discourse of 'terrorism', as a preliminary step to developing more adequate tools for the understanding of insurgency.

Constructing insurgency

For one counter-insurgency 'expert', Peter Janke, Irish Republicanism has attracted to the movement 'petty criminals and thugs', it relies on 'young boys and women' and its 'godfathers' use 'the innocent, the impressionable and the disadvantaged in the most unscrupulous manner' (Janke 1979:15). The motivation for such pathological behaviour is, according to Janke, 'an embittered idealism which goes back generations' (ibid.). No doubt, all insurgent movements have attracted such adverse and patently implausible comments at one time or another. In the Irish situation, the counter-factual case made itself present the following year, when ten IRA prisoners held at the Long Kesh or 'Maze' prison in Northern Ireland died in a drawn-out and dramatic hunger strike. Such commitment to a cause, whether one would agree with its objectives or not, could hardly be the action of 'criminals and thugs' or the 'innocent and impressionable'. To construct a more adequate image of insurgency, however, we need to turn to the question of identity and the formation of *political identities* in particular.

It was once common to believe that identity was a function of predefined social roles, that it was part of the innate 'essence' which constitutes a 'person'. Today, we are more likely to view identity as something more unstable and fluid than this. Thus, for example, Kwame Appiah's essay on African identities seeks to deconstruct the notion of a unitary, essentially fixed African identity, with its essentialised and totalising concept of group identity (Appiah 1995). The new post-structuralist views stress, rather, the fractured nature of subjectivity and the concept of multiple identities. As Chantal Mouffe writes, 'The "identity" of such a multiple and contradictory subject is therefore always contingent and precarious' (Mouffe 1993:77). This anti-essentialist approach to identity implies 'acknowledging the contingency and ambiguity of every identity' (ibid.:76). As against the notion of subject as a rational and transparent agent, this position leads us to examine the multiple relations of subordination people are subjected to and the complexities of contestation that emerge from this dynamic. Thus Irish Republicans can be seen as subject to at least four sets of interpellations, including nationalism, Catholicism, socialism and a 'physical force' ideology. We cannot assume a unity or homogeneity of these elements and need instead to examine their unstable and always constructed conflictual convergence at different historical periods. Rather than seeking orderly binary oppositions, we should perhaps be more open to ambiguity, multiplicity and fragmentation in analysing political identities.

Many of the chapters in this book are about narratives of identity formation, in particular how insurgent political identities are constructed, deconstructed and reconstructed through struggle. Identities emerge through difference and are always relational. Thus, identity is always partial and contingent. In other words, there is no identity outside of its context or, as Ernesto Laclau puts it, 'Identity depends on conditions of existence which are contingent, its relationship with them is absolutely necessary' (Laclau 1990:21). Identity formation is therefore always an incomplete process, a point worth bearing in mind when we read that this or that movement is 'essentially' about this, that or the other. We need to foreground Laclau's dictum that 'identities and their conditions of existence form an inseparable whole' (ibid.). Thus we shall see to what extent Irish Republicanism, for example, is shaped by its 'conditions of existence' in terms of the role of the British state in Ireland, particularly in the North, rather than springing from the eternal mists of Irish prehistory. Against the discourse of 'terrorism', which perceives Irish nationalism as emerging from the 'terrorist' subject, we need to follow Laclau in seeing any identity as being 'merely relational and would therefore not be what it is outside the relationship with the force antagonizing it' (ibid.).

Poststructuralist and, more clearly, postmodernist theory has forced us to rethink the basic categories of social and political analyses we have been used to. However, to announce the end of the subject precisely when women and the ex-colonial peoples are finding and asserting their identity is a position that is not without problems. Difficulties with an essentialist concept of 'womanhood' notwithstanding, there is a thriving women's movement in many countries. As Bobby Sayyid puts it, while the West or the rich countries of the North discard the old certainties of modernity, 'others who cannot bear the world without foundations retreat into "ancient" myths, search for a rock upon which they can base their identity' (Sayyid 1994:278). The new 'politics of difference' at the centre is matched by a new 'politics of authenticity' at the periphery. The uneven yet combined character of global development paradigms are manifest here too. Thus Islamisms might not be simple pre-modernist meta-narratives, and despite all the emphasis on the recovery of original identities, anti-imperialism remains an underlying position. As Sayyid shows, if we examine the 'conditions of existence' within Islamism and not just its form or content, we can see how it is constituted from a position of weakness, as one means of radicalising the process of decolonisation and of decentring the West.

State and terror

General Jorge Rafael Videla, the head of the Argentinian military junta that had seized power from the discredited government of the widow María Estela Martínez de Perón in March 1976, declared that 'A terrorist is not just someone with a gun or a bomb but also someone who spreads ideas which are contrary to Western and Christian civilisation.' To purge society of these elements and this cancer from within its midst, Videla stated openly that 'as many people will die in Argentina as is necessary to restore order'. While declaring his 'respect for human rights', Videla went on to launch the 'dirty war', which entered the annals as one of the clearest cases of state terror in the contemporary era. As one strategic theorist, M.L.R. Smith, puts it somewhat clinically, 'the concentration on sub-state organisations inhibits the analyst from viewing the place of terrorism as an instrument of policy available to state and non-state actors alike' (Smith 1995:230) and that is the dimension we now need to examine.

The Latin American dictatorships of the 1970s and early 1980s were international laboratories of repression and powerful symbols of state terror. As Jean Franco writes, 'the death camps were governed with a curious mixture of bureaucracy and sadism. The sordid bloodshed and torture were systematized, and euphemistic language ... gave the barbarous proceedings a certain routineness and legitimacy' (Franco 1992:106). A powerful signifier in this bloody field of state terror were the *desaparecidos* or disappeared ones. The state policy of clandestinely engineering the 'disappearance' of suspected 'subversives' and random citizens played a central role in the panoply of repression and terror unleashed by the Latin American dictatorships of this period. The regimes played a cat-and-mouse game with the relatives of the disappeared, denying the existence of captives or any knowledge of those executed and saying instead that they must have been killed by the insurgent organisations. More often than not, those disappeared who were held captive – whether they be found 'guilty' or otherwise – would be swept aside, as an inevitable consequence of the war against 'subversion'. As a result of the twin operations of repression and disappearance, 'these desaparecidos inhabit a space where they are neither dead nor alive; they can reappear, they can also be killed. Their death and their life is suspended, deferred' (Laclau and Zac 1994:34). This logic dominates society and instils cultures of fear, which maintain negative effects for many years.

The reigns of state terror which have dominated various periods of world history operate on the basis of human fear, which, like Foucault's conception of power, is both produced and productive (or active). Cultures of fear produce a new political praxis based on a 'routinised' and wholesale abuse of human rights, with the power of the state taking on a sublime, unquestioned aspect. Then, as Norbert Lechner writes, 'Violence is attributed not to the dictatorship but to chaos, the enemy that infiltrates and subverts the established order' (Lechner 1992:31). In the discursive construction of political violence, the state portrays itself as representative of order against the chaos of the insurgents outside the city gates. As the victims of this new 'order' are broken by torture, before being made to 'disappear', the discourse of the aggressor-state becomes public currency – that is 'they must have done "something" to be punished in such a manner'. As effective as the ceremonies of public execution in a previous era, the new regimes of terror in countries like Argentina even led to a new term, the so-called 'dirty war', to describe their handiwork.

In his study of 'spectacle, psychosexuality and radical Christianity' in the Argentinian 'dirty war', Frank Graziano (1992) goes a long way in helping us understand the practices of terror from a cultural perspective. Graziano traces the messianic mythology of the perpetrators of the 'dirty war' by showing the context in which torture and execution could become 'holy acts'. The atrocities of this period are seen as political strategies based on a symbolic construction of the enemy within. In the military narrative of the 'dirty war'. the *desaparecidos* and *detenidos* (detained ones) had sinned against God and thus fully merited the horrific treatment they received. This was divine will at work (on earth) and while the war may have been 'dirty' it was also cleansing. As Graziano explains, the absolutely disproportional relations between the level of force deployed and the level of possible threat from the victims was deliberate, 'dramatic action was utilized to accomplish some objective greater than the simple apprehension of an unresisting victim ... the excess was strategic' (ibid.:65). Indeed, the whole theatrics of the 'dirty war' were designed to cow a civil society which in the late 1960s and early 1970s had dared to show a dangerous level of activity, autonomy and projection. In the words of Foucault, the carnival of reaction and repression was designed not only to punish a real or imaginary transgression but 'to bring into play, at its extreme point, the dissymmetry between the subject who has dared to violate the law and the all-powerful sovereign who displays his strength' (Foucault 1977:49). In conclusion, any consideration of political violence must take into account the possibility, perhaps the ultimate certainty, of state terror when faced with insurgency, be it that of the dissident intellectual, the militant worker or the armed activist or revolutionary.

Reading insurgency

One way of misreading insurgency is the attempt by various counter-insurgency theorists to subsume all low-intensity wars under a general umbrella and to seek a general theory of the 'causes' of political violence. The contorted discourse and the narrow, at times contrived, policy prescriptions of this school are a major impediment to clarity of understanding. As M.L.R. Smith argues, 'the damage caused to the decent study of low intensity wars by the decontextualisation of conflicts as a result of terrorist study methodology, seen in the superficiality of some works in this area, has been vast' (Smith 1995:231). Each of the contributors in this volume draw explicitly from detailed examinations of the context of political violence they are concerned with. We take seriously the motivation of those engaged in political violence, rather than dismiss them as psychopaths and thereby end up not contributing to any clarity of understanding and relevance of ensuing political interventions. In the field of political conflict, ideology plays a crucial role and we are thus concerned with what John Cash calls the 'battle within discourse over different forms of signification, communication and subjection' (Cash 1996:61). The struggle for hegemony, which all forms of politics are about, has a moral and intellectual dimension, which should be at the forefront of our concerns.

It makes obvious sense to argue that any account of political violence should include, as a primary source, the participant's own accounts. Only thus can we trace the management of meaning of political violence. As David Moss notes, 'the making and unmaking of meanings must be regarded as essentially interactive, carried out through exchanges within the community of armed struggle, between the members and their opponents and among the opponents themselves' (Moss 1989:6). Practitioners of political violence need to constantly (re)interpret the sense of their actions. Yet we should also be aware that violence is usually only a part, often a small one, of the broader construction of political identity. Nor should we neglect the modes of being and communication addressed by psychoanalysis in addressing the question of insurgency. Although often repressed in social theory, this dimension may help us better understand the 'extraordinary' in the construction of identities. As Cash has argued, we need to address 'the structuration process through which unconscious rules integral to the organisation of political subjectivities ... are drawn upon in the making of political conflict' (Cash 1996:56).

One of the most interesting recent accounts of the making of political violence and identity formation has been Alan Feldman's *Formations of Violence* (1991). This is an account or narrative of the body and political violence in Northern Ireland, but it develops a methodology of wider applicability. It helps us understand that political agency is not a given but permanently constructed through diverse practices. What Feldman proposes in essence is 'a genealogical analysis of the symbolic forms, material practices, and narrative strategies through which certain types of political agency are constructed' (ibid.:1). This proposal takes us back to Foucault's move from archaeology to genealogy, with its concerted concern with the historical transformations in the discursive practices of orders of discourse and their relationship to wider processes of social change. In a general sense, Foucault's view of power leads us to pay greater attention to the element of discourse in social analysis, but also, at the same time, to focus more attention on power in discourse analysis, not forgetting that power is also spatialised, with the body itself becoming a spatialised unit of power. For the counter-insurgency theorists, the 'nature' of insurgency is explained through various a-historical conspiracy theories. The community is seen as a passive and gullible entity *vis-à-vis* the insurgent's malevolent external manipulations or threat. As Frank Burton writes, 'There is no suggestion that the guerrilla is part of his [sic] community or that his [sic] causes can be intellectually grasped and rationally embraced by that community' (Burton 1978:119). Rather than reduce the insurgent to a 'pathological conundrum' (ibid.), we need to turn to a narrative of insurgency. Narratives are enacted and acquire culturally situated meanings, and in most communities affected by insurgency we see the development of an oral tradition, which is itself a powerful narrative genre. Only by focusing on this range of sources will we get 'behind the mask' of the insurgent. As Feldman puts it, when we deal with the events of political violence as narrative it is necessary to 'view narrativity and emplotment as the organization of events into a configurational system, a mode of historical explanation, a normative intervention' (Feldman 1991:14).

Making peace

Insurgents may be defeated or they may defeat the incumbent regime, but they might, with a given balance of forces, end up negotiating peace. In recent years, from South Africa to Central America, from the Middle East to Northern Ireland, peace processes have ensued from conflicts previously assumed to be intractable. There are internal specificities behind this process, such as politico-military stalemates and more external influences, like the end of the Cold War. Some years ago, Bernard Crick reflected on 'the high price of peace' (Crick 1990). The underlying theme which Crick explored was the possibility of a non-zero-sum political game, that is, where all might gain, rather than one person's or party's gain being automatically another's loss. He states that 'My moral is not peace at any price but the terribly high price and unpredictability of victory if it comes to winner take all' (ibid.:269). The turn to peace can come from war-weariness, a fear of losing all if hostilities continue and from genuine convictions that a peace process could prosper and could deliver a viable and 'honourable' historic compromise. As Crick notes, 'The highest price of peace is likely to be giving up hopes of victory, a realisation of the limits of power' (ibid.).

There are now many accounts of how peace might be achieved in civil war situations. For William Zartman, 'Internal conflicts are marked by intensity and commitment that ... so lock the parties into opposition and hostilities' (Zartman 1995:20) that they cannot get out of the situation unaided. This is certainly the case sometimes, but there are many other cases where the internal dynamic was sufficient to spur negotiations, albeit with external parties engaged as mediators at crucial points along the way. Also on a pessimistic note, Zartman's survey concludes that 'at best, internal conflicts are simply subsumed back into normal politics' (ibid.:333). This would, however, seem to be quite an achievement. Zartman's hankering for the Cold War era seems apparent when he rules that 'It is hard to crush the rebels' (ibid.). The whole gist of the case studies he organises is that compromise is possible and no one should be seeking to 'crush' anyone else. Where we can agree wholeheartedly with Zartman is when he says that 'In the long run, all solutions are only experiments' (ibid.:24). This is almost universally the case, and it is what makes the conflict resolution process so politically and intellectually exciting, precisely because the mould is sometimes broken and we can imagine a different future.

If we broaden our analysis, we need to consider how societies without fear might be reconstructed, remembering how central 'fear' is to authoritarian regimes. Referring to the new democracies in Latin America, but from a point of broader relevance, Lechner points out that now 'we may exclude subjectivity as a private affair, but sooner or later it will reappear in the political arena as rank irrationality. The subjectivity we repress returns to haunt us' (Lechner 1992:34). The disappearances and the torture, the no-warning bombs and the kidnappings, leave traces which do not disappear overnight. (Ir)rational fears of what our 'enemies' might do if we lay down our arms have powerful political and psychological effects. Negotiations entail trust and this is hardly a characteristic of the war years. Certainly there is nothing pointing towards a smooth and peaceful transition beyond armed conflict and, as Corradi puts it, 'The deconstruction of cultures of fear is a long, fragile and incomplete process' (Corradi 1992:285). It is of course possible, and the example of South Africa's slow but steady exorcising of the past, and the construction of a new democratic order, shows that it can be done. One precondition is to take the political aspirations of the insurgent movement seriously.

Peace, as we have learnt, is more than just the absence of war, it entails an active process of construction in the discursive and extra-discursive domains. If we learn nothing else from a critical reading of the counter-insurgency or 'terrorism' literature, it is that nothing can be gained at least in the long term, from labelling insurgents as criminals, psychopaths or murderers, though short-term political advantage may be gained by the regime. However, with a longer-term view it is clear that regimes which refuse to recognise a legitimate interlocutor may only postpone the inevitable, with the ensuing years of accumulated bitterness and distrust making a democratic settlement that much more difficult and fragile. Within insurgent movements, conversely, we have seen a rise of a new realism and a forsaking of absolutism. Politics as the art of the possible is understood and democratic compromise is not automatically translated as cowardly betrayal. The democratic terrain, procedures and discourse are the privileged planes for full settlement, including the subjective aspects of the situations which gave rise to insurgency or civil war in the first place.

References

Appiah, K.A. 1995: 'African Identities' in L. Nicholson and S. Seidman (editors), *Social Postmodernism: Beyond Identity Politics*, Cambridge: Cambridge University Press.

Burton, F. 1978: *The Politics of Legitimacy: Struggles in a Belfast Community*, London: Routledge & Kegan Paul.

Cash, J.D. 1996: *Identity, Ideology and Conflict: The Structuration of Politics in Northern Ireland*, Cambridge: Cambridge University Press.

Corradi, J. 1992: 'Toward Societies Without Fear' in J. Corradi, P. Fagan and M. Garretón (editors), *Fear at the Edge: State Terror and Resistance in Latin America*, Berkeley: University of California Press.

Council of Europe 1981: *Conference on the Defence of Democracy Against Terrorism in Europe: Tasks and Problems*, Strasbourg: Council of Europe.

Crick, B. 1990: 'The High Price of Peace' in H. Gilliomee and J. Graziano (editors), *The Elusive Search for Peace: South Africa, Israel and Northern Ireland*, Cape Town: Oxford University Press.

Fanjul, J.M. 1981: 'Nature of Terrorism' in Council of Europe, *Conference on the Defence of Democracy Against Terrorism in Europe: Tasks and Problems*, Strasbourg: Council of Europe.

Feldman, A. 1991: *Formations of Violence: The Narrative of the Body and Political Terror in Northern Ireland*, Chicago, IU: University of Chicago Press.

Foucault, M. 1965: *Madness and Civilization: A History of Insanity in the Age of Reason*, New York: Random House.

Foucault, M. 1977: *Discipline and Punish: The Birth of the Prison*, Harmondsworth: Penguin.

Franco, J. 1992: 'Gender, Death and Resistance: Facing the Ethical Vacuum' in J. Corradi, P. Fagan and M. Garretón (editors), *Fear at the Edge: State Terror and Resistance in Latin America*, Berkeley: University of California Press.

Graziano, F. 1992: *Divine Violence: Spectacle, Psychosexuality and Radical Christianity in the Argentine 'Dirty War'*, Boulder, Col. Westview Press.

Herman, E. and O'Sullivan, G. 1989: *The 'Terrorism' Industry: The Experts and Institutions that Shape our View of Terror*, New York: Pantheon.

Janke, P. 1979: 'Ulster: A Decade of Violence' in *Conflict Studies*, no. 108, pp. 1–24.

Laclau, E. 1990: *New Reflections on the Revolutions of Our Time*, London: Verso.

Laclau, E. and Zac, L. 1994: 'Minding the Gap: The Subject of Politics' in E. Laclau (editor), *The Making of Political Identities*, London: Verso.

Laqueur, W. 1996: 'Postmodern Terrorism' in *Foreign Affairs*, vol. 75, no. 5, pp. 25–36.

Lechner, N. 1992: 'Some People Die of Fear: Fear as a Political Problem' in J. Corradi, P. Fagan and M. Garretón (editors), *Fear at the Edge: State Terror and Resistance in Latin America*, Berkeley: University of California Press.

Macdonell, D. 1986: *Theories of Discourse*, Oxford: Basil Blackwell.

Moss, D. 1989: *The Politics of Left-Wing Violence in Italy, 1969–85*, London: Macmillan.
Mouffe, C. 1993: *The Return of the Political*, London: Verso.
Pêcheux, M. 1982: *Language, Semantics and Ideology*, London: Macmillan.
Sayyid, B. 1994: 'Sign O'Times: Kaffirs and Infidels Fighting the Ninth Crusade' in E. Laclau (editor), *The Making of Political Identities*, London: Verso.
Smith, M.L.R. 1995: 'Holding Fire: Theory and the Missing Military Dimension in the Academic Study of Northern Ireland' in A. O'Day (editor), *Terrorism's Laboratory: The Case of Northern Ireland*, Aldershot: Dartmouth.
Van Creveld, M. 1991: *On Future War*, London: Brassey's.
Visker, R. 1995: *Michel Foucault: Genealogy as Critique*, London: Verso.
Wardlaw, G. 1982: *Political Terrorism: Theory, Tactics and Counter-measures*, Cambridge: Cambridge University Press.
Wilkinson, P. 1981: 'Admissibility of Negotiations Between Organs of the Democratic States and Terrorists' in Council of Europe, *Conference on the Defence of Democracy Against Terrorism in Europe: Tasks and Problems*, Strasbourg: Council of Europe.
Zartman, W. (editor) 1995: *Elusive Peace: Negotiations and End to Civil Wars*, Washington, DC: The Brookings Institution.

2
Private, Public and Political: Learning Processes of the Revolutionary Left in Argentina[1]

María Matilde Ollier

The processes of deradicalisation undergone by survivors of the Argentinian Revolutionary Left (RL)[2] have been characterised by the decisive influence of the interplay between different modes of learning carried out by them in the private, public and political spheres. And the result of this interaction was the liberalisation and democratisation of their political identities – that is, a shift towards new understandings and an appreciation of liberalism and democracy. At the same time, I find that these identity formations are incomplete processes, which must be understood in relation to society as a whole. In brief, in this chapter I trace the political learning processes of survivors after the annihilation of the RL in Argentina.

Public and private spheres could also be named as civil society. However, I decided to use private and public spheres instead of civil society for a number of reasons. For instance, I consider it much clearer to separate some dimensions such as the family (where the action of the state does not reach easily) from that of the school. The relation between private and public is part of different perspectives in political science and here I follow Norberto Bobbio (1989) in noting the difficulties of clearly delineating the boundary between private and public. I present three spheres: the private, public and political. The *political sphere* embraces the instances of political power (that is, parties, guerrilla groups, armed forces, the state). At the other extreme, the *private sphere* encompasses areas such as family, friends, couples, neighbourhoods and psychotherapy. Finally, I speak of a *public sphere* to refer to social space that is formed by school, university, church, psychotherapy, 'catacomb universities' and areas of culture – that is, literature, cinema, theatre and music. I hypothesise that what human beings learn in these three dimensions or spheres shapes their political identities.

During the 1960s and 1970s, the RL in Argentina formed the largest guerrilla grouping in the Southern Cone of the Americas. Guerrillas, leftist activists and their actions were crucial for Perón's return to Argentina after seventeen years of exile, and consequently for the restoration of democracy in 1973 (see Gillespie 1982, Viola 1982, O'Donnell 1982 and Ollier 1986, 1989). The RL played a key role in forcing the break of the Peronism versus anti-Peronism dilemma in Argentinian politics and facilitated the transition from military government. However, the guerrilla movement in particular and the RL in general also fuelled the political violence which, at least in part, led to the military coup in 1976. From 1974 until 1978, these groups endured increasing repression and were eventually destroyed. In the process, some surviving members of the RL left behind their revolutionary goals and established ties with people who came from different political traditions. And consequently, a few years later many members of the former RL became some of the most enthusiastic proponents of democracy. How do we account for the process of learning which led them to return or rediscover liberal and democratic values? To answer this question requires extending our view to encompass the entire processes of political identity formation within the RL, society and the historical evolution of Argentinian politics.[3] Under the first authoritarian military regime (1966–73) considered here, the combination of the political learning of political élites and particular social conditions (that is, large explosions of social protest and the emergence of a radicalised labour leadership that contested the authority of traditional leaders) opened up space for the entrance of the RL into the political arena. Under the second military regime (1976–83), another type of élite political behaviour in tandem with changing social and political conditions (that is, a demobilised society and the failure of Peronism in office) led to the annihilation of the RL. Ultimately, such conditions permitted the survivors of the RL to insert themselves into areas of cultural and public resistance, and to favour the moves made by the military regime towards liberalisation and democratisation. Just as radicalisation was framed by more extensive processes concerning the polarisation of civil society and political classes, conceptual changes by the survivors of the RL cannot be separated from the larger processes of Argentinian democratisation. The formation and transformation of the political identities of survivors should be understood within the context of the regime itself. I would argue that political learning regarding the processes of transformation of the RL is a lifelong process.

Political learning is understood here as the processes through which people organise certain understandings (values, ideas, beliefs) and perceptions (images) about the political world. In a very general way, I understand political identities to be the instance of the identification of survivors with real or symbolic political collective actions. This identification is composed of multiple variables. Here, I consider the ideological and political universe, values and the way of doing politics. People can change their perceptions, comprehension and ways of doing politics and, therefore, their political identities. However, early learning also possesses an important persistence and influence on them. Thus, there is a combination of changes and continuities in processes of identity formation. And the outcome of such a combination depends on the manner in which individuals resignify values, ideas and ways of conducting politics, according to their political experiences and their reading of such experiences within the societies and contexts in which they live.[4]

Macro-political context

The transition of our protagonists from a revolutionary to a non-revolutionary phase must be understood within the context of the military regime and its transition.[5] The macro-political context can be divided into two periods. The first is from the 1976 military coup to 1981, when general Viola became president. This was the beginning of the political opening. The second period encompasses Viola's fall until the change of regime. During this latter period, two episodes, namely the *Porteñazo* and the war in the South Atlantic, revealed and at the same time, produced new political positions among the protagonists.

In this subsection I argue that while the development of the RL must be framed by the dynamic of Argentine politics, the disappearance of the RL and the methodology used for its annihilation were also crucial for strengthening and giving credibility to the political opposition, for weakening the military government and for giving value to the democratic regime. Within this process, the RL was part of both the social and cultural opposition, as well as the human rights movement, which struggled against the regime and framed the transition to democracy.

The military's triumph over the RL was in fact a political defeat, in so far as the regime could not achieve two key objectives: legitimisation of its fight against the guerrillas and a tutelary position in Argentina's institutional future. In the beginning, the RL was the only faction clearly opposed to the regime. However, given that the junta chose terrorism as a means to combat the RL, the human rights issue became of crucial importance within the political process and eventually turned against the government itself. An active role in the campaign against human rights violations was played by the survivors who fled into exile, including former political prisoners and *desaparecidos* who had been released. This action of bold resistance to the dictatorship proved to be effective with human rights campaigns emerging in different countries (for example, Mexico, Sweden, Spain, Israel) and the international press beginning to show concern about violations of human rights and democratic freedoms, which became a considerable problem for the regime. The strategy of the armed forces in annihilating the RL and depoliticising civil society had not taken into account that the subject of human rights would emerge into prominence. The military's assumption that the political struggle could be won solely through military means was ultimately proven false. By ruling out political struggle in its confrontation with the RL, the military regime caused, as an unintended consequence, the organisation of an opposition field which emerged as an alternative.

Under the authoritarian regime, a dispute took place between the three main groups of civilian political élites over two issues, namely the transition to democracy and the nature of democracy. The civilian allies of the regime, grouped in the *Movimiento Nacional de Opinión* (MNO), backed the main plan of the armed forces, which involved the retention of the Argentinian military as 'guardians' of the nation and favoured the exclusion of the other two major political parties – the Radical Party and the Justicialist Party. A second group were the potential negotiators with the regime, mainly Balbín and some Peronist leaders. While they moved within the restrictions set by the junta in one sense (that is, legitimisation of the war against guerrillas), they did not accept the armed forces' tutelary role in the transition to democracy. Finally, there was a third group which encompassed party leaders such as Alfonsín (Radical Party), Ubaldini and Bittel (Peronist Party), Alende (Intransigent Party) and other leaders from the Socialist and Christian parties. The basic demand of this group was for general elections without any kind of control from the army. The political transformations of the former members of the RL overlapped with the rise of this latter group.

The year 1979 marked two important milestones. On the one hand, some members of the third political group and the human rights movement began to emerge as a democratic front, of which some survivors of the RL were party to. On the other hand, the mission sent by the Inter-American Commission (IC) yielded important results. Crucially, Adolfo Perez Esquivel was awarded the Nobel Peace Prize, illustrating an international recognition of the Human Rights movement in Argentina, which the military read as a condemnation.[6] Two years later, in 1981, with Viola's assumption of the presidency, the transition to democracy began. According to O'Donnell, Schmitter and Whitehead (1986), the sign of the beginning of the transition was when the regime modified its own rules in order to confer more guarantees to individual and groups rights. The appointment of Viola was the result of a dispute among the different military factions, and between them and other social and political groups. The political 'opening' proposed by Viola met with resistance from some sectors within the junta and General Galtieri emerged as Viola's main rival. On behalf of the civilian parties, Balbín and Bittel decided to take action by creating the Multipartidaria (Multiple Party Assembly), as a means of negotiating the transition with the Viola faction (see González Bombal 1991). The second group and the regime therefore began to converge and signalled a possible route to democracy. In the end, however, the entire scheme failed due to the opposition that Viola's plan raised within the military, and also due to Balbín's death which made Viola's mission impossible.[7] Although before his death, Balbín had shown a moderate attitude in the course of the negotiations held with the regime, a part of Argentinian society used him as a symbol to express their disgust towards authoritarian rule. Civil society had begun its resurrection.

On March 30, 1982, the Confederación General del Trabajo, Brasil (CGT, General Workers' Confederation), called for demonstrations in the streets of Buenos Aires. The so-called *Porteñazo*[8] could be considered the starting point of renewed political activity among the capital city's citizenry. The *Porteñazo* was a clear sign that fear alone could no longer be used by the regime to stifle popular dissent, it was a sign that social discontent was now beginning to reemerge and that civil society had sprung back to life. With international opinion focused on the Argentinian human rights issue and the struggle against the guerrillas over, the regime had little chance to use violence to suppress the opposition of groups without guerrilla sympathies, as it had done during the 'dirty war'. Even so, the junta decided that it was necessary for the regime to return to its 'foundational principles', those which had been the rationale for their intervention. Galtieri showed signs of planning a new type of 'transition' that would be fully controlled by the government and the armed forces, which was scheduled to start in two years' time (Fontana 1984). The political parties decided to resist this plan and opened a new period of uncertainty, which led, three months after Galtieri's assumption and three days after the *porteñazo,* to the Malvinas (or Falklands) War. The Argentinian transition has conventionally been seen as a 'transition through breakdown'. However, to conceive of the transition as a result of the collapse of the regime implies that collapse was the starting point of the transition and says nothing about the *causes* that led the junta to engage in the war that, in turn, brought about its collapse. If the regime was unable to manage the transition in 1982, it was because it had failed previously to deal politically with the opposition, who, acting on different levels (social, cultural and political), had begun to enjoy a consensus and put down roots in some segments of Argentinian society.

The chief goal of the Malvinas/Falklands War launched in April 1982 was a political one – that is, to recover the legitimacy of the military government and to achieve a return to the very 'foundations' of the *Proceso*. It has also often been written that the Argentinian transition was solely a consequence of the Malvinas defeat. I would argue that the key to understanding the transition is the search for the causes that led the junta to engage in war in the first place. Therefore, as Brysk (1994) points out, the loss of the war did not cause but only accelerated the transition. According to him the collapse of military dictatorship and the transition to democracy were the combined result of economic decline, external military defeat and a domestic legitimacy crisis. Moreover, the continuous appeal of the armed forces to a state of war is essential for an understanding of the political opposition of the period, including the role played by the survivors of the RL. If the war against the 'subversive enemy' who dwelt within a defenseless society was the chief argument of the armed forces for intervening in the political arena in 1976, once again war – now against an external enemy – was the military's card to restore their legitimacy and ensure their perpetuation. In both cases, the values at stake were the 'National Being' and 'Nationality'. In the run-up to the Malvinas/Falklands War, social and political discomfort was growing, whereas discord between factions within the armed forces had declined after Viola's fall. Undoubtedly the military gambled. Once the war was won, they had planned on calling for a return to democracy, justifying the crimes of the 'dirty war', and securing a place for themselves in the future institutional framework.[9] However, from their defeat in Malvinas in June 1982 until the mass protest march organised by the Multipartidaria, on 16 December, consensus around the government's actions declined steadily, culminating in neighbourhood revolts known as *vecinazos*.[10]

In order to carry out their ultimate goals, the military would have had to have successfully put down the international human rights movement; to quash definitively the Justicialist and Radical parties; to disrupt the domestic human rights movement; and to eliminate every sign of cultural dissent in order to build a 'new type of citizen', based on a homogeneous stereotype of the 'perfect individual'. For this was the ultimate conception of this profoundly totalitarian regime, which disregarded the recognition of diversity within society that is the very basis of democratic rule. Diversity means the existence of conflicts. It was this rationale of opposition to all forms of conflicts and dissent, hidden beneath the military's transition plan, which led the regime to its final collapse. The ignominious military débâcle in the Malvinas/Falklands War put a seal on the defeat already suffered by the armed forces in the political arena prior to the war.

Transition from revolutionary political identity

During their revolutionary stage, politics was the axis of the identity of the survivors of the RL. Everything referred to the revolution, from friends, partners and family to work and almost every aspect of life. Therefore, starting in 1976, when the political and public spheres were strongly repressed and controlled by the armed forces, not only did the RL's revolutionary political identity increasingly lose meaning, but also their identities as a whole. There was a profound crisis of identity. In order to survive, individuals had to reshape their sense of self. If they were no longer revolutionary political activists as in the past, who were they? I argue that the starting point of this transition from revolutionary identity to a post-revolutionary one was made possible by the nature of the crisis of rupture with the revolutionary project. This was an identity crisis which embraced the meaning of the private, public and political for the survivors in particular, and for Argentinian society more generally. The crisis was caused by three levels of political breakdown – external (macro-political context), internal (revolutionary group) and interior (the 'political being' of every individual). As a result of this crisis the former members of the RL redefined the meaning of their lives and came to recognise themselves through a new subjectivity. In the Argentina where the survivors grew up, became revolutionaries and eventually gave up that identity, the interplay between their learning carried out in private, public and political dimensions was crucial for rebuilding their new political identity. Let us now examine each sphere in more detail, beginning with the political.

Political sphere

In order to make sense of their political and ideological past, the survivors of the RL had to solve the dilemma created by two contradictory movements. On the one hand, they had to criticise the authoritarian regime and, on the other hand, they were therefore compelled to criticise their own past. Despite their left-wing training within the 'Friend versus Foe' paradigm, some of them could and did perform this double and contradictory movement.[11] I argue that through a critique of their own authoritarianism they undermined authoritarian legitimacy.

Catastrophe writ large forced the survivors to reevaluate politics and their concept of political struggle. And this process was diametrically opposed to that of the military. In contrast to the confidence that the revolution had generated during the first authoritarian military regime, assertiveness had to be relinquished under the second. However, the first reaction of the RL to the 1976 *coup d'état* was confrontation. Even though they had a clear perception of how serious the situation had become, the PRT/ERP did not give up armed struggle. Immediately following the coup, Santucho issued a document titled '*Argentinos, a las armas*' ('Argentinians, rise up in arms') but promptly thereafter there was a shift in the party's position. The Montoneros underwent an even more complicated process of internal debate on the coup. Although the degree of reaction varied, the constituent members of the RL seemed to have gone through similar sensations of fear, uncertainty, anguish and relief. Whatever options there were for introspection and self-criticism for survivors of the RL, it was carried out until 1981, only within limited circles (Sarlo 1988). During the first few years after the *coup d'état*, the process of political–ideological experience involved several aspects:

- the urge to preserve themselves;
- a feeling of failure;
- the loss of the influence of their collective reference (even those who remained in their organisations experienced the loosening of ties with them);
- the beginning of deep criticism of their past (for example, errors, dogmatism, excessive sense of adventure, militarism, inopportuneness of the use of arms). Though most of them maintained their

fundamental belief in Marxism, realism began to prevail over revolutionary heroism and zeal.

One of the first consequences that emerged from the defeat of the RL was the fact that the set of representations provided by their groups, which had given the survivors the clues to understand the world from a certain standpoint, were now left up to the individual. Even those who stayed within the group had to revise their actions because of the magnitude of their defeat. Hence, we could say that the transformation of the political identities of the survivors began in a more individual context *vis-à-vis* their own thoughts, ideas and uncertainties: 'What happened when one was no long a member of the tribe but still possessed all its instruments? The answer is obvious, one's ideas become exposed to critical thought' (Juan). This perception was different for those who had been imprisoned for many years and maintained links with their collective entities, until their release and even afterwards. For many it was time to think by themselves. However, when interpreting political reality, their minds still operated within the language of Marxist theory. Deprived of the major influence of 'the political line' imposed by the leaders of their respective organisations, the survivors still defined the world with the tools with which they had learned collectively. Therefore, in the search for reasons underlying their defeat, many pointed out only tactical mistakes.

Conversely, for those who did not leave their organisations, 'the political line' was still present, but its power was diminishing. A striking paradox resulted – leaving the organisation did not necessarily imply abdication of the RL approach, whereas remaining within it did not mean maintaining one's ideas unaltered. Even so, we should take into account that at this early stage, the sensation of being overtaken was still stronger than any controversy over one's own past. As a result, many members of the RL understood their experience in terms of defeat or failure, rather than the product of erroneous conception. The catastrophe and political disruption had been so pronounced that even those who remained in their organisations were bound to face some degree of criticism for their political radicalisation. Within this context, the strategic use of arms in political struggle began to be revised. Those who were guerrillas began to soften their view on armed struggle as a means of social transformation: 'Armed struggle had been central to our conception. Now I was considering it was just one way of resisting among others. If it could be avoided, much better. I criticised European [insurgent] groups like the IRA, who had been fighting for so many years!' (Rodolfo).

Isolation was even more pronounced for those who stayed in Argentina. Most of them had lost contact with their closest relations in addition to the loss of their collective entities. Chances to gather and debate were easier for those who were in exile, and it obviously implied fewer risks. Soon the survivors heard criticisms from people belonging to other progressive but not necessarily revolutionary groups. This contestation with other political experiences, from within Argentina or from other countries, eventually brought the survivors to re-evaluate their own actions and take a new approach to their past. Observing the activity of the leftist parties in other countries provided them with further comparative elements that helped in their revision. This diversity of perspectives and situations showed them that changing political reality was not an easy task. Little by little, the criteria of truth which had been the basis of their revolutionary identity were being dropped. No longer were there absolute facts in politics, or an infallible theory. Others who disagreed with them were not just cowards, but people with different points of view. Many of those in exile became aware of the disappointments and bitterness that many revolutionary processes had led to: 'We noticed that our generational experience had been shared by others, by South Africans, Americans. There was a lot in common. The discovery made us relinquish any alleged possession of the truth. It was time to slow down and realise the world was something more diverse than our rights and wrongs' (Susana). Self-confinement, imposed by harsh repression, restricted the chances of such discussion in Argentina. Some of the survivors who remained decided to travel and get in touch with old friends and acquaintances overseas. They discovered the importance of dialogue and contestation with other opinions, and were willing to break the sectarianism in which they had been bound. At first, there was a gap between political action and theory in this respect. Being a revolutionary or a Marxist did not mean one was irrevocably right. The survivors still subscribed to the Marxist paradigm, but had been forced to give up revolutionary political practice. This implied that the conception that sustained their ideological radicalisation was retained although they had had to give up their political radicalisation.

As a result of these other critiques, the survivors began acquiring new terms to understand politics. Hermetic revolutionary language was being gradually left aside. To quote: 'I started reading Octavio Paz, Bobbio, Max Weber and that brought a huge change in my political conception. I was speaking another language and feeling further apart from that stiff discourse' (Simón). In another sense, we must also take into account that the self-criticism engaged in by the survivors during the years 1976–9, took place simultaneously with similar developments in the leftist movements in many other places. Moreover, regimes in the so-called Third World that combined authoritarianism, nationalism and socialism (as in Iran) had brought little hope. These failures undergone by the left were observed during overseas visits made by members of the RL. Of course, these new developments did not occur without internal frictions and certain events did lead them to evoke their old entrenched convictions. This was true among those who were frankly critical about the action displayed by their groups. At this point a number of them gave up some of the categories that had served as the basis for their political identifications (such as Peronism, Leninism, Maoism, Trotskyism), while retaining the tradition which identified them from an ideological standpoint, that of 'practical politics,' namely Marxism. Others did not abdicate their identity (such as 'Montoneros', 'PRTists', and so on) but were beginning to reformulate it. In general terms we could say that by the year 1981, most of the RL's survivors, in one way or another, were supporting democracy and carrying out an even more radical process of introspection concerning the revolutionary groups they had been part of. Slowly they began to extend their criticism to Marxism as well.

One of the crucial points that initiated the process of revision and criticism was each member's own personal experience, not conceptual but factual, which aroused their reappreciation of individual freedoms and civil liberties. To all of them it became clear that freedom had to be a founding value of any new order that Argentinian society would choose for itself. For those outside of Argentina, the joy of living in freedom was experienced wherever they went. The experience of individual freedom left a strong imprint on those who still acted within the organisations of the RL. However, if we analyse these testimonies in detail, we realise that the sensation also implied freedom from the control of their organisations, in addition to the oppression they felt in Argentina. The dimension of individual freedom led them to a broader appreciation of 'bourgeois liberal' democracy, concerning institutional rules, political activities and an open cultural life at all levels. Isolated, politically and ideologically, the survivors came to appreciate the value of certain institutions formerly regarded as 'bourgeois'. I refer not only to democracy, but to the simple right of habeas corpus and legal institutions that the RL had previously scorned. The revolutionary organisations had prevented them from focusing on matters considered irrelevant such as civil liberties, individual rights and other such institutions. This new appreciation, which was the result of their own personal learning, led the survivors of the RL from socialist utopia to the vindication of an abstract form of democracy.

During the second period (1981–3), it is possible to observe the political and ideological learning process that led the survivors to appreciate the democratic alternative as the key for solving the deep-rooted conflicts in Argentina. After 1981, such learning was based on their revaluation of individual freedom, the discovery of the importance of politics and the questioning of national–popular thought. All former members of the RL appreciated the advantages of democratic rule as compared to the autocracy of the military regime. However, once the question was raised in terms of authoritarianism versus democracy, such a dichotomy would also come to affect the authoritarianism within their own former political organisations. Sooner or later they would find themselves compelled to criticise the actions of their own groups and particularly the authoritarian conception of politics they had supported. Most of the survivors still subscribed to Marxism. However, they had already begun their revision of the idea that the working class was the revolutionary force meant to change society, one of the foundations of Marxist thought – 'dictatorship of the proletariat'. During these ideological transformations, both the *Porteñazo* and then the Malvinas/Falklands War took place. I refer to this war here in order to show the changes undergone by the survivors. In so far as they were halted from carrying out a revolutionary war, their ideological radicalisation underwent modifications. The military conflict in the South Atlantic definitely awakened two essential sentiments, *nación* (nation) and *pueblo* (people), that the RL shared not only with most Argentines across the political spectrum, but also with the military themselves. What is more, I would argue that the *pueblo/nación* couplet was an essential principle upheld by practically all of Argentinian society during those years. This amalgamation of people and nation also led the military to seek active popular support for the war. According to RL ideology, the 'social question' (the people) converged with the national question (the nation).

Those who supported the war did so because they understood it from a populist point of view, as an issue pertaining to the struggle against imperialism. The military, they thought, were now on the side of the nation. The national–popular core of those holding these sentiments was still alive. Nonetheless, it is also true that the nationalist sentiment of the exiles blended with their pining for home. The positions supported by the survivors in exile towards the Malvinas/Falklands War ranged from support to dissent, with intermediate positions between both ends. Those who stood in that middle ground between support and disagreement had already begun their introspection on the matter of democracy and linked it to the question of nationalism raised by the conflict. They thought that by supporting the war there could be a new chance to reach an agreement between the political parties and to force the military to discuss the transition to democracy. There was another group who refused to support the war despite the fact that their nationalism was absorbed at a tender age in primary school: '*las Malvinas son Argentinas*' ('the Malvinas islands belong to Argentina'). Others, however, felt no nationalism at all and objected to the notion that the war was a just cause. The Malvinas/Falklands War is crucial in so far as it allows us to understand:

1. The tension caused by the passage from the old dilemma, liberation versus dependency, to a new one, authoritarianism versus democracy; and from a perspective linked to their political action rather than from an ideological perspective.
2. The questioning of two concepts, *pueblo* (people) and *nación* (nation). The Malvinas elicited many to question the association of *pueblo* = *nación*. Such questions meant a significant change in their ideological vision, since it meant questioning one of the pillars of the revolutionary identity – the figure of the people.

To sum up, reaction to the Malvinas/Falklands War shows that different ideological positions were supported by survivors of the RL. Some were extremely ambiguous, and faced a dilemma between their early socialisation and their political rationality, which included the possible outcome of a military victory. Had the armed forces of the junta won, the consequences would have been terrible for Argentinian society. Some had no doubt and were against the war from the beginning. Nonetheless, for most of them, their political identities had been affected. Moreover, for some of them, their identity *qua* Argentinian suffered a deep crisis. For many, the national–popular view began to undergo sweeping changes. The war also increased the hope for democracy and the possibility for revolution became more remote. The left's faith in the concept of 'the people' as the repository of 'the truth' had been definitively shaken.

Public sphere

The RL survivors and followers, among other progressive people, contributed to the organisation of a micro-sphere of public resistance against the military regime. Here, public resistance is taken to be the micro and semi-public defence of a different discourse, concerning the public, private and political, from that of the regime. This alternative discourse was created and supported by former revolutionary activists, along with people from other sectors of the cultural field. Resistance activities included covert study groups in different disciplines and research institutions, literature, theatre, psychotherapy, the rock music scene and cinema. With the intention of subsisting as intellectuals, some former RL members were integrated into various independent research institutes such as CLASCSO (Consejo Latinoamericano de Ciencias Sociales: Social Science Latin American Council), FLACSO (Facultad Latinoamericana de Ciencias Sociales: Latin America School of Social Science), CEDES (Centro de Estudios de Estado y Sociedad: Centre for Studies on Society and State) and CISEA (Centro de Investigaciones Sociales y Económicas: Centre for Social and Economic Research). They also organised some study groups which were useful to connect up with former militants. There were also study groups of literature and writing workshops. This movement as a whole was called '*universidades de la catacumba*' or 'graveyard universities'. The research institutions and the study groups comprised the most varied of subjects. Many survivors thus become part of a small world that was able to oppose and resist the regime's mono-narrative discourse. Through their own cultural activities, they learned new values and were part of the creation of a new public sphere.

Under the authoritarian regime and according to the dictatorship's view of the cultural system there was a 'false' or 'illegitimate culture' and another 'true' or 'legitimate culture'. According to this discourse, the false culture was opposed to the 'natural spirit of our nation'. It represented the foreign. One culture excluded the other. Conflict was inherent to Marxism/Communism – the ultimate enemy of the military crusade – and it was the core of the false culture. The military's political, social and cultural diagnosis was that violence in Argentinian society was the result of conflict. Therefore, censorship had as a goal the elimination of all symbolism and expression of conflicts in order to build, in this way, a homogeneous, coherent and peaceful society according to the norms of the 'legitimate' Argentinian culture and lifestyle. To achieve this, it was necessary to discipline and regiment every cultural manifestation and every small part of the public sphere that could survive outside of this meta – narrative. Thus, some survivors tried to bring out conflicts and to support a different identity from that proposed by the regime – because the first (that is, conflicts) questioned the 'peacefulness' of Argentinian society and the second (that is, another identity) questioned the notion of 'homogeneity' and its coherence. Given the nature of censorship (see Sosnowski 1988) inspired by the foundational project of the armed forces, all those that engaged in its subversion were transformed into public resistance activists. However, the situation for former RL members was extremely dangerous. In order to effectively implement the military's concept of the Argentinian cultural universe, public education (which had the largest number of students) was headed by people of well-known conservative political activism and lineage. National universities and higher education institutions were occupied by the army and the police. For many years, a colonel of the army was in charge of the Secretary of Social Communication, part of the Ministry of Education, where censorship and the ideological control of teachers and professors was exercised. This was also where denunciation was encouraged. State television stations were monopolised by the government and each branch of the armed forces took control of one of them. Self-censorship reached the private press. Literature and art were treated according to their impact on the public. The censorship of movies was as severe as TV censorship. Despite the long blacklist of actors, singers, directors and writers who were prohibited, the theatre had a little more freedom. Thousands of books considered subversive were confiscated and some of them were burnt in public, others in private.

The public resistance of the survivors in defence of even a word different from that of the regime's discourse concerning the private, the public and the political was organised in two opposing discourses – the permitted and the prohibited. There were organised spheres where censorship was displaced and therefore could be avoided. Public resistance, under its different guises to the regime, was organised in these micro contexts (Bermeo 1992). A central issue became *what* could be said with a certain guarantee of surviving, and *how*. Beforehand, there was not a clear delimitation between *what* and *what not*, and between *how* and *how not*. As Avellaneda (1989) argues, the ubiquity of censorship raised its effectiveness. Given that the military tried to impose its will across society, the survivors of the RL resisted by offering a concrete alternative in each place where the regime imposed itself over the population. They resisted in different ways, but all activities had a basic axis – to question the conservative Catholic paradigm the regime wanted to impose over society.

The different dimensions of the resistance implied some resignifications and new learnings, the central axis of which was the re-creation of a small public sphere. The contents of such public space were the valorisation of one's own word as well as the words of 'others', and the value of similarities and differences. For the survivors of the RL, both elements were the basis of their personal liberalisation and the rupture (incipient of course) with a homogeneous conception of the private, public and political spheres. From the most absolute imposition of silence, survivors could listen and speak some words. New discourses and values emerged from this silence and hence their strength was sometimes hard to explain. To carefully scrutinise every word they were to utter led them to think carefully. The visible fear of being repressed enclosed another hidden one, which implied the political responsibility of what to say. *What to say* showed them the relevance of some basic values that had to be preserved – that is, life, freedom and communication with others. There was a concerted attempt to recover the value and meaning of the public sphere. The public and private were abolished not only by the logic of war, but also by a revolutionary conception. The latter made the public and private spheres that were entirely dependent on politics. Thus, some survivors were passing from a revolutionary conception of politics – understood as a fight to accumulate power in order to capture state power and to achieve social and national liberation – to a conception of politics as the creation of a public sphere where public words and identity existed, a more plural public sphere, built upon differences, negotiations and non-violence.

They learned to value their individual and public words above political collective work and weapons. Language emerged as the only way to fight. This was the beginning of the valuation of dialogue and, as we will see later, the responsibility for individual and personal words without the need for any collective framework. The creation of 'words' began to be valued. To recognise the value of the public word implied a vindication of freedom of speech (the words of 'others') and the relevance of dialogue. Fighting for the liberalisation of the regime, the survivors began their own processes of liberalisation. They passed from fighting to take power for national and social liberation to fighting for the building of the public sphere. This support for small-scale activities in the private/public sphere was combined with another vision of politics as 'the game of the possible'. The limits of *what to say* and *how* went further. In this fashion, a certain pluralism, debate and dialogue were made possible, in the midst of the government's considerable attempts to homogenise and silence civil society. In this sense, cultural resistance functioned as a way of liberal and democratic learning. Some survivors of the RL now began to accept political pluralism.

Private sphere

The increase since 1976 of psychological therapy and new therapeutic techniques reveals a greater affection for private issues, not only by those who belonged to the RL, but for large layers of Argentinian society. Moreover, they are inner quests directed to each of their most intimate selves. Under the military regime, the struggle for the meaning of privacy was one of the axes of liberal and democratic resistance to the regime. This private resistance, in its attempt to rethink personal life, has as an axis its problematisation. The persecution of psychologists would become a central task for censorship and repression. Nevertheless, psychoanalysts continued their labour, helping many members or former members of the RL. For many survivors, therapy represented concrete help through the figure of the analyst. Psychotherapy was part of an impoverished public resistance precisely because this was a regime that tried to impose a homogeneous vision of life. In order to confront the child-care view of life that the dictatorship had imposed, psychotherapy had to confront the vision of the private world where questions were not allowed, and therefore therapy became the place for a new search and for new questions. In order to confront the firm creed that was supposed to guide personal conduct, the psychological realm emerged as a sustaining aid, without anguish, for uncertain human beings. The homogeneity that the regime wanted to impose functioned as a mirror of the RL's own militant ideology. The revolution also demanded an ideal human type. The homogeneity of the future society, without conflicts, was core to the revolutionary belief. Therapy put into question the old schemes, which were the foundation of their revolutionary political activity. Paradoxically, psychotherapy also questioned their revolutionary private life scheme. Psychotherapy questioned the lifestyle of militants on two points, sexuality and family. Therefore, psychotherapy could be seen as:

1. the place of the word in a society where it was prohibited;
2. the place of conflict, under a political regime which suppressed it, and therefore the place of the *problematisation* of private and emotional life;
3. the place of plurality, under a regime which attempted to homogenise;

4. the place of thought and reflection about the private, under a regime where such thought was under suspicion;
5. the place of emotional and rational protection, under a regime whose goal was isolation.

Thus, within the therapy sessions, survivors made a double movement – criticising/questioning the values of both their own revolutionary ideology and the ideology of the authoritarian regime.

We will see that the learnings of new values and views were motivated by recurrent psychotherapy. In therapy, the survivors redefined the directions of their lives and recognised themselves in a new subjectivity. These operations – redefinition of life and subjectivity – bore a key lesson in the private dimension that placed them far away from the values, about private life and the affective world, upon which their revolutionary militancy rested.

When the collective dissolves – that is, the collective identity that sustained the person – each must look for ways and means of personal reconstitution. There is a need and a practice for preservation and personal repair. The military regime thought that the elimination of the political sphere, through strong control and repression of public activities, would force people to live only private lives and that, further down the road, society would finally become totally depoliticised. This objective failed, however. Within their private domain, in which they had been forced to live due to the repression, many Argentinian leftists, whether intentionally or not, began a process of identity transformation and repoliticisation. From 1976 onwards, several spaces appeared, adding to those already there, where sectors of the Argentinian middle class worked, rethought and relearned new means of understanding and living their private lives. The locations were quite diverse, such as fitness centres and therapy groups. These were new spaces that, in turn, provided new learnings, allowing the development of small private spaces, where not only survivors of the RL, but also certain sections of the progressive middle class, sought to reorient their lives. What had changed so drastically for all of them? The 'back to me' theme is what in one way or another occurred to each one. Defining the 'self' is not an easy task. Psychotherapy defined the private realm, which contributed to the self-perception of their own individualities, as the step prior to the recognition of diversity; the pillar of the liberalisation of their lives. The role of psychotherapy was very important in the process of the reconstruction of the self. The result is a bundle of issues dealing with private life, including therapy, employment and money, which all in turn contributed eventually to changes in political conceptualisation.

It was clear to all that life as a militant was the reason why they had initiated analysis: 'I believe I entered into therapy during a brutal crisis, a consequence, in part, of that cycle of risk, fear, thrill, uncertainty, imbalance that political militancy was, and the *coup d'état* that followed' (Mariano). The need for analysis was the result of the rupture which forced them to pass from a life based on an absolute truth to one sustained in a political and personal vacuum. A strong confusion or a certain intuition about 'something must be, or must have been, profoundly wrong in my life' were the feelings and thoughts that took our protagonists to therapy. Part of the crisis is the state of confusion they found themselves in: 'I felt bad after leaving the militancy, I went back to therapy, another analyst. I asked him to understand, I was very confused' (Ramón). All this soul-searching led to:

- A *valorisation of private life, simply life, and the human being*, as opposed to the subordination of private life to revolutionary political life, the latter being considered superior. Merely attending therapy, whatever the results, implied attributing to private life, feelings and affections at an elevated position. Therapy was the place from which the right to privacy was revindicated. For the former revolutionary heroes, visiting a place to talk about pain already implied that something had begun to change within them.

    When one of them says, 'Therapy helped me detect states of mind I wouldn't let myself accept. I learned to feel and express what I feel' (Luis), it is because a crucial change produced itself in his place in the world. This process gave legitimacy to a privacy which possessed its own logic and an autonomous dynamic that is absolutely personal. There was an instance of valuation of the individuality in this introspection: their pain, their losses, their deficiencies.

    Therapy began to put into question the heroic paradigm of revolutionary life as the only one worth living. As they scrutinised this paradigm they began to look at themselves more humanly. And the mystique about the revolutionary personality began to crumble.
- *Prioritising the individual instance*, as opposed to the social and collective force. Individual desire appeared in their consciousness with a force that went beyond revolutionary obligations. Through psychotherapy, the need to do those things that they truly wanted to do and which were not linked to the revolution surfaced: 'The psychoanalyst wanted me to follow what I believed in, if I didn't

believe in certain values I had to find myself and make a life that was more in tune with what I wanted to do' (Alberto). It was necessary to find themselves as individuals, to seek their own desires and needs. And new processes of change based on individuality began to grow new roots, motivations and commitments, different from those proposed by social change.

All these learning processes began to take an important place in each person's private scene. They began to discover that individual change was also relevant. There was then a sense of urgency *vis-à-vis* the new commitment – a commitment with themselves as opposed to commitment with the collective, society, the poor, and so on.

- *The search for truths as opposed to the established truth.* The beginning of therapy necessarily implied a new search. The motive for consultation was always an old wound which demanded changes, even in the outlook of one's own life. Those changes led, consciously or not, to a search. That search was the possibility of receiving new discourses, of being open to new possibilities. Some saw it clearly, while others just lived it.

Those who in therapy had the opportunity to rethink the place of private life, later rethought political action, at least in the sense that they were both lived by the revolutionaries: 'Therapy helped me with life itself. The valorisation of private life, I think, leads to another way of thinking' (Fernando). To think about the private also obliged them to think about the public and the political. They learned that how they had defined and lived private life affected how they defined and lived public life. They also learned that during therapy they had seen the private and the public as separate spheres, but that in each of their subjectivities they would connect and had to be negotiated. How a person defined and lived the private dimension is tied to how they defined and lived life in public, and vice versa. Analysis allowed for personal balance and therapy helped to conceptualise the changes and openings, but also to understand the old attachments, as to 'why I did what I did'; that it was not just omnipotence.

The crucial point that led to this analysis was the learning of a new subjectivity. They emerged as individuals. They understood, together with the experience of the terrible isolation and solitude of the military regime, that they 'are' more than and beyond political/revolutionary beings. They were forced to reveal their individual selves to themselves. This individual, who began to model him/herself on their own selves was – in my understanding – the cultural base that interacted *vis-à-vis* the demand for political citizenship. This profound, individual revelation led the survivors to value the liberties of 'bourgeois liberal democracy', which they had despised so much. Having been freed through their own recognition, to continue along this new track was fundamental for their political change, for their definitive valuation of citizen rights.

Concluding words

The learning processes carried out by the survivors of the RL in the private, public and political spheres intertwined with the transition from revolutionary identity. The end result was the liberalisation and democratisation of their political identities. When democracy finally arrived in 1983, a different politics could be distinguished among the survivors from the perspective of the public and political spheres – that is, the value of individual freedom, of the word, of dialogue and negotiations, and a questioning of the national–popular couplet. They had passed from fighting to take power for national and social liberation to struggling for the building of the public sphere. They also began to understand politics as 'the art of the possible'. In this way they valued democracy as the best political regime for Argentina. From the private sphere they learnt to value private life, the individual and the search for life as opposed to its subordination to the revolution, the collective and the established truth. These lessons led them to a new subjectivity and a new definition of life. Both sets of changes led them away from the foundation of revolutionary thought. Private learning, in my understanding and theirs, had profound repercussions on the way we understood political action, principally on two points: *liberalisation* and *democratisation*.

Notes

1. My sincere thanks to Ernesto Cabrera and Gretchen Helmke for their useful comments. This work is part of a larger research project on the formation and transformation of survivors of the Argentinian RL and is partially based on 23 life histories. In this particular study, I explain the limitations of the methodology that I have used. Rather than concentrating on developing a 'causal explanation' or 'the psychological determinants' of political values, ideas and ways of doing politics, the study is basically a description and an interpretation of the entire process of survivor's identity formation (Ollier 1997).
2. The RL believed in revolution – through armed struggle, insurrection, integral war, etc. – to seize power and construct a socialist state. The members of the RL included: Fuerzas Armadas Revolucionarias (FAR,

Revolutionary Armed Forces), Fuerzas Armadas Perónistas (FAP, Peronist Armed Forces), Montoneros, Vanguardia Comunista (VC, Communist Vanguard), Partido Comunista Revolucionario (PCR, Revolutionary Communist Party), Fuerzas Armadas de Liberación (FAL, Armed Forces for Liberation), Partido Revolucionario de los Trabajadores (PRT, Workers's Revolutionary Party) and its guerrilla group Ejército Revolucionario del Pueblo (ERP, People's Revolutionary Army), Poder Obrero (PO, Worker's Power), *Partido Socialista de los Trabajadores* (PST, Workers's Socialist Party), and Política Obrera (PO, Worker's Politics). In addition, theoretically oriented groups such as Praxis and those organisations that had relations with armed revolutionary groups (that is, youth organisations, neighbourhood associations, university groups, political parties, trade union organisations) can also be categorised as being part of the RL. These groups belonged to the same period of Argentine history, emerging in the period between the Cuban Revolution and the Cordobazo (an important social uprising) in 1969, and growing in number until the death of President Perón in 1974.
3. In general, the literature about the RL either refers to a radical stage itself or to its later transformation – see, for example, the works of Gillespie 1982, Giussani 1984, Bonasso 1984, Hilb and Lutzky 1984, Ollier 1986, Seoane 1992, Moyano 1995 and Diana 1996. And the literature on the transformation of the left in the Southern Cone of the Americas emphasises the ideological aspects of this change – for example, see Moulián 1982, García 1986, Barros 1986, Flischfish 1986, 1987, Packenham 1986, Reader 1987, Pecaut 1990, Walker 1990.
4. My perspective on this must be placed at an intermediate point between old and new theories about political learning and socialisation. I concur with older analyses that support the idea that experiences during childhood and adolescence are determinants for the formation of individual political identity – for example, Greenstein 1965, Hess and Torney-Pwra 1967, Easton and Dennis 1989. However, there are other studies about political learning during adulthood, such as Danziger 1971, Sigel 1982 and Bermeo 1992, who consider that socialisation occurs throughout life, a point which also has to be taken into account.
5. Different perspectives have focused on the political processes between 1976 and 1983. See for example Fontana 1984, 1986, 1990, Acuña and Smulovitz 1991 and González Bombal 1991.
6. For example, at that time, Pérez Esquivel was a victim of arbitrary detainment and torture. However, the report issued by the IC mission was even more severe than expected.
7. Balbín was the only one in a condition to articulate a transition through a pact. His death revealed both the renewed democratic expectations of the population and the fact that fear had begun to recede (Aliverti 1987). On Viola's arrival at the burial, the crowd shouted threateningly, '*Se va a acabar/se va acabar/la dictadura militar*' ('It shall end/it shall end/the military dictatorship shall come to an end') (Jordán 1993:290). Paradoxically, Viola eulogised the best ally of his transition plan to democracy.
8. *Porteñazo* derives from *Porteño* which is a name given to the inhabitants of Buenos Aires.

9. According to Fontana (1986), the popular endorsement of the war was widespread but not total. Opposition to the war was severely silenced and isolated.
10. *Vecinazos* (from *vecino*, meaning neighbour) were the movements of protest from the neighbourhoods in the Gran Buenos Aires against tax increases (see González Bombal 1988).
11. The 'Friend versus Foe' paradigm refers to the conception of politics as war. The opponent is considered an enemy, therefore he/she must be annihilated at whatever cost.

References

Acuña, C. and Smulovitz, C. 1991: *Ni olvido ni perdón? Derechos Humanos y tensiones cívico militares de la transición argentina*, Buenos Aires: Estudios Cedes (July).
Aliverti, E. 1987: *El archivo de la década*, Buenos Aires: Cuatro Editores.
Avellaneda, A. 1989: 'The Process of Censorship and Censorship of the Proceso: Argentina 1976–1983' in D.W. Foster (editor), *The Redemocratization of Argentine Culture 1983 and Beyond* (proceedings of an international research symposium), Arizona: Arizona State University.
Barros, R. 1986: 'The Left and Democracy: Recent Debates in Latin American' in *Telos.*, 68(2), pp. 49–70.
Bermeo, N. 1992: 'Democracy and the Lessons of Dictatorship' in *Comparative Politics*, April, pp. 273–91.
Bobbio, N. 1989: *Democracy and Dictatorship: The Nature and Limits of State Power*, Minneapolis: University of Minnesota Press.
Bonasso, M. 1984: *Recuerdos de la muerte*, Buenos Aires: Bruguera.
Brysk, A. 1994: *The Politics of Human Rights in Argentina: Protest, Change and Democratization*, Stanford, Calif.: Stanford University Press.
Danziger, K. 1971: *Socialization.*, Harmondsworth: Penguin.
Diana, M. 1996: *Mujeres Guerrilleras*, Buenos Aires: Planeta.
Easton, D. and Dennis, J. 1969: *Children in the Political System*, New York: McGraw-Hill.
Flisfisch, A. 1986: *El socialismo y la preferencia por la democracies*, Chile: FLACSO (July).
Flisfisch, A. 1987: *Los ideales y la izquierda: la racionalidad del cambio*, Chile: FLACSO (october).
Fontana, A. 1984: 'Fuerzas Armadas, Partidos Politicos y Transición a la Democracia en Argentina, 1981–1982', Working Paper No. 28, Notre Dame, NB: The Helen Kellogg Institute for International Studies, University of Notre Dame.
Fontana, A. 1986: 'De la Crisis de Malvinas a la subordinación condicionada', Working Paper No. 74, Notre Dame, NB: The Helen Kellogg Institute for International Studies, University of Notre Dame.
Fontana, A. 1990: *Percepción de amenaza y adquisición de armamentos: Argentina 1960–1989*, Buenos Aires: Estudios Cedes.
Foster, D.W. (editor) 1987: *The Redemocratization of Argentine Culture 1983 and Beyond*, (proceedings of an international research symposium), Arizona: Arizona State University.
García, M.A. (editor) 1986: *As Esquerdas e a Democracia*, Rio de Janeiro: Centro de Estudos de Cultura Contrmporânea (CEDEC).

Gillespie, R. 1982: *Soldiers of Perón. Argentina's Montoneros*, Oxford: Clarendon Press.
Giussani, P. 1984: *Montoneros: La soberbia armada*, Buenos Aires: Sudamericana Planeta.
González Bombal, I. 1988: *Los vecinazos y las protests barriales en el Gran Buenos Aires, 1982–83*, Buenos Aires: Ed. del IDES.
González Bombal, I. 1991: *El diálogo politico: la transición que no fue*, Buenos Aries: Estudios Cedes.
Greenstein, F. 1965: *Children and Politics*, New Haven, Cann.: Yale University Press.
Hess, R. and Torney-Purta, J. 1967: *The Development of Political Attitudes in Children*, Chicago, IU: Aldine.
Hilb, C. and Lutzky, D. 1984: *La Nueva Izquierda argentina: 1960–1980*, Buenos Aires: Centro Editor de América Latina.
Jordán, A. 1993: *El Proceso 1976–1983*, Buenos Aires: Emecé Editores.
Moulián, T. 1982: 'La crisis de la izquierda' in *Revista Mexicana de Sociologia*, vol. XLIV, no. 2, April–June, pp. 649–64.
Moyano, M.J. 1995: *Argentina's Lost Patrol: Armed Struggle 1969–1979*, New Haven, Cann.: Yale University Press.
O'Donnell, G. 1982: *El estado Burocrático–Autoritailo. Triunfo, Derrotas y Crisis*, Buenos, Md Aires: Ed Belgrano.
O'Donnell, G., Schmitter, P. and Whitehead, L. (editors) 1986: *Transitions from Authoritarian Rule: Prospects for Democracy*, Baltimore: Johns Hopkins University Press.
Ollier, M.M. 1986: *El fenómeno insurreccional y la cultura política*, CEAL (Centro Editor de América Latina), Buenos Aires: Colección Biblioteca Politica.
Ollier, M.M. 1989: *Orden, poder y violencia (Argentina, 1968–1973)*, Vol. 1/2, CEAL (Centro Editor de América Latina), Buenos Aires: Colección Biblioteca Politica.
Ollier, M.M. 1997: *Dimensions of the Political Learning Process: The Private, The Public and The Political – The Survivors of the Argentinian Revolutionary Left, 1966–1996*, Notre Dame, NB: University of Notre Dame.
Packenham, R. 1986: 'The Changing Political Discourse in Brazil, 1964–1985' in W.A. Selcher (editor), *Political Liberalization in Brazil*, Boulder, Colo and London: Westview Press.
Pécaut, D. 1990: *Os intellectuals é a política no Brasil: Entre o pôvo e a nação*, São Paulo: Editora Atica.
Reader, K. 1987: *Intellectuals and the Left in France since 1968*, New York: St Martin's Press.
Sarlo, B. 1988: 'El campo intelectual: un espacio doblemente fracturado' in S. Sosnowski (editor), *Represión y reconstrucción de una cultura: el caso argentino*, Buenos Aires: Editorial Universitaria de Buenos Aires.
Seoane, M. 1992: *Todo o Nada: La historia secreta y la historia pública del jefe guerrillero Mario Roberto Santucho*, Buenos Aires: Planeta.
Sigel, R.S. (editor) 1989: *Political Learning in Adulthood: A Sourcebook of Theory and Research*, Chicago, III: University of Chicago Press.
Sosnowski, S. (editor) 1988: *Represión y reconstrucción de una cultura: el caso argentino*, Buenos Aires: Editorial Universitaria de Buenos Aires.
Viola, E. 1982: *Democracia e autoritarismo na Argentina Contemporanea*, São Paulo: Universidad de São Paulo.
Walker, I. 1990: *Socialismo y Democracia. Chile y Europa en Perspectiva Comparada*, Santiago: CIEPLAN/HACHETTE.

3
Political Processes and Identity Formation in El Salvador: From Armed Left to Democratic Left

Gerardo L. Munck and Dexter Boniface

The left in El Salvador has undergone some major changes since the 1970s when, confronted with a repressive political system, it abandoned its belief in the possibility of attaining socialism through peaceful means and took up arms. Unable to stage a revolution, it subsequently negotiated a peace accord with its former enemies, laid down arms and became a major force behind the transition to democracy in the late 1980s. Finally in the 1990s, having abandoned violence as a political instrument and successfully undergone a transformation from a guerrilla force to a political party, the left movement began to face a challenge that affected its identity as much as the cycle of political violence did during the 1970s and 1980s – that of defining a socialist agenda in a post-Cold War era. In short, the issue of political violence and subsequently the search for progressive options in a neoliberal age have been the crucibles wherein the identity of the left has been shaped and reshaped during that time.

Focusing on these three main turning points in the recent evolution of the Salvadorian left, this chapter seeks to show how the left's very identity has undergone some very significant changes. Our approach to the study of identity formation firmly rejects the view that identities are either fixed or primordial. Rather, we see identity as something that is configured and reconfigured in the context of dynamic political processes and thus consider the left in relation to the key issues it has faced over time. These issues, it bears stressing, are hardly peculiar to the left in El Salvador. Indeed, because similar issues were confronted by the left, particularly throughout Latin America but also in other Third World societies, the trajectory of the left in El Salvador is somewhat of a microcosm of that of developing societies. The Salvadorian left, thus, not only constitutes an interesting case study in itself, but also opens a window on to its changing identity, roughly since the military coup of 1973 in Chile brought Salvador Allende's experiment with electoral socialism to an end.

Turn to arms: the end of socialism through peaceful means

The first turning point we are concerned with is the turn to arms by Salvadorian leftist groups, a development that can be understood in terms of the rise of opposition to the governing alliance between the military and oligarchy in the late 1960s, and the reaction to these opposition forces by Salvadorian élites. Ever since the peasant insurrection of 1932 was violently suppressed, in an episode that became known as *la matanza* (the massacre), this inter-élite alliance had held political power, determined to retain the status quo by whatever means were necessary (Baloyra 1982). This included, in part, attempts to forestall the advance of opposition forces through the recourse to blatantly rigged elections. A landmark election in this regard was that of 1972, when José Napoleón Duarte, a leader of the Christian Democrats and presidential candidate of a three-party coalition, was prevented from taking office. Indeed, thereafter, electoral fraud became even more pronounced, with the government merely announcing the number of seats given to each party without compiling and publicising general election results (Stanley 1996: chapter 3). But the response of the élites to the rising opposition also took a more sinister turn, with the increased use of repression by both state and private actors associated with the ruling status quo. Thus in 1966, Colonel Rivera oversaw the creation of the National Democratic Organisation (Organización Democrática Nacionalista – ORDEN), a paramilitary organisation aimed particularly at eliminating the opposition in the countryside. In addition, starting in the mid-1970s, a number of extra-governmental organisations or death squads, such as the Anti-Communist Armed Forces of Liberation by Wars of Elimination (Fuerzas Armadas de Liberación Anticomunista de Guerras de Eliminación – FALANGE) and the White Warriors Union (Unión de Guerreros Blancos – UGB), became active in the repression of the opposition (Stanley 1996: 101–5).[1]

The impact of the closed and repressive nature of the political system on the left was quite dramatic. Until then, the dominant force on the left since the 1930s, the Communist Party of El Salvador (Partido Comunista de El Salvador – PCS), had espoused an electoral strategy. That is, it had sought to achieve socialism through peaceful and democratic means. But as the left, as well as centrist forces, became a target of repression in the late 1960s and as the fraudulent character of the electoral process was driven home in 1972, the futility of such thinking was revealed. A similar message came from other quarters, when the Marxist government of Allende in Chile, a crucial point of reference for the left seeking an alternative to the Cuban model of armed insurrection, was overthrown in a military *coup d'état* in 1973.[2] The lesson of developments in both El Salvador and Chile was very clear: democratic channels were not a realistic option for those pursuing a change of the status quo.

This realisation rapidly changed the configuration of the Salvadorian left. As it became clear that socialism through peaceful means was not a viable route, other options were pursued, and the choice rapidly became framed as a continuation of a failed electoral strategy or a turn to arms. This new thinking on the left was first manifested through the formation of various guerrilla organisations that splintered from the PCS, which continued to advocate an electoral strategy. Then, following a massacre in the Plaza Libertad in 1977, even the PCS abandoned its commitment to an electoral route and began organising a guerrilla force. The turn to arms had been completed and by early 1980, with the failure of an attempt at reform launched in the wake of the October 1979 coup by colonels and captains representing a moderate faction of the Armed Forces, civil war had become all but inevitable.

The significance of these developments for the identity of the left deserves some comments. As is well-known, the break-up of the PCS did not result in one single military organisation but rather five distinct guerrilla groups, each with their own unique profile (see Figure 3.1). The most fundamental split, however, was that between the first two guerrilla groups to be formed: the Popular Liberation Forces (Fuerzas Populares de Liberación – FPL) and the People's Revolutionary Army (Ejército Revolucionario Popular – ERP).[3] On the one hand the FPL, formed in 1970, favoured a prolonged engagement (*guerra popular prolongada*), as in Vietnam and China, and were quite willing to follow Moscow's lead on international issues. On the other hand, the ERP, formed in 1971, favoured decisive guerrilla action that would lead to the seizure of power (a '*foco*' strategy), as in Cuba and Nicaragua and, being hesitant about embracing a Marxist–Leninist ideology, were more nationalistic.[4] These two guerrilla groups would be the dominant groups throughout the 1980s. Indeed, while the other three groups retained distinct profiles, they were more or less aligned in ideological terms with these two main groups. Thus, both the National Resistance

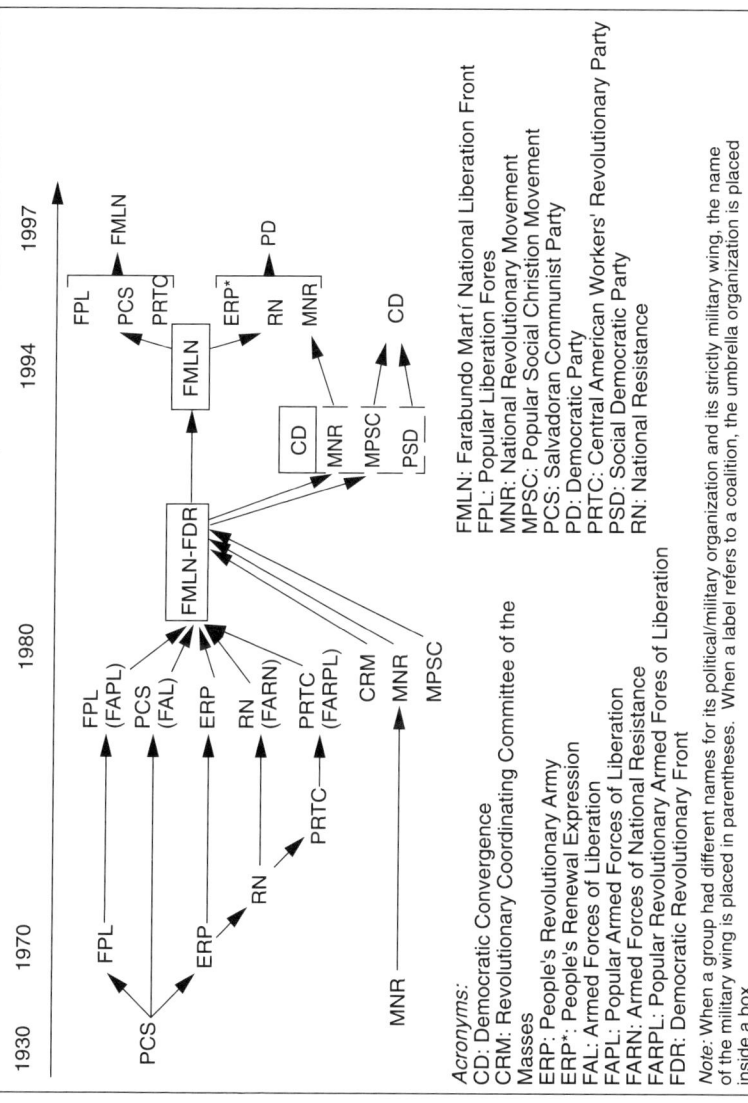

Figure 3.1 Evolution of Leftist Organizations in El Salvador

(Resistencia Nacional – RN), which split from the ERP following the execution of poet Roque Dalton in 1975, and the Central American Workers' Revolutionary Party (Partido Revolucionario de Trabajadores Centroamericanos – PRTC),[5] shared much in common with the ERP. In contrast, when the PCS – a distinctively pro-Moscow organisation – turned to guerrilla activities, it quite naturally was ideologically close to the FPL.[6]

Though some steps were taken to coordinate the activities of these five groups, it is important to stress the limits of the convergence among the various guerrilla organisations. The five groups certainly had an interest in coordinating their actions in pursuit of a common goal – that is, the overthrow of the government. Thus, when Fidel Castro made it clear that his condition for supplying the guerrilla forces with weapons and other needed resources was the formation of a unified command structure, the Farabundo Martí Front for National Liberation (Frente Farabundo Martí para la Liberación Nacional – FMLN) was formed in October 1980 as a military structure that overarched the five politico-military organisations. This formal unity of the guerrilla forces, however, was not the result of some consensus that did away with their differences, and these variances continued to affect how the war was conducted and how the left would eventually confront the post-civil war period. Despite the formation of the FMLN, the five guerrilla groups were maintained as distinct organisations, turning the FMLN into a body that coordinated distinct organisations rather than an 'organic unit' (Prisk 1991:28). Real power, in short, continued to lie in individual politico-military organisations and especially within the FPL and the ERP.

The maintenance of various leftist organisations, each with their distinct leaders, profiles and strategies, should not obscure, however, what was the main change in the identity of the left during the 1970s. Differences within the left aside, practically the entire left movement turned to arms and the rise of an armed left was extremely significant. The resort to violence could be justified as a strategic choice, which was adopted in the face of a new environment, that did not allow for the pursuit of change through peaceful means and was consistent with the left's basic identity as a force for change. Indeed, the left did justify its use of violence, either in terms of the need for revolutionary change to bring about the sought-after goal of socialism, or more poignantly in terms of the present need to resist the use of 'unjust violence'.[7] But if the turn to arms could be seen as an extension of the same politics of the left only through different means, it had unintended consequences on the very politics and identity of the left.

The impact of the turn to arms was clearly evident in the recourse to violence as a way to resolve internal differences among the guerrillas themselves. Within the ERP, the most obvious example was the 1975 'execution' of the popular revolutionary poet Roque Dalton on the spurious grounds that he had committed 'treason' against the revolutionary forces. Within the FPL, the most notorious example of intra-guerrilla violence was the assassination of an important leader of the organisation, Mélida Anaya Montes (alias 'Ana María') in 1983, presumably by Salvador Cayetano Carpio (alias 'Marcial'), one of the founders of the FPL (Castañeda 1993:101–2, 130–2, 351–7). An effect of the turn to arms, in short, was the spillover of violence to internal practices.

But even more crucially, the turn to arms led to a weakened link between the guerrilla forces and their supporters. To be sure, the conduct of war was not carried out in full isolation from the need to mobilise support for the left. Indeed, the politico-military organisations that made up the FMLN not only formed military wings but also a set of popular or mass organisations that were politically coordinated by the Revolutionary Coordinating Committee of the Masses (Coordinadora Revolucionaria de Masas – CRM).[8] The CRM, in turn, joined forces with the National Revolutionary Movement (Movimiento Nacionalista Revolucionario – MNR) and the Popular Social Christian Movement (Movimiento Popular Social Cristiano – MPSC),[9] to constitute an umbrella organisation, the Democratic Revolutionary Front (Frente Democrático Revolucionario – FDR), which was formed in April 1980 for all non-guerrilla components of the left and that became the non-militarised counterpart of the FMLN (see Figure 3.1). But the left did increasingly lose contact with the masses, as the logic of war increasingly clashed and overrode the logic of mass mobilisation.[10] As the key decision-making power was centralised in the military command structure of the FMLN and its constituent organisations, the popular mass-based organisations rapidly ceased to exist as effective entities, while the FDR was little more than an organ for international diplomacy. Even if the left movement had turned to arms for strategic reasons, the means did affect its very identity. For even if the worst distortion of armed struggle – militarism or the use of violence as an end in itself – did not develop, a politics of deliberation, persuasion and organising was increasingly replaced by a politics of force and war. The turn to arms had changed the meaning of left politics.

Negotiating peace: from revolution to democracy

The turn to arms set the trend for the Salvadorian left for several years to come. Starting in January 1981, the guerrillas and government forces became locked in a conflict that would dominate Salvadorian politics throughout the 1980s. There were several initiatives aimed at resolving the civil war, but for a variety of reasons conflict resolution appeared to be an elusive goal for a long time. Indeed, it was only starting in late 1987 that a series of changes began to open the way for the peaceful resolution of conflict, centred around the signing of a peace accord in January 1992.[11]

The reasons behind the peace negotiations were complex, responding in part to external and domestic developments. On the part of the defenders of the status quo, this included changes whereby the United States of America, which had been a firm opponent of negotiations during the Reagan administration, started to show signs of flexibility under President George Bush. Indeed, as the Soviets started to withdraw from Central America following Gorbachev's rise to power, and as progress in Nicaragua was forthcoming in the context of the regional peace accord being brokered by Costa Rican President Oscar Arias, the reduction of the stakes of the regional conflicts generated a climate in which the USA finally started to support, if reluctantly, a negotiated settlement in El Salvador.

Within El Salvador, there were also some crucial changes on the right that opened the way for peace negotiations. Roberto D'Aubuisson, a man widely seen as instigator of the activities of death squads, was replaced at the head of the right-wing National Republican Alliance (Alianza Republicana Nacionalista – ARENA) party, by a more moderate and US-educated conservative, Alfredo Cristiani. This shift, responding to the rise of those elements within ARENA with urban and industrial rather than traditional agricultural concerns, allowed the party to improve its electoral fortunes.[12] Indeed, ARENA emerged as El Salvador's strongest party, winning an important victory in the March 1988 election for the legislative assembly and electing Cristiani as president in March 1989. The good electoral performance of ARENA was quite important, in that it gave the civilian right greater confidence in their ability to operate successfully in some future democratic system, while also putting the Cristiani-led government in a stronger position than the previous government to confront the military and negotiate with the left-wing guerrillas.

Finally, there were also significant developments that led the left movement to undergo a deep rethinking of their attitude towards violence. The first move came from the FMLN's allies in the FDR. Taking advantage of the results of the regional peace negotiations and specifically the signing of the Esquipulas II accord,[13] the FDR's two main leaders, Guillermo Ungo and Rubén Zamora, decided to explore their electoral possibilities and to that end returned to El Salvador from Mexico in November 1987 to form the Democratic Convergence (Convergencia Democrática – CD), a three-party coalition.[14] These two top leaders of the FDR had previously abstained from participation in elections and their decision to retake the path of institutional, democratic politics had a profound effect on the FMLN. It was a sign of the changing tide and made the FMLN leadership acutely aware of the fact that the continuation of a costly civil war with no end in sight translated into a loss of prestige and popular support.[15] For the first time, if still decreeing a transportation boycott, the FMLN decided not to oppose the democratic left's participation in the 1989 presidential election.

The process of change within the left thus had its roots, at least in part, in certain strategic considerations. The FDR leaders were taking advantage of new opportunities which had not been present in the early 1980s. The FMLN, for its part, was responding to the perception that the conflict they were engaged in had become stalemated and that the option of revolution seemed out of reach, as well as to the mounting evidence that the continuation of fighting under these circumstances was likely to eat away at their popular support. This calculus carried all the more sway, moreover, as the FDR leaders not only showed that there were other options to continuing fighting but also that the electoral avenue offered some real opportunities for advancement. Thus, as in the turn to arms in the 1970s, strategic considerations had again played an important role in the politics of the left.

But there was more to the changes on the left in the late 1980s than a strategic response to a changing political environment. For the left movement in El Salvador was also engaged in an ideological critique of the centrality of revolution and a revaluation of democracy as a goal in itself. In this regard, the left in El Salvador was not alone, but was rather part of a broader process of rethinking and renewal of the left throughout Latin America, a process that was given impetus early on by the auto-critique by elements of the Socialist Party in Chile, concerning their role in the breakdown of Chilean democracy. This process was subsequently given greater force as a result of the move towards electoral democracy in Sandinista Nicaragua, along with the collapse of communist-led regimes in Eastern Europe in 1989.[16] Indeed, when the Salvadorian left abandoned its prior commitment to arms and its search for revolution, it was actually part of a worldwide critique of revolutionary politics and a revaluation of democracy.

In sum, the Salvadorian left underwent a second major change in its identity, a change that was undoubtedly driven by strategic considerations, that is, by their assessment of the improbability of revolution, but also by a distinct process of ideological change that led to an increasing appreciation for democracy.[17] As a result, the armed left that had emerged in late 1970s was transformed into a democratic left in the late 1980s and early 1990s.

The dilemmas of a democratic left: socialism in a neo-liberal age?

The shift from armed left to democratic left has been in many regards a smooth process. First of all, the left became a key force behind the prolonged negotiations that led to the signing of a peace accord in January 1992.[18] Subsequently, it demobilised its military apparatus and began transforming itself into a legal political party. Thereafter, this party contested power within a reconstituted political arena and emerged from the 1994 elections as El Salvador's second-strongest political force.[19] But inasmuch as the left successfully transformed itself into a democratic force and as the problem of violence ceased to be the dominant issue on the political agenda, the left movement was forced to confront an issue that would go to the very heart of its identity. Put succinctly, as violence was replaced by democracy, the left had to turn its attention to an issue that has till recently troubled left forces worldwide, that is, it had to search for and define just what progressive options existed in an age in which neo-liberal thought has emerged as hegemonic.

The challenge of defining leftist options within the context of democracy led very quickly to disagreements among the five groups that made up the FMLN. The first disputes emerged over the question of participation in the new legislature's Leadership Council. But the source of division actually went beyond the strategic question of how best to play an oppositional role and was actually rooted in deeper disagreements about ideology and the very goals that would define the left's agenda. These divisions were in some sense nothing new, as the above discussion of the differences between the two main guerrilla groups, the ERP and the FPL, shows. What was different was that divisions which throughout the 1980s had been subsumed for the most part under the strategic imperative of operating in a society wracked by political violence came to the fore as democratisation proceeded.

In the new context of democracy, the left would undergo a fairly thorough process of reorganisation. Divisions within the FMLN over basic ideological issues became apparent in late September 1993, when the ERP announced that it was formally abandoning Marxist–Leninist beliefs and espousing social democracy, thus distinguishing itself from the FPL, which continued to support a fairly orthodox Marxist perspective. Then in December 1994, a formal split occurred, as the ERP leader Joaquín Villalobos announced his group's withdrawal from the FMLN and the RN followed suit a few days later.[20] This process of reorganisation continued throughout 1995, as the ERP joined forces with the RN and the MNR to form the centre-left Democratic Party (Partido Democrático – PD) in March 1995. Soon after, the FPL (the largest group on the left), the PCS (the left movement's oldest organisation) and the PRTC[21] disbanded and reorganised into a single, left-oriented party in August 1995, that retained the FMLN label. The landscape of the left had changed quite considerably (see Figure 3.1).[22]

As had been the case in its prior turning points, the transformation of the Salvadorian left in the 1990s reflected broader regional trends. After a period in which the problem of violence had dominated its agenda, the left movement now had to face an issue that was once again critical for its identity – that is, the definition of an agenda of change which could be advanced within a new context of democracy, but also of neo-liberal ideas. In other words, having contributed to the rise of democracy, the left had to confront the question of just what their utopia consisted of and what socialism would mean in the new post-Cold War world. In response to this question, the Salvadorian left, much as the left throughout Latin America, split between modernising and orthodox sections, that is, with the first group abandoning their prior agenda of socialism and Marxism, out of considerations of both necessity and conviction, for the more moderate agenda of social democracy,[23] while the second group continued to espouse a radical ideology and to cling to the possibility of sweeping transformations.

When viewed in a regional perspective, however, there is an interesting contrast between the relative success of the new centre-left and left parties in El Salvador and most of Latin America. Indeed in this regard, El Salvador has diverged from a trend which has seen the modernised and moderate left doing extremely well, as the experience of countries like Chile and Brazil shows.[24] In contrast, the FMLN did considerably better than the PD in the March 1997 municipal and legislative elections. Barely losing to ARENA, the FMLN gained 32 per cent of total votes and increased its representation in the Legislative Assembly from

14 to 27 seats. The PD, on the other hand, was not able to reach the 3 per cent threshold required for parties to be legally recognised and has remained a party only as a result of ARENA's intervention on the PD's behalf.[25] The evolution of the left in El Salvador, then, raises some very interesting questions. Most critically, there is a sense in which El Salvador has come full circle, as indicated by trends such as the hardening of the left but also of the right, the polarisation of the electorate and the lack of viability of the social democratic left. The question, then, is whether it will be able to avoid a renewal of the cycle of frustrated reform and radicalisation that led these Central and Latin American countries down the road of violence in the late 1970s, or in other terms, whether it will provide a more positive example of the search for change within democracy than that offered by Allende's Chile.[26]

Conclusion: moving beyond political violence as a basis of identity

Since the 1970s, the left's identity has undergone fairly dramatic transformations in the context of three distinct moments. First, the left was drawn towards the use of violence, as violence became the only option through which they could pursue their political agenda in the 1970s and thereby became an armed left. Thereafter, as the odds that armed struggle would lead to revolution diminished throughout the 1980s and as democracy became increasingly valued as a goal in itself, the left started to become a force for peace and democracy and began a process of transformation from armed left to political party. Once this transformation was accomplished, that is, once the left had completed its change from armed left to democratic left, and accepted that political conflicts had to be limited and channelled within democratic institutions, its distinct stance towards political violence ceased to be the dominant axis around which identity was defined. Indeed, the Salvadorian left in the 1990s has had to face a question which had never really emerged with clarity during the prior period and that had been subsumed under the strategic imperative of operating in a society racked by political violence – that is, the question of what the goals of the left are and whether its ostensible goal of socialism continued to be a defining feature.

It is in this new context of peace and democracy that the Salvadorian left has undergone its deepest crisis of identity, as some segments have abandoned the goal of socialism, a criterion it used to be defined by until the collapse of state socialism in the East and when it embraced social democracy. So far, the dominant groups of the left have resisted this trend quite effectively. It remains an open question at this point in time, however, if the orthodox left in El Salvador will continue to resist the pressures toward social democracy, or if its greater participation in government as a result of its successes in the 1997 elections and its aspirations in the context of the 1999 presidential elections will also gradually force it to rethink what socialism means and what kind of progressive politics is actually feasible in this day and age.

Notes

1. Though ORDEN was dissolved as a legal entity after 1979 it continued to operate independently of the government. Indeed, one of the organisation's members, Roberto D'Aubuisson, would become El Salvador's most notorious abuser of human rights.
2. The significance of developments in Chile for El Salvador is evident in a statement of Miguel Castellanos, an activist in the Popular Liberation Forces (FPL), one of the first guerrilla groups to emerge during this time period. He argues that 'To a great degree, the overthrow of Allende showed the invalidity of the PCS's thesis', that is, of its advocacy of an electoral strategy (Prisk 1991:11). From a different perspective, centrist politician Napoleón Duarte was arriving at a similar conclusion. As he put it, 'Many people concluded that the powers ruling El Salvador would never permit votes to defeat them. Change had to come by other means' (quoted in Manwaring and Prisk 1988:18).
3. While the FPL was a political/military organisation, it spawned a strictly military wing that had a different name: the Popular Armed Forces of Liberation (Fuerzas Armadas Populares de Liberación – FAPL).
4. Castellanos of the FPL thus argues that 'Ideologically they [the ERP] weren't Marxist–Leninists' (Prisk 1991:37). On the differences between the FPL and the ERP, see NACLA (1982) and Montgomery (1995:chapter 4).
5. The PRTC was originally formed in early 1976 as a regional, that is, Central American, party. After October 1980, however, the party increasingly disbanded international ties and organised exclusively in the domestic context of El Salvador.
6. As in the case of the FPL, these political/military organisations also had strictly military counterparts with distinct names. The military wing of the RN was called the Armed Forces of National Resistance (Fuerzas Armadas de Resistencia Nacional – FARN), that of the PRTC the Popular Revolutionary Armed Forces of Liberation (Fuerzas Armadas Revolucionarias Populares de Liberación – FARPL), and finally, that of the PCS's armed wing the Armed Forces of Liberation (Fuerzas Armadas de Liberación – FAL).
7. As one priest who had turned to liberation theology stated, 'I am against violence, but even more against unjust violence. There is another *matanza* going on in the countryside. If the solution to this is Marxism, let it come, rather than what is here' (quoted in North 1981:77).
8. The mass organisations coordinated by the CRM were the Popular Revolutionary Bloc (Bloque Popular Revolucionario – BPR), formed by the

FPL in 1975; the 28th of February Popular Leagues (Ligas Populares 28 de Febrero – LP-28), formed by the ERP in 1978; the United Popular Action Front (Frente de Acción Popular Unificada – FAPU), formed by the RN in 1974; and the National Democratic Union (Unión Democrática Naciónal – UDN), formed by the PCS in 1967. Only the Popular Liberation Movement (Movimiento d!e Liberación Popular – MLP), formed in 1979 by the PRTC, was not linked to the CRM.
9. The MPSC, led by Rubén Zamora, was formed by dissidents within the Christian Democratic party in early 1980. The MNR, led by Guillermo Ungo, had been formed earlier, in 1965.
10. Similar trends have also been found among other guerrilla groups in Latin America. See, for example, the discussion of the Montoneros in Argentina in Gillespie (1982).
11. For an extended discussion of the failure of compromise during the 1981–87 period and the changes that subsequently made possible the peaceful resolution of conflict, see Munck (1993:77–81) and Munck and Kumar (1995).
12. Since 1982, elections had been held on a regular basis, but the FMLN had alternated between boycotting and sabotaging these elections. If abstention was in many ways a choice, it is also important to stress the sense in which the left was essentially forced to abstain from participation because the government could not ensure the physical protection of leftist candidates. Indeed, it is hard to support the view that these elections were democratic.
13. The Esquipulas II accord was signed by the elected presidents of Guatemala, El Salvador, Honduras, Nicaragua and Costa Rica in August 1987. On the Central American peace process, see Child (1992) and Dunkerley (1994:40–6).
14. The CD was founded in 1987 by Zamora, of the MPSC, Ungo, of the MNR, and Mario Reni Roldán, head of the new Social Democratic Party (Partido Social Democrático – PSD).
15. The growing popular sentiment for peace in the mid-1980s was clearly an important factor behind the resolution of the civil war. By 1987, 83 per cent of the Salvadorian population supported negotiation (Karl 1992:151), and FMLN campaigns of destroying bridges and power plants became increasingly unpopular.
16. On this regional process of ideological change, see Touraine (1988:chapter 13), Lechner (1988), Cavarozzi (1992, 1993), Castañeda (1993) and Pelletier (1996).
17. A clear statement of the various strategic and ideological considerations that led to the abandonment of arms by the Salvadorian left is provided by Villalobos (1989), a leader of the ERP.
18. On the negotiation of the peace accord, a process that took place over a period of 21 months, from April 1990 to January 1992, and on the subsequent implementation of the accord, see Karl (1992:154–60), Munck (1993:81–6) and Stahler-Sholk (1994:9–23).
19. For the purpose of the 1994 elections, the left formed a coalition, made up of the FMLN, the Democratic Convergence (CD), and the National Revolutionary Movement (MNR), which supported Rubén Zamora for president. In the first round Zamora received 25 per cent of the votes, in con-

trast to the 49 per cent going to the ARENA candidate, Armando Calderón Sol. In the run-off election, between the two top vote-getters, Zamora received 31.7 per cent of the votes while 68.2 per cent went to the victor, Calderón Sol. In the 84-seat unicameral legislature, the FMLN's 21 seats were second only to the ARENA's 39 seats. On the 1994 elections, see Stahler-Sholk (1994:23–34).
20. As part of its transformation the ERP underwent a name change, from People's Revolutionary Army to Renovating Expression of the People (Expresión Renovadora del Pueblo – ERP). The acronym, however, remained the same: ERP. On the differing positions held by groups within the FMLN and the break-up of the FMLN, see Vickers and Spence (1994:10–11), Vilas (1995), and Spence *et al.*, (1997:20–1, 24–7). For the views of the social democratic left, see Villalobos (1992). For the views of the orthodox Marxist sectors, see the writings of Shafik Handal (Handal and Vilas, 1993), the leader of the PCS that was closely associated with the position of the FPL.
21. The PRTC, which had originally formed as a splinter of the ERP and followed the ERP's lead, had increasingly come under the sway of the PCS. Rather than joining the PD, thus, it followed the PCS and the FPL into the FMLN.
22. With the break-up of the FMLN, the FMLN's legislative bloc was divided. The PD bloc controlled seven seats formerly held by the ERP and the RN, while the FMLN controlled fourteen seats previously held by the FPL, PCS and PRTC.
23. The new thinking on the left is well captured by Przeworski (1991:chapter 3, 1993) and Casteñeda (1993).
24. In Chile, while the renewed left, represented by the Party for Democracy (PPD) and the Socialist Party (PS), has gained over 20 per cent in elections held since 1989 and has been part of the governing coalition along with the Christian Democratic Party, the orthodox Communist Party has only hovered around 5 per cent. In Brazil, while the Labour Party (PT), which has only gradually undergone a renewal process, has done very well in elections, it was the Social Democratic Party (PSDB) led by Fernando Cardoso that came to power in 1995 as part of a fairly conservative coalition of forces.
25. The basis for a cooperative relationship between ARENA and the PD was established soon after the 1994 elections. In a conflict that precipitated the break-up of the FMLN, the ERP and RN representatives in the new legislature supported the ARENA candidate to the presidency of the National Assembly, Gloria Salguero Gross, against the objections of the FMLN hardliners. In return, the ERP–RN had members elected as vice-president and secretary of the assembly.
26. While El Salvador diverged from the pattern set by South American countries, its evolution closely parallels that of Nicaragua. In Nicaragua, as in El Salvador, a guerrilla movement, the Sandinista Front of National Liberation (Frente Sandinista de Liberación Naciónal – FSLN), became a political party that contested power through democratic elections. Following the inauguration of democracy through an election that saw the rise of a right-wing coalition to power in 1990, the FSLN also split into two new parties, giving rise to the orthodox FSLN and the social democratic

Sandinista Renovation Movement (MRS) in February 1995. And thereafter, the parallel continued, with the orthodox left out-polling the moderate left. Indeed, in the elections of October 1996, the FSLN held its ground as the second political force, with its leader Daniel Ortega coming in second in the presidential race, while the FSLN gained 37 seats in the 93-seat unicameral National Assembly. Meanwhile, the MRS's presidential candidate, Sergio Ramírez, got less than 0.5 per cent of the votes, and the MRS gained only one seat in the legislature. Thus, the same questions that emerge from a consideration of the evolution of the left in El Salvador apply to Nicaragua.

References

Baloyra, E. 1982: *El Salvador in Transition*, Chapel Hall, NC: University of North Carolina Press.

Castañeda, J.G. 1993: *Utopia Unarmed. The Latin American Left After The Cold War*, New York: Knopf.

Cavarozzi, M. 1992: 'The Left in Latin America: The Decline of Socialism and the Rise of Political Democracy' in J. Hartlyn, L. Shoultz and A. Varas (editors), *The United States and Latin America in the 1990s*, Chapel Hill, NC: University of North Carolina Press.

Cavarozzi, M. 1993: 'The Left in South America: Politics as the Only Option' in Menno Vellinga (editor), *Social Democracy in Latin America. Prospects for Change*, Boulder, Colo: Westview Press.

Child, J. 1992: *The Central American Peace Process, 1983–1991*, Boulder, Colo: Lynne Rienner Publishers.

Dunkerley, J. 1994: *The Pacification of Central America*, London: Verso.

Gillespie, R. 1982: *Soldiers of Perón – Argentina's Montoneros*, Oxford: Clarendon Press.

Handal, S. and Vilas, C.M. 1993: *The Socialist Option in Central America: Two Reassessments*, New York: Monthly Review Press.

Karl, T.L. 1992: 'El Salvador's Negotiated Revolution' in *Foreign Affairs*, vol. 71, no. 2, Spring, pp. 147–64.

Lechner, N. 1988: 'De la revolución a la democracia' in Norbert Lechner (editor), *Los patios interiores de la democracia. Subjetividad y política*, Santiago: FLACSO.

Manwaring, M.G. and Prisk, C.E. (editors) 1988: *El Salvador at War: An Oral History of Conflict from the 1979 Insurrection to the Present*, Washington, DC: National Defense University Press.

Montgomery, T.S. 1995: *Revolution in El Salvador. From Civil Strife to Civil Peace* (2nd edn), Boulder, Colo: Westview Press.

Munck, G.L. 1993: 'Beyond Electoralism in El Salvador: Conflict Resolution Through Negotiated Compromise' in *Third World Quarterly*, vol. 14, no. 1, pp. 75–93.

Munck, G.L. and Kumar, C. 1995: 'Civil Conflicts and the Conditions for Successful International Intervention: A Comparative Study of Cambodia and El Salvador' in *Review of International Studies*, vol. 21, no. 2, April, pp. 159–81.

NACLA 1982: 'The Revolution Stumbles' in *NACLA Report on the Americas*, vol. 16, no. 2, March/April, pp. 23–31.

North, L. 1981: *Bitter Grounds: Roots of Revolt in El Salvador*, Toronto: Between the Lines.

Pelletier, S.R. 1996: *Revolution Reassessed. Democracy and the Left in Contemporary Central America*, Amork, NY: M.E. Sharpe.

Prisk, C.E. (editor) 1991: *The Comandante Speaks: Memoirs of an El Salvadoran Guerrilla Leader*, Boulder, Colo: Westview Press.

Przeworski, A. 1991: *Democracy and the Market. Political and Economic Reforms in Eastern Europe and Latin America*, New York: Cambridge University Press.

Przeworski, A. 1993: 'Socialism and Social Democracy' in J. Krieger (editor), *The Oxford Companion to the Politics of the World*, New York: Oxford University Press.

Spence, J., Dye, D.R., Lanchin, M., Thale, G. with Vickers, G. 1997: *Chapúltepec: Five Years Later – El Salvador's Political Realities and Uncertain Future*, Cambridge, Mass: Hemisphere Initiatives.

Stahler-Sholk, R. 1994: 'El Salvador's Negotiated Transition: From Low Intensity Conflict to Low Intensity Democracy' in *Journal of Interamerican Studies and World Affairs*, vol. 36, no. 4, Winter, pp. 1–59.

Stanley, W. 1996: *The Protection Racket State. Elite Politics, Military Extortion, and Civil War in El Salvador*, Philadelphia, Pa: Temple University Press.

Touraine, A. 1988: *The Return of the Actor. Social Theory in Postindustrial Society*, Minneapolis: University of Minnesota Press.

Vickers, G. and Spence, J. 1994: 'Elections: The Right Consolidates Power' in *NACLA Report on the Americas*, vol. 28, No. 1, July/August, pp. 6–11.

Vilas, C.M. 1995: 'A Painful Peace. El Salvador After the Accords' in *NACLA Report on the Americas*, vol. 28, no. 6, May/June, pp. 6–11.

Villalobos, J. 1989: 'A Democratic Revolution for El Salvador' in *Foreign Policy*, vol. 74, Spring, pp. 103–22.

Villalobos, J. 1992: *Una revolución en la izquierda para una revolución democrática*, San Salvador: Arcoiris.

4
South Africa: From 'Racial Conflict' to Democratic Settlement[1]
Alan Emery and Rupert Taylor

Why were the widespread expectations of racial conflagration in South Africa misplaced? This chapter contests the conventional wisdom in South African studies that the country was trapped in an irresolvable 'white' versus 'black' politics, with additional racial conflicts as the country's most likely future. Such apocalyptic scenarios were flawed precisely because they overlooked the transformative changes in 'white' and 'black' politics. In this chapter we argue that resolution of the conflicts through democratisation was tied to shifts in collective identities away from 'race'. In both 'white' and 'black' communities, an emergent non-racialism was created during the course of political struggle in the 1980s. Democratic settlement, then, rested on a partial transcendence of racial definitions of South African society.

Prior to the democratic settlement, there is no doubt that most analyses of the conflict in South Africa were framed in terms of 'race', Politicians, media pundits and academics, all in varying degrees, and with few dissenting voices, have rendered accounts of the conflict in terms of either 'race relations', or in terms of 'black' and 'white', with a 'black majority' confronting a 'white minority'. Underlying such accounts, whether popular or scholarly, has been the presumption that South African politics is transparent and fully understandable in terms of 'race', with conflictual behaviour being seen to flow from the different 'nature' of racial group identities. The dominant approach has been to see the character of the conflicts in South Africa in terms of 'rigid identities' in a seemingly 'irresolvable zero-sum conflict' – that is, where political gain for one group implies loss for the other. Hence, many prophets of doom foretold an inevitable apocalyptic 'race war'.

The view that intractable identity issues dominate and frame South African politics is hardly surprising as Afrikaner nationalism, which swept the National Party (NP) to power in 1948, was institutionalised through the ascendancy of a racially exclusive polity cast in 'black' and 'white' (Carter 1958). Apartheid was a set of state policies advancing Afrikaner ethno-national interests and 'white' privilege, through 'black' exclusion and economic exploitation. With racial distinctions taken as the basis of the distinctiveness of identities and separateness in community life, racialism was legally constructed and upheld by the apartheid state. The Population Registration Act of 1950 laid the groundwork in creating the racial categories and segregation that came to guide nearly all state policy – that is, 'White', 'Coloured', 'Indian' and 'Black'. In addition, the Prohibition of Mixed Marriages Act of 1949 and Immorality Amendment Act of 1950 imposed mandatory rules governing personal relationships. Other apartheid legislation worked to racially limit access to residential areas, public and private services, and amenities. These racist laws served to heighten racial consciousness, to give 'race' social and cultural connotations (Kuper 1960). In short, 'race' was entrenched as the basis for access to power, resources and socio-economic prosperity or impoverishment.

In line with state policy, the NP persistently defined and emphasised the situation in terms of 'race' and propagated the view that interracial contact leads inevitably to conflict (Verwoerd 1966). With South African society being cast in such antagonistic form and given the large-scale, socio-structural inequalities between 'black' and 'white', many 'whites' were ever fearful of a 'black uprising', and ever vigilant of a 'terrorist war' (Hanf et al. 1981:206–9). The prospect of black majority rule was constructed to be a nightmare scenario. Indeed, even at the time of the April 1994 democratic elections, some 'whites', consumed with apocalyptic visions, were 'stockpiling dry goods or even arranging to be abroad for election week' (Johnson 1994:6).

Correspondingly, the conventional theoretical wisdom in South Africa studies since the 1960s was that the country could not democratise peacefully because of 'the zero-sum communal conflict' between 'black' and 'white' or, more specifically, between a 'white' racial-nationalism, primarily embodied by the NP, and a 'black' anti-colonial struggle for independence, primarily embodied by the African National Congress (ANC). Several influential studies written by Pierre van den Berghe in the 1960s stressed that political change in South Africa could not be peaceful; that 'The opposing forces of Afrikaner and African nationalism have become increasingly polarized ideologically' (van den Berghe 1965:182); and that 'A South Africa divided against itself awaits its impending doom' (van den Berghe 1967:110).

Needless to say, the view that violence was the only route forward became the accepted norm in much intellectual thinking. The country was seen to be a fraction away from revolution and, as John Brewer wrote, 'in the late 1960s and early 1970s the overthrow of apartheid in South Africa was thought to be inevitable' (Brewer 1989:2). From the Marxist perspective, apartheid was interpreted as a form of super-exploitation, which '*only* revolutionary action on the part of the black masses ... inextricably linked to a socialist economic strategy' could smash (Asheron 1969:55–6, Legassick 1974). In the 1980s Brewer himself captured the sense of time running out by subtitling an edited collection of essays as *Five Minutes to Midnight*. Many political scientists erroneously subscribed to the view of Arend Lijphart that 'In the extreme cases of plural societies such as South Africa, the outlook for democracy of any kind is extremely poor' (Lijphart 1977:236).

In the 1990s, the dominant vision continued to be one of viewing South Africa in terms of mobilised racial blocs – Afrikaner versus African nationalism – a position supported within academic circles by the application of plural society theory and, more recently, conflict modernisation theory. Notable recent works that have advanced this standpoint include Hermann Giliomee and Lawrence Schlemmer's *From Apartheid to Nation-Building* (1991) and Milton Esman's *Ethnic Politics* (1994). This overriding perception of South Africa and its prospects, though, clearly confronts a major problem. For how can they begin to explain – outside of believing in a world of 'miracles' – the way in which the democratic settlement in South Africa was made *possible*? Where did the social forces for peace come from?

The source of the problem here is not hard to trace, for the conventional wisdom rests on a particularistic and highly contestable reading of identity politics – that is, it clearly rests on the objectification of collective identities, whereby people are seen first and foremost to have separate racial group identities. Thereafter it presumes that South African politics can be reduced to those totalised racial identities, which have to be examined and understood as an unchanging phenomenon. This, however, is not a position that can be defended with any intellectual sophistication. It is not hard to show that people's identities are more fluid, fractured and precarious. This can be revealed by directly addressing the central question of the extent to which the conflict in South Africa can be seen in terms of 'black' and 'white'. Are the collective identities which have been assumed to 'underpin' South African politics what the dominant story has suggested? Should politics be reduced to issues of 'black' versus 'white' identity? Or is an alternative and more complex analysis necessary?

Transformation of 'white' politics

As far as the supposed 'white' bloc is concerned, a most significant transformation in the identity of the former ruling NP occurred during the 1980s. This transformation involved the complex unfolding of interests, as the NP moved from being a populist Afrikaner ethnonationalist party to one dominated by broader 'white' racial concerns that were coupled with conservative class interests. Under F.W. de Klerk, the party dropped its racial exclusivism and became more or less multiracial in its outlook. Central to this shift was the 'modernisation' of South African society – that is, economic growth, increasing levels of urbanisation and educational provision, and a changing class structure (Waldmeir 1997:22–36, Crankshaw 1997) – with what were once marked economic differences between Afrikaners and English speakers rapidly diminished. The differential in per capita income, having been two to one in 1948, was virtually eliminated by 1980. These social forces came to impact upon the social bases and politics of the NP.

Indeed, in the 1980s there were two other crucial and interrelated changes. First, there was the break-up of Afrikaner nationalism as a coherent political force. In March 1982, the NP split up and the right-wing Conservative Party (CP) was formed later that year. This was in reaction to the limited reform moves of P.W. Botha, specifically the establishment of the racially-based tricameral parliament (the 1983 Constitution), with separate houses for 'Whites', 'Coloureds' and 'Indians', but not for 'Blacks' (O'Meara 1996:251–316). For the *verkramptes* (reactionary Afrikaner nationalists), such 'power-sharing' was seen to involve losing control over the state and with it 'white' self-determination. Second, there was the development of a new NP constituency around an emergent multiracial, conservative class politics. Prior to the 1980s, class cleavages within the Afrikaner community did little or nothing to affect voting behaviour, but in this decade there were dramatic changes in the class and 'ethnic' composition of the NP. Historically, it was the party of the poor 'white' Afrikaner, but by the end of the 1980s this was no longer the case. Within Afrikanerdom, much of the working-class vote went over to the Conservative Party, whereas amongst English-speaking 'whites', approximately 20 per cent of the working class and over 40 per cent of the professional and managerial class switched allegiance to the NP. In 1977, the NP attracted over 85 per cent support from Afrikaners (Lemon 1987:98) and by 1989, this had fallen to under 50 per cent (O'Meara 1996:400).

Underlying this convergence was a move away from ethno-national identity politics towards developing a middle-class agenda, with the state drawing the corporate world into the policy-making process and the NP championing a market-orientated economy (Schrire 1991). More broadly, this transformation can be traced in party propaganda and discourse from the 1970s onwards, through a decline in ethno-nationalist sentiment around *volks*-unity, and the rise of multinationalist and conservative class concerns. The NP's 1974 election manifesto reveals a concerted effort by its leadership to persuade their Afrikaner following to accept multilingualism, calling for 'National Unity' between Afrikaans and English-speaking 'white' South Africans. By 1986 in contrast, speeches at the Federal Congress made no mention of the claim that Afrikaners were a distinct group from English-speakers and NP documents separated the term 'nation' from its past exclusivist cultural overtones.

The Afrikaner power élite moved to redefine their interests less in terms of symbolic meaning and historic identity and more through pragmatic rationality and scientific reasoning. Heribert Adam had identified this trend as far back as 1971 in his book *Modernizing Racial Domination*, wherein he argued that South Africa was governed by a pragmatic oligarchy, capable of altering the mould of social organisation from a race-based to a class-based one. After 1982, with the far-right ideologues out of the NP, there was room for the *verligtes* (enlightened Afrikaner nationalists) to push ahead with new thinking. For, as early as 1977, 'even to the most obtuse [*verligte*] members of the Afrikaner intelligentsia the moral perversity and intellectual bankruptcy of apartheid had become clear' (Shingler 1994:20). Debates around the 1983 Constitution had involved the NP in attempting to reconcile apartheid with liberal democratic principles, by drawing on concepts of cultural pluralism and consociationalism, with notions of multi-ethnic rule as opposed to majority rule. Given the high level of popular resistance to the tricameral parliament, there was a move to explore the idea of voluntary (instead of statutorily defined) group membership, in order to search for a new constitutional model that, although committed to a group-orientated view of power-sharing, would get away from conceiving of groups as legally defined categories (Taylor 1990). With growing international isolation, economic sanctions and ever-mounting internal resistance, it was increasingly apparent that the costs of apartheid domination were too high and that apartheid ideology was incapable of providing answers. As long as the state maintained a commitment to a racial division of powers, it fell well beyond the bounds of respectability and was unable to find legitimate negotiating partners.

In February 1990, F.W. de Klerk un-banned the ANC, Pan-Africanist Congress (PAC) and South African Communist Party (SACP), released Nelson Mandela along with other political prisoners and then moved to repeal apartheid legislation. F.W. de Klerk declared that, 'I have an obligation to lead South Africa into a new era of its history ... The old one has finally passed' (in W.J. de Klerk 1991:173). The NP opened its doors to all South Africans, abandoning formal reference to any overt racial group politics, and projected a 'new' South Africa in which power would be shared *with* 'black' people. Implicit in this shift was a dawning recognition that attempts to reconcile 'group rights' with individual rights were impossible, as in the South African context 'group rights' were so closely associated with past racial exclusiveness. In the process of four years of constitutional negotiation (1990–4), key negotiators within the NP came to see all South Africans as individuals with common interests and accepted that a constitutional state, in which individual rights are protected in a Bill of Rights, provides sufficient safeguards for human liberty (Asmal 1993).

The role of dissident Afrikaner intellectuals was important in promoting sustained public dialogue concerning the direction of the whole Afrikaner nationalist project, suggesting that real benefits could be gained by changing track and exploring alternatives. They argued that Afrikaner cultural and social identity, redefined and broadened, might survive in a democratic South Africa – see for example, the work of Johan Degenaar and Willie Esterhuyse of the University of Stellenbosch. More generally, within apartheid 'civil' society, the need to go beyond apartheid was increasingly recognised. The Dutch Reformed Church officially moved in 1986 to question the theological justification for apartheid, while leading members of the 'white' establishment travelled to Lusaka (from 1985) and Dakar (July 1987) to meet the ANC. New thinking was also encouraged within the Afrikaner *Broederbond* (League of Brothers), whose members included the NP's inner circle and which, under J.P. de Lange, set out to encourage dialogue with 'black' South Africans through a confidential network of discussion groups (Schutte 1995:155–61, Waldmeir 1997:51–3). Gradually, the real and imagined risks of an inclusivist alternative for South Africa was eroded in the perception of key NP members and some supporters, resulting in greater susceptibility to change (see Adam 1971:118).

Beyond the dissent and questioning in Afrikanerdom, it is also necessary to recognise the presence of other progressive white South Africans and their role in attempting to push the centre of 'white' politics towards embracing a democratic society (Jaster and Jaster 1993). To the left of the NP, it is important to point:

- the Progressive Federal Party (PFP) and later the Democratic Party (DP) – which gained 20 per cent of 'white' support in the last 'whites-only' election of 1989;
- sections of the press (for example, *Rand Daily Mail*, *Weekly Mail*);
- certain institutes (for example, South African Institute of Race Relations, Christian Institute);
- the churches (for example, South African Council of Churches, Southern African Catholic Bishops Conference);
- the student movement (for example, National Union of South African Students);
- the End Conscription Campaign – which supported 'white' conscripts who refused military service in the South African Defence Force (SADF).

The English-language universities, in particular, also became sites of struggle against the apartheid state (Shear 1996). Such forces worked for the articulation and organisation of anti-apartheid opinion, and in different ways and with varying success challenged what it meant to be a 'white' South African.

In sum, the intransigence and homogeneity of 'white' politics should not be exaggerated; there has been no universally accepted measure by which 'white' society defined itself and not all those designated as 'white' supported apartheid. It should not be presupposed that the 46 years of highly repressive apartheid rule were marked by the 'white' population being moulded into a single unified societal bloc, despite the fact that most 'whites' did benefit during the apartheid system (some quite significantly) when compared to the vast majority of people deemed 'non-white'.

Rejection of 'black' politics

As far as the supposed 'black' bloc is concerned, here too a mistaken exclusivism has been assumed, for the ANC has not viewed the struggle against apartheid as a 'racial conflict' – such a definition of the conflict has been imposed by others. To suggest that the ANC is an 'ethnic political movement', with Nelson Mandela being an 'ethnic politician', or to talk of 'black resistance', 'black opposition', or 'black protest', is to miss the vital significance of non-racial politics and vision (Frederikse 1990). As one activist puts it, 'Mandela ... is not concerned with colour, he is not concerned with black or white' (in Hanf et al. 1981:353). More broadly, the ANC has seen itself as a voice for all people and foresaw a common society in which everyone has the right to full participation in government. The Freedom Charter, which was adopted by an alliance of progressive forces in late June 1955, stated that 'South Africa belongs to all who live in it, black and white' (Suttner and Cronin 1986:262).

The adoption of the Freedom Charter led to a split in the ANC and the formation of the PAC, which had a stronger nativist–African vision and objected to the participation of 'whites' in the anti-apartheid movement – similar to the policy adopted by the Zimbabwe African National Union (ZANU) during the post-colonial struggle for liberation.[2] In contrast, the ANC, in its opposition to apartheid, increasingly rejected racial segregation and encouraged organisational openness. It also moved further and further into multiracial alliances: in 1969, the External Mission of the ANC opened its membership to 'non-Africans' – akin to the policy of the Zimbabwe African People's Union (ZAPU). Accordingly, the South African case cannot and should not be reduced to a 'black' versus 'white' conflict. During the course of struggle against the apartheid state, the terms of conflict were increasingly transformed, since resistance was not built primarily around viewing the struggle as one 'between two races for domination ... [but as] a struggle between the protagonists of racial domination and the advocates of racial equality' (Asmal et al. 1996:41).

In terms of the armed struggle against apartheid – which followed the banning of the ANC in 1960 and was waged between 1961 and 1990 – South Africa never witnessed a 'revolutionary war' as such (Lodge 1986). With the apartheid state's capability to call up 400 000 combat-ready troops, there was no possibility of overthrowing 'white' domination militarily. Many years went by without Umkhonto we Sizwe (MK), the ANC's armed wing, being responsible for any shootings or explosions inside the country. The climax of the armed struggle came in 1986, but through the use of superior force and terror, and by labelling the ANC/MK as 'terrorists', the apartheid state managed to contain guerrilla activity. In total the MK trained over 12 000 guerrillas, of which over half had been deployed in South Africa. However, between 1976 and 1989, the MK was involved in no more than 800 incidents and a former Commissioner of Police only attributed 153 deaths to alleged 'acts of terror' (Barrell 1990, Asmal et al. 1996:41), and around 700 MK combatants were captured or killed by the SADF (Barrell 1990:64). The numbers killed in the armed struggle between the MK and the security forces stand in contrast to the thousands killed by the systemic violence of apartheid:

- over 700 dead in the Soweto uprising of 1976;
- over 4000 dead during the insurrectionary period of 1984–8;
- over 16 000 dead in political violence in KwaZulu-Natal;

From the ANC's perspective, the armed struggle was certainly not part of a 'race war'. Whilst on the ground, particularly in the townships, there was a popular conception of revolutionary action, key strategists within the ANC (and the apartheid state) never believed 'that Umkhonto we Sizwe was going to march into Pretoria with its banner flying and its guns held high' (Ellis and Sechaba 1992:173). Rather, the MK took up arms 'to create the conditions for credible peace', in order to force changes to avoid 'race war'. MK activity was guided by the belief that they 'should not foster the kind of bitterness that might lead to race war in South Africa' (Barrell 1990:4,70, Barrell 1993). The enemy was not seen to be 'whites', but the apartheid system, and the MK focused most of its armed activities on 'hard targets' – that is, military, police, state infrastructure – generally avoiding civilian casualties. In MK training camps, 'the history of the ANC ... was taught to MK cadres ... [the] non-racial policy of the ANC, that it is not a white skin we are fighting, we're fighting the system that is unjust. We want to remove that system. After that we say South Africa belongs to all of us, black and white' (Mills and Burrows 1996:29). The MK itself was non-racial in membership, having 'white' soldiers and for years one of its key commanders – Joe Slovo – was 'white' (Kasrils 1993, Slovo 1995).

Beyond the struggle being waged by MK combatants, the ANC sought to get involved and establish a social base inside South Africa by promoting a network of civic organisations to oppose the apartheid state (Mbeki 1996:46). To this end the ANC infiltrated some of its activists back into the country. Here, it was recognised that the way forward in challenging apartheid had to rest on developing an emancipatory approach, concerned with realisation of the potential for an alternative democratic system – with the capacity to challenge racial constructs of Self and Other – in order to move away from a racialised understanding of South African society. Crucially, it increasingly came to be recognised that 'For a resistance project to succeed, a logic different to that of apartheid discourse had to be developed, a logic which would not simply constitute a reversal of that project' (Norval 1996:171–2). The answer was a strident non-racialism, premised upon the principled rejection of 'race' and a discourse of equality. Thus, as an ideal, non-racialism envisages a democratic South Africa in which racial categories and divisions have been swept away by the forging of a common South African identity (van Diepen 1988). In practice, non-racialism 'as a method embodies the process of pulling black and white together so that they jointly dismantle apartheid' (Patrick Lekota, Delmas Treason Trial, April 1988).

The influence of the ANC's non-racialism culminated in the context of growing opposition to the 1983 Constitution, with the formation of the United Democratic Front (UDF), where the need to create an embryonic, new democratic and non-racial state was of central import. A confidential UDF discussion paper of May 1985 'argued that the new strategy would link the destruction of apartheid to the creation of a new society' (Mufson 1990:105). Anti-apartheid resistance in the 1980s centred on the UDF, an umbrella organisation made up of hundreds of affiliated organisations (Lodge and Nasson 1991). At inception, the UDF had over 575 member organisations, rising to around 800 at its height in 1986 and involving around three million people. Most affiliates were student and youth groups, but also included were civic organisations, women's groups, political groups, workers' groups and religious organisations. The UDF mobilised initially around local material concerns, but by 1985 it was unambiguously out to achieve the end of apartheid, through the construction of an inclusivist, democratic nation-building project. This project was carried forward by developing parallel non-racial institutions and services as concrete examples for the future, as in the offering of alternative legal, medical, educational, health and welfare services.

The UDF effectively used its organisational cohesion and resources to pose the most sustained challenge to the apartheid state (Price 1991), and its success was in large part attributable to its commitment to internal non-racial democratic organisation. The UDF recruited members from all the apartheid-designated 'race' groups, and promoted non-racial organisation and mobilisation throughout the country. For

Source: South African History Archive 1991, p. 41.

example, 'white' South Africans held regional executive committee positions in the UDF and campaigns were explicitly focused on building a non-racial outlook in the 'white' community (Lazerson 1994) – as in the 'Call to Whites' campaign of 1986 (see UDF poster, p. 64). A non-racial politics opened the ground for greater resource mobilisation, especially with regard to the freedom to operate and increased funding. The severe restrictions imposed by the apartheid state on the right to organise, speak and demonstrate were not so easily applied to progressive organisational work that involved 'white' people. Non-racial politics was also attractive to many international funding agencies – at its height, the UDF budget was over R2 million, with over R200 million donated to organisations aligned with the Front (Marx 1992:139). Not surprisingly, 'With its financial resources, the UDF was able to gain considerable publicity and to offer various services, thereby encouraging the affiliation of many more local groups' (ibid.:144).

The UDF as a genuine mobilisation of popular resistance was united under a unifying ideology. Diverse at the local level, at leadership level a network of activists linked the resistance together, and at top-management level, where cross-racial cooperation was necessary for effective mobilisation and organisation, people consciously came together to actively challenge and transform the terms of conflict, in the course of which they transformed themselves – this was indeed '*the future non-racial and democratic South Africa in embryo*' (Patrick Lekota 1984 quoted in Norval 1996:241).

Alongside the UDF, the Congress of South African Trade Unions (COSATU) also arose to place stress on non-racial inclusivism. The unions had developed through a decade and a half of struggle to build strong and democratic shop-floor organisations, and COSATU was formed in 1985 through a merger of the non-racial Federation of South African Trade Unions and the National Union of Mineworkers (Baskin 1991). By 1990 COSATU's paid-up membership was well over a million. Initially the labour unions had not entered the formal political arena because of the potential threats this might pose to their continued existence. The UDF's success in opposing the state, however, created the conditions for a more active political role by the labour movement – which included 'the development of alliances and the building of alternative structures within civil society' (Cooper 1996:56). Unions used their power in the economy selectively and strategically, further alienating capitalists from the state with large-scale strikes, stay-aways and boycotts, while calling for the end of apartheid.

From the mid-1980s however, the apartheid state moved to curtail the rapid formation of the UDF's alternative structures of 'people's power', through the use of emergency powers – detaining or restricting over half of the UDF's national executive committee members and banning the Front in 1988. In fact, between July 1985 and December 1988, innumerable organisations were restricted and around 41 000 people were detained (Webster and Friedman 1989:22). Nonetheless, the project of democratisation through non-racialism continued in the work of an array of organisations, namely, civic associations, student movements, women's organisations, religious groups and progressive professional associations. Finally, in 1989, the UDF formed an alliance with COSATU through the Mass Democratic Movement and then effectively un-banned itself with the grass-roots Defiance Campaign, which saw mass protest in all of South Africa's major cities against racially segregated hospitals, schools, buses and beaches (Collinge 1989).

In sum, the anti-apartheid struggle was carried forward by many non-governmental and voluntary organisations in numerous spheres of life, which – whether the strategic focus be on structures or restoring relationships – worked on a non-racial basis to redress the inhumanity of apartheid, and build a new moral, political and social order. In cities, towns and townships, in factories and in non-governmental organisations, there was an emerging – if at times and in places rather fragile – non-racial democratic society, an aggregate of networks and institutions, independent of and set against the apartheid state (Pandor 1996). In particular, the aims to break former racial stereotypes, to promote justice and freedom, and to realise a substantive vision of non-racial democracy – involving a significant number of 'white' professional people (for example, doctors, lawyers, clergy, academics, psychologists and social workers) – were advanced through:

- conflict mediation work by the Centre for Conflict Resolution;
- the activities of people's organisations, such as the National Education Crisis Committee;
- the contribution of service organisations, such as the Legal Resources Centre;
- the attempts of 'think-tanks' to influence public opinion and target policy-makers, through publications of the Institute for a Democratic Alternative for South Africa;
- consciousness-raising work, as undertaken for example, by the Black Sash (for more details see Winkler *et al.* 1987).

The ideological hegemony of apartheid tended to circumscribe the possibilities for envisaging a non-racial future – indeed to Andries Treurnicht, former leader of the Conservative Party, there was 'no such thing as a non-racial society for South Africa' (Treurnicht 1988:8). However, the apartheid state was unable to enforce racial thinking on all its subjects – there were always sites for contesting the dominant framework of assumptions, notably through interpersonal contacts, informal groups and other broad social entities. As resistance to apartheid grew, the type, quality, number and influence of these sites expanded. Thus, over and above the armed struggle, all this active participation in establishing non-racial democratic organisations constituted a limited revolution against racism. It played a crucial role in creating the possibility of a non-zero-sum outcome to transition by pushing the exclusivist apartheid state to place more inclusive constitutional changes on the agenda.

Conclusion

As we have argued above, the South African case cannot be simply reduced to a 'black' versus 'white' conflict. The view of there being a 'white' bloc and a 'black' bloc had never been accurate and became less so during the course of the 1980s. As argued above, a 'black' versus 'white' representation of the conflict is erroneous, as it rests upon accepting preexisting and totalised constructs of Self and Other, which do not in fact correspond to sociological realities. The conflict in South Africa has have not been primarily between 'blacks' and 'whites', but between all those who supported a non-racial democracy and those who did not. As has been argued, conceptualising South African politics in terms of racial blocs requires imposing inappropriate and rigid categories which deny internal differences and cross-cutting commonalties. Specifically, the transformative changes in the identities of the NP and organised resistance politics need to be acknowledged and fully investigated – and scholarly understandings of conflict in South Africa and its transformation can only be advanced through such a recognition. This involves problematising how group identity politics were constructed, deconstructed and reconstructed.

It was precisely because the conflicts in South Africa did not conform to a rigid 'black' versus 'white' pattern, and that this reality was increasingly seen to be so, that the transition occurred. The NP's successful purge of its *verkrampte* constituency 'from above' paved the way towards accommodating demands for inclusion 'from below'. It was the inclusivism of non-racialism, however, that made it possible for a negotiated settlement to be found – as one member of the apartheid state's covert negotiating team with Mandela and the ANC expressed:

> Non-racialism was very important in finding a solution to the conflict in the country. Our interactions with the ANC leadership inside and outside [the country] demonstrated clearly to us that, while we disagreed with the ANC on many matters, especially on the nature of the economy, we would be accepted by them in an ANC government.
> (Personal interview 1996)

The South African transition required an acceptance of reciprocal recognition among equals – that is, that 'white' South Africans (especially NP members) come to see 'black' people (especially African National Congress supporters) as South Africans of equal standing and vice versa. Democratisation required collective action from above and below to redefine the nature of the conflict away from 'race' and while this project is neither complete nor consolidated – it is in fact rather fragile – no settlement could have been *possible* without the positive impact of non-racialism.

Notes

1. The authors are grateful for the comments of Jacklyn Cock, Anthony Egan, Adrian Guelke, Tara Linh Leaman, Aubrey Lekwane, Tom Lodge, Jens Meierhenrich, Jo-Ansie van Wyk and Elke Zuern.
2. The Zimbabwean war of liberation ended in 1979 and the country gained independence on 18 April, 1980, according to the tenets of the Lancaster House Constitution, which was a negotiated settlement agreed to by the former colonial power Britain, ZANU, ZAPU and the Rhodesian regime (that had instituted apartheid-like policies and maintained racist discrimination in all sectors of society).

References

Adam, H. 1971: *Modernizing Racial Domination: The Dynamics of South African Politics*, Berkeley: University of California Press.

Asheron, A. [pseudonym of Maud, R.] 1969: 'Race and Politics in South Africa', *New Left Review*, no. 53, pp. 55–67.

Asmal, K. 1993: 'Making the Constitution', *Southern African Review of Books*, vol. 5, no. 3, pp. 3–4.

Asmal, K., Asmal, L. and Roberts, R.S. 1996: *Reconciliation Through Truth: A Reckoning of Apartheid's Criminal Governance*, Cape Town: David Philip.

Barrell, H. 1990: *MK: The ANC's Armed Struggle*, Johannesburg: Penguin.

Barrell, H. 1993: 'Conscripts to Their Age: ANC Operational Strategy 1976–86', unpublished PhD thesis, Oxford University.

Baskin, J. 1991: *Striking Back: A History of COSATU*, Johannesburg: Ravan.
Brewer, J. 1989: 'Introduction' in J. Brewer (editor), *Can South Africa Survive? Five Minutes to Midnight*, London: Macmillan.
Carter, G. 1958: *The Politics of Inequality: South Africa Since 1948*, London: Thames & Hudson.
Collinge, J. 1988: 'Defiance: A Measure of Expectations', *Work in Progress* (Johannesburg), vol. 61, pp. 5–8.
Cooper, D. 1996: 'War of Position and Movement: Reflections on Central Europe 1917–21 and the South African Trade Union Movement 1973–94', *South African Journal of Sociology*, vol. 27, no. 2, pp. 55–71.
Crankshaw, O. 1997: *Race, Class, and the Changing Division of Labour Under Apartheid*, London: Routledge.
de Klerk, W.J. 1991: *F.W. de Klerk: The Man and His Times*, Cape Town: Tafelberg/Jonathan Ball.
Ellis, S. and Sechaba, T. 1992: *Comrades Against Apartheid: The ANC and the South African Communist Party in Exile*, London: James Currey.
Esman, M.J. 1994: *Ethnic Politics*, Ithaca, NY: Cornell University Press.
Frederikse, J. 1990: *The Unbreakable Thread: Non-Racialism in South Africa*, London: Zed.
Giliomee, H. and Schlemmer, L. 1991: *From Apartheid to Nation-Building*, Cape Town: Oxford University Press.
Hanf, T., Weiland, H. and Vierdag, G. 1981: *South Africa: The Prospects of Peaceful Change*, London: Rex Collings.
Jaster, R.S. and Jaster, S.K. 1993; *South Africa's Other Whites: Voices for Change*, London: Macmillan.
Johnson, R.W. 1994: 'South Africa: On the Eve', *London Review of Books*, vol. 16, no. 8, pp. 3–6.
Kasrils, R. 1993: *Armed and Dangerous: My Undercover Struggle Against Apartheid*, Oxford: Heinemann Educational.
Kuper, L. 1960: 'The Heightening of Racial Tension', *Race*, vol. 2, no. 1, pp. 24–32.
Lazerson, J. 1994: *Against the Tide: Whites in the Struggle Against Apartheid*, Boulder, Colo: Westview Press.
Legassick, M. 1974: 'South Africa: Capital Accumulation and Violence', *Economy and Society*, vol. 3, no. 3, pp. 253–91.
Lemon, A. 1987: *Apartheid in Transition*, Aldershot, Hants: Gower.
Lijphart, A. 1977: *Democracy in Plural Societies: A Comparative Exploration*, New Haven, Conn.: Yale University Press.
Lodge, T. 1986: 'A Crisis, But Not Yet Ripe for a Revolution', *The Age* (Melbourne), 15 July.
Lodge, T. and Nasson, B. 1991: *All Here and New: Black Politics in South Africa in the 1980s*, Cape Town: David Philip.
Marx, A. 1992: *Lessons of Struggle: South African Internal Opposition, 1960–1990*, New York: Oxford University Press.
Mbeki, G. 1996: *Sunset at Midday: Latshon'ilang'emini!*, Braamfontein, Gauteng: Nolwazi.
Mills, G. and Burrows, D. (editors) 1996: *In Their Own Words: Personal Recollections of South Africa's Wars of Liberation*, Johannesburg: South African Institute of International Affairs.

Mufson, S. 1990: *Fighting Years: Black Resistance and the Struggle for a New South Africa*, Boston, Mass.: Beacon Press.

National Party 1974: *Election Manifesto 1974*, Cape Town: Information Service of the National Party.

Norval, A. 1996: *Deconstructing Apartheid Discourse*, London: Verso.

O'Meara, D. 1996: *Forty Lost Years: The Apartheid State and the Politics of the National Party, 1948–1994*, Johannesburg: Ravan.

Pandor, N. 1996: 'Prospects for a Sustainable Civil Society: African National Congress Perspective' in H. Kotze (editor), *Consolidating Democracy: What Role for Civil Society in South Africa?*, Stellenbosch: Centre for International and Comparative Politics.

Price, R. 1991: *The Apartheid State in Crisis: Political Transformation in South Africa, 1975–1990*, New York: Oxford University Press.

Schrire, R. 1991: *Adapt or Die: The End of White Politics in South Africa*, New York: South Africa Update Series, Ford Foundation–Foreign Policy Association.

Schutte, G. 1995: *What Racists Believe: Race Relations in South Africa and the United States*, London: Sage.

Shear, M. 1996: *WITS: A University in the Apartheid Era*, Johannesburg: Witwatersrand University Press.

Shingler, J. 1994: 'Nationalism and Apartheid, 1948–1989: The Growth of Dissent within the Afrikaner Intelligentsia' in D. O'Meara (editor), *The Politics of Change in Southern Africa* (Collected Seminar Papers vol. 1), Montreal: Canadian Research Consortium on Southern Africa.

Slovo, J. 1995: *Slovo: An Unfinished Autobiography*, Johannesburg: Ravan.

South African History Archive (Poster Book Collective) 1991: *Images of Defiance: South African Resistance Posters of the 1980s*, Johannesburg: Ravan.

Survey of Race Relations (annual): Johannesburg: South African Institute of Race Relations.

Suttner, R. and Cronin, J. (editors) 1986: *30 Years of the Freedom Charter*, Johannesburg: Ravan.

Taylor, R. 1990: 'South Africa: Consociation or Democracy?', *Telos*, vol. 85, pp. 17–32.

Treurnicht, A. 1988: 'Cover Story Interview', *Inside South Africa*, vol. 2, no. 6, pp. 8–11.

van den Berghe, P. 1965: *South Africa: A Study in Conflict*, Middletown: Wesleyan University Press.

van den Berghe, P. 1967: *Race and Racism*, New York: John Wiley.

van Diepen, M. (editor) 1988: *The National Question in South Africa*, London: Zed.

Verwoerd, H.F. 1966: *Verwoerd Speaks: Speeches 1948–1966* (edited by A.N. Pelzer), Johannesburg: Afrikaanse Pers Boekhandel.

Waldmeir, P. 1997: *Anatomy of a Miracle: The End of Apartheid and the Birth of the New South Africa*, London: Viking.

Webster, D. and Friedman, M. 1989: 'Repression and the State of Emergency: June 1987-March 1989' in G. Moss and I. Obery (editors), *South African Review 5*, Johannesburg: Ravan, pp. 16–41.

Winkler, R., van der Merwe, H. and Geldenhuys, O. 1987: *An Overview of Peace Initiatives, Movements and Organizations in South Africa*, Cape Town: Centre for Intergroup Studies.

5
Northern Ireland: From Long War to Difficult Peace?
Ronaldo Munck

When the Cold War ended and various conflicts around the world entered a settlement phase or 'endgame', most observers thought that Northern Ireland would be a hard nut to crack. It seemed that the intensity of the struggle was such that deadlock would prevail for many years to come. Yet those closer to developments on the ground had already detected a move away from the 'long war' towards a difficult 'peace process'. It is the seemingly intractable nature of the conflict in the north of Ireland which makes it a particularly interesting case study, this and the longevity of the insurgent force, the Irish Republican Army (IRA), whose history and mythology have had considerable impact on the international stage. This chapter examines the character of Irish Republican discourse, its internal political currents and its relations with the British state, before embarking on an analysis of the peace process, which began when the IRA declared a cessation of armed actions in August 1994.

The state of Northern Ireland, which has been the site of the modern IRA's struggle since 1970, was born in 1920 under difficult circumstances. With an objective basis in uneven development, which made it the most industrialised part of Ireland, the northern state was created through a violent process of national partition and anti-nationalist 'pogroms'. This almost permanent 'state of exception' never obtained the consent of the nationalist minority population and thus never achieved full legitimacy at home or abroad. Northern Ireland was indeed a 'Protestant state for a Protestant people', as one of its leaders once notoriously declared, although the religious label was also primarily a national one. Remaining part of the United Kingdom, when the majority of the country won its independence through a bloody war, followed by an internecine conflict between compromising and 'true' nationalists, the six counties of the north-east which became Northern Ireland were bound to see conflict. Unwilling to coopt its Catholic-nationalist minority and unable to decisively defeat its insurgent organisations, the state would increasingly rely on repressive measures and structural discrimination against the insurgents and nationalist populace.

The origins of the IRA itself date from the same period, although its prehistory can be traced to various nationalist movements of the nineteenth century. The failed uprising of Easter 1916 – heralded by Lenin – led to a consistent war against Britain from 1918 to 1920, spearheaded by a movement which became known as the 'Irish Republican Army'. Partial victory, partition and civil war followed. The IRA was re-formed and turned towards the communist tradition in the 1930s, and launched a small-scale campaign during the Second World War. Defeat, depoliticisation and disenchantment ensued, which were not broken but reinforced by the 1956–62 Border Campaign. A renewed turn towards the communist tradition in the 1960s led to a split in the Republican movement in 1970. While the 'Official' wing drifted out of the Republican orbit, the Provisionals ('Provos') proved a hardy offshoot. Northern Ireland had also experienced a civil rights campaign in the late 1960s along North American lines, but the state responded with repression. This is the crucible out of which the modern IRA was created, although this organisation itself was a key player in the unfolding history of Northern Ireland from 1970 to 1994.

Jumping to the conclusion of our story, the IRA declared a historic cessation of hostilities in 1994. None of its objectives had been achieved, yet this was no simple defeat as the organisation had the personnel and *matériel* to continue its armed campaign for many years to come. International developments certainly had an impact – for example, the negotiated settlement in South Africa which would bring the African National Congress (ANC) to power, the moves towards peace in Central America between former Cold War enemies and the then hopeful moves made in the Middle East between Israel and its Arab neighbours. Within the organisation itself, there had also been a gradual rethink from the 'quick hard push' line of the 1970s and the 'long war' perspective of the early 1980s. The spectacular growth of the Republican political party, Sinn Féin, had lent credence to the viability of a democratic political path. It was understood among Republican circles that war was a continuation of politics by other means and the objective a political one. It was also recognised that the struggle could not be won by military means alone and that armed conflict could/would have a dangerous and destructive dynamic. And in order to understand the evolution of this thinking we will need to examine in considerable detail the discursive formation of Irish Republicanism.

Method

Since the 1970s, there have been many 'histories' of the IRA and countless analyses of the conflict in Northern Ireland or the 'Troubles'. We need to self-consciously reflect on the methods used in these studies before proceeding to our own analysis. The standard histories of the IRA (for example, Bell 1979, Coogan 1980, Bishop and Mallie 1987) focus almost exclusively on personalities and events, creating a seamless narrative akin to a thriller. There is little space here for discourse and internal contradictions as the military story unfolds in a glowing romantic light. A few recent studies of Irish Republicanism (for example, Burton 1978, Feldman 1991, White 1994) have begun to address the question of ideology more critically and centrally. There is now a growing interest in the neglected dimension of women's participation in the nationalist movements (for example, Ward 1983) and in the Northern 'war zone' in particular (for example, Aretxaga 1997). There are also studies by journalists (for example, Toolis 1995, O'Brien 1995) who considerably add to our understanding of the movement. There is even a brave attempt to address the military dimension of the struggle (Smith 1995), albeit with inevitably restricted sources. For all this, the general literature is dominated by a superficial view, whether hostile or sympathetic, which barely begins to scratch the surface of Irish Republican political-identity formation.

Michel Foucault's theory of discursive practices allows us to go beyond the 'history of ideas' approach to Irish Republicanism. Whereas the history of ideas focuses on continuity and the coherence of a discourse, Foucault stresses the element of discontinuity – that is, 'a discursive formation is not an ideal, continuous, smooth text that runs beneath the multiplicity of contradictions and resolves them in the calm unity of coherent thought' (Foucault 1972:155). This would seem to be the assumption behind many histories of nationalism and nationalist movements. Foucault, to the contrary, argues that 'contradictions are neither appearances to be overcome, nor secret principles to be uncovered' (ibid.:151). The latter idea seems to underlie the critical accounts of Republicanism, which seek its essence or secret. Our analysis of Republicanism will not draw a rigid line between true and false elements, following the 'science versus ideology' tradition, but rather seek to determine the conditions of its existence, its mode of operation and its transformations. We do not construct homogeneity and continuity, but instead investigate contradictions and discontinuities.

In analysing Irish Republicanism we are also engaging in an exercise of 'deconstruction', to borrow a Derridean term (see Derrida 1980). This method, to simplify, works through an 'in-worming' or internal subversion of the text. It uncovers suppressed contradictions and undermines any thought system based on supposedly unassailable first principles. Once a discourse is decentred in this way, its premises can be questioned and its consistency challenged. The moments of indeterminacy in a discourse can thus be exposed to critical analysis, to reveal its presuppositions and limits. The founding myths upon which a discourse's system of meaning is constructed must necessarily be deconstructed in this process. In refusing the urge to 'totalise' a system, deconstructionists emphasise rather plurality and heterogeneity, hesitation and indeterminacy. Deconstruction, perforce, rejects the self-definition of a discourse and its rigid boundaries separating truth from falsity. Thus deconstruction of Irish Republicanism would pursue the various ramifications of this discourse and ascertain the extent to which these contradictory elements subvert the logic of the system.

Republicanism, as all ideologies, must 'recruit' subjects through the process Louis Althusser once dubbed 'interpellation' (Althusser 1971). An individual may be subject to more than one such interpellation, by legal, familial or political institutions, for example. Thus, Irish Republicans would need to be seen as subject to a diversity of interpellations. As Terry Eagleton notes, ideology is not a seamless web embracing all of life, but is rather 'a heterogeneous, contradictory formation, a question of constant struggle at the level of signifying practices' (Eagleton 1981:141). Republicanism cannot thus be seen as a simple, homogeneous unity, a transcendental ideology as it were. It is composed, rather, of distinct, often contradictory elements. It reflects the lived relations of Republicans to their world, not in some simple, transparent manner, but conflictually. Republicanism is an ideology of rebellion and contestation, but it is also 'conservative' in many senses as well. It is through the process of interpellation that Republicanism takes on meaning, for, as Pêcheux argues, 'a meaning effect does not pre-exist the discursive formation in which it is constituted. The production of meaning is an integral part of the interpellation of the individual as subject' (Pêcheux 1982:187).

Republican discourse

This investigation into Irish Republican discourse seeks to distinguish four sets of interpellations or sub-ensembles of Republican ideology:

1. Nationalism, seen as a key motivating and unifying factor from the 1920s to the present;
2. Catholicism, which has had varying ideological influence and continuous social influence;
3. Socialism, present at various points of history in various guises;
4. Republicanism proper, by which we mean commitment to a particular form of government and the use of 'physical force' as a legitimate political principle.

Through a process of 'binding', the four elements of Republicanism we have identified are unified in practice. Lacan refers, in another context, to a 'binding of representations, binding of meanings, which finally confers a certain stability' (cited in Laplanche and Leclaire 1972:18). The contradictory unity of a discourse such as Republicanism is maintained through a process of displacement during periods of stability, although the opposite occurs during crisis periods as we shall see, when inherent contradictions become exacerbated.

In interviews with Republican activists from the 1920s and 1930s (see Munck and Rolston 1987, from which subsequent quotes are taken) we found that it was nationalism which invariably motivated those joining the Republican movement. Thus Liam Mulholland, a leader of the movement in Belfast, recalls how 'The overriding thing that made people join the IRA, especially in the North, would be the national question. We were very conscious of the fact that we were under the domination of England [and] that domination was brutal'. Another volunteer, Charlie McGlade, said that 'their idea of joining the movement was to get trained and equipped to go out and fight to free Ireland'. Inevitably, the Republican movement's nationalism led to a general blurring of class and political divisions, as its members concentrated on 'freeing Ireland'. Yet nationalism and freedom could assume different meanings in Irish Republican discourse. The Republican movement drew its strength from the working class and small farmers, a social base which imbued the movement with a dynamic quite different from that of constitutional nationalism. Peadar O'Donnell, a Republican–socialist leader of the 1930s, referred to 'Fenian Ireland, the Ireland of the poor', thus drawing a clear link between nationalism and the subaltern classes.

Nationalism was also the mainstay, perhaps the only element, of the Provisional IRA's ideology in the early 1970s. It sought a 'Third Way' between capitalism and communism in the nationalist (to some extent Theirdworld 1st) tradition. The keynote of all Republican discourse was 'the nationalist people' or 'national-minded people'. Hunger-striker Bobby Sands expresses the continued importance of nationalism, 'I believe and stand by the God-given right of the Irish nation to sovereign independence' (Sands 1981:7). The Republican balance sheet of the 1981 hunger strike, in which Bobby Sands and nine of his comrades fasted to death, contrasted the attitude of 'the ordinary nationalist people of Ireland' with the 'refusal of the Irish nationalist establishment' to support the prisoners' demands (*Iris* 1981:2). Language here seems stretched to breaking point, with the same word – 'nationalist' – carrying quite different connotations, beyond the distinction between 'good' and 'bad'. Yet this is precisely what we can expect if we follow a post-Saussurean view of language as de-centred signifiers with an infinite structure of possible meanings. Nationalism is a fluid and floating signifier, which takes on different 'meaning' in different periods and as part of different discourses.

Most Irish Republicans are Catholics but the influence of religion goes beyond this. Frank Burton, in an ethnography of a Republican community in Belfast, claims that 'IRA ideology emerges from, fits into and capitalizes on [the Catholic *Weltanschauung*]' (Burton 1978:6). There is indeed a certain 'fit' between Catholicism and Republicanism, but we must not ignore the contradictions that are present too. Thus Jack Brady, an activist from the 1930s, tells how 'I'm a Catholic but I'm not tied to the dogmatism of the Catholic church' (Munck and Rolston 1987). Most Republican activists (as against supporters) show an uneasy balance between 'public' political beliefs and 'private' religious beliefs, usually resolved by keeping the two in separate compartments. Certainly few would allow the political pronouncements of the Church to sway them. For the more recent period, Kevin Toolis, an astute observer of Republicanism, notes that:

> Irish Republicanism is imbued with the culture and imagery of Catholicism. During the 1981 Hunger Strike, West Belfast was covered in murals depicting the emaciated IRA hunger-strikers as the martyred Christ figure. In the informer war, the powerful Catholic sacrament of confession and its sub-elements of recanta-

tion, repentance, redemption and absolution, subconsciously guided the IRA.
(Toolis 1995:224)

Socialism, or at least social radicalism of some sort, has always been an integral element of Republican discourse. As Jack Brady, a Republican activist in the 1930s, recalls, 'With unemployment and poverty, a kind of social conscience was creeping over everybody, we needed a better appeal than the national policy of Sinn Féin' (Munck and Rolston 1987). A social crisis was causing a rearrangement of the diverse component elements of Republican discourse. There emerged a type of 'Social Republicanism' (see Patterson 1989), which continued to resurface until the present day. The influence of 'Third World' national liberation struggles was a significant, if not dominant, element in this process. Socialism was probably an ethical objective for most Republican activists but there was also a feeling that class struggle would detract from the overriding national and military objectives. Politics was essentially a private affair; like religion, it caused divisions – whereas the imperatives of a military organisation required unity. Contemporary Republicans have more wholeheartedly embraced the socialist language, yet, as we shall see below, there was a decisive turn in the 1980s towards nationalist unity through the 'pan-nationalist front'.

Irish Republican discourse is also embodied in the military, political, youth and cultural organisations which make up 'the movement'. It is this material element – the organisational imperative, we could call it – which links the three interpellations of Nationalism, Catholicism and Socialism and gives them coherence. Although the strictly political dimension of Republicanism – pursuit of a particular form of government for Ireland – should not be ignored, the unity of Republican discourse is constructed through the material practices of the organisation. Organisational unity is cemented through the various symbols and rituals of Republicanism, including the parades and commemorations, the funerals and the cultural gatherings (see Goldring 1982). The overwhelming importance of the organisation and its unity stem, ultimately, from the 'physical force' or 'armed struggle' function and purpose of the Republican involvement. The 'revisionist' leaders of the Second International, who held that the movement was everything, would be well-understood by Republicans. Tradition for Republicanism has helped perpetuate a feeling of resistance and ensured organisational continuity, but it has also created a certain lack of political imagination and has acted as a heavy weight holding back political innovation and change.

There is a tendency in most accounts of Republican discourse to seek single factors to account for difference. Thus, Robert White refers to 'the timing and the geography of recruitment' (White 1993:131), which he sees as creating four blocs of Republicans, on the basis of pre- or post-1969 recruitment and northern versus southern origins. Yet these binary opposites occlude much more than they illuminate and cannot account for much of the debates in the 1980s, often between post-1969 northern Republicans. Other authors, such as Bob Purdie (1980) and Henry Patterson (1989), view Republicanism through a Marxist grid in a reprise of the old 'science versus ideology' opposition. To say that Republicanism is not 'really' socialist hardly adds to our understanding. Republicanism is a revolutionary nationalist ideology with all that that entails. Our own analysis has shown that the unity of Republican discourse is a contradictory one, with shifts and displacements occurring in periods of crisis. No single unbroken thread or myth of origins can unite the Irish Republicanism of the French Revolution period with that of today. Its current 'conditions of production' (Foucault), even its whole meaning, is different for different periods. Our stress is necessarily on the continuous (re)making of Republican discourse.

Something usually submerged in most accounts of discourse is the question of violence. In an original analysis of the 'Troubles', Feldman has highlighted the symbolic construction of violence and the inadequacy of structural accounts, and points to 'the growing autonomy of violence as a self-legitimating sphere of social discourse and transaction' (Feldman 1991:5). The British government coined the phrase of an 'acceptable level of violence' to describe phases of the 'Troubles' which did not surpass the level of violence the state could live with. Republicans, for their part, lived with violence daily both as victims and practitioners, and thus became adept at distancing techniques. Killing was 'stiffing' or, more bizarrely, dying was 'gone for one's tea'. Violence, as Foucault noted in relation to power, has been productive and not merely repressive. As Feldman notes, 'Political violence reorganises the material world into a phantasm, into a spectacle of historical transformation' (Feldman 1991:80). The 'Troubles' became almost a theatre of violence and repression a self-contained world of action and reaction. It was Republicans, who ultimately broke that spiral of violence and started the dynamic towards a peace process.

Republican currents

The path to peace has, however, been a long one and has passed through a fierce ideological struggle within the Republican movement.

It has been common amongst commentators to distinguish between Republican 'doves' and 'hawks', the latter being 'harder', more militarist and 'ultimatist'. However, this distinction is purely subjective and usually based on superficial knowledge of the internal political dynamic of the Republican movement. I would propose instead a distinction first used in relation to the German Green Party, the notably successful ecological movement (see Scott 1991). The Greens were seen to have a fundamentalist (or *'fundi'*) wing which would admit to no dilution of principles and a realist (or *'realo'*) tendency which was prepared to compromise over ecological demands and participate in institutional politics. While the *fundis* are essentially utopian in terms of both ends and the means to pursue them, the *realos* seek pragmatic changes and are less pessimistic about achieving change through institutional means. On the Republican side of the 'sectarian divide' in Northern Ireland, proponents of the *fundis* would include splinter groups such as the Real IRA, Continuity IRA and the Irish National Liberation Army (INLA), and the *realos* would now be the majority in Sinn Féin and the IRA. For the *fundis*, engagement with institutional politics means a loss of principles and an inevitable decay of the mass movement, whereas for the *realos* the only realistic means to change things is through a flexible policy of political pressure combined with mass mobilisation.

For the Irish Republican *fundis*, the absolute end is of course 'the Republic' as defined in the movement's theology. Clare O'Halloran has written in this regard of 'the primacy of rhetoric and the rejection of compromise' (O'Halloran 1987:157) in Irish nationalism. As the means to obtain the mythical Republic, 'physical force' is and always was the only way. The 1986 Sinn Féin debates, on whether to drop the traditional 'abstentionist' policy in southern elections, is indicative of this mindset. For one conference delegate, going into Leinster House (the southern parliament) was 'betraying the Republic', while others described 'abstentionism' as 'a fundamental cornerstone' of Irish Republicanism and said dropping it would mean 'forgetting everything the men of 1922 died for' (Sinn Féin 1986:24). The Irish Republican *fundi* discourse is all about ill-defined and ultimately theological inalienable 'principles', which cannot be 'betrayed', with the dead generations being called up as witnesses. The *fundi* position, by its very nature, cannot be debated or proven wrong. It is a defensive discourse, well suited to a movement used to periodic setbacks and defeats, but it was hardly adequate to bring to a conclusion a conflict which had gone on for over 20 years and which was obviously stalemated.

In 1986, there was another Republican split with the small *fundi* breakaway, Republican Sinn Féin, setting itself up as a 'pure'

Republican alternative to an organisation already beginning the long process towards a peaceful resolution. The parting of ways was over 'abstentionism', which had now been abandoned, but the differences went further. For Ruairi O Brádaigh, leader of the breakaway:

> I would feel that when people depart from fundamental principles, basic principles, that they are in a gradual slope and that going looking for permits for Easter lilies [used to commemorate the 1916 Rising] in the South ... it follows the next thing is looking for permission for the RUC [Royal Ulster Constabulary] to honour people whom the RUC killed in the North.
>
> (O'Brien 1995:278)

An outsider may not see the logic of this slippery slope or understand the peculiar emphasis on symbols. To a Republican, however, these are matters of principle. Max Weber refers appropriately to an 'ethic of ultimate ends' (*Gesinnungsethik*), according to which all pragmatic considerations are suspended in the face of a single and absolute imperative. In pursuing the ultimate objective, the *fundis*, like these Republican 'rejectionists', turn their backs on possible gains in the 'here and now'. One is reminded of George Orwell's somewhat overstated dictum, that 'behind every revolutionary lies the secret expectation that nothing can be changed'.

The Republican '*realos*' who had gradually been achieving hegemony over the movement, culminating in the 1986 split, had rather, a very Nietzschean 'will to power'. For Gerry Adams and Martin McGuinness, 'abstentionism' was not a 'principle' but a theological shackle in the ability of a movement to advance politically. McGuinness, in a keynote address to the 1986 conference, denied that the new leadership was 'egging the Republican movement into a constitutional path' and maintained that 'the war against British rule must continue until freedom is won', and to those wavering, declared, 'Don't go my friends. We will lead you to the republic' (Mallie and McKittrick 1996:40). So the price for a realist acceptance of participating in constitutional politics was a continuation of the armed struggle and a reaffirmation of the mythical Republic. The turn towards realism was, as one would expect, contradictory and incomplete, being constantly subject to fierce rearguard action by the keepers of the faith. A *realo* in one context could become a born-again *fundi* in another. Overall, however, there was a recognition that, as Mark Swilling wrote about South Africa, 'If you gear your whole organisation to the impossible, you are trying to commit your followers to a faith in something which you cannot demonstrate is possible now and so you will remain marginal' (Swilling 1992:51).

There were a number of issues which became the site of an ideological struggle between the *fundi* and *realo* Republican tendencies. We will explore two of these sites, namely the character of British interests in Ireland and the significance of moves towards an integrated Europe. For one contributor to a Republican journal (McThomas 1992), the reasons for the British presence in Ireland were perfectly clear: there was an economic motive, a strategic motive and a political motive – that is, the 'demonstration effect' of withdrawal in Britain itself. There is a *mélange* of outdated analysis here (physical occupation is not necessary for capitalist domination today) and a serious lack of proportion (no state would maintain a conflict such as this to keep up a 'laboratory of repression'). It seems that Republican discourse was wrong-footed by a claim by British politicians in 1990 that Britain had 'no selfish strategic or economic interest in Northern Ireland'. A more realist analysis was however surfacing and other Republicans argued that 'British interests in Ireland might be more *ad hoc* and contradictory than the above analysis allowed', and these authors called for an 'opening up of our analysis, making it more fluid, less "necessitarian"' (McClelland and Dowd 1992:13). However, the traditional 'conspirational/necessitarian' view prevailed, even if a submerged unspoken alternative was floating around.

On the question of Europe we see, as expected, all the 'little Irelander' reactions, which often made Republican discourse sound like anti-European conservative discourse in Britain. Thus, in the 1989 Sinn Féin European Parliament election manifesto, it is argued that in the process of European integration, Ireland was bound to 'increasingly become not just a dependent colony but part of NATO territory' (Sinn Féin 1989:8). Ironically, these Republicans themselves hold high the flame of neutrality in Ireland, even when the 'actually existing' Republic had long since reduced it to a token utilitarian policy. The theological/imperialist reading of Europe can be contrasted to one emerging from the prisons (from where critical analysis had emerged in the past), which argued that European unification would represent 'a political reality with which we would have to come to terms ... it would be ... vitally important ... for our movement' (Campbell 1992:24). Indeed, tacitly accepting this case, Sinn Féin has since opened a European Office keen to exploit whatever discontent there might be, at all levels, with Britain's role in Ireland. Again the 'necessitarian' approach – things are bad necessarily and will always remain so

– is challenged by a more nuanced and fluid approach to issues. The driving force for moves beyond theological certainties is usually practical politics and the need to broaden alliances.

Another area where 'revisionist' Republican thinking emerged was in relation to Ireland's Protestant minority, which is of course the majority population within the state of Northern Ireland. For long, Republicans were content to repeat clichés, that northern Protestants would negotiate democratically only when their British underwriters withdrew their troops from the streets and the like. Then in 1991, a 'Derry Protestant' wrote in a Republican journal that there was a problem in democrats 'making their voices heard over the noise of the armed struggle and in the context of the established assumption that Republicans are opposed to Protestants' (A Derry Protestant 1991:12). Once all the parallels were with the Algerian *colons* (French settlers) and other settler populations. Now there was a belated common-sense recognition that 'many IRA activities from the northern Protestant perspective are seen to be sectarian' (McLaughlin 1991:16). Yet the implications of that statement and the lessons of the break-up of Yugoslavia seem not to have fully sunk in. Indeed, the logic of war is very difficult to reconcile with the logic of democratic compromise. The part-time local British army soldier was seen as part of the military apparatus and not as a Protestant farmer or office worker, who might feel under threat from Irish Republicanism.

A submerged but constant feature in all the debates was the question of the armed struggle, with other issues often serving as sounding boards for this underlying fundamental issue. The new leadership had to deal not only with the traditionalist 'abstentionist' tendency, but also a much more pervasive 'militarist' faction. In this case, which came to a head in 1985, the conflict was over the use of scarce resources such as money and personnel – that is, whether the priority would be Sinn Féin's electoral drive or the IRA's function as the 'cutting edge' of overall Republican struggle. The militarist logic was to use the recently acquired heavy weaponry for an all-out military assault on the British state. They conceived the struggle as a zero-sum conflict, with every element dedicated to mere politics detracting from the military campaign. The leadership, on the other hand, had by now recognised that the conflict could not be settled by military means alone and that any escalation by the IRA could be easily met by the British state. In these circumstances, an attempted revolt by the militarist faction was quickly quelled by the new politico-military leadership. Before we return to the means whereby this leadership came to the peace process, we need to examine relations between the Irish Republican movement and the British state.

Republicanism and the British state

All discourses are relational and any serious consideration of Irish Republicanism needs to consider its relations to the British state. Surprisingly, this element has been neglected and on the whole Republicanism has been dealt with as a self-contained universe. Recently, however, Anthony McIntyre has argued persuasively that 'The modern Republican movement has persistently been the product of British state strategies rather than a body which has existed for the sole purpose of completing the "unfinished business" of uniting Ireland' (McIntyre 1995:98). Like any political force, the Republican movement has been shaped – right down to its structures, procedures and symbols – by the force it opposes. Going back to 1916, we see the IRA setting up as a military body with a discursive formation not unlike that of the imperialist military apparatus it opposed. It is not a timeless tradition which has imposed its tempo on the Republican movement, its discourse and psyche, but the ups and downs of its relations with the British state. As in war, so in peace, it was the British state which indirectly, but sometimes directly imposed the modalities and dictated the pace.

McIntyre correctly, if somewhat bluntly, states that 'The history of the modern Republican movement – from the early 1970s – has basically been one of adapting to survive in the face of British state strategies' (1995:102). The British state has always had a consistent counter-insurgency strategy to deal with the Republican threat in Ireland. This has included military measures, security legislation and various political initiatives designed to outflank or marginalise Republicanism. These have not always worked and they have often had contradictory effects, but the point is that the British state was the dominant player for all except a brief year or so at the start of the 'Troubles' when the IRA offensive was launched. With the British state developing a panoply of measures designed for the containment of the Republican movement, the latter could but try to evade these. So at different times, the Republican movement tried to broaden its social base in the south of Ireland, turned to a radical brand of 'Social Republicanism' or went for a pan-nationalist alliance against Britain. This was not usually due to far-sighted thinking, but rather, as McIntyre puts it, 'the consequence of a body following the line of least pressure and appearing on that part of the stage least protected by the British state' (ibid.:102).

Republicans also face the 'Other' of Ulster unionism, whose historic mission is to maintain the link with Britain. Its so-called Loyalist (to the British crown) wing launched a vicious campaign of assassination of ordinary Catholics at various key points of the 'Troubles', which locked Republicans into a sectarian war regardless of their intentions. With or without assistance from the British state (and the evidence now points to with), Loyalists were effectively able to distract Irish Republicanism from its historic mission to unite 'Catholic, Protestant and Dissenter' in a new democratic Ireland. However much the Republican movement portrayed its struggle as one against British imperialism, in practice it impacted most on the local Protestant population, which provided the personnel for the police and the local part-time regiments of the British army. For their parts, the Loyalists sought in their discourse to dehumanise the nationalist people. As John Cash notes in his recent analysis of Unionist ideology, their attitudes towards Republicanism are 'organised by unconscious rules which have sadistic and dehumanising processes at their core' and 'such a construction is spread along a chain of signifiers' from the IRA to the nationalist community as a whole and in this way, 'they are all gathered under the one dehumanising construction and viewed as both alien and "preferred-dead"' (Cash 1996:183).

To an outside observer the main characteristic of the 'Troubles' in Ireland has been the violence of the conflict. Violence is usually just seen as a symptom of a 'sick society' or, more crudely, the self-interested product of the 'godfathers of violence' running the IRA. As Anne Norton writes: 'Violence in its myriad forms ... appears to be, without ambivalence or ambiguity, a simple act of opposition and destruction' (Norton 1993:145). Yet, if we follow Foucault's conception of power and extend it to the question of violence, we might conceive it as productive in the political sense. In this conception, following Norton, 'violence is taken as a species of inscription and an act of authority. Acts of violence, like acts of speech and writing, invest the material with meaning by giving it structure' (ibid.:145). The history of the IRA's dealings with common crime in the nationalist areas is a good example of this process. In a previous study (Munck 1988) I have shown in some detail how the IRA established its legitimacy by becoming the political authority and police in nationalist areas. The real, yet symbolic, physical punishment of offenders, from tarring and feathering to 'knee-capping', represents just such an inscription on the body of insurgent political authority.

The military confrontation between the IRA and forces of the British state acquired a dynamic of its own, if always reflecting underlying political developments. This gave rise to the phenomenon of 'militarism', which meant an almost exclusive emphasis on military means by Republicans. Yet we need to note that this is a political strategy and not just a political deviation which was overcome in the 1980s with the electoral successes of Sinn Féin. Indeed, the politics of militarism spring from a strongly held belief that only military force will dislodge the British presence in Ireland. It is not that the means are confused with the end, but a recognition that the end can only be achieved by force. It is thus that the whole issue of cease-fires take on such a politically fraught connotation. Republican strategy was always a joint political/military one and the problem was that for many years the political discourse was simplistic and unrealistic. When the time came for a cessation of the Republican military campaign in the early 1990s (see next section), it was not out of outright military weakness, but from a realistic political appraisal of the balance of forces and the movement's political prospects.

In its sometimes open, sometimes covert, war with the Republican movement the British state was prepared to use such levels of force as it could get away with politically. Studies of the British army (Hamill 1985), the covert security services (Dillon 1988, Urban 1992) and Loyalist paramilitaries (Dillon 1992) all show the panoply of repressive measures which were brought to bear on Republican activists. As Desmond Hamill writes, 'In the dark shadows of the undercover war, it was accepted that no quarter would be given. "You cannot bring home the bacon," commented one police officer, "unless you cut the pig's throat"' (Hamill 1985:291). Others, while denying that there was an official 'shoot to kill' policy when dealing with Republican suspects, admit that the security forces had been told to 'take the gloves off'. So it was the Republicans who were able to seize the discursive high ground, with their drive for a peace process from the late 1980s onwards. Although atrocities occurred (Birmingham and Enniskillen come to mind), it is probably more remarkable that the Republican movement did maintain political control over the IRA campaign. Ultimately, when the IRA obtained its (in)famous consignments of heavy Libyan weaponry in the mid-1980s, it did not launch the all-out guerrilla war it was undoubtedly capable of carrying out.

Finally, where the Republican movement most interacts with the British state is at the local or community level. This is the front line of the politico-military confrontation, where identities are constructed and discourses developed. In one of the better ethnographies of a community in conflict, Burton (1978) has traced the complex interplay between the IRA, the residents, the British army and the Loyalist gangs in a Belfast area. The political significance of the community is its ability to withstand assault and 'soak up' repressive coercion. This crucial element, which Burton perhaps excessively attributes to a Catholic social structure, has meant that Republican areas have 'resisted enough of the external pressure (riots, gun-battles, assassinations, internment) to make the continuation of the war a possibility' (ibid.:3). In the ebb and flow of the conflict, the IRA was always mindful of its complex and often contradictory relationship with the community. Far from being some alien excrescence, as many commentators from the outside argued, the IRA was very much part of a certain 'fit' between Republican ideology and the broader Catholic communitarian context it operated within. As in all conflicts, the physical aspect was often less important than the discursive struggle over 'hearts and minds'.

That a community which perceived itself to be under siege by state and para-state forces would throw up activists was not surprising. Here again, too much emphasis has been laid on 'tradition', the fact that many IRA activists had older family members in the organisation, for example. In fact, in the construction of insurgent identities, the state played a crucial role through its blanket use of repressive measures such as house-to-house searches and arrests. In Northern Ireland arrests were akin in their function to public executions in Foucault's description, 'Its aim is not so much to re-establish a balance as to bring into play, at its extreme point, the dissymmetry between the subject who has dared to violate the law and the all-powerful sovereign who displays his strength' (Foucault 1977:48–9). It was on the streets that Republican identity was constructed and not through the misty myths of origin of the Irish nation. While arrests were individual acts, they also took on a collective meaning in the nationalist community. Arrest and interrogation were, in brief, a seminal experience in the formation of Republican identity. As Feldman puts it, 'it is crucial to understand the function of arrest as a biographical experience capable of generating collective political meanings' (Feldman 1991:97).

Republicans and peace

From around 1990 onwards, many of the above tendencies flowed into a new situation and this confluence led to the so-called 'peace process'.

Since 1969, the conflict between the Irish Republican movement and the British state had seen clearly defined phases and shifts in the balance of forces. An early phase of Republican ascendancy had caught the British state unawares, but this was followed by a concerted and largely successful effort to contain Republicanism. The reorganisation of the IRA in the late 1970s and the dramatic hunger strike of the early 1980s (see O'Malley 1990) put Republicanism back in the running. However, breaking out of containment did not lead to a new Republican ascendancy, but rather to a political and military stalemate (albeit with fluctuations) *vis-à-vis* the British state. In terms of our discourse analysis, the nationalist element became totally preeminent. The socialist interpellation was almost totally defunct after the cataclysmic international transformations of 1989. Catholicism was not particularly important *per se* but it did lead to a communitarian aspect, which took the nationalist community's war-weariness seriously. Finally, the element of 'physical force' was being reconsidered, as the diminishing political returns of the military campaign were becoming plain to see.

The Republican movement's turn towards 'electoralism' in the 1980s must be seen in the context of the 'long war' strategy then being developed. In retrospect, the notion of a 'long war' seems less of a new strategy than an attempt to explain away the failure of the oft-predicted 'victory' of the 1970s to materialise. The implicit notion of an integrated politico-military strategy, as advocated in international guerrilla strategy, did not really come to fruition. If anything, the concept of a 'long war' tended to marginalise the role of Sinn Féin within the overall Republican strategy – that is, because the electoral turn was still conceived *within* a world-view which was profoundly militaristic. Thus Sinn Féin signally failed to develop realistic and relevant socio-economic policies beyond that of pious platitudes. This was due not only to militarism, it also stemmed from the nationalist optic which united 'left' and 'right' Republicans. In a rapidly integrating world, clinging to the narrow boundaries of the nation state was a major stumbling block to the development of radical democratic politics. In the south of Ireland, this failure was most manifest, with Sinn Féin failing abysmally to capitalise on the social contradictions engendered by dependent capitalist development. In the North, the political limitations of Sinn Féin were masked by the adoption of a 'gas and water' municipal socialism, embraced enthusiastically by the new generation of Sinn Féin councillors.

During the 1980s, the IRA had clawed back from its bleak defensive period of the 1970s. The determination was to wage a more selective 'political' war, rather than the 'total onslaught' of an earlier era. There were spectacular successes, particularly in Britain, and war material had become sophisticated and more than sufficient for its purposes. Yet, through all its multifaceted arenas, from 'shoot to kill' to draconian legal measures, the British state hit back. By the early 1990s there was undoubtedly a certain war-weariness, if not amongst the hardened IRA volunteers, then certainly within their community support base. That is where the political stalemate comes in, because for all its electoral advances, Sinn Féin could not unblock the political situation. Therefore, a new initiative was called for. From the socialist camp there was nothing new on offer, so clearly the dominant discourse would be from the familiar territory of Irish nationalism. Given the new international dispensation and traditional Republican alliances, the role of the United States was to be crucial.

When the 'Troubles' began in 1968–9, the international context had considerable bearing on the local northern Irish situation. In 1988–9, the emerging realisation that the war had to end was equally influenced by the new international context (see Ryan 1994). A key factor was the collapse of the Soviet Union and the associated discrediting of the 'non-capitalist development' path and the new post-Cold War era which became manifest with the Gulf War of 1991. Not only was the military might of Western imperialism clear for all to see, but it also achieved a certain moral regeneration. The whole concept of national liberation began to seem a quaint anachronism to many one-time progressives. In Ireland, Republican eyes turned towards the incipient demilitarisation of struggles in South Africa, Palestine and El Salvador. Pragmatism was boosted by changing international realities and by late 1993, the Republican press was noting how 'All across the world, direct and indirect dialogue is used as a means to end seemingly intractable conflicts ... Conflict areas throughout the world are being transformed from theatres of war into political arenas' (*An Phoblacht/Republican News* 11 November 1993).

This is not the place to rehearse the complex history of the so-called 'peace process' in Northern Ireland (for more details see Mallie and McKitrick 1996 and O'Brien 1995). Our purpose is the more limited one of seeing how the early signs of a 'new departure' in Irish Republicanism in the mid-1980s came to fruition in the 'peace process' of the 1990s. Republican discourse took a decisive turn between the *Scenario for Peace* document (Sinn Féin 1987) and *Towards a Lasting Peace* (Sinn Féin 1992). For many commentators on the left, the shift from a language of 'victory' to one of 'democratic compromise' masked a simple 'drift towards respectability' and provided an opportunity to lecture Republicans on 'the dangers of opportunism' (Ryan 1994:74). From this perspective, Gerry Adams is simply the latest in a long list of Republicans who have eventually succumbed to the discrete charms of democratic constitutional nationalism and, maybe, when looking back from the future, that may indeed prove to be the case. However, there are sound arguments to see the 'new departure' of the 1990s as a decisive shift towards a realism which is more likely to have a fundamental impact on Irish politics.

The 1992 Sinn Féin Ard Fheis (conference) adopted the document *Towards a Lasting Peace* (Sinn Féin 1992) in a move which appeared to mark a break, albeit partial, with the earlier 'theological' discourse of the party. Previous programmes tended towards 'absolutist' and rhetorical arguments about self-determination and national 'rights'. It was hard in previous formulations to find a coherent statement on how a British withdrawal might actually be achieved and conducted according to a timetable. In fact, they were totally superficial on the post-withdrawal scenario and left their own supporters quite unable to deal with the 'power vacuum' or 'blood-bath' scenarios. In contrast, the watchwords of the 1992 document were pragmatism and flexibility. Certainly the traditional themes of self-determination and Irish national sovereignty were rehearsed, but we also see a move towards a new realist terrain.

Towards a Lasting Peace recognised implicitly that Irish Republicanism might come to play only a catalyst role in the conflict over the north. It had become clear to many Republican realists that it would not be they who would reap the fruits of 'victory', the meaning of which was becoming quite fuzzy. Reflecting this, the document called on the British and Irish governments to initiate a peace process, possibly under the auspices of the European Union or with the mediation of the United Nations. The traditional nationalist discourse of Irish Republicanism is at least in part contested, if not replaced, by a new democratic discourse. For example, the once cavalier attitude towards the northern Protestant minority was replaced by a clear recognition that 'peace in Ireland requires a settlement of the long-standing conflict between Irish Nationalism and Irish Unionism. We would like to see this conflict, often bloody, replaced by a process of national reconciliation, a constructive dialogue and debate' (ibid.:3). In terms of the broader principles of how politics is or should be conducted, it is argued in the document that 'it is necessary to break out of the present conception of politics in Ireland, where one person's gain is conceived automatically as another person's loss' (ibid.:14). It is a far cry from the 'ultimatist' arguments of fundi

Republicans to recognise that all lose from a continuation of the conflict and all might gain from its resolution.

As an 'all or nothing' conception of struggle began to cede ground to the terrain of democratic compromise, so the question of methods of struggle began to be reconsidered. In 1992, it was already stated that 'the development of ... an alternative [to the armed struggle] would be welcomed by Sinn Fein' (Sinn Féin 1992:10). Towards the end of 1993, Gerry Adams concluded talks with the middle-class Catholic Social Democratic Labour Party's (SDLP's) leader John Hume, which aimed at establishing a nationalist consensus. At first, reactions were sceptical about the prospects for the resulting Hume–Adam proposals for bringing about peace. However, Hume successfully put this on the agenda of the Dublin government and in bilateral negotiation with the British government, a commitment to Irish national self-determination was obtained. Furthermore, it was established that a termination of the IRA campaign would allow Sinn Féin to attend the negotiating table. The result was the Downing Street Declaration, which Sinn Féin did not reject outright; instead they sought a process of 'clarification' *vis-à-vis* the more ambiguous formulations in the Declaration.

Negotiations continued into 1994 and 'clarifications' were obtained all round. After what appeared like a setback at Sinn Féin's conference in Letterkenny in June, when the Declaration was still not accepted, the IRA made a historic announcement at the end of August that it was ceasing hostilities. The 'long war' was replaced by 'long negotiations' – with more to be gained from unarmed alternatives than from armed struggle. The unilateral and complete cessation of Republican military operations was called on the basis of the 'potential of the current situation and in order to enhance the democratic peace process' (*The Sunday Tribune* 1995). Republicans felt that the forces of Irish nationalism, both at home and abroad, could create the conditions for a lasting settlement. That this might not mean a united Ireland in the short to medium term was also accepted. It would seem that 25 years of armed struggle had 'won a draw', as Britain recognised the validity of Irish nationalist aspirations and Irish Republicans accepted that there was no 'quick fix' to resolve the pro-British sentiment of a minority of the people in the island of Ireland.

After 25 years of intense and bitter struggle, what have Republicans achieved? They have not been defeated by a powerful enemy and they have placed the 'national question' firmly on the agenda. They have also made it impossible for Northern Ireland to return to the 'sectarian statelet' it was for 60 years. However, the unravelling of the 'peace process' since August 1994, through the Canary Wharf bombing and repeated Unionist triumphalism at Drumcree during the 'marching season', made it clear how little some things change. British stalling on negotiations led Republicanism to the tried and tested 'message in a lorry' at Canary Wharf. Unionist fears of a British 'sell-out' led to the most aggressive Orange 'parading' for many years, including murder, church burnings and mass intimidation. Eamonn McCann feels understandably that the peace process has not faltered but failed due to its being based on and thus entrenching sectarian divisions: 'Far from being designed to loosen the grip of sectarianism on the minds of men and women, the process accepts sectarianism as a natural, central, permanent fact of Northern Irish life' (McCann 1995). Republicans for their part have accepted that 'an agreed Ireland needs the allegiance of varied traditions to be viable' (*The Sunday Tribune* 1995) – a statement that departs dramatically from traditional Republican discourse. The challenge for mainstream Republicans will be to find ways of moving beyond the zero-sum conception of politics in practice and not just in rhetoric, in opposition to the die-hard-actions of Republican *fundis*, as in the Omagh bombing of 1998. Overwhelming public outrage over Omagh led to a cease-fire being called by most Republican *fundis*, including the Real IRA and the INLA.

For Irish Republicans, as Gerry Adams admitted, 'The road to peace was always going to be difficult. What we are attempting to do is very ambitious, as well as risky and dangerous' (Adams 1996). One possibility is that the Republican movement could be sidelined now that its most manifest expression – IRA action – has been largely muzzled. Going back to the old status quo – a bloody stalemate – seems hardly possible, given the dramatic change in political alignments. Clearly a return to previous practice by Republicans would represent a major obstacle to the historic compromise(s) necessary to establish an agreed Ireland in the foreseeable future. Conversely, the huge leap taken by Republicanism over the past decade, as explored in the pages above, places the movement in the positive column of that historic project. A more decisive move on to the democratic terrain – and this should be conceived of as civil society as a whole and not be reduced to the constitutional – to reclaim the original Republican project, would place the contemporary Republican movement in a pivotal political role. The poverty of political thought induced by centuries of colonialism, the disaster of partition and the heavy blanket of nationalism versus Unionism leave the terrain open for a fresh and bold approach out of the dead end of the recent past.

Endgame?

On Good Friday 1998, a historic agreement was signed between the Northern Irish political parties and the British and Irish governments. Was this the 'endgame', the winding down of a 30 (or 300) year-old conflict, a basis for historic compromise between Irish nationalism and pro-British Unionism? For Irish Republicanism it was a 'transition phase' towards Irish unity and for Unionists it represented Republican acceptance of the continued British presence in the north of Ireland. In fact, what was put together by the two governments, with American and European blessing and backing, was a hybrid political being. Both governments agreed that the future status of Northern Ireland would be decided by its inhabitants, the famous 'consent' principle. This is a fluid, labile and indeed 'provisional' status for a territory, quite in keeping with the postmodern era. It is now the political process, or to be precise, struggle, which will decide the future of the north and to what extent all-Ireland dimensions develop. A new horizon of possibilities opens up, in which demilitarisation is possible, but by no means guaranteed. For the time being, the proponents of war are a small minority, but a genuine political solution is still a long way off.

In May 1998, a reconvened Sinn Féin Ard Fheis in Dublin ratified the Good Friday Agreement by a majority so large that it was hard to tell whether it was 96 or 97 per cent of the delegates who voted in favour. Proceedings opened with a warning to never confuse principles with tactics. The delegates had little problem with the idea of Sinn Féin taking its seat in the new Northern Assembly. They did have some reservations in recommending voters in the south to discard the (in)famous Articles 2 and 3 in the Constitution, which lay claim to the whole island of Ireland. In fact, the amended articles are a far better expression of the democratic nationalist aspiration to Irish unity, as they are couched in the language of citizenship and not as a territorial imperative. The situation now facing Irish Republicanism seems to be how it will reconstitute itself as a radical opposition within the broad nationalist consensus. For a generation of activists, now in a position of leadership, politics had been seen, to put it crudely, as a continuation of war by other means. Now the traditional Republican agenda, like that of Unionism, is at a cross-roads and the political clock cannot be turned back to before Good Friday 1998, but the future can only be an uncertain one.

Now, nearly a year since the Good Friday agreement was signed, much has changed but much remains the same. The British and Irish governments (with US backing) seem firmly committed to a lasting 'solution'. On the ground, people have got used to a 'post-war' situation and community politics is flourishing. However, only a bare majority of Unionists now support the agreement and Loyalist groupings (new or reconstituted) engage in sectarianism and promoting the stand-off at Drumcree (where Orangemen insist on their 'God-given' right to march through nationalist areas) continues and will probably flare up again. On the nationalist side there are divisions as the Irish government pressurises the IRA to hand in weapons before a political settlement is established. Republicans are uneasy and sometimes frustrated. The mould of nationalist/unionist politics has not been broken and politics seems to be a continuation of war by other means. It is a very cold peace but better than a hot war. Some organisations such as the small Continuity IRA keep to the *fundi* faith but on the whole realism prevails in Republican circles. Certainly, the Republican movement in 1999 has come a long way from the small band of 1969, which was nearly condemned to oblivion. Whether it can now develop a new radical democratic discourse more in keeping with the tradition of Wolfe Tone, the founder of modern Irish Republicanism, remains an open question.

References

Adams, G. 1996: 'Adams insists SF does not advocate armed struggle' in *Irish Times,* June 20.
A Derry Protestant 1991: 'Reaction to Sinn Fein Policies in the Protestant Community' in *Starry Plough*, vol. 1, no. 2 pp. 10–12.
Althusser, L. 1971: 'Ideology and Ideological State Apparatus' in L. Althusser, *Lenin and Philosophy and Other Essays*, London: New Left Books.
Aretxaga, B (1997) *Shattering the Silence. Women, Nationalism and Political Subjectivity, in Northern Ireland*, New Jersey: Princeton University Press.
Bell, J. 1979: *The Secret Army. The IRA 1916–1979*, Dublin: Academy Press.
Bishop, P. and Mallie, E. 1987: *The Provisional IRA*, London: Corgi.
Burton, F. 1978: *The Politics of Legitimacy: Struggles in a Belfast Community*, London: Routledge.
Campbell, B. 1992: 'Voices from the Edge' in *An Glor Gafa*, vol. 4, no. 1.
Cash, J. 1996: *Identity, Ideology and Conflict: The Structuration of Politics in Northern Ireland*, Cambridge: Cambridge University Press.
Coogan, T.P. 1980: *The IRA*, Glasgow: Gollanz.
Derrida, J. 1980: *Positions*, Chicago, ILL: University of Chicago Press.
Dillon, M. 1988: *The Dirty War*, London: Hutchinson.
Dillon, M. 1992: *Stone Cold. The True Story of Michael Stone and the Milltown Massacre*, London: Arrow.
Eagleton, T. 1981: *Walter Benjamin or Towards a Revolutionary Criticism*, London: New Left Books.

Feldman, A. 1991: *Formations of Violence: The Narrative of the Body and Political Terror in Northern Ireland*, Chicago, ILL: University of Chicago Press.
Foucault, M. 1972: *The Archaeology of Knowledge*, London: Tavistock.
Foucault, M. 1977: *Discipline and Punish*, London: Penguin.
Goldring, M. 1982: *Faith of Our Fathers: The Formation of Irish Nationalist Ideology*, Dublin: Repsol.
Hamill, D. 1985: *Pig in the Middle: The Army in Northern Ireland 1969–1985*, London: Methuen.
Iris 1981: 'Editorial' in *Iris*, no. 2, Dublin: Sinn Féin.
Laplanche, J. and Leclaire, S. 1972: 'The Unconscious: A Psychoanalytic Study' in *Yale French Studies*, no. 48, pp. 118–75.
McCann, E. 1995: 'Managing Sectarianism' in *New Statesman and Society*, 25 August.
McClelland, M. and Dowd, C. 1992: 'British Strategy in Ireland: Imperialist Plan or Crisis Management' in *Starry Plough*, vol. 2, no. 1, pp. 3–14.
McIntyre, A. 1995: 'Modern Irish Republicanism: The Product of British State Strategies' in *Irish Political Studies*, no. 10, pp. 99–121.
McLaughlin, M. 1991: 'Protestantism, Unionism and Loyalism' in *Starry Plough*, vol. 2, no. 2, pp. 13–16.
McThomas, H. 1992: 'What are the British Doing in Ireland?' in *Starry Plough*, vol. 2, no. 1, pp. 10–12
Mallie, E. and McKittrick, D. 1996: *The Fight for Peace: The Secret Story Behind the Peace Process*, London: Heinemann.
Munck, R. 1988: 'The Lads and the Hoods: Alternative Justice in an Irish Context' in M. Tomlinson, T. Varley and C. McCullagh (editors), *Whose Law and Order? Aspects of Crime and Social Control in Irish Society*, Belfast: Sociological Association of Ireland.
Munck, R. and Rolston, B. 1987: *Belfast in the Thirties: An Oral History*, Belfast: Blackstaff Press.
Norton, A. 1993: *Reflections on Political Identity*, Baltimore, Md: Johns Hopkins University Press.
O'Brien, B. 1995: *The Long War. The IRA and Sinn Fein from Armed Struggle to Peace Talks*, Dublin: The O'Brien Press.
O'Halloran, C. 1987: *Partition and the Limits of Irish Nationalism*, Dublin: Gill & Macmillan.
O'Malley, P. 1990: *Biting at the Grave: The Irish Hunger Strikes and the Politics of Despair*, Belfast: Blackstaff.
Patterson, H. 1989: *The Politics of Illusion: Republicanism and Socialism in Modern Ireland*, London: Hutchinson Radius.
Pêcheux, M. 1982: *Language, Semantics and Ideology*, London: Macmillan.
Purdie, B. 1980: 'Reconsiderations on Republicanism and Socialism' in A. Morgan and B. Purdie (editors), *Ireland: Divided Nation, Divided Class*, London: Ink Links.
Ryan, M. 1994: *War and Peace in Ireland, Britain and the IRA in the New World Order*, London: Pluto.
Sands, B. 1981: *The Diary of Bobby Sands*, Dublin: Sinn Féin.
Scott, A. 1991: *Ideology and the New Social Movements*, London: Unwin Hyman.
Sinn Féin 1986: *The Politics of Revolution*, Dublin: Sinn Féin.
Sinn Féin 1987: *Scenario for Peace*, Dublin: Sinn Féin.

Sinn Féin 1989: *Sinn Féin: European Parliament Election Manifesto*, Dublin: Sinn Féin.
Sinn Féin 1992: *Towards a Lasting Peace in Ireland*, Dublin: Sinn Féin.
Smith, M.L.R. 1995: *Fighting for Ireland? The Military Strategy of the Irish Republican Movement*, London: Routledge.
Swilling, M. 1992: 'The Dynamics of Reformism' in A. Callinicos (editor), *Between Apartheid and Capitalism: Conversations with South African Socialists*, London: Bookmarks.
'*The Sunday Tribune*' 1995: 'The IRA Peace Document', 23 April.
Toolis, K. 1995: *Rebel Hearts. Journey within the IRA's Soul*, London: Picador.
Urban, M. 1992: *Big Boys' Rules: The Secret Struggle Against the IRA*, London: Faber.
Ward, M. 1983: *Unmanageable Revolutionaries: Women and Irish Nationalism*, London: Pluto Press.
White, R. 1993: *Provisional Irish Republicans: An Oral and Interpretative History*, Westport, Conn.: Greenwood Press.

6
Ethiopia: Success Story or State of Chaos?

Aregawi Berhe[1]

After the collapse of Colonel Mengistu Haile Mariam's seventeen-year-old military dictatorship in May 1991, Ethiopia appeared to take a new direction of peaceful and democratic transition, with the Tigray People's Liberation Front (TPLF) taking the lead in determining crucial political matters.[2] By 1989, through managing to control its ethnic base area of Tigray (a northern region of Ethiopia) and in the attempt to capture power in the whole of Ethiopia, the TPLF hastily formed an umbrella organisation – the Ethiopian People's Revolutionary Democratic Front (EPRDF) – in conjunction with three weaker organisations, namely: the Ethiopian People's Democratic Movement (EPDM),[3] the Oromo People's Democratic Organisation (OPDO) and the Free Officers Movement (FOM).[4] These three organisations were supported by the TPLF even in their creation. The decision on the part of the TPLF to form this (unequal) alliance was based on a number of strategic considerations. Primarily, it was designed to outmanoeuvre the other competing popular political organisations – such as the Oromo Liberation Front (OLF) in the south and east, and the Ethiopian People's Revolutionary Party (EPRP) in the central highlands and adjoining provinces. This political manoeuvre, coupled with its military dominance, enabled the TPLF-led EPRDF to defeat the forces of the military junta, known as the Derg (or Committee), and capture state power in May 1991. Nonetheless, the politics of exclusion soon ignited animosity between the EPRDF and numerous other ethnic and multi-ethnic organisations like the OLF, the Afar Revolutionary Democratic Union (ARDU), the EPRP, the Ethiopian Democratic Union (EDU) and the All Ethiopian Socialist Movement (MEISON) – all of which were either marginalised or banned from the post-Mengistu political process.

Given the post-Cold War geopolitical scenario, it was essential for the victorious TPLF-led EPRDF forces to secure the backing of the USA, its European allies and Israel (who were content with the fall of the former pro-Soviet military regime), in order to consolidate their position. The USA in particular spared no time in supporting the militarily stronger TPLF. And it was ironic to observe the so-called 'Stalinist TPLF' – seen at the height of the Cold War as terrorists by the 'free democratic Western alliance' – being supported by the USA and Western European countries as it ascended to power. The TPLF and its affiliate organisations went on to unilaterally create a transitional government in 1991 – installing a new constitution and implementing a highly controversial policy of ethnic politics, which grants the right of secession to the over 80 ethnic groups in the country (1995 Constitution, Art. 39, No. 1). The restructuring of the Ethiopian state, or, as some would like to call it, 'the democratisation process', proceeded in accordance with the dictates of the EPRDF-led transitional government, with the leadership of the TPLF at the helm of the new political set-up. Finally in August 1995, a new government was declared 'elected' with the same political grouping in office. The post-Mengistu political processes, including the formation of the sovereign Eritrean state in 1991 (see Hagos 1995), as one could anticipate, have led to serious confrontations between the new regime in Addis Ababa and a multitude of opposition groups of various political and ideological persuasions.

Needless to say, whenever such conflicting political, social, cultural and economic interests lack space for compromise or broad-based consensus, and when local governance proceeds without deliberation or consultation at the popular level, long-term peace drifts out of reach. If the absence of war does not necessarily mean peace, then today's Ethiopia (where the seeds of yet another cycle of civil war and ethnic conflict are being sown) certainly illustrates this argument. Before moving on to an examination of the 'democratisation process' in post-Cold War Ethiopia, I shall provide a brief analysis of the emergence of the TPLF as a political force, which will induce a greater understanding of the machinations of the power-at-work.

Origin and rise of the TPLF

The formation and development of modern Ethiopia, with the subsequent shift of power from its traditional location in the north (mainly Tigray, Gonder and Wollo) to the south (Showa), left the Tigrayans in particular in multifaceted, disadvantageous positions. When the

Showan King Menelik, the architect of modern Ethiopia, assumed power in 1889, his long-term strategy was to systematically divide and weaken the Tigrayan monarchy, whom he evidently considered to be a dangerous rival power. To control the Tigrayan overlords, Menelik devised political, diplomatic and military stratagems by appointing his cronies to key positions in Tigray, thereby undermining the autonomy enjoyed by the Tigrayans. Also as part of his scheme, Menelik drove a wedge between the traditionally homogeneous Tigrayans, who, if united, could mount resistance and reclaim the central position from him. Thus, repression of the power-contenders and concurrently their civilian followers was severe.

Emperor Haile Selassie, who took over and ruled the country for over four decades (until his overthrow in 1974), pursued Menelik's policy of divide and rule towards the Tigrayan political elites. He imposed the Amharic language in the fields of education and all workings of the government as a compulsory requirement to any official communication. Even in the Ethiopian Church, Amharic replaced Geez and ordinary Christian Tigrayans had to learn Amharic, otherwise they would fall off their spiritual track. They were also required to pray for the emperor's long life. Almost all ministerial power was given to the members of the Amhara ethnic group – mainly from Showa – except for one or two posts, spared for Tigrayans, which in most cases had been symbolic rather than dealing with real power. The numerous other ethnic groups were even treated as if they did not qualify in the politics of power. The repression of Tigrayans did not stop there: peasants had to pay numerous, unaccounted tributes, not only to the central government, but also to a number of local officials who were keen to retain their former status – including the Ethiopian Orthodox Church which had effectively legitimised the hegemony of the Showan–Amhara ruling class.[5]

As the domination and exploitation of the Tigrayans (who still believed themselves to be at the centre of the Ethiopian nation) deepened, concomitantly, intolerance and tension mounted throughout Tigray, taking the form of counter-hegemonic ethno-nationalism. By the middle of 1942, peasants from five out of eight districts (Raya, Enderta, Kilete-Awlaelo, Agame and Tembien), mobilised by hereditary leaders and radical nationalists like Bellata Haile-Mariam Reda, ignited a revolt, known as '*Woyane*', meaning rebellion. The *Woyane* continued until 1943, when the British Royal Air Force (RAF) intervened to suppress the uprising. The RAF, together with the ground forces of Haile Selassie, devastated parts of Tigray including the market-places of

Mekele, the capital of Tigray, through air bombardment (Public Record Office, ref. Fo371/35607). The defeat of the *Woyane* was another misfortune that brought about a series of vengeful measures. Organised plunder, side by side with vandalism, had been carried out by the emperor's army, whose mission was to punish the Tigrayan people so that they could never rise up again. The process of repression continued, reinforced every time not only by up-to-date military and police measures, but also by the recurring natural calamities the government never cared to arrest. Comparatively speaking, Tigrayans led the most impoverished life and hundreds of thousands of them were forced to migrate all over the country in search of seasonal or long-lasting employment.

Thus, one of the most fundamental factors of the recent conflicts in Ethiopia, and specifically the armed struggle in Tigray, stems from the fact that power in all its aspects (political, economic, social, cultural, historical, religious) was the monopoly of one domineering national élite, namely the Showan–Amhara ruling group. This elite considered itself to be the core element for the building of Ethiopian nationalism, hence the claim to, and appropriation of, the leadership and its privileges. As John Markakis critically observes, 'the process of the national integration was tantamount to assimilation into the culture of the empire builders' (Markakis 1990:73).

The Marxist military government, led by Colonel Mengistu, which succeeded the emperor, declared that it would represent an oppressed class of multinational and multi-ethnic social forces. Yet, Mengistu's regime in no time revealed itself as essentially no different from the previous regime towards the assertive ethnic-nationalists, only this time accompanied by the harshness of a military dictatorship. This military regime was not only repressive, but also, throughout its reign, exceptionally brutal in its use of sheer military force and police terror against all national and ethnic groups that dared raise the democratic question of self-determination or autonomy – even those that conformed their presence within the framework of the then Ethiopian state. Tigrayans, together with their affinitive neighbours the Eritreans, were the first targets of the new repression. There was thus a proliferation of liberation movements especially in post-revolutionary Ethiopia, namely, those of the Oromos, the Afars, the Sidamas, the Ogadens, the Tigrayans and the Eritreans, who had all opted for secession. This was an inevitable reaction to the unbridled domination by the Showan–Amhara aristocracy and here lies the root cause of much of the ethnic strife and secessionist tendencies that have threatened to crack the bondage Ethiopians have developed over thousands of years of coexistence. Thus, the conditions for the struggle of ethnic-based national self-determination were created which partially explains why the TPLF and the Tigray Liberation Front (TLF) came into existence, and why the TPLF managed to effectively mobilise the people of Tigray against the military dictatorship ruling Ethiopia.

Unlike the Tigrayan peasant uprising of 1943, which could not survive the joint onslaught by Haile Selassie's ground forces and Britain's RAF bombers, the radical Tigrayan nationalists of the early 1970s devised a coherent strategy to challenge national domination. It began by creating a clandestine force, namely the Tigrayan National Organisation (TNO), to conduct political struggle in the urban areas. Later, in February 1975, a rural-based armed struggle was launched; a well-coordinated endeavour led by the TPLF. As a left-oriented nationalist movement fighting for the right to self-determination, from the beginning the TPLF concentrated on two basic tactics of mobilising the people against the regime.

Throughout the sixteen years of armed struggle, the mobilisation process of the TPLF was based on a hybrid of two ideologies, nationalism on one hand and class struggle on the other. This form of struggle greatly helped the TPLF to confront the military regime, which also pursued a similar double-edged mobilisation process – 'Ethiopian *Tikdem*' (that is, Ethiopian nationalism) on the one hand and Marxism–Leninism (Soviet version) on the other. These two ideologies may appear incompatible, especially when stretched to their extreme limits, however at a certain level of social interaction where material conditions are intrinsic to national domination, their relationship was positive. As Markakis puts it, 'uneven development and material disparity distinguish not only regions and ethnic groups but social classes as well, and condition class attitudes to political phenomena, nationalism included' (1990:273). The TPLF's combination of both ideologies as a guiding method of struggle enabled it to successfully mobilise the Tigrayan people on its side and build a strong peasant army ahead of the other movements such as the OLF, the ALF or even the EPRP.

By the mid-1980s the TPLF had created a strong support base and an army. Unlike the government forces, which employed strict conventional warfare, the TPLF, combining guerrilla and mobile warfare, cleared all government troops from Tigray by the end of 1989 and began marching to the centre of Ethiopia, targeting Addis Ababa, the capital city of Ethiopia. Since it could not accomplish this broader task as a Tigrayan (single-ethnic) organisation, it forged an 'Ethiopian

Front', namely the Ethiopian People's Revolutionary Democratic Front (EPRDF) – comprising the Ethiopian People's Democratic Movement (EPDM), a small splinter group from the EPRP (hardly known by the Ethiopian people) and the Oromo People's Democratic Organisation (OPDO). In the eyes of the vast majority of Ethiopians, the TPLF's advance outside Tigray was a purely militaristic strategy, which created fear and anxiety among other ethnic and multi-ethnic movements that had also been fighting the Mengistu military regime. Although these movements were not as strong militarily as the TPLF, they nevertheless had a social base and political programmes that at least put them in a position to negotiate the military march through their respective socio-political domains. Obsessed with its military victories and the taste of power, the TPLF, led by Meles Zenawi, seemed to pay no attention to the amelioration of this situation that had the potential to trigger future conflicts. Just a week after the desperate flight of Colonel Mengistu into exile in Zimbabwe on 28 May 1991, the TPLF, under the guise of its nominal umbrella organisation, the EPRDF, won the war and managed to capture the capital, Addis Ababa, with little resistance.

Unfolding of a crisis

So far, it appears to be a success story for the TPLF. However, that is not what matters most. The armed struggle for self-determination was waged by and for the people of Tigray. For the people who paid dearly to bring the struggle to a successful end, what does this change entail? What are the gains for the Ethiopian peoples as a whole, who fought the military regime, each in their own way, to make it possible for the TPLF-led EPRDF to seize state power in Ethiopia? Have they got what they sought to achieve, in the form of peace, democracy, respect of human rights, rule of law and equal opportunity and security to prosper? It is by critical treatment of these questions that we should appraise the direction in which Ethiopia is heading.

True, it was the combined effort of the Ethiopian peoples and various liberation movements, albeit with the significant military role played by the TPLF, which brought the seventeen years of the Derg's military dictatorship and reign of terror to an end. Most Ethiopians welcomed the change, genuinely hoping that whoever came to power this time would not be as horrendous as the military junta. In the beginning, no one seemed to contest that this was a positive achievement, although some people had reservations because of the TPLF's wavering stand on Ethiopian unity and its ideology,[6] which from the beginning was ultra-left but now appeared to embrace the Western liberal democratic and 'free market' model. Many foreign governments, with the USA taking the lead, also offered instant recognition to the new rulers, assuming that they would easily join their club of acolytes, unlike the 'pro-Soviet' military dictators.

The concern of the USA-led Western powers was obvious. They wanted to arrest the expansion of 'Islamic fundamentalism' in the aftermath of the Cold War, which was seen to be posing a serious challenge to their cultural values and a threat to their material interests, in and around the Middle East and the Horn of Africa. Sudan, where an Islamist government had gained ground and which occupied a strategic position in the Horn of Africa, had to be checked from influencing the region. The USA found the TPLF a better organised and manageable military force in Ethiopia, which could accomplish the strategic tasks it wanted to pursue. Despite its leftist rhetoric, Zenawi's TPLF swiftly came to terms with the USA and has become an ally in harnessing the anticipated opposition from the other Ethiopian political forces and the people at large. The USA was more than willing, therefore, to facilitate the seizure and consolidation of power in Ethiopia by the TPLF.

As the forces of the TPLF and EPLF were closing in on Addis Ababa and Asmara respectively, on 27 May 1991 in London, Herman Cohen, US Assistant Secretary of State for Africa, met with leaders of the militarily stronger TPLF, OLF and EPLF together with delegates from the collapsing Derg, ostensibly to negotiate a peaceful transition of power. Other political forces that could have affected Ethiopia's future were ignored in the process and a golden opportunity for a far-reaching political settlement was brushed aside in favour of a more short-sighted military solution. Even then at the end of May 1991, before a negotiated settlement was reached, after spending a night in the American Embassy in Khartoum, Zenawi suddenly showed up in Addis Ababa to head the forthcoming Ethiopian government.

The USA and its allies spent no time in according the new regime diplomatic recognition as well as financial aid. US military and technical experts, including constitutional advisers, began flowing to Zenawi's administration within months of taking office. In an interview with the *Ethiopian Commentator* (*EC*), Marc Baas, US Ambassador to Ethiopia said, 'The overall policy of the US towards Ethiopia is to promote the process of democratization in this country and the opening up of the free market economy. We have done a great deal in the last year [1992]. I have signed agreements for over 105 million dollars in emergency food and humanitarian assistance, in addition to over 170 million dollars of development assistance' (*EC* 1993:31–2). The commitment of the USA to hook Ethiopia into its globalisation 'programme' and orbit lies in the fact that in terms of geopolitics, Ethiopia is an important country in the continent of Africa – that is, coping with peacekeeping, hosting mediatory talks between contesting African political actors and tackling the Islamist state of Sudan and similar radicals in Somalia (with the cooperation of Uganda, Eritrea and Egypt for which the EPRDF regime is reportedly remunerated by US$100 million worth of military aid a year by the Americans).

The TPLF-led EPRDF regime, with its extremely narrow and uncertain social base, is confronted internally with the opposition of the Ethiopian people who denied it the mandate to rule the country on the one hand, and externally with the pressure the USA exerts to fight the proxy war with Islamist Sudan on the other. Prime Minister Zenawi's choice appears to be repressing the opposition at home and following US policy. The net result is that in a relatively poor country like present-day Ethiopia, which is confronted by a range of internal and external problems, a stable government, if not impossible, is less likely to emerge. People who argue that the current government is better than the former military regime of Mengistu should understand that the fall of one form of dictatorship does not necessarily mean a transition to a democratic and peaceful system of governance. While Mengistu was pro-Soviet, Zenawi is pro-West, with little improvement in the overall socio-political condition and upward mobility of the peoples of Ethiopia. In fact, in today's Ethiopia, an unprecedented wave of resistance is in the making. The EPRP in the west, the OLF in the south, the Ogaden National Liberation Front (ONLF) in the south-east, the Afar Revolutionary Democratic Front (ARDF) in the east, have all stepped up their fight against the EPRDF. Many other political organisations, including the Oromo National Congress (ONC), the Southern Ethiopian People's Democratic Union (SEPDU) and the All Amhara People's Organisation from within, and the Tigrayan Alliance for National Democracy (TAND), the Tigray Tigrigni Ethiopia (TTE), the Ethiopian Medhine Democratic Party (MEDHINE) and many others from outside the country, are pressing hard to bring about a fundamental change in Ethiopia. All these organisations have been calling publicly for peace, reconciliation and stability. The EPRDF, however, has remained deaf to all popular calls for peaceful change and has continued to push the country towards an eventual state of chaos and civil war.

The unyielding response of Zenawi's regime to all the popular and legitimate calls by greater and greater numbers of the peoples of

Ethiopia and related political organisations could also be scrutinised from another dimension. In 1985, a party officially known as the Marxist Leninist League of Tigray (MLLT) was established within the TPLF, with Zenawi as its chief ideologue. In its constitution, this party declared that the 'MLLT, as the core of the future Ethiopian Marxist Leninist Party, is the only correct party free from all sorts of revisionism (Trotskyism, Maoism ...) that could constitute a proletarian–peasant dictatorship to liberate the Ethiopian people' (MLLT 1985:1). Any other political organisation that did not correspond ideologically to the MLLT was labelled 'reactionary' and 'anti-people', and hence had to be 'cleansed'. In an interview with *The Independent*, at the end of 1989, the present Prime Minister of Ethiopia, Zenawi, asserted that 'the Soviet Union and other Eastern bloc countries have never been truly socialist. The nearest any country comes to being socialist as far as we are concerned is Albania' (*Dowden* 1989). For him only this party could lead to a 'fully democratic state' (ibid.). The officially published programme and declarations of the MLLT and TPLF are no longer visible since Zenawi joined the camp of the USA and he prefers not to even mention that he was a radical Marxist. Eclectic as they appear, Zenawi's policies have nevertheless succeeded in drawing the whole country into a veritable state of chaos and confusion. I will now look into some of the practical measures and policies employed by the TPLF-led EPRDF in Ethiopia's complex power politics.

Tinkering with democracy

After years of struggle, the time for Zenawi's 'fully democratic state' and its 'revolutionary' slogans of democratic rights, national equality, freedom of expression and organisation, rule of law and human rights came to be tested – rights for which the people struggled for decades and wait in earnest for their realisation. Regrettably, the EPRDF leaders took no time to prove that in practice they were no different from their predecessors, the military dictators. As they grabbed power, they began a systematic offensive campaign against legitimate democratic organisations which had, like the TPLF-led EPRDF, fought the Mengistu regime and with whom they were expected to build an all-inclusive, stable system of governance. For example, one of their malicious and unfounded accusations was directed towards the EPRP, an organisation which had the potential to pose a serious challenge, associating it with the defunct military dictatorship of the Derg by claiming, that 'in April 1991 EPRP forces in Gondar province united with the Derg forces to fight side by side against the EPRDF' (EPRDF *News Bulletin* 1991:6). So in order to silence any opposition elements within the country and deny freedom of expression which could perhaps lead to mass mobilisation against their unpopular policies, the EPRDF leaders embarked upon a reign of terror that began with opening fire on peaceful student demonstrators from the Addis Ababa University, only a few days after they seized power.

Encouraged by opposition parties within and outside the country, many papers critical of the government began to emerge. Yet, whenever critical remarks against the government appeared, the respective editors, journalists and publishers were immediately dragged off to prison, accused of negative campaigning against the government. According to an Amnesty International report, 'since October 1992, over 100 journalists and publishers of private newspapers and magazines in Addis Ababa have been arrested and a score or more others have been summoned for interrogation. Two journalists have "disappeared"' (Amnesty International 1995:10). Thousands of members of political organisations, unions and associations, which pose a serious challenge and espouse different programmes from that of the EPRDF, are at present languishing in prisons and detention centres. In the same report, Amnesty International revealed that over 20 000 officials and members of the OLF, AAPO, EPRP, ONLF and Southern Ethiopian Political Parties were detained without due process of law and subjected to harsh imprisonment and torture (ibid.:13–27). After giving details of gross violations of human rights, including names of people killed by EPRDF forces, the Ethiopian Human Rights Council (EHRCO) states that, 'The rigid, self-righteous and uncompromising position of those in power and their apparent determination to hold the monopoly of power by any means is matched by the thwarted peace efforts and frustrated ambitions of the opposition parties' (EHRCO 1994). In the same vein, in its resolution of 1996, the European Parliament 'calls on the Ethiopian authorities to guarantee complete freedom of expression and action to the Ethiopian Teachers Association and considers that civil society's democratic rights and independence must be fully respected' (European Parliament 1996: Resolution on Human Rights in Ethiopia 13[d] B4-0930/96, No. 2). From day one in power, the EPRDF has been unpopular basically because it came to power through military force and remained in power using the same instruments of force that brought it to power. This partially explains why the EPRDF is engaged in the gross violation of human and democratic rights, despite its rhetoric to the international community to the contrary. The democracy talked about by the EPRDF and its allies is nothing more than a fashionable, 'paper formality' which camouflages the true character of its leadership.

Formation of the transitional government and a new constitution

With the blessing of the US administration and its allies, the dominant TPLF-led EPRDF – representing one nationality in a country of no less than eighty nationalities and ethnic groups – was left alone to determine the future of the others. After the TPLF controlled Addis Ababa without difficulty, it swiftly established the Transitional Government of Ethiopia (TGE). Based upon the official London agreement of May 1991 between the TPLF-led EPRDF, OLF and EPLF, which was hosted by the US Assistant Secretary of State for African Affairs, a peace conference was held in Addis Ababa in July 1991 to create the TGE. Twenty-five political organisations, most of them ethnic-based and tutored by the TPLF, and some newly formed, like the ONLF, attended the conference. A hastily prepared charter for the transitional period was adopted by the conference. Many long-standing national and multinational political organisations like the EPRP, MEISON, ARDF and the Tigray People's Democratic Movement (TPDM), among others, which had been excluded from being part of the London treaty, saw what appeared to be a dubious scheme of the TPLF-led EPRDF and boycotted the conference. As the monopoly of power by the TPLF was becoming more evident, within months of the TGE's formation, most of the organisations which signed the charter, including the OLF (a participant in the London agreement) withdrew from the TGE and joined the ranks of the opposition. Terence Lyons correctly points out that 'the EPRDF led throughout this transition period and capitalised on its commanding position to consolidate its power. The party dominated the political landscape by virtue of its military power' (Lyons 1996:121). According to the charter, a Council of Representatives (CR) composed of 87 members was formed, and 32 seats were allocated to the EPRDF and its leader Zenawi, who became the president of TGE. Key posts such as Foreign Affairs, Defence and Security were held by members of his organisation, the TPLF. The other 55 seats and remaining ministerial posts were shared among 22 organisations, most of which were formed later on with assistance from the EPRDF. Henceforth, the EPRDF took the lion's share of the seats in the CR and with a private army of its own, which was declared as the national army, hardly any opposition could stand in its way. And thereafter, the formation of the new constitution followed.

The Ethiopian people are familiar with written constitutions since the reign of Emperor Haile Selassie. However, these constitutions were delivered from above and as governments came and went, so did the 'constitutions of Ethiopia'. What is more, these constitutions range in content and form, from monarchic to communist, and were granted by the rulers to the people, and not formed through consultation and participation of the people or their legitimate representatives. In fact, each government came up with its own 'new' constitution, tailor-made to suits its reign, and thus it has been evident that the function of such constitutions has only been to protect the power and privilege of the rulers rather than working as constraints over their power. The EPRDF's process of creating a new constitution was not in any way different from that of its predecessors.

In August 1992, the EPRDF, acting in the name of the TGE, established a Constitution Drafting Commission by Proclamation No. 24/1992. However, there was no fair and democratic selection procedure for membership of the Commission through which opposition groups could have expressed their views on this matter of national importance. Despite vehement criticism from the opposition groups and legal scholars on the deliberate stifling of this democratic procedure, members of the Commission had already been hand-picked by the leader of the EPRDF, Zenawi, and set to carry out the drafting of the new constitution. The effect this kind of selection procedure has on the nature and content of the constitution is a controversial subject, as one could argue that the essential thing is whether the draft constitution leads to empowering the manifold peoples of Ethiopia and instituting democracy. Be that as it may, the Commission did not acquire even a semblance of legitimacy that could enable it to seriously communicate with the wider population. The main demand of most of the peoples and political groups, both within and outside the country, concerned peace. The plea made by human rights organisations, along with legal and constitutional experts and academics, was that the Commission should include members of the opposition and independent experts. The TGE, however, showed no interest in such appeals and went on with its dubious, if not Machiavellian, plan of consolidating its own exclusive power base.

The next move of the TGE was to go ahead with regional elections for a Constituent Assembly, which would endorse the newly crafted constitution. In early June 1992 the OLF, which has a long-standing social base among the Oromos, who constitute the majority of the Ethiopian peoples, withdrew from the election process and joined the numerous opposition political groups operating outside the country. Then on 21 June 1992, regional voting day, only the EPRDF and a few ethnic organisations affiliated with it appeared on the ballot, once again failing to provide for the popular participation of the peoples of Ethiopia and the opposition forces during the so-called transitional period. 'The electorate's choice was basically between the EPRDF and their allies or no vote', proclaimed the Norwegian Observer Group (1992:12).

Aware of the fact that the democratisation process was derailed by the EPRDF, with the obvious intention of monopolising power and legalising it through the drafting of the new constitution without the participation of major national and multinational organisations, nine political organisations – EPRP, MEISON, EDU, MNCPE, EPDM, OLF, ARDU, TTE, SEPDU – met in Paris in March 1993 and agreed to convene an all-inclusive Conference for Peace and Reconciliation. They forwarded their invitation to Ethiopian political forces including the EPRDF, which rebuffed the invitation denouncing it as an 'anti-government campaign'. Thirty-four political organisations and movements responded positively to the call and were due to convene in Addis Ababa in December 1993. Pressed by national and international public opinion, the EPRDF could not stop the convening of the conference, rather it devised other means of sabotaging this effort at stimulating the democratic process, out of fear that the impact of this event could exert pressure on its continued dominance and hold over power. As the delegates of the opposition political parties arrived in Addis Ababa for the conference, TGE agents picked them up from the airport and the hotels they were staying in and crammed them into jail. The conference had to proceed, but without the leaders of the major political parties who could have made the difference in the outcome of the conference. Without the participation of important organisations like the OLF, MNCPE, COEDF, among others, the conference inevitably failed to accomplish the objectives set for it at the Paris meeting, although it was able to set up a loose front called the Coalition of Alternative Forces for Peace and Democracy in Ethiopia (CAFPDE). Still worse, some of the leaders who went to attend the conference – like Abera Yemane Abe of MEISON (All Ethiopian Socialist Movement) – are still in jail without any due process of law.

Keeping the remaining opposition parties at bay, the TGE went on with the elections for the Constituent Assembly that endorsed the

EPRDF-authored constitution. *Africa Confidential* reports on the proceedings as follows: 'Without the main opposition movements, the results of the elections are a foregone conclusion. In June's constituent assembly elections, the EPRDF parties took 89 per cent of the seats' (*Africa Confidential* 1995:2). As head of the TPLF-led EPRDF and President of the TGE, Zenawi became the Executive Prime Minister of the 556-seat Federal Assembly. As events revealed, the new constitution, no matter what was inscribed in it – among other things appearing to 'defend the rights of citizens' – was no more than a piece of paper (like Haile Selassie's and Mengistu's constitutions before it), which could only serve the interests and image of the ruling élite.

Ethnic polarisation

The TPLF-led EPRDF came to power promising, among other things, the right to self-determination, including and up to secession, for which it had fought rigorously for sixteen years and at great cost. So it is not surprising when Article 39, No. 1 of the EPRDF-engineered new constitution reads that 'Every nation, nationality and people in Ethiopia has an unconditional right to self-determination, including the right to secession.' This may lead to the notion that unlimited political rights are granted to all the nationalities in Ethiopia. In practice, however, the EPRDF seems to show no concession to other forces which put forward the same demand. To this effect, it declared war on the Ogadeni National Liberation Front (ONLF), in 1998 while the intensity of the war and its heavy cost were continuously reported even in the government's newspapers (see issues of the *Ethiopian Herald*, January–February 1997). One is then bound to wonder what the principles of the EPRDF are regarding the right to self-determination and ask how the EPRDF reconciles its theory and practice of self-determination, in particular Article 39 of its new constitution. Unfortunately, the EPRDF does not provide a clear explanation to this riddle, nor to a number of pertinent political and economic questions raised below, therefore compelling us to make our own conclusions. It is fair to admit, however, that there is no easy answer or solution to such complex issues of self-determination, inter-ethnic accommodation and power-sharing in a country with more than eighty ethnic-based 'nationalities' and a grim history of decades of repression and insurgency. Nevertheless, from my experience of the unfolding Ethiopian saga, I believe that genuine democratic endeavour could pave the way to reach an acceptable solution. Undoubtedly, this would be an arduous and time-consuming process, with many debates of what 'genuine democracy' would be in the Ethiopian context, but there are no short cuts to long-term peace and stability. The contradictory position of the EPRDF regarding self-determination, however, lacks both a genuine approach and the democratic participation by the peoples of this deeply divided land.

As we have noted earlier, the TPLF, before and after establishing the EPRDF in 1991, obviously understood that as an ethnic-based national movement its social base was restricted to Tigray, with a population of about four million in a vast country of 55 million people, and that the question of its legitimacy and authority was at stake. When it became apparent that Mengistu's regime was collapsing, a power vacuum was imminent, and that it was a better-organised military force when compared to the other opposition movements of the time, the TPLF made a swift advance to the capital, in the name of the EPRDF, which was created rather late in the day to extend the image of a multinational force. The strength and participation of the EPDM (composed of about two hundred members) and the OPDO (formed by just a few POWs from the military regime), the organisations that helped the TPLF form the EPRDF, were only nominal. Suddenly the TPLF found itself in a sea of people it had never seen fit to mobilise or organise during its struggle for liberation and whose allegiance had been to other political organisations, most of which had been antagonistic to the TPLF-led EPRDF. The gallant TPLF army, which expected to get a warm hero's welcome for its front-line sacrifices in getting rid of the military dictators, had to suffer verbal and at times physical attacks from the non-Tigrayan majority of Ethiopians.

Having failed to anticipate the results of its capture of state power, the TPLF hastily declared the right to self-determination, including secession, and invited all ethnic groups in the country to organise on an ethnic basis and join the EPRDF – without fully thinking through its application and consequences. The EPRDF leaders naively hoped that the newly formed 'ethnic organisations', which understandably lacked the necessary organisational experience and capacity to run their own affairs by themselves, would rush to join the EPRDF in the citadel of power, and thereby enable them to draw from a wider support base and develop the legitimacy needed to rule the country over the long term. Contrary to the expectations of the EPRDF leaders, many ethnic organisations began to demand their version of self-determination, including secession, without even considering their politico-economic viability as independent nation states. The Ogadeni, the Oromo, the Afar and the

EPRP are, at the time of writing, engaged in armed struggle against the TPLF-led EPRDF regime. Many others are waging a propaganda war from within and without the country, some of which are contemplating armed confrontation, openly stating that those who come to power through force of arms can only be removed by arms.

The EPRDF's ethnicised political device, which was cobbled together in order to generate legitimacy and consolidate its hold on power, has proved not only to be a failure, but also a thorn in the side of the regime. The no less than eighty ethnic groups in Ethiopia, which thought to exercise the unlimited political, economic and social rights that go as far as secession to form a nation state, as inscribed in the new constitution, have become unmanageable largely because of the ill-conceived experiment of ethnicised political management attempted by the EPRDF. This is why we find, these days, a new wave of ethnic-based 'national' challenges launched by the Afars, Ogadenis, Oromos, Sidamas and Beni Shangulis, to mention but a few.

Ethnic-based 'nationalism', is generally seen as a reaction to national domination or oppression. What the EPRDF is fostering is an exclusional logic, reflected in many ways by all the nationalist actors and expressed as 'Us' versus 'Them'. 'At the heart of nationalism,' argues John Keane, 'is its simultaneous treatment of the Other as everything and nothing. The Other is seen as a knife in the throat of the nation' (Keane 1995:193). Or, as Peter Alter argues, 'Nationalism, to all intents and purposes, means undisguised political egoism. As an ideology it preaches solidarity with and willingness to make sacrifice to one particular social group' (Alter 1994:118). Carried away by its military success, the TPLF opened up a Pandora's box that it cannot control, except perhaps by sheer force, which obviously creates countervailing forces that could very well bring about its demise.

To fight domination or oppression and opt for an egalitarian state of federated relationships based on democratic coexistence is desirable, if not imperative. However, to go the further step and opt for secession, brushing aside centuries-old social, economic and political interdependence, is problematic to say the least. Failing to learn from the humiliating defeat of former dictators or even from the chaotic predicament of neighbouring Somalia, the EPRDF leaders are keen to promote the ethnic factor by pushing it to its extreme limit. At least two instances of this short-sighted ethnic policy could be referred to:

1. instructing and pressing the South Ethiopia People's Democratic Coalition (SEPDC), composed of thirteen ethnic organisations, to be

represented in the national assembly on a single-ethnic basis rather than as a multi-ethnic coalition;
2. forcing the multinational Ethiopian People's Democratic Movement (EPDM), which was initially TPLF's junior partner in forming the EPRDF, to only represent the Amhara ethnic group and to change its name to the Amhara National Democratic Movement (ANDM).

Such actions clearly reflect how far Zenawi's government is bent on promoting ethnicity, which leads to exclusionary politics and divisions in Ethiopia, simply in order to maintain its rule.

Another significant political force marginalised by the EPRDF's ethnic politics is the whole spectrum of multi-national political organisations. This section of the Ethiopian political scene puts emphasis on the unity of the people and the integrity of the country as one 'national' entity. Some of these organisations, like the EPRP and MEISON, have a long history of struggle no less than that of the TPLF. These multi-national forces have been at loggerheads with the TPLF ever since its inception and their relationship worsened even further when it seized power. Despite the hostility reflected on both sides, these organisations have taken the initiative to negotiate peacefully with the TPLF. The Paris Peace and Reconciliation Conference of March 1993 and the Carter Peace Centre Conference of February 1994 could be referred to as some of the constructive endeavours on the part of these multinational opposition parties. None of these peaceful attempts seem to have convinced the EPRDF leaders, while anger and/or frustration is mounting in the quarters of the opposition, as well as with the peace mediators. In a letter written to the opposition organisations on 18 March 1994, former US President Jimmy Carter stated that 'the negotiation with the government could not proceed further because of President Meles's unwillingness to proceed on the proposed terms of negotiation'.

When the paths to the negotiated settlement of existing conflicts are closed and state repression becomes the response to peaceful initiatives, what could be the next plausible step of these numerous multi-ethnic organisations? How can we influence the current leaders to get on to a democratic track and avoid violence as a means to achieve political ends? Such are the questions revolving in the minds of many concerned indigenous scholars these days and a number of proposals are being put forward. Some propose a 'comprehensive national civil disobedience organized at the grass roots level' (Araya 1996:32) as the only hope for Ethiopia's predicaments. There are many others who argue that power-holders, as a rule, listen only to countervailing power and therefore the only remaining option to set Ethiopia free from the shackles of 'the dictators' who remain deaf to the repeated calls for peace is to use force. Whichever direction the unfolding struggles may take, Ethiopia seems to face yet another catastrophe, perhaps far worse than the present chaotic situation.

Breaking out of cycles of conflict

No matter how complex this question appears to be and given that the solution is not within easy reach, the need to confront it, however, is indisputable. The present political crisis in Ethiopia basically emanates from the unbridled desire of the TPLF's leaders to monopolise power in all its aspects, as was evident in the practice of their predecessors. This impasse has two major effects:

- on the conflict of the EPRDF with the opposition forces on one hand; and
- on the mounting tension among ethnic groups on the other.

This crisis has also been aggravated by the one-sided intervention of the US administration and its allies, who have ignored the democratic will of the majority of the peoples of Ethiopia and the key role of the opposition forces who represent them. Intellectuals, who for various reasons support the EPRDF, are worsening the crisis by blindly defending the very incorrect policies which have been adopted and which are recreating conflicts in an already deeply divided country. Perhaps Ethiopia's leaders love adulation and will be swayed by less critical remarks like that of Stephen Ellis, who with carefully selected words declares that 'Ethiopia is experimenting with an ethnically based constitution which to an outsider, looks hazardous. But perhaps it looks different to those who live in Ethiopia' (Ellis 1996:271). Ironically, while Ellis writes about 'the atrocities committed in the name of Islam in Algeria and Egypt' (ibid.:272), he does not refer to what accompanied the 'experiment in Ethiopia' – that is, a catalogue of war-related atrocities perpetrated on the Oromos, Ogadenis and Afars in the south and east, combined with a plethora of human rights violations, 'disappearances', large-scale imprisonment and torture – in short, organised state terror throughout the country, including Tigray, the ethnic base area of the TPLF. Adhana Haile Adhana goes even further and tells us that 'In politics, the Ethiopian peoples have already stepped in the

"Garden of Eden"' (Adhana 1995:93), displaying an opportunist position without content, which even Zenawi himself would not dare utter.

In response, forces within the broad-based opposition are regrouping and reorganising themselves to wage a struggle for political space. Some of them have already formed alliances, like the Coalition of the Ethiopian Democratic Forces (COEDF), and have undertaken a political offensive, with civil disobedience as one of their tactics. Others like the OLF, ARDU and ONLF are already engaged in armed struggle in the southern and eastern parts of the country. Worst of all, ethnic tensions are mounting sharply every day across the land. The fatally simplistic ethnic policy of the EPRDF has created an unmanageable crisis never experienced in the history of Ethiopia. To assert their 'independent' identity and justify their claim to statehood of their own (no matter the viability of the imagined state), almost all the ethnic groups have come forward with their exclusive agendas. The present chaotic predicament reminds many Ethiopians of their history during the 'Era of Princes' from the middle of the seventeenth century to the middle of the nineteenth century, when, as Markakis puts it, 'provincial rulers waged a protracted struggle for supremacy ... central power was entirely eclipsed and the throne itself remained vacant' (Markakis 1990:15). The unfolding, exclusionary ethnic agendas of contemporary Ethiopia pretend they have nothing socially, politically, economically, historically or culturally in common with their other ethnic compatriots.

In failing to realise the extent to which ethnic claims could be stretched, the EPRDF leaders are frantically trying today to reverse the proliferation of ethnic movements by launching state repression instead of committing themselves to democratic dialogue to stop the rot. These leaders should have better grasped by now, how ethnic sentiments can be destructive, simply by looking at the horrific realities in Rwanda, Somalia or the former Yugoslavia. As Eugeen Roosens critically observes, 'the study of ethnic phenomena reveals how far ethnic ideology and historical reality can diverge from each other; how much people feel things that are not there and conveniently forget realities that have existed' (Roosens 1989:161). It is only through constructive engagement in a democratic and rational dialogue that one can make people feel the positive side of their history and appreciate harmonious relationships and unity.

Contrary to the preposterous position of Adhana and his likes who proclaim that Ethiopia is stepping into a democratic 'Garden of Eden', the gross violation of human and democratic rights – essentially acts of state terrorism – perpetrated by Zenawi's regime is so alarming that almost every organisation concerned with human rights in Ethiopia is expressing its concern, including Amnesty International, the European Parliament, the Ethiopian Human Rights Council (EHRCO), the International Federation of Journalists (IFJ) and Africa Watch, to mention but a few. In its *A Worldwide Survey* annual report for 1993, the Committee to Protect Journalists (CPJ) wrote that 'For the second year running, Ethiopia held more journalists in prison than any other country in Africa' (CPJ 1994:6–7) and provided the list of journalists in prison as of March 1994, which ranked Ethiopia second in the world in relation to this particular violation of human rights. Prisons are overcrowded, there is no fair trial and according to the EHRCO (1996;13), over 35 000 cases are being handled by only five courts. Of the several thousand detainees who have been accused of committing human rights violations and war crimes during the rule of the Derg regime, a considerable number have not yet been formally charged, even six years after its fall. No plausible reason has been given for this delay, except maybe that the present leaders do not want to set a legal precedent that could be used against them in the event that they lose their hold on power.

In countries with very low economic development, like Ethiopia, contention over scarce economic resources, mainly land, also helps to consolidate ethnic alliances. 'The longing for material goods does not by itself produce ethnic identity or ethnicity ... Ethnicity, however, is directly concerned with group formation, and thus with power relation' (Roosens 1989:158). The political élite – in this case forces within the opposition – fill the gap of political leadership in the ethnic-based uprising for their own purposes and self-interested motives. With the forthcoming battles over state power intensifying, the devastation of the country's human and material resources, including the structure of the state itself (as in Somalia), is a very real probability if events are allowed to spiral out of control.

On the part of most of the opposition forces there seems to be a growing realisation of the imminent danger of large-scale violent conflict if the current situation is allowed to continue. The biggest threat is posed, however, by the emergence of organised groups of ethnic-based 'national' extremists, some of whom adopt the corrosive ideologies of racism, chauvinism or religious fundamentalism, and negate the basic principles and tenets of democracy. Therefore, a very heavy burden of responsibility rests on the democratic opposition forces, the only bloc – if organised along a common democratic front – which could prevent these extremist forces (who found fertile ground to grow in as a result of the terminally flawed ethnic policy of the EPRDF), from dictating the terms of Ethiopia's political struggle for survival in the twenty-first century. It is only genuinely committed democratic forces which can forge a political mechanism capable of empowering the diverse and disparate peoples of Ethiopia, so that they can exercise their political, social, cultural and historical rights in creating a truly dynamic and all-inclusive constitution, that is, one that will permanently enable them to influence the conduct and modality of any future government that is set up through a democratic mandate. It is only such democratic forces which could envisage a positive and less destructive policy of self-determination, a notion which has galvanised almost the entire country, and help create unity within all the cultural, linguistic, religious and historical diversity, and forge respect and tolerance for all. In a democratic system, self-determination and national unity are two concomitant categories and not mutually exclusive notions as the extremists want us to believe. Yet, under the present dictatorial system of the EPRDF, self-determination, like all democratic rights, will always suffer the effects of repression, hence inducing a series of confrontations that will remain the source of fragmentation and recurring conflict.

Epilogue: the Ethiopian–Eritrean crisis of May 1998

Before we embark on investigating the causes and implications of the conflict between Ethiopia and Eritrea, it is very important in the first place to have a thorough understanding of the nature and evolution of the relationship between the forces involved in the conflict, namely the governments of Ethiopia and Eritrea, whose core elements are the TPLF and the EPLF respectively.

Relations between two fronts

The struggle against the military dictatorship of Mengistu brought the two nationalist forces, the TPLF and the EPLF, closer together to basically form a military alliance since the mid-1970s. Politically, the TPLF supported the struggle for Eritrean independence from Ethiopia, while the EPLF reciprocated by supporting the self-determination of Tigray within the Ethiopian political framework. During the same period, the TPLF also strove to maintain a relationship with the ELF, another contending nationalist force in Eritrea, but this relationship was affected by a number of problems from the beginning which led to animosity and finally in 1981 it was completely broken, as war erupted between the ELF on one side and the EPLF and TPLF on the other. Militarily, the ELF was defeated and forced out from its base area. This war, no doubt, enabled the EPLF to control the entirety of rural Eritrea with no contending force. So much so, that the TPLF also emerged as a sole force in Tigray, after driving out the forces of the Ethiopian Democratic Union (EDU) and the Ethiopian People's Revolutionary Party (EPRP). All this political manoeuvring was done through the use of sheer military force.

The EPLF in Eritrea and the TPLF in Tigray were now the only well-organised military forces, which would determine the ensuing struggle against Mengistu's military regime and evidently the future political and geographical shape of this region. Given that they were fighting to topple the same military dictatorship of the Derg, it was quite rational to form a military alliance and effectively coordinate their military activities. Since the formation of the TPLF in 1975, both the TPLF and the EPLF started as intimate partners of struggle against the military regime of Mengistu. They effectively coordinated their military assaults, with each participating in the other's theatre of operation, as one army under one command. Together they shed blood in one or other front against the same enemy. Nevertheless, they appeared to have nothing in common politically, with their political agendas or programmes being mutually exclusive – that is, the EPLF striving for the independence of Eritrea from Ethiopia and the TPLF opting for the self-determination of Tigray within the bounds of Ethiopia. Furthermore, serious differences along political lines had emerged, which resulted in the severing of relations quite a few times, until military necessities forced them to work together again. A remarkable breaking-off of relations took place in 1985, when the Zenawi group created a Stalinist party known as the MLLT (referred to above) within the TPLF and characterised the EPLF leadership as being bourgeois puppets of imperialism and incapable of realising Eritrean independence. To make matters worse, the TPLF had harboured leftist ELF splinter organisations, like Sageme and the Democratic Movement for the Liberation of Eritrea (DMLE), with the aim of supplanting the EPLF. For its part, the EPLF had closed the outlet to the Sudan, which the TPLF was using to transport relief aid for the 1985 famine victims in Tigray. Despite the occasional emergence of such acrimonious differences, relations between the two fronts appeared to run smoothly, basically because of the dictates of military realities in the face of a common enemy and with the operative logic of 'an enemy's enemy is my friend'.

Despite the fact that inter-front relations appeared to be rectified, the political scars which were caused by 'ideological daggers' were so deep that severe differences were bound to reemerge at any moment, especially when there was no dire threat from a common enemy calling for an alliance. On the other hand, the existence of radical Eritrean opposition fronts, even at a distance, were constant reminders of the threat that the TPLF in collaboration with ELF splinters could pose to the very existence of the EPLF as a political force in Eritrea. Bogged down by its own internal contradictions and rejected by the majority of Ethiopian peoples, who could not bear its authoritarian rule, the Derg failed to resist an offensive and was even unable to complete the (then ongoing) London peace negotiations sponsored by the USA in May 1991. The short-sighted external sponsorship of the fronts with military muscle, the TPLF and the EPLF, during these negotiations – which excluded countervailing democratic political forces – happens to be one of the seeds of the prevailing instability in the region.

In any event, the military alliance enabled both the EPLF and the TPLF to get rid of Mengistu's military regime and establish an EPLF-led government in Eritrea and a TPLF-led EPRDF government in Ethiopia in May 1991. As in the case of the TPLF-led EPRDF (discussed above), the formation of an independent government in Eritrea was concluded without the participation of major political forces, which had a meaningful share in the struggle and had significant constituencies. These political forces are still banned from working inside their respective areas and are forced to operate as an opposition from outside. Had these political groups been included in the USA-sponsored London talks and hence in the transitional process (supported by some European governments) – which was subsequently manipulated by the EPLF and the TPLF – it would have been possible to strictly define the nature and modalities of the relations between Ethiopia and the newly emerging state of Eritrea, thereby avoiding any ambiguity (real or false), which evidently appears to be the cause of the current border war.

EPLF and TPLF in power

The joint military venture of the EPLF and the TPLF was based on the exceptional determination of their armies and the full cooperation of both peoples who despised the Derg military regime, which had helped both the EPLF and the TPLF to assume power in Eritrea and Ethiopia respectively. The TPLF immediately transformed itself from a nationalist into the 'multinationalist' organisation known as the EPRDF. Without consultation with the Ethiopian people concerned, the EPRDF under Meles undertook two highly sensitive measures, which affected the inner sensibilities of many Ethiopians. These measures were:

- the endorsement of Eritrea's independence in the name of the Ethiopian people without their mandate;
- the policy to restructure the political set-up of the whole country on an ethnic basis.

These and other undemocratic, non-consultative measures carried out by the EPRDF were from the start in direct confrontation with the majority of the Ethiopian peoples, and the major political and civic organisations representing them. Equally, the EPLF under Isayas Afewerki totally rejected even a symbolic participation of opposition parties and civic groups in the political process shaping the newly independent Eritrea.

These two developments in Ethiopia and Eritrea, which have generated substantial opposition from all parties and civic groups which (for obvious reasons) do not comply with the enforced political processes, exert immense pressure on both governments, constantly placing them in highly precarious positions. Although the defiance is more vigorous and visible in opposition to the EPRDF, both were compelled by the volatile circumstances to renew their alliance by signing a military pact – with a wider scope of security and intelligence schemes and, this time round, power politics and diplomacy included. The fact that the EPLF had a more experienced army and relatively advanced military organisation than that of the TPLF-led EPRDF placed it at a vantage point to manoeuvre and take advantage of the relationship, which has led to the present crisis. Some of the major factors that contributed to the outbreak of the current conflict include:.

1. When the EPLF seized power in Eritrea, it immediately took the drastic measure of expelling Ethiopians who had been established there for years without the faintest idea that one day they would be treated as foreigners. Many lost their jobs while others could not take their property with them. The EPRDF government took no measures to defend the rights of its citizens and in fact it stood by the side of the EPLF government in condemning those Ethiopians as associates of the defunct Derg (EPRDF *News Bulletin*, 30 August 1991). At the same time, Eritreans in Ethiopia were treated respectfully.
2. Ever since Eritrea declared independence, a number of pertinent issues including the status of Eritreans living in Ethiopia who

hitherto had Ethiopian citizenship and the privileges that go with it had never been clearly defined – particularly in the sphere of property ownership, trade and government job opportunities. By contrast, in Eritrea, the privileges an Eritrean would enjoy *vis-à-vis* those of an Ethiopian, or any other foreigner for that matter, were set in place. This unequal state of affairs obviously enabled Eritreans to benefit from greater privileges than their Ethiopian counterparts.
3. During the march to Addis Ababa in May 1991, an EPLF mechanised brigade took active part in the action and, subsequently, part of this brigade remained in Addis Ababa to take care of Zenawi's security. The obscure presence and free mobility of this mechanised contingent was opposed even by the TPLF army, including the Defence Minister Seye Abreha, who was subsequently removed from his post as he could not go along with this intrusion into his professional domain.
4. Eritrean opposition parties, including those favoured by the TPLF leadership (which were and are still banned in Eritrea), were also forced to close their offices and leave Ethiopia. Some of the opposition, specifically the ELF–RC members, were even detained until they were rescued by human rights organisations like Amnesty International, before they were eventually declared 'disappeared'.
5. Until last year, Eritrea had no currency of its own. The EPRDF allowed it to use the Ethiopian Birr through which the Eritrean government would purchase Ethiopian products that earn foreign currency (for example, coffee, hide and oil seeds) and export it to earn hard currency for its own use, obviously depleting Ethiopia's foreign exchange earnings. When the Eritrean government issued its own currency called Nakfa, the expectation was that it would circulate on parity with the Birr. However, such expectations in the face of stiff global economic realities proved to be hollow – the Nakfa had to find its rightful place way down below the Birr and Eritrea had to bear the burden of yielding its own products for export. This matter was perhaps the most serious incident which induced the EPLF government to go for the war option.
6. The border issue, which had never been addressed in any conventional way since Menelik II and the Italians signed a treaty at Wuchale on 2 May 1889, could not have led to war because the TPLF and EPLF governments had not even discussed it seriously, unless, that is, they wanted it as a pretext to cover up the dire root causes of the war – namely, the internal economic and political instability on both sides of the 'disputed border'. The question of who started the

war in May 1998 is not important and perhaps even academic, simply because both governments had been creating the conditions for war by forging an unbalanced and unfair relationship that was liable to break any moment when confronted with hard economic and political realities – conventionally referred to as 'national interests'. Driven by overambitious pipe dreams of lifting their nations to the level of Hong Kong in one go, each set of political leaders was rushing to claim and control whatever resources were available within their geopolitical vicinity. Naturally, this state of affairs led to angry confrontations, including armed clashes in places like Humera, Badema and Bada for one reason or another. In his recent interview of 25 June 1998 with Florence Aubenas (a French journalist), Isayas refers to an incident in July 1997, when two Ethiopian battalions entered Eritrea from Tigray, as one such instance. Meles, on the other hand, in his interview with *Asser*, flatly denied the occurrence of any clashes or even differences and went on to deceive the Ethiopian people, declaring that 'our relations document is signed with ink and blood' (*Asser* 2nd/No. 9, December–February 1998).

7. Ever since the Italians set foot in what is now known as Eritrea and began to carve out its boundaries since the late 1890s, with the exception of Menelik II, no other Ethiopian leader has recognised an independent Eritrea, let alone a demarcated border between Ethiopia and Eritrea. This is not to say that the border issue of Eritrea was without controversies. For most of Eritrea's existence as an entity, it was a provincial matter that had been settled by local administration. Once Eritrea declared independence, the first task of both governments should have been to clearly demarcate the border by defining or redefining it, instead of letting any one of them claim whatever land they believed to be 'theirs' and picking this or that map which supported their desires.

As a way of addressing the nature of the current conflict, it is worth noting that the border issue was just one element which could have been resolved through mediation or arbitration and certainly not, by any means, the only cause driving the conflict. The May 1998 war that erupted along the Ethiopian–Eritrean border area was, therefore, not simply caused by a border disagreement, although the border dispute may have partially contributed to the conflict. As I have tried to explain earlier, the root causes of this conflict lie in the economic and political contention of the two governments – which are indulging in combat as a way of resolving their respective internal and external problems. This is coupled with their incapacity to devise a comprehensive and integrated scheme *vis-à-vis* their respective peoples and intelligentsia, in order to address the deep-rooted socio-economic problems that the societies they claim to represent are confronted with and to forge a viable means of democratic cooperation as opposed to conflict and short-term manoeuvrings.

The future: which way out?

An answer to this difficult question is not within easy reach and we are once again confronted with a dangerous impasse which we cannot avoid facing. In a nutshell, this 'border conflict' is between two autocratic governments and not between the peoples of Ethiopia and Eritrea, simply because these two peoples who are found across the arbitrary colonial border, created by the Italians in the late 1800s, have lived together in harmony for centuries and have never clashed as peoples of two separate entities. Eritrea as a separate entity was the creation of Italian colonialism and prior to this period, although there was no central power that fully controlled the periphery, Christianity in the highlands, Islam in the lowlands and eighteenth-century emperors, had progressively managed to unite these peoples in social, political, economic and legal aspects of life in this currently 'contested region'. They certainly have much more in common than what exclusionary politicians of the contemporary era try to construct or deconstruct.

For a 'brief' period of six decades, Italian occupation attempted to alter a centuries-old system of peasant production and close-knit relations with the land. This was followed by the manoeuvrings of a more recent set of political masters. Yet history, geography, and most importantly the social ties that still exist, strive to survive and maintain their continuity despite the changes and difficulties. Today, we have an independent Eritrea, but socially and economically it is tightly interwoven with Ethiopia. Had this evidently historical relationship been based on publicly defined pacts and regulations made with the consent of both peoples and the participation of the hitherto outlawed opposition political parties, then at least we would not have arrived at the present chaos and we could have instead been moving in the right direction of peace, stability and development. An integral requirement to accomplish such a complex task and to overcome the current difficulties both within and between Ethiopia and Eritrea, is the formation of two governments that have the trust of its peoples, created through unimpeded popular participation, together with respect for the rule of law, human rights and democratic freedoms, and whose goals are not merely power-based, but justice-oriented – harnessing political power for development, long-term peace and stability.

Notes

1. The author was one of the founders of the TPLF and a member of its Central Committee for over ten years.
2. I will not go into the history of the military dictator Mengistu's rise to power and the subsequent demise of the Derg (the military council which later on became the Worker's Party of Ethiopia) in this chapter. For more details regarding background history, see the works of Halliday and Molyneux (1981), Keller (1988), Clapham (1988) and Markakis (1990).
3. The EPDM later transformed itself into an ethnic-based organisation called the Amhara National Democratic Movement (ANDM).
4. The FOM was formed by prisoners of war (POWs) while the government's army was in total disarray.
5. This class was more of a traditional political élite coming from the province of Showa in the Amhara region. The life of the ordinary Showan, however, was as wretched as that of the rest of the Ethiopians.
6. See *Manifesto* of the TPLF, vol. 1, p. 24, published in February 1976, which declared that the first task of the TPLF would be 'the establishment of an independent democratic republic of Tigray'. This was the stand of the present EPRDF leaders and was a point of difference with the author who consistently fought for a democratic unity of Ethiopia.

References

Adhana, Haile A. 1995: 'Tigray: The Emergence of a Nation within the Ethiopian Polity', paper presented at the August conference on Ethnicity and the State in East Africa, Addis Ababa, Ethiopia.
Africa Confidential 1995: September, vol. 36, no. 19.
Alter, P. 1991 : *Nationalism*, London: Edward Arnold.
Amnesty International 1995: *Ethiopia, Accountability Past and Present: Human Rights in Transition* (April – AI Index: AFR/25/6/95), London: AI.
Araya, M. 1996: 'Ethiopia's Fate and Her Democratic Forces' in *Ethiopian Review* (Los Angeles), September, pp. 30–2.
Clapham, C. 1988: *Haile Selassie's Government*, Longman: London.
CPJ 1994: 'Ethiopia: Attacks on the Press in 1993' in *A Worldwide Survey* (March), New York: CPJ.
Dowden, R. 1989: 'Tigrayans Home in on Ethiopian's Lifeline', Interview with Meles Zenawi, Prime Minister of Ethiopia in *The Independent* (London), 28 November, p. 19.
EHRCO 1994: 'The Human Rights Situation in Ethiopia' in *Report No. 7* (August), Addis Ababa: EHRCO.
EHRCO 1996: 'The Human Rights Situation in Ethiopia' in *Report No. 10* (September), Addis Ababa: EHRCO.

Ellis, S. 1996: *Africa Now: People, Policies & Institutions*, London: James Curry for Ministry of Foreign Affairs.
Ethiopian Commentator (Michigan) 1993: 'Interview with M. Baas, US Ambassador to Ethiopia' (May).
EPRDF 1991: *News Bulletin* (May).
European Parliament 1996: *Resolution on Human Rights in Ethiopia* 13(d) B4-0892, 0917 and 0930/96.
Hagos, T.W. 1995: *Democratization? Ethiopia (1991–1994) : A Personal Interview*, Cambridge, MA: Khepera Publishers.
Halliday, F. and Molyneux, M. 1981: *The Ethiopian Revolution*, London: Verso.
Keane, J. 1995: 'Nations, Nationalism and European Citizens' in S. Periwal (editor), *Notions of Nationalism*, Budapest: Central European University Press.
Keller, E.J. 1988: *Revolutionary Ethiopia: From Empire to People's Republic*, Bloomington, MN: Indiana University.
Lyons, T. 1996: 'Closing the Transition: The May 1995 Elections in Ethiopia' in *Journal of Modern African Studies*, vol. 34, no. 1, pp. 121–142.
Markakis, J. 1990: *National and Class Conflict in the Horn of Africa*, London: Zed.
MLLT 1985: *Constitution of the Marxist Leninist League of Tigray* (July – Tigrigna edition).
Norwegian Observer Group 1992: 'Local and Regional Elections in Ethiopia 21 June 1992' in *Human Rights Report No. 1*, Oslo: Norwegian Institute of Human Rights.
Roosens, E. 1989: *Creating Ethnicity: the Process of Ethnogenesis*, London: Sage.

7
Palestinian Authority, Israeli Rule: From Transitional to Permanent Arrangement?[1]

Mouin Rabbani

Apart from a privately organised reunion for Israeli, Palestinian and Norwegian veterans of the covert Oslo negotiations, the third anniversary of the 13 September 1993 Israeli – Palestinian Declaration of Principles on Interim Self-Government Arrangements (DOP) passed without notice. In Israel, the recently installed government of Prime Minister Binyamin Netanyahu was in no mood for festivities. This is only partly because it had been elected in 29 May on a platform which unambiguously rejected the partnership between Israel and the Palestine Liberation Organisation (PLO) embodied by the DOP. More to the point, Netanyahu had only days previously shaken hands with Yasir 'Arafat in full public view, in that brief instant parting company with a year's worth of sound bites promising that relations with the Palestinians would be fundamentally different under his regime. Notably, neither Ariel Sharon nor any other ultra-rejectionist cabinet member saw fit to tender their resignation in protest. Any ceremony proclaiming the merits of political accommodation and coordinated action against Palestinian radicalism would therefore have only heightened the new government's reputation for shallow opportunism and the opposition's calls for Netanyahu to beg for forgiveness at Yitzhak Rabin's graveside.

In the autonomous Palestinian enclaves, it would probably have required armed force to assemble a crowd large enough to make speeches commemorating the DOP media-worthy. Despite the redeployment of the Israeli military out of large sections of the Gaza Strip and most West Bank cities, and the assumption of power within these areas by the Palestinian Authority (PA), Israeli control over Palestinian lives is exercised with greater vigour than at any time since the occupation began in June 1967. Where the DOP initially enjoyed general popular acceptance, there now remain only a handful of Palestinians prepared to defend it in private. Although most ascribe their disillusionment to the conduct of the Israeli authorities, the performance of the PA or both, an increasing number are concluding that Israeli and Palestinian practices are on the whole consistent with the accord and the arrangements it has produced. Even so, gradually, appeals for the faithful implementation and proper stewardship of the DOP are giving way to demands for its fundamental reconsideration.

In contrast to most Palestinian exiles, who virtually from the outset rejected the DOP because it failed to address their rights and in so doing relegated them to the furthest margins of the Israeli–Palestinian equation, the popular reassessment of this agreement within the occupied territories has been a slower and altogether more complex process. Although the DOP provides for neither the decolonisation of the West Bank and Gaza Strip, nor Palestinian self-determination, the majority of Palestinians in these territories accepted the PLO's argument – that in the context of the 'New World Order' this was an offer which could be neither refused nor improved upon, and that despite its shortcomings, it created a new dynamic which would ultimately result in the establishment of an independent Palestinian state. No less importantly, repeated PLO proclamations that the transitional phase would above all be characterised by tangible improvements in the quality of life (specifically personal security and economic prosperity) were eagerly embraced by a population driven to utter desperation by the relentless escalation of Israeli repression and a stagnant *intifada* – for more details see Graham Usher (1993).

The warm welcome accorded to Yasir 'Arafat and his entourage of soldiers and bureaucrats when they entered Gaza in July 1994 revealed the high hopes that Palestinians continued to attach to the DOP, even though little had been achieved in the intervening months to inspire popular confidence. Largely isolated from direct contact with the PLO apparatus throughout the period since 1967, residents of the occupied territories generally retained an idealised notion of its character and capabilities. Those with a more nuanced view tended to assume, for any variety of reasons, that the PA would be more responsive to popular opinion than the PLO and additionally felt a moral obligation to give the historic leadership an opportunity to succeed. Only a small minority insisted that 'Arafat and his lieutenants signed on to the DOP primarily in order to revive their own flagging fortunes and would be reduced to junior partners in the administration of Israeli rule.

The rude awakening experienced by many Palestinians during the first year of autonomy did not fundamentally alter the popular consensus in favour of the DOP. When all was said and done, autonomy was considered the lesser of two evils when compared to direct Israeli occupation, while PA mismanagement and misconduct could be rationalised as the 'product of inexperience and individual maleficence', and the deteriorating economic situation attributed to 'Israeli restrictions and the donor community's inertia'. At the same time, Palestinian expectations were visibly lowered and further depressed by the continuation of Israeli policies, which seven years earlier had produced the *intifada*. The PA's inability to confront a very palpable Israeli hegemony, set against its very public cooperation with Israel's security forces – most notably the 'joint patrols' – increased the damage to its reputation.

With hindsight the period between the signing of the 28 September 1995 Interim Agreement (or 'Oslo II') and the suicide bombings, carried out by the Islamic Resistance Movement (HAMAS) and Islamic Jihad in February and March of 1996, represents the high point of the DOP. Faced with mounting criticism of its strategy, performance and conduct, the extension of autonomy to West Bank cities allowed the PLO to claim that Gaza–Jericho was only a beginning, while the January 1996 elections for an 88-member Palestinian Council and Yasir 'Arafat as *ra'is* of the Palestinian Executive Authority endowed the PA with sorely needed political legitimacy.[2] The smooth transition from Rabin to Peres, after the former's November 1995 assassination by a Jewish extremist and Israeli public reaction to this event, increased hope among Palestinians that Israel was serious about reaching a genuine peace. Meanwhile, the Palestinian opposition's decision to boycott the self-rule institutions, and implicit neglect of the bread-and-butter issues within the domain of these institutions, led to its further marginalisation and increased dissent within its diverse ranks.

The unprecedented Israeli siege of the occupied territories imposed in the wake of the suicide bombings constituted a turning point for Palestinian public opinion. Essentially, the hermetic closure of the West Bank and Gaza Strip, and the policy of 'separation' subsequently pursued by Israel, served to remove any remaining ambiguities about the nature of post-Oslo Israeli–Palestinian relations. Equally, this period – which saw an unprecedented PA campaign against anyone and anything currently or formerly Islamist – left little to the imagination *vis-à-vis* the PA's own role within this relationship. And in conclusively demonstrating that Palestinian economic fortunes remain a function of the Israeli–Palestinian balance of power – that is to say at the total mercy of Israel – 'separation' has reestablished for Palestinians the connection between political context and quality of life which the PLO had done its best to sever. That the siege was imposed and institutionalised by the most liberal government in Israel's history undermined the DOP's credibility even further.

While Palestinians were subject to a myriad of Israeli restrictions, affecting virtually every aspect of daily life prior to autonomy, the Interim Agreement has formalised the fragmentation of the occupied territories into zones of Palestinian and Jewish settlement – and the atomisation of Palestinian society – resulting from Israel's post-1967 policy of 'creeping annexation'. This is most evident in the West Bank, where only approximately 3 per cent of the total surface area, comprising the majority of Palestinian towns, is under full PA control (that is, 'Area A'). Because the towns are non-contiguous and given that the Israelis remain in command of the road network connecting them, all movement of goods and persons in and out of (or between) these enclaves can be interdicted at will. In the villages, most of which fall within 'Area B' (altogether comprising approximately 27 per cent of the West Bank), the situation is more serious. Here, the PA has only civil and police powers, while Israel remains responsible for 'internal security' – the meaning of which it is free to define. According to the terms of Oslo II therefore, Israel can – and routinely does – continue with land confiscation, mass arrests, demolition of houses, defoliation, prolonged curfews, arbitrary violence and any other measures it sees 'legally' fit to impose on the pretext of security. As the roads connecting villages to each other, nearby towns and often their agricultural lands remain in Israeli hands, periods of 'internal closure' have been particularly devastating, with villagers unable to tend crops and livestock, market perishable goods, purchase foodstuffs or obtain essential services such as hospitalisation, which are available only in the towns. The realities of power in 'Area B' are underlined by reports of Israeli soldiers preventing Palestinian policemen from reaching villages to mediate violent family disputes and even placing them under curfew along with the rest of the population.

The largest portion of the West Bank, about 70 per cent of its surface area, is classified as 'Area C'. Comprising of Jewish settlements (including the centre of Hebron), water-rich areas, border regions, main roads, and most lands outside Palestinian municipal and village boundaries (but also several Palestinian villages), 'Area C' is a contiguous whole which surrounds both 'Area A' and 'Area B' in their entirety, and parcels them into isolated enclaves. Pursuant to Oslo II under exclusive Israeli control, it is not subject to restrictions regarding the further expansion of Jewish settlements or indeed anything else. No less importantly and in accordance with the Interim Agreement, jurisdiction over the settlements has been formally transferred from the civil administration of the military government within the occupied territories to the state apparatus within Israel, consolidating their position as integral, undifferentiated components of Israeli territory and public administration. 'Area C' also includes the numerous 'by-pass roads' that were constructed during the past several years, at an enormous cost in terms of Palestinian land-loss – in order to erase the boundaries between Israel and the settlements, to provide easy access between settlements in a manner which 'by-passes' Palestinian enclaves and to physically isolate the latter. In mid-September 1996, a new road costing US$40 million, including the largest tunnel yet constructed by Israel, was opened in the West Bank, in order to integrate the Gush Etzion settlement bloc near Bethlehem more fully with metropolitan Jerusalem. Speaking at the opening ceremony, Jerusalem Mayor Ehud Olmert asserted that this road, which reduces the distance between the two communities to a ten-minute drive, would make Gush Etzion 'a permanent part of Israel' (*Palestine Report* 1996:4). To emphasise this point, Hebron Mayor Mustafa Natshe was forbidden from using this road several days later.

Although 'internal closure' has thus far been imposed as an extraordinary rather than a permanent measure, the separation between East Jerusalem and its annexed environs – comprising roughly 20 per cent of the total surface area of the West Bank – and the rest of the West Bank has been fully institutionalised. As a 'final status' issue, Jerusalem is in fact simply excluded from the terms of the Interim Agreement. Without an Israeli permit, which as a rule is virtually impossible to obtain, Palestinians may neither enter the Jerusalem area nor pass through it. Permanent military checkpoints on most primary and secondary roads leading out of the West Bank, backed up by other forms of border surveillance, constant patrols within Jerusalem, along with stiff fines and prison sentences for violators (to say nothing of vicious physical assault by members of the notoriously thuggish *shmar gvul* or border police), have ensured that few Palestinians venture today into, the city. Ironically, it is a city which has, throughout the occupation functioned as their political, economic, cultural and institutional capital, and to which they enjoyed virtually unrestricted access, that is, prior to Oslo. Advanced surgery at al-Maqasid hospital, prayer at al-Aqsa Mosque or the Church of the Holy Sepulchre and shopping on Salah-al-Din street, activities that West Bank Palestinians could undertake at a moment's notice until recently, have now become the stuff of nostalgia and dreams.

The closure and the associated Israeli 'final offensive' against the Palestinian community within Jerusalem's municipal boundaries have driven the latter to the brink of defeat. Severed from daily contact with the West Bank population, which is approximately ten times its own size and the main market for its goods and services, and encircled by a triple ring of rapidly expanding Jewish settlements, East Jerusalem has become a ghost town with an economy in name only. Increasingly certain that they will never live under Palestinian administration unless they move to Ramallah, and in order to elude Israel's systematic and accelerated campaign to deprive Jerusalemites of residency and property rights, a growing number (how many it is impossible to determine) are in the process of resolving what they perceive as a hopeless predicament by applying for Israeli citizenship or simply emigrating abroad. Such measures to secure individual futures in turn only strengthen Israel's control of the city and its outskirts. The widespread despair and feeling of powerlessness – reflected in the reportedly steady rise of property sales to institutions representing Jewish settlers – has all but overwhelmed more steadfast Palestinians, reducing them to waging a desperate struggle to prevent further erosion of Arab rights in the city, rather than, as most initially hoped, using the DOP to turn the tide against Israeli colonisation. While past experience (for example, the period prior to the *intifada*) suggests that such despondency eventually translates into popular resistance, mass action has in the past generally failed to reverse previously inflicted damage.

The Gaza Strip, a contiguous if oddly shaped entity, 80–5 per cent of which is 'Area A' – with most of the remainder classified as 'Area C' – is where self-rule began and consequently the laboratory for Israel's post-Oslo policies. Technically immune to 'internal closure', it has instead been transformed into the world's largest prison camp. Entirely surrounded on three sides by several layers of electrified razor wire and a heavily patrolled coastline on the fourth, entry and exit of goods and persons is strictly controlled by a series of permanent Israeli and Palestinian checkpoints. In principle, only senior PLO and PA officials ('VIPs'), a select number of Palestinian businessmen and drivers with prior clearance, and a constantly varying quota of married fathers over the age of 30 with 'clean' security records and permits to contribute to the Israeli economy may pass.[3] The latter, who require employment in the Israeli labour market primarily because of Israel's systematic 'de-development' of the Gaza Strip, have been left with no other means of subsistence – for further details, see Roy (1994). Therefore, they must leave and return on a daily basis, through a separate and considerably more arduous crossing point. In practice, Israel has on several occasions prevented Yasir 'Arafat from leaving Gaza, banned several senior PA officials from doing so for prolonged periods – including Social Affairs Minister Intisar al-Wazir ('Umm Jihad') for attempting to smuggle several students to Birzeit University in the West Bank – and routinely prevented most or all workers from reaching their jobs for prolonged periods. With respect to goods, Israeli products as a rule have unrestricted entry to the Gaza Strip, while imports from other countries often experience bureaucratic 'warfare' and associated highly exorbitant storage costs. For example, the PA was recently forced to burn US$3 million worth of sheep carcasses donated by Saudi Arabia on the occasion of the Muslim feast of *'Id al-Adha* after these spoiled while awaiting entry permits. Israel's policy on Palestinian exports similarly seeks to ensure continued dependence upon Israel and prevent the emergence of a distinct and recognisably Palestinian economy. According to Palestinian economists, it is both quicker and cheaper to import Spanish rather than Gaza tomatoes in the West Bank, while efforts to build trade relationships independent of Israel are routinely sabotaged. In one instance, a Palestinian agricultural cooperative was reportedly informed that if it did not sell its strawberry crop to the state marketing agency, AGREXCO, at a higher price than that being offered by a European importer, the strawberries would not be allowed passage to the Israeli port of Ashdod on 'health grounds'. It appears likely that economic considerations have played their part in Israel's refusal thus far to open a 'safe passage' between the Gaza Strip and West Bank, as stipulated in the agreed-upon Interim Agreement.

While the various forms of closure are imposed on security pretexts, senior Israeli military and intelligence officers have pointed out that no suicide bomber has ever applied for a permit to enter Israel, and that no Palestinian with a valid work permit has been convicted of 'terrorist' charges. Such officers are inclined to see closure as a misguided and ultimately counterproductive political response to an essentially military challenge on the ground. Other observers have argued that closure is, or at least has become, a political strategy rather than a security tactic, the economic consequences of which – for example, massive unemployment in the Gaza Strip, widespread poverty throughout the occupied territories and a rapidly growing PA budget deficit which is paralysing its ability to deliver services[4] – makes further violence more rather than less likely.

Although no longer physically present, Israeli administration remains very much in evidence within the PA areas as well. Birth certificates, identity cards, driving licences, bureaucratic application forms of various sorts and even Palestinian passports must all be registered with and approved by the military government in order to attain official status (and often retain Hebrew alongside Arabic on Palestinian documents as a means of controlling the Arab Palestinian population). The difference here is that Palestinians outside Jerusalem now conduct such procedures through the PA rather than directly, leading to considerable delays and frustration, and numerous reports of favouritism and administrative corruption.

Because the relevant international conventions and safeguards are not incorporated into the DOP, which furthermore has no enforcement mechanisms, Israel has been able to continue disregarding applicable standards of international conduct, and thereby make the gross imbalance of power between itself and the PA the Agreement's operative terms of reference. It is aided in this by an international community even less inclined to intervene today than in days past. This is partly because the PLO has itself accepted the existing arrangements but, more importantly, the USA (with Western Europe characteristically acquiescing despite its misgivings) views Israeli regional hegemony as vital to its geopolitical interests and the region's stability, and consequently will allow nothing to obstruct Oslo's continued implementation.

If the PA could initially count on public support in the occupied territories, because most inhabitants had simply not read the DOP or believed it would be overtaken by an inexorable dynamic leading to Palestinian statehood, its prestige has been shattered by reality. Instead of the much-vaunted improvements in the quality of life intended to underpin the interim stage, most Palestinians are today significantly poorer than before Oslo. What Palestinian leaders have endlessly hailed as the inevitable prelude to 'a Palestinian state with its capital in Jerusalem,' is in fact a succession of isolated enclaves physically detached from Jerusalem. With the PA additionally incapable, in fact as well as in perception, of effectively challenging Israeli policies or mobilising the 'international community' to do so, the belief that no agreement at all would have been preferable to the present arrangements is slowly but surely gaining ground.

The PA's own approach to government and state-building, its relationship with Israel and the role of the opposition have all contributed substantially to the growing pessimism. Best characterised as an elected autocracy, the PA's *ra'is* possesses a seemingly limitless capacity for micro-managing the public and private sectors, and some would say, consequently, an equally impressive ability to coopt, marginalise or otherwise outmanoeuvre his critics with comparatively little violence, though not without acrimony. 'Arafat brooks no opposition to his own person or position as uncontested leader, and has moved quickly and decisively to crush such dissent by whatever means necessary. Most of the violence and brutality meted out by his security forces – which is documented by the human rights community, and includes the systematic torture of prisoners and at least eight deaths in detention – has been aimed at improving the PA's standing *vis-à-vis* Israel and the West, or can be attributed to the machinations of its numerous 'security services' which have all but obtained a licence to run amok, rather than directly bolstering his rule. Nevertheless, the relatively widespread campaign of intimidation and the fact that people either care little for the above subtleties, or see repression as primarily directed at those involved in the struggle against a continuing and increasingly intolerable Israeli occupation, have served to further undermine the PA's legitimacy.

The elections of 20 January 1996, monitored by the European Union and rather hastily certified by it as free and fair,[5] have strengthened perceptions of a 'vibrant Palestinian democracy'. While the PLO's traditional pluralism continues to survive in attenuated form, 'democracy' is permitted only to the extent that it respects autocracy. Concerning freedom of expression, for example, Iyad al-Sarraj, the appointed PA ombudsman, was arrested in May 1996 following a critical interview in the *New York Times* which offended 'Arafat. Released after submitting a public apology, he was promptly re-arrested after explaining that he never intended to insult the *ra'is* but otherwise stood by his denunciations of PA misconduct. Charged this time with dealing with drugs, planted in his mental health clinic presumably by PA security, and physically tortured in addition, international pressure was brought to bear, which eventually secured his release. In August 1996, PA security forces confiscated and banned books by the preeminent Palestinian intellectual, Edward W. Said, which unequivocally denounce both Oslo and 'Arafat (Shanahan 1996:24). If only because their actions have not been officially disavowed and the books remain unavailable, claims by senior officials that this was a rogue operation have been met with disbelief.

The Palestinian media meanwhile promote the personality cult of the leader as faithfully as any of its Arab counterparts, replete with all manner of pomp and circumstance. Palestinian television (coincidentally headquartered in 'Arafat's office) broadcasts several songs of praise daily, along with any number of additional eulogies. The media's responsibilities were emphasised when Mahir al-'Alami, night editor of *al-Quds* newspaper, was arrested by the PA's Preventative Security Agency for relegating to an inside page a statement by Greek Orthodox Archbishop Theodorus likening 'Arafat to the first Muslim conqueror of Jerusalem, Caliph 'Umar bin al-Khattab.

The judiciary has fared little better. As Usher (1996:21–34) has pointed out, the plethora of Palestinian security services – most recently augmented by *jihaz amn al-jami'at* or the Universities Security Agency – are lawless in the term's technical sense, in that they and their activities are neither regulated by legislation nor subject to regular legal review. In mid-August 1996, however, the Palestinian Supreme Court agreed to hear a case brought against the PA by ten Birzeit University students, who had been detained without charge or trial since the suicide bombings of February–March. When the court ordered their immediate release, its president, Amin 'Abd-al-Salam, was immediately forced into retirement and his ruling ignored. In other cases, suspects have been arrested, charged, tried, convicted and sentenced within hours by the utterly farcical 'State Security Courts'.

Hopes that the Palestinian Council would act as an effective counterweight to the executive branch have on the whole failed to materialise:

- First, its powers of legislation are substantially restricted by, *inter alia*, the corpus of Israeli military orders which remain in force,
- Second, 'Arafat had successfully coopted several of its most prominent independents and Islamists, including 'Abd-al-Jawad Salih, Hanan 'Ashrawi[6] and 'Imad al-Faluji into his cabinet, as the ministers for Agriculture, Higher Education and Communications respectively;
- Third, the Council is thoroughly dominated by 'Arafat, who typically gets his way and, without exception, disregards decisions he does not like;
- Fourth, 'Arafat has cleverly resurrected the PLO Executive Committee since the elections and PA critics are seen off with the observation that the PLO represents the entire Palestinian people, and is furthermore the PA's source of authority, while detractors from within the PLO are informed that the Palestinian Council is the only directly elected Palestinian body.

Even if devoid of results, substantial debate and criticism are however possible within the Palestinian Council. It also appears to be getting more restive in reaction to the growing frustration of its members and popular cynicism – in a recent public opinion survey 46.7 per cent stated that the Council 'represents the people well but with no effect' (Rabah and Shanahan 1996:20).[7] There are certainly prominent PA officials who do take a principled stand in tune with critics from among the general public, against the crass cronyism and corruption of the 'Arafat-led status quo. As a case in point, 'Arafat won approval for his controversial new cabinet in the Palestinian Legislative Council by a vote of 55 to 28 and with three abstentions, a year after legislators had demanded that the then sitting cabinet be dissolved due to a widening corruption scandal. The current 'victory' was not achieved without a contentious debate and heated criticism, which pointed to the fact that 'Arafat's expanded cabinet reshuffle had done nothing to address the serious allegations of widespread government corruption, as it included certain ministers of the previous cabinet who had been the subjects of a scathing report made in 1997[8] by a special legislative investigating committee, which in fact recommended that three ministers be put on trial. In apparent protest at 'their re-appointment, Hanan 'Ashrawi (since 1996 the Minister for Higher Education, who had been earmarked in the reshuffle for the Tourism portfolio) and 'Abd-al-Jawad Salih refused to take up their posts in the new cabinet, which included an additional ten new ministers whom many suspect of having being 'bought off'. Complaining against the rampant corruption *and* mismanagement of the Middle East peace process according to US and Israeli dictates, 'Ashrawi (who will continue to represent Jerusalem in the Palestinian Legislative Council) warned in a CNN interview, that the substantial vote against the cabinet was 'a warning signal ... that this government has to face the serious expectations of the people'. She also told Reuters that 'I believe when people called for change they didn't ask for additions. They asked for change in the ... status quo, but what we see now is maintaining what existed [and] adding people to it.' And to reporters in the West Bank Town of Ramallah, she said, 'I assured President 'Arafat that once he conducts ... genuine reform, I will be willing to help him.' According to Associated Press, Minister of Agriculture 'Abd-al-Jawad Salih announced his resignation by calling the cabinet reshuffle a 'tragedy' and saying that 'Arafat had thwarted efforts to fight corruption by protecting high-ranking officials.

A subsequent poll showed that almost 57 per cent of Palestinians believed that the cabinet reshuffle would not improve the PA's performance, while more than 71 per cent intimated that corruption would either increase or remain at the same level. And according to a Reuters report, even some members of 'Arafat's own FATEH faction, which dominates the legislature, voiced criticism – with one leading activist cynically suggesting during the debate, that 'Arafat be named as the permanent "God" of the Palestinian people', a statement that almost brought about a fist fight. Independent lawmaker Hassan Khreisheh said that legislators had come under intense pressure over the past few days to approve the government and that 'The vote wasn't democratic ... it was according to games played outside the institutional framework through encouragement and intimidation at times.' He stated: 'I will never give my confidence to a government that was formed with this mentality.'

Although the Palestinian Council may eventually develop into a significant forum, the more likely sources of opposition are to be found on the streets of Palestine. Denied the all-too-visible perks and privileges of self-rule, but paying a terrible price for the DOP's implementation – including tax arrears Israel was unable to collect during the *intifada* but which are now being collected by the Authority – many have come to view the PA and its omnipresent security forces with bitterness and contempt. Undermobilised and provided with no meaningful role in national reconstruction, the process of state-building for such people is all too easily obscured by the realities of easy money being amassed by monopolists and others popularly derided as 'mafias'. People no longer speak of the venality of individual PA officials and hangers-on, but rather point their finger at the apparatus itself. While Palestinians do not belittle the significance of being able to walk certain streets more safely than before and enjoy a day at the beach, 'this is not what we fought and died for' has become a national refrain. According to a recent poll, 68.5 per cent of those describing themselves as 'not well-to-do' are pessimistic about their future. By contrast, 54.9 per cent of the 'well-to-do' remain optimistic (Rabah and Jamal 1996:10–11).

Throughout the West Bank and Gaza Strip, the feeling of abandonment is palpable. The Islamist opposition (held responsible for provoking the closure and contributing to Netanyahu's rise) and the radical left (whose basically unmodified political sloganeering seems primarily irrelevant to everyday realities) are on the whole not considered viable alternatives to the PA. Asked which Palestinian movement they trust most, 34 per cent chose FATEH, 6.5 per cent HAMAS, 2.8 per cent the PFLP and 29.4 per cent 'I do not trust anyone' (Rabah and Shanahan 1996:22). When asked which leader they trust most, 38.5 per cent chose 'Arafat, 3.0 per cent Shaikh Ahmad Yasin, 1.4 per cent George

Habash and 20.5 per cent 'I do not trust anyone'. The mainstream FATEH movement, which has become increasingly marginalised with 'Arafat's transformation from the leader of a national movement to head of government and with the attendant decline of factional politics, must itself be considered a potentially volatile force. A broad national front – including elements from FATEH, the Palestine People's Party (the pro-Oslo former Palestine Communist Party), independents, along with sections of the Islamist and secular opposition – may yet coalesce around a programme of self-determination and democracy, but faith in Oslo and a piece of the PA pie would first have to be definitively terminated (and particularly in the case of FATEH it must achieve its independence from the PA) for this to occur. Overall, the outlook for Palestinian democracy is bleak. Many democrats fear that if reforms (they are currently unable to impose) are not institutionalised before 'Arafat's departure from the scene, the following deluge will be characterised by a bitter war of succession in which – aside from foreign interference – politics will play a relatively minor role compared to petty power rivalries and the frenzied struggle for access to the sources of wealth for the long term.

Nevertheless, so long as continued Israeli hegemony remains the basis for Israeli–Palestinian relations, Palestinians will continue to struggle for their national rights. This is because Palestinians are not simply fighting for an ideal, but against a reality whose removal is a prerequisite for the resumption of normal life and freedoms. The conviction that neither Peres nor Netanyahu were ultimately prepared to transcend Palestinian authority under Israeli rule left many Palestinians basically indifferent to the outcome of the 1996 Israeli elections. Once Netanyahu, flanked by right-wing hardliners Ariel Sharon (of Shabra and Shatilla 'fame'), Rafael Eitan and Benny (the son of Menachem) Begin, actually assumed office, and *with more precision and clarity than his predecessors*, enunciated a programme that left no room for doubt as to his real intentions, the mood turned increasingly sour as the last vestiges of hope disappeared rapidly within the first 100 days of Likud rule. Over a period of several months, as Netanyahu and his 'Strangelovian' sidekick Dore Gold trotted the globe and sweet-talked into the global media's microphones in order to peddle their peculiar interpretation of 'reciprocity', its meaning was made very clear on the ground in diametrical opposition to the spirit of Oslo:

- Labour's settlement expansion would be accelerated and even extend to the Gaza Strip;

- the closure would be extended, not removed;
- no additional redeployment from either Hebron or 'Area B' and 'Area C' would occur until the unilateral concession made by gullible Israeli doves, the Interim Agreement, was renegotiated.

With his constant refrain of no statehood, no Jerusalem, no return and more settlements, Netanyahu sent a clear message that the final status was already in place and not subject to further negotiation. He not only made 'Arafat appear totally powerless, but in his gravest error to date, pretended that the latter did not exist, reducing him to a supplicant and repeatedly humiliating him. Routinely coating his rejectionist policies with multiple layers of provocation, something the more politically aware and experienced Peres generally avoided, Netanyahu turned the occupied territories into a boiling cauldron. Furthermore, the PA came to be increasingly seen as a direct accomplice to these extremist policies, cooperating with Netanyahu's army of occupation, protecting the expansion of Jewish settlements and receiving absolutely nothing in return, while preventing Palestinians from fighting back. In the summer of 1996, clashes between demonstrators and PA security forces in the northern West Bank appeared to be a foretaste of things to come.

The standing ovation Netanyahu received from the US Congress for explicitly rejecting compromise over Jerusalem only strengthened 'Arafat's conviction that a crisis would be required to ensnare Netanyahu, concentrate American minds and strengthen his position among the Palestinians. He thus first went over Netanyahu's head, obtaining a public commitment from Israeli President Ezer Weizmann to meet him if the Prime Minister would not and then followed this up with a call for a national commercial strike on 29 August 1996. Within days it produced the long-awaited encounter, but nothing else. When this was followed by the Israeli demolition of the Burj al-Luqluq centre for handicapped children within Jerusalem's Old City and loudly announced plans for additional settlements, culminating in the extension of a tunnel excavated alongside the Haram al-Sharif complex into the heart of East Jerusalem, the long fuse that was lit on the White House lawn three years previously touched a powder keg of popular Palestinian bitterness and frustration.

What followed from 23 to 26 September 1996 was neither an organised uprising nor an entirely spontaneous revolt. Rather, the opening provided by the PA's calls for Palestinian protests was utilised by students at Birzeit University (with the backing of FATEH's *shabiba* movement) to take on the Israeli military, despite initial attempts by PA forces at the scene to prevent them from doing so. When Israeli soldiers at the al-Bira checkpoint responded with indiscriminate gunfire against the stone-throwing students, several PA policemen were shamed by the demonstrators into returning fire to defend them or otherwise joined the fray. Immediately thereafter, the West Bank Commander of the Palestinian police, Haj Isma'il Abu-Jabr, almost ignited his second civil war when he arrived to threaten those who continued firing with punishment. He was unceremoniously chased away and other orders to desist were similarly ignored. Subsequently, the Preventative Security Force *(jihaz amn al-wiqa'i)*, which is almost entirely composed of hardened FATEH militants from inside the occupied territories, joined the exchanges of fire with Israeli troops, as an organised force.[9]

The clashes, which actually began in East Jerusalem the previous day, quickly spread to Bethlehem, the Gaza Strip and finally the rest of the West Bank. Involving civilian demonstrators and security forces alike on the Palestinian side, and heavy machine guns and helicopters on the Israel side, the pitched battles resulted in approximately 80 Palestinian and 15 Israeli dead, and 1200 Palestinian and 50 Israeli wounded – the worst bloodshed the occupied territories have witnessed since the June 1967 war.[10]

Despite having encouraged Palestinian protests, the PA leadership was reeling from the intensity of events and its inability to control either its forces or population. Nevertheless and with characteristic acumen, 'Arafat quickly turned the crisis to his advantage. Holding out against Netanyahu's desperate appeals for a meeting and thus turning the tables, he forced the amateurish Israeli leader to publicly demonstrate that Israel remained committed to its partnership with the Palestinians and that it viewed 'Arafat as the key Palestinian player in this relationship. 'Arafat then quickly moved to quell the protests and rein in his forces, holding out the prospect of progress at the Washington summit as an incentive. For the moment at least and despite the dismal failure of the summit, his own standing and particularly that of the security forces have soared.

The September 1996 rebellion, while revealing internal fractures within the PA, appears to have consolidated the relationship between it and the new Israeli government. Both sets of leadership have made it clear that the continued implementation of Oslo is their strategic priority. The problem is that in the absence of meaningful progress on the ground, there is a very real possibility that Palestinian streets will eventually explode once again, perhaps augmented by another round of active participation by armed elements from within the PA. In such a scenario, if the new security arrangements in place are upheld, this makes a direct confrontation between the PA and Palestinian citizens virtually inevitable. If this disintegrates into armed conflict and Israel attempts to reoccupy the enclaves, Palestinians are quick to point out that it took Israel only six days to defeat the Arab world but six years to conquer the Gaza Strip – which is reportedly full of unregistered weapons smuggled in or sold by Israeli *agents provocateurs* in early 1994 in anticipation of a inter-Palestinian civil war.

Few who have followed developments in the 'peace process' thus far, particularly since the imposition of 'separation', can realistically claim that it will result or could have resulted in anything approaching Palestinian self-determination. Rather, what is emerging is a series of 'Arabistans' reminiscent of the Bantustans of the apartheid era in South Africa, ruled by a native authority but subject to overall Israeli politico-military control. These may yet and probably will be extended territorially in the context of a permanent settlement, but in functional terms they are most unlikely to change. Netanyahu's October announcement that Israeli troop redeployment in Hebron will be followed by an immediate transition to final status negotiations should be interpreted in this context and if the PLO rejects the 'New Middle East', the current situation will be frozen in place like a festering sore. Even then, however, it is almost impossible to conceive of circumstances – including the above scenario – in which the PLO would renege on Oslo and its renunciation of resistance, and return instead to an active, armed struggle against occupation. Therefore, so long as Israeli rule continues to accommodate Palestinian authority, the future of the DOP will come to rest upon the ability of Israel and the PA to jointly control an increasingly disillusioned and restive Palestinian population.

Epilogue

Almost from the moment it was signed on 13 September 1993, the Israeli–Palestinian Declaration of Principles on Interim Self-Government Arrangements (DOP) or 'Oslo agreement' has by common consensus been 'in crisis' and 'on the verge of collapse'. Since the election of Netanyahu as Prime Minister of Israel in May 1996, these dire warnings have gradually been replaced by the more morbid diagnosis of a 'clinically dead' or more simply 'deceased' process. Simultaneously, opportunities for renewed global euphoria and self-congratulation, such as that presented by the adoption of the Protocol Concerning the

Redeployment in Hebron on 15 January 1997, are increasingly fewer, farther between and shorter in duration. Rather, it is the armed confrontations which erupted throughout the occupied Palestinian territories in September 1996 which are viewed as the shape of things to come.

From the perspective of Palestinian national rights and Israeli–Palestinian reconciliation, the above nuances are somewhat trivial, because Oslo was a dead letter from the outset. The essential prerequisite for a durable resolution of this conflict, namely Palestinian self-determination, was purposely left unmentioned in both the DOP and each of the subsequent Israeli–Palestinian agreements. No less importantly, these texts have consistently been implemented in a manner designed to make the prospects for its attainment ever more remote. It is in this respect worth remembering that:

- Oslo was the brainchild of the 'dovish' wing of the Israeli Labour Party;
- all but one of the relevant agreements were concluded prior to the November 1995 assassination of Yitzhak Rabin;
- since his assumption of power Netanyahu has made more compromises with Oslo than it has with him.

In practical terms, Netanyahu's main deviation from his predecessors has been in the substantively insignificant realms of attitude and rhetoric. The more germane policies of accelerated colonisation, economic warfare, systematic abuse of human rights and an increasingly formalised system of apartheid were, along with the fundamental Zionist principle of non-recognition of Palestinian national rights, inherited from the most left-wing or 'liberal' government in Israeli history. While the Netanyahu regime's methods are certainly more aggressive in style, hostile in intent and provocative to say the least than those of the suave Peres, the available evidence conclusively demonstrates that the former basically picked up where the latter had left off. Repeated claims by the extremist–militant settler lobby, that the previous government was in fact more responsive to their demands than the current one, only serve to underline the point that in its broad outlines Netanyahu's programme is novel only in so far as it is being implemented by a relative novice to the game of *realpolitik*. It remains to be seen whether the removal of Netanyahu from office in May 1999 will substantially alter Israeli positions.

While the crisis in Palestinian rights is real enough, it is not this which has been exercising the minds of most commentators and causing them to predict Armageddon. Rather, their concerns are for the integrity and sustainability of what is conventionally termed the peace process itself. From this perspective, a tangible, reciprocal, and most importantly, dynamic process of expanding self-government for Palestinians and increasing security for Israelis, which culminates in a permanent settlement based upon the principle of land for peace, forms the inviolable prerequisite for the successful implementation of Oslo. The fundamental breakdown of this formula, symbolised by Israel's systematic procrastination in redeploying its forces away from Palestinian population centres and represented most visibly by Palestinian suicide bombings in Israeli cities, is widely considered a harbinger of catastrophe. Some observers have opined that the relevant agreements are themselves too vague and self-contradictory to produce the required results, and were thus a recipe for failure all along. More often, however, the gloomy forecasts derive from a perceived refusal by the parties directly involved to respect deadlines and commitments explicitly agreed upon, and by their violations of what is held to be the spirit of Oslo. Netanyahu's current insistence on retaining absolute control of a minimum 60 per cent of the West Bank, at least throughout the interim phase, and the refusal by his US patrons to force the implementation of the further Israeli troop redeployments as agreed upon in the Hebron Protocol and simultaneous insistence on a monopoly of sponsorship of the Oslo process, are likened to the final nails in the 'Nordic coffin'.

To the extent that adherents of Oslo view it as a framework for the comprehensive resolution of the conflict between Zionism and the Palestinians, and more generally as a key link in producing an overall Israeli–Arab settlement, it has indeed failed them. Thus, while Oslo's proponents generally consider a two-state solution as the most desirable, if not the only viable formula for a permanent settlement, they are faced with the uncomfortable reality that the only 'partitionist' solution on offer is one in which the pre-1967 boundaries have become wholly irrelevant. Rather, the West Bank and Gaza Strip (excluding Jerusalem and its environs) have themselves already been effectively partitioned into an emaciated and fragmented Palestinian entity, along with a recently contrived Jewish province known to its inhabitants as 'Judea–Samaria–Gaza' and which has been wholly absorbed by the Israeli state. The Palestinian entity, a state in name only and an ethnic reservation in all but name, will furthermore exist within rather than alongside its more powerful and less generous neighbour. Needless to say, this reality has put existing Arab–Israeli peace treaties under considerable strain, rather than paving the way for additional agreements and expanding opportunities for cross-regional trade, the manufacturing industry, tourism and other forms of cooperation, such as in science, technology, education and the arts.

It is of course true that the dispossession of the Palestinian people long preceded Oslo, but the 'Bantustanisation' of the question of Palestine is its direct and intended outcome. In this regard, few arguments are as disingenuous as those which place the blame for the current crisis solely or primarily on Netanyahu's shoulders (as if it began only after his May 1996 election) and which guilefully claim that had the Labour Party been reelected, Peres would in effect have entirely reversed the course that both Rabin and he had chosen from 1993 onwards. It is indeed true that Israeli negotiators during the Rabin–Peres years made numerous intimations to their eager (to say nothing of gullible) Palestinian interlocutors at Oslo and during subsequent sessions, which collectively could be interpreted as a commitment to implement UN Security Council Resolution 242 in a manner not entirely inconsistent with the international community's interpretation. More importantly, however, such confidences were never made formal and any resulting documents never ratified, whilst the official agreements which did result from such negotiations, each superseding its predecessor, progressively constricted the possibilities for meaningful decolonisation and loosening the Israeli stranglehold over the Palestinian polity. The metamorphosis of Oslo's withdrawal clause into a three-stage redeployment, the scope of which was subsequently left to Israel's sole discretion by the United States, is but a case in point. No sooner did the ink on such agreements dry than their implementation, determined primarily by the gross imbalance of power between Israel and the Palestinians, which removed from any form of international arbitration, ensured that in the absence of an Israeli civil war or full-scale Arab–Israeli hostilities, UN Resolution 242 would in reality remain but ink on a meaningless piece of paper.

While Oslo has set back the cause of Palestinian self-determination by at least a generation, it has also failed to develop into a process leading to a viable Israeli–Palestinian 'permanent settlement' and is therefore in a seemingly permanent state of crisis, nevertheless it would be a mistake to conclude that its demise is imminent. The revolutionary transformation of Israeli–Palestinian relations heralded in the Norwegian capital was ultimately the product of more significant changes in the regional and global balance of power, symbolised by the disintegration of the Soviet Union and establishment of US hegemony worldwide, the Gulf crisis and the bankruptcy of the PLO. As such, the Israeli–Palestinian arrangements which have been established since 1993 will more likely than not survive in their fundamental respects so long as the current regional and international orders perpetuate themselves.

With the Palestinians being incapable of challenging the status quo and Israel refusing to offer a permanent settlement acceptable to any Palestinian leadership intent on surviving legitimately on an electoral mandate, and the USA having made a strategic choice to substitute the illusions of process for the requirements of peace, the current impasse will continue for quite some time. More to the point, what is today an impasse is likely to become a permanent arrangement of sorts, or rather a pattern of relations, sustained by and ultimately dependent upon the regional and global balance of forces which produced it in the first place. In this scenario, further political violence initiated by various detractors of the *de facto* partition of the occupied territories and further procedures of normalisation among those of its beneficiaries are to be expected. A piecemeal expansion of the territory under PA rule, together with a unilateral and successful declaration of Palestinian statehood within these enclaves (perhaps giving way in due course to Jordanian supremacy in at least the West Bank 'Arabistans'), and Israeli annexation of a sizeable portion of the occupied territories, are developments which can all be easily contained within the current framework, even if accompanied by periodic frenzies of organised blood-letting. While the possibility of full-scale hostilities leading to mass expulsions along the lines of 1948 and 1967 can of course not be dismissed, barring extreme developments, an Israeli politician proposing the reconquest of Jabalya and the Nablus Qasaba is more likely to be sent to a psychiatric ward than to the elected office of prime minister.

Ultimately, the balance of power which has resulted in the formalisation of Palestinian dispossession must and will change, if sanity and justice are to prevail at the end of the day. Indeed, there are subtle indications that every 'latest' crisis with Iraq and with small bands of Islamist radicals means that the question of Palestine continues to play a central role in regional politics and retains a capacity to serve as a unifying factor for the Arab and Muslim world. Stronger yet, it appears to be a catalyst for the reordering of regional and perhaps eventually of international alliances. To simply conclude, however, that several million Israelis can never succeed in permanently subjugating several hundred million Arabs and that in view of the current disheartening situation, any strategic change is by definition welcome, would be disastrous. If the conflict were merely one of numbers, Israel would never have been established and bad situations, furthermore, seem to have a habit of getting worse. Instead, Palestinians must seek to actively influence the impending changes to their advantage and in doing so, they must themselves propose agendas, rather than continue to be relegated to the margins of the designs of others:

- First and foremost, the Palestinian people must reestablish a national framework on sound democratic foundations with a pluralistic/multicultural content, which accommodates or rather reunites its increasingly disparate and apathetic elements. Unless and until this cardinal challenge is effectively addressed, the remobilisation of the Palestinian masses is a non-starter and internal strife a constant threat, rendering all other efforts futile and doomed to failure.
- Second, the strategic choices and partnerships made during the past decade need to be critically reassessed and appropriate conclusions drawn. The propositions that Palestine will be liberated by Saddam Hussein, Uri Savir or Dennis Ross have all been tried and failed miserably. Rather, it was as the common cause of the Arab world, as the international symbol of the struggle against dispossession, military occupation and Western hypocrisy, and as a result of alliances with popular movements within Europe and North America, that the claim for Palestinian self-determination became internationally accepted and Israel came to be a pariah state. While unprecedented access to the corridors of power in Washington and elsewhere may be a welcome addition, it is a poor substitute. Furthermore, one need only look at the Zionist experience to conclude that the neglect of basic strategic alliances reduces rather than enhances the meaning of such access.
- Finally, Palestinians need to think imaginatively about the struggle for self-determination. Statehood, which during the past decade has effectively displaced self-determination in official Palestinian parlance, is probably imminent but in its present form certain to be meaningless as an adequate response to the question of Palestine. Partition, which in fairness to the proponents of statehood was considered to be the same, had much to recommend it between 1974 and 1993, but as a result of Oslo it is no longer a viable option. The reason for this is the incontrovertible transformation of Israel and the occupied Palestinian territories into a Mediterranean version of South African-style apartheid. A struggle against apartheid requires diverse strategies and different resolutions than a struggle against

military occupation. It is time that these options are considered seriously by those engaged in the struggle for democracy and justice for all in this embittered and deeply divided land.

Notes

1. Previous versions of this chapter appeared in Rabbani (1996a, 1996b).
2. *Ra'is*, which can be translated as both 'president' and 'chairman', is for this reason the term used to designate 'Arafat's status in the otherwise English-language Interim Agreement. The Palestinian Executive Authority is the PA's executive branch (i.e. cabinet) and the Palestinian Council, informally known as the Legislative Council, is a PA body – not to be confused with the Palestine National Council (PNC), which serves as the supreme authority of the PLO.
3. The same holds true for passage from the West Bank to Israel, but on account of the longer border and hilly terrain, this practice is much more difficult to enforce.
4. The financial costs of closure, adding up to several million dollars a day (US$6 million according to a PA estimate) during periods of full closure, far outweigh the total volume of donor assistance. The costs of closure, are moreover, generally borne by individual families and firms, whereas donor assistance is largely disbursed to the PA and other institutions, many of them from bilateral or multilateral sources. Also, donor assistance cannot cover long-term structural damage in terms of reduced investment, delays to infrastructural projects and the like. The vast increase in the PA's budget deficit (in early September 1996 it was US$136 million, or approximately 40 per cent of the annual budget) is primarily on account of reduced tax receipts.
5. While voting day appears to have been free of systematic irregularities, the electoral process raised basic questions about the freedom and fairness of the elections, which still remain to be addressed.
6. 'Ashrawi is a well-known Palestinian spokeswoman, as well as being a respected human rights and women's rights activist and educationist.
7. Public opinion polls are by nature problematic and particularly so in circumstances such as those in Palestine. Nevertheless, questions which do not directly address the leader's status or basic policies often provide a useful indication of popular thinking.
8. This report categorically stated that corruption, mismanagement and inefficiency were rampant throughout the PA and estimated that nearly 50 per cent of its annual budget of US$800 million was being squandered. While the general thrust of this milestone is accurate, it is lacking in many of its details.
9. Subsequent claims to the effect that 'Arafat had the night before ordered his praetorian guard, Force 17, to 'defend themselves' if fired upon are in my view *ex post facto* rumours intended to demonstrate that the PA was in full control of events and should therefore be credited for them. At the same time it does appear that the PA, once confronted with the irreversible fact of imminent involvement by sections of its security forces, provided tacit authorisation.

10. According to the Palestinian human rights community, 60 per cent of the injured suffered head and chest injuries, and 40 per cent of the injured were children. Moreover, most Palestinian dead appear to have been killed by single bullets, indicating a shoot-to-kill policy carried out by Israeli snipers (with or without official sanction) rather than indiscriminate fire.

References

Palestine Report 1996: 'Israel Confiscates 1,000 Acres' vol. 2, no. 14, 6 September, p. 4.

Rabah, J. and Jamal, M. 1996: 'Well-to-do Palestinians More Optimistic' in *Palestine Report* vol. 2, no. 14, 6 September pp. 10–11.

Rabah, J. and Shanahan, C. 1996: 'JMCC Public Opinion Poll' in *Palestine Report* vol. 2, no. 13, 30 August, pp. 20.

Rabbani, M. 1996a: 'Palestinian Authority, Israeli Rule: From Transitional to Permanent Arrangement' in *Middle East Report* vol. 26, no. 4, pp. 2–6, 22.

Rabbani M. (with Aarts, P.) 1996b: 'Palestijns gezag onder Israelische Overheersing' in P. Aarts and M. Rabbani (editors), *Waar ligt de grens? Kritische beschouwingen over het Vredesproces tussen Palestina en Israel*, Coutinho: Bussum.

Roy, S. 1994: *TITLE*, Washington, DC: Institute of Palestine Studies.

Shanahan, C. 1996: 'PA Bans Books by Edward Said' in *Palestine Report,* vol. 2, no. 13, 30 August, p. 24.

Usher, G. 1993: 'Why Gaza Says Yes, Mostly' in *Race and Class*, Jan–March, no. 35, p. 68.

Usher, G. 1996: 'The Politics of Internal Security: The PA's New Intelligence Services' in *Journal of Palestine Studies* vol. XXV, no. 2, Winter, pp. 21–34.

8
Somalia After the Cold War: Anarchic Factionalism, Intervention or Peacemaking?

Abdullah A. Mohamoud

By the early 1990s, politico-economic conflicts and power struggles which had beset Somalia since the late 1970s finally engulfed the country in a disastrous civil war. Consequently, it led to the overthrow of the military regime of Siyad Barre, disintegrated central authority and caused the state of Somalia to cease existence as a politically organised national entity. Eventually, the ensuing carnage, unprecedented in the history of Somalia, resulted in more than 30 000 combat-related deaths, while another 300 000 died of starvation and famine-related diseases (Sahnoun 1994). Nonetheless, as the conflicts continued unabated, so too did the mounting casualty rate of daily victims among the hapless civilian population. For almost two years, that is, from January 1991 to December 1992, the human suffering inflicted upon civilians as a result of armed conflicts remained largely unpublicised. Eventually, heightened media publicity on the 'forgotten' Somali tragedy led to international humanitarian intervention in 1992, spearheaded by the global superpower, the United States of America. Ostensibly, among other factors, the international community intervened in Somalia so as to restore law and order, and eventually reestablish central authority. In short, this ambitious project ended in a total fiasco, forcing the United Nations to terminate its international peacekeeping mission on 4 March 1995. Regrettably, after spending more than US$3 billion, the UN left Somalia in a situation no better than the one it was in earlier and which prompted the intervention in the first place (*Horn of Africa Bulletin* 1995:20).

By the beginning of 1998, although the intensity of the conflicts in the country had gradually subsided, the underlying reasons for the conflicts had not disappeared altogether. While these underlying factors are both historical and structural in content – that is, underlying historical factors being internal/indigenous and the structural factors being largely external in character – others can be described as momentary episodes. In Somalia indigenous, conflict-related, historical and structural problems are confined in the main to ecological conditions and the praxis of pastoral nomadism they have spawned and perpetuated as a means of living. Pastoral production – which still remains the economic activity of most inhabitants even in the 1990s – is an economy of scarcity and survival, a 'mode of production', which has been a source of conflict among Somali pastoral nomads for centuries. Closely related to this simple subsistence-based nomadism is the character of societal organisation of the Somalis, which is a system based on lineage segmentation.

Critical episodes of an external character in Somalia include a series of interventions, namely, colonial occupations, Cold War geopolitical impact and last but not least, the USA-led UN humanitarian intervention. Each of these phases played a critical role in adding fuel to the fires of ongoing, survival and politico-economic power-based conflicts. At present, even though all three recent external interventions are 'past history', each one of them has left behind a deleterious legacy which still feeds conflicts in Somalia, as well as in the Horn of Africa subregion.

The basic issues addressed in this chapter are the decisive historical, structural and conjunctural factors which have cumulatively led to fragmentation of the state as an organised societal force in Somalia. To search for answers to this central question, we need to go beyond the often repeated claims of journalists and occasional armchair observers that the nature of the problem in Somalia is the re-emergence of unsettled scores of 'primordial clan animosities'. These so-called experts, who regularly inform the international media, argue that the revival of the recalcitrant political behaviour of tradition, which segments the Somali people into units of hostile clans, is in fact the 'real' causal force for the current upheavals and fragmentation of the state. Even now, as I illustrate below, certain established scholars in Somali studies continue to reiterate similar arguments. The dilemma of state disintegration in Somalia requires detailed historical and structural analysis of indigenous realities, as well as innovative and alternative thinking. First of all, this chapter discusses a number of academic debates on the fragmentation of the Somali state, followed by an examination of the historical and structural problems that the peoples and their rulers have had to endure. The second section of the chapter presents an overview of the deleterious effects of external momentary episodes, before finally going on to a critical evaluation of the short- and long-term feasibility and success of ongoing attempts at peace and reconciliation undertaken by Somali factional leaders.

Somali state fragmentation

In Somali studies, debates concerning the fragmentation of the Somali state have been partially addressed through scholarly debates. The most significant intellectual battle is between two major schools of thought. Traditionalists focus more on sociological aspects of state fragmentation, presuming that 'the causes' that have led to the demise of the state in Somalia are internal, lodged in the traditional clan system and Somali cultural praxis. Put more plainly, from a sociological viewpoint the Somali people were not structured as a single political entity, but organised along divisive lines of clans and lineage (see, for example, Lewis 1961, 1988, 1994a,b and Ahmed Samatar 1988, 1991, 1993).

Since the 1980s, this traditionalist line of approach in explaining the implosion of the Somali state has come under severe criticism from the transformationist school of thought, spearheaded by the brothers Ahmed and Abdi I. Samatar. The transformationist school of thought accounts for the demise of the state primarily as a result of economic competition and internal élite rivalries. Scholars from this tradition emphatically argue that among other factors, the ongoing fragmentation of the nation state in Somalia is not 'caused' by the survival of patrimonial kinship structures. Instead, they argue that it is a 'transformation' brought about through the introduction of complex systems such as the world capitalist economy, the imposition of the modern concept of nation state, and the recently constructed and 'politicised' concept of clanism (see Abdi Samatar 1989, 1992, 1993 and Ahmed Samatar 1988, 1989, 1993, 1994). They also contend that the manipulation of clan ties by dominant social groups for their narrow interests, especially state élites and merchants, has led to the degeneration of Somali politics and has nothing to do with the impinging 'primordial' structures of 'the society'.

In a nutshell, both major debates advance scholarly explanations of the causes of the contemporary state collapse in Somalia. However, it is a fallacy to maintain, as traditionalists argue, that the cause of the present state fragmentation in Somalia is exclusively rooted in the 'primordial' clan system and lineage order. This single variable explanation is in fact an example of circular reasoning. Furthermore, the traditionalist thesis denies both structural conditionality and social contingency. By contrast, the transformationists have touched on crucial issues which I believe are central to understanding the fragmentation of the state in Somalia. Their discussion centres around economic competition and elite rivalry. For example, both factors were discussed in internal historical processes as well as in external structural changes. In this respect, the thesis of the transformationists is superior to the sociological explanation offered by the traditionalists because it takes into account concrete political and economic interests. For example, the transformationists indicate how contests among dominant social groups for the control of state power, as well as its resources and opportunities, gradually but progressively imploded the very existence of centralised structures. Accordingly, incessant pursuit of private profit is the primary source of contemporary social upheavals and state fragmentation in Somalia.

Nevertheless, my critique of both debates of Somali scholarship is that neither clan divisiveness as claimed by traditionalists nor class exploitation as argued by transformationists can sufficiently explain why the central government and state structures fragmented. It is a fact that both clan and perhaps class factors are part and parcel of a complex, multi-layered series of events that led to fragmentation of the state in Somalia. I find that the most decisive elements that determined the break-up of the state in Somalia are:

1. The historical continuity of private pursuit partially addressed by the transformationists;
2. Post-colonial public pursuit or irredentist expansion (which neither traditionalist or tranformationist scholarship has so far considered in relation to contemporary state fragmentation in Somalia).

Structural poverty of pastoral economic existence

The first factor, which I term *private pursuit* or 'spoils politics', due to the lack of a better designation, is compelled by the scarcity of resources in pastoral existence. As noted earlier, pastoral nomadism is an economic activity which is meagre and only fit for basic sustenance and survival. This means that it is an economic activity which does not produce a surplus. Moreover, the production of this historic means of existence is very much dependent on the vagaries of nature and the environment – that is, the yearly availability of water and pasture. If, for instance, it does not rain at all in a given year, this will mean death for the livestock and destitution for the nomads. If it however rains little, which is the norm rather than the exception, this will mean fierce competition among the pastoral nomads for sheer survival. The fragility of economic life among pastoral nomads is what makes compromise and sharing hardly possible. Instead, fierce group or individual pursuit is seen as the only way to appropriate scarce resources for the purpose of survival. From the point of view of Somali pastoral nomads, private pursuit is regarded as a rational form of survival, which cannot be avoided. Even the impact of colonialism, which lasted from 1885 to 1960, and the more recent penetration of the global market economy have not reduced much of the acute scarcity of this pastoral 'mode of production'. Colonialism had to a greater extent commoditised livestock and pastoral production, but this did not help transform basic scarcity – that is, the underlying environment-based structural conditions. Consequently, scarcity and the perpetual instability of pastoral production remained the same and so too did its concomitant private pursuits to which the groups and individuals helped themselves for generations as a means for survival.

Since Somalia attained statehood, private pursuit and fierce competition over natural resources have been a marked feature among Somali élite behaviour. Every élite person within the government believed he represented the interests of his particular kinship and lineage members – that is, he is in the government not as a national figure but as a clan representative. The additional wealth which the state obtains mainly through foreign aid was seen as similar to water and pasture, which Somalis competed for in the pre-state era. Abdi Samatar notes that 'the state, which mediates conflicts between classes in advanced capitalist societies, was here the object and the prize of the struggle (appropriation of the state)' (Abdi Samatar 1989:110). With a philosophical world-view, the Somali people normally regard pasture and water as the God-given wealth of every pastoral Somali and not property of a specific group (Lewis 1988:9). The practical idea behind this vision is that each and every pastoral Somali has a private right to appropriate a slice of this gift from God. This view is in line with the egalitarian principle of traditional social order among Somali people. However, this consideration becomes more problematic with respect to the public wealth of a modern nation state. If the people perceive the property of the state through this lens, then the creation of public wealth will not be possible. This perception has led to plundering of the national wealth without any qualms. No Somali feels guilty in the unlawful appropriation of public wealth and the people do not see it as robbery. On the contrary, any person holding public office in the government is encouraged to get rich and also to help his kin-relations at the same time. If he does not, his colleagues and the public will consider him to be not manly but a weak and cowardly person. This public attitude towards state wealth is probably what made the national coffers empty.

Deleterious effects of colonialism

The second factor, which I call *public pursuit*, was a national political preoccupation and the declared objective of every government since independence. This public national aspiration was the dream of a 'Greater Somalia', which had solely dominated the foreign policy and political agenda of the Somali leadership since the late 1960s. Rulers of Somalia have pursued the unification of the Somali-inhabited 'missing territories' from the moment the Republic attained its independence and until its dissolution.

However, this predicament that the Somali leadership confronted was not of their own making – it was the legacy of the colonial dismemberment of the country. In the closing decades of the nineteenth century during the 'scramble for Africa', competing imperialist powers parcelled the country into five parts. With respect to the rest of sub-Saharan Africa, this five-fold partitioning of Somalia was an exceptional case. The rival foreign powers at the time were Britain, Italy, France and Ethiopia. After decolonisation, British Somaliland in the north and Italian Somaliland in the south merged and became the Republic of Somalia. However, this unification was not at all complete, since three areas which Somalis inhabited still remained under foreign domination that is, – the eastern regions of Ethiopia, Djibouti and the northern frontier district of Kenya. Subsequently in 1977, Djibouti achieved its independence from France, but its president declined a merger with the Republic of Somalia and instead maintained strong ties with their former colonisers.

After decolonisation, Somalia was the only country in sub-Saharan Africa which rejected the status quo of the frontiers demarcated by departing colonialists. This outright rejection was resented by neighbouring countries, the Organisation of African Unity (OAU), as well as the former colonial countries in Western Europe. Nonetheless, the Somali leadership insisted that the colonial borders were artificial and unlawful, and that they would not prevent them championing the cause of self-determination for all Somalis who remained under foreign rule. This political stand caused the newly independent state of Somalia a great deal of problems. Within three years of independence in 1960, Somalia was embroiled in border skirmishes with Ethiopia.

These incidents urged the ruling leadership to procure large stocks of military armaments by all means possible for eventual war with the neighbouring countries. To this end, late in 1963, the government refused an offer of more than US$10m in military assistance from three Western countries – the USA, West Germany and Italy – because it was considered too little. Instead, the government accepted a larger Soviet military aid package, estimated to be around US$30 million (*Africa Report* January 1964). In the same year, the Somali government – resenting the unilateral decision of the British government to let Kenya annex the northern frontier district inhabited by Somalis – severed diplomatic relations with Britain. This decision also cost the government of Somalia dearly because it put an end to aid from Britain, which the Republic urgently needed at that time.

From these early years after independence – which was crucially needed for the consolidation of internal social–political cohesion and domestic resource exploitation – the Somali government embarked on a mission of external irredentist expansion. This irredentist politics was in contrast to that of other ruling élites in the rest of sub-Saharan Africa, who not only agreed to abide by the frontiers inherited in the aftermath of colonialism but also occupied themselves with what they perceived as the utmost priority for their newly independent countries – namely internal social cohesion, nation-building and economic development or creation of domestic wealth. In contrast, the Somali political elites considered pursuing irredentist expansion as a process of nation-building. From their point of view, the Somali nation was fragmented beyond the borders of the Somali Republic and needed reunification.

Indeed, irredentist activities have been a unique feature of the Somali Republic since independence. It is however this quest which had, from early on, militarised the political process in the country. Domestically, pursuing the goal of a 'Greater Somalia' had been a strategy used by the ruling élites in Somalia as a positive function for internal social stability and as a principle of rule or legitimisation of power. Externally, it was viewed as a very serious national preoccupation, which every Somali leader must continue to advocate. For example in 1967, when Premier Mohamed Haji Ibrahim Egal signed a peace treaty with the government of Kenya in Arusha, Somalis reacted with condemnation. The public saw this policy of *détente* as tantamount to selling out Somali territory to Kenya. It is this public anger, among other factors, which led the military to topple the civilian government of Premier Egal. The military takeover of state power demonstrates the paramount public commitment not only to the Pan-Somali cause but also to the increased militarisation of national politics from that time onwards. At the time, militarisation of state politics both for internal suppression and external preparation for war was greatly helped by the high levels of superpower rivalry in the region of the Horn of Africa and around the Gulf of Aden. Both superpowers and their allies were willing to provide generous military assistance to Somalia at one time or another. This support enabled Somalia to build up one of the largest and well-trained armies in sub-Saharan Africa. Nonetheless, in order to raise such a well-trained modern army in preparation for combat, the government had to divert a significant portion of its revenues away from taking care of the immense internal socio-economic problems. Somalia was and is one of the poorest countries in sub-Saharan Africa, yet its defence expenditure was ranked highest, with 25 percent of its annual budget going to defence and security (Marte 1994:221). It is even argued that central authority in Somalia actually started fragmenting as a consequence of the Ogaden adventure of 1977–8. The Ogaden region under Ethiopian control evokes a very special affinity not only to the nation as a whole but particularly to the then president of the military regime, Said Barre, who had family connections to the dominant clan residing in the area. In fact, the mother of Barre was from Ogaden, whose clan populated most of the area and after which the region was named.

However, what is also evident is that the successive Somali governments did not engage in irredentist activities simply to liberate land and their Somali inhabitants. To a lesser extent, both material interests and religion also played a significant role. For example, the Ogaden area is believed to hold oil and gas reserves, and also other rich mineral resources. The exploitation of these resources after the unification of this region with the Republic of Somalia can be viewed as a 'rational temptation' for Somali élites, a significant factor which is determined by the acute scarcities of pastoral existence. In addition, saving Muslim Somalis from the clutches of Christians was another important aspect and should not be underestimated, given the historical animosity between Muslim Somalis and Christians, be they Ethiopian, British, Italian or French colonialists. For example, in the sixteenth century, a Muslim leader named Imam Ahmed Gurey waged a holy war (*jihad*) against Ethiopians with the aim of subduing them and converting them to Islam. Similarly, in the late nineteenth century, another powerful Muslim Somali leader, Sayyid Mohamed Abille Hassan, emerged and also waged a 'holy war' in order to drive all the Christian colonisers out of Somalia. Thus, all factors, land and people, material interests and religion, have in combination motivated successive Somali governments to engage in decades-long irredentist activities against neighbouring countries.

Irredentist politics was perceived as a legitimate public pursuit with which the leadership had to comply. It was also a test of the extent to which a leader could be considered a Somali nationalist. For instance, another case of public disaffection with a leader can be cited here. During the Ogaden war in 1977 and 1978, when the army was defeated and failed to unite the region with the Republic, the public turned their outrage to Barre's leadership, which culminated in an abortive coup in April 1978 with the involvement of high-ranking army officers. Elite preoccupation with the struggle for Pan-Somali unification dominated politics in the country since the late 1960s, however the impact of this phenomenon on the recent fragmentation of the state has not yet been researched.

It is now evident that successive Somali governments pursued this irredentist expansion to the neglect of domestic issues. Rhetoric aside, no effective internal social cohesion was promoted, neither was there an allocation of adequate time, energy or resources to cope with important social questions. From time to time, irredentist expansion served the cause of national unity but this was only a temporary affair. Somali governments were not too concerned either with the exploitation of domestic resources or economic development. After decolonisation, the Somali Republic inherited a very backward and underdeveloped economy largely based on pastoral nomadism. The revenue generated by this anaemic means of production was not enough even to cover the cost of running the administration of the state, let alone ensure expanding the productive base of the economy. It is this resource scarcity which conditioned Somali administrations to stay firmly hooked on budgetary support in the form of loans and grants from former colonial powers and Cold War rivals. Worse still, the foreign aid received for development was not put into the creation of domestic national wealth but was siphoned off by competing élites. It is for this reason that Somalia is dubbed 'the graveyard of foreign aid' among certain circles in the Western press (Omar 1992:88).

Episodes of the cold war and of 'humanitarian' intervention

The conflicts in Somalia also have other external dynamics. In addition to the deleterious impact of the colonial legacy, the politics of the

Cold War and the seemingly philanthropic USA-led UN 'humanitarian intervention' of more recent years have played determinant roles in perpetuating hostilities. During the Cold War era, Somalia was a theatre of superpower rivalry for strategic advantage and the state was a pawn of this bipolar politics. This means that the conflicts among domestic forces, as well as between Somalia and neighbouring states, such as Ethiopia, were constantly meddled with by external patrons. Needless to say, the foreign forces involved in these conflicts first and foremost served their own geopolitical interests and only second the domestic interests of their clients.

Foreign involvement in Somali political and social affairs' has a long history, going back, arguably, to the eighth century BC, when Persian traders and Arab Muslims in the nearby regions migrated to Somalia for economic and religious reasons. Since then, foreign influence in modern Somalia has been a significant factor in the dynamics of domestic politics. In the 1960s, Somalia became an independent state at a time when the Cold War was at its peak. The involvement of countries of the Western bloc, particularly the USA, was largely motivated by the need to contain Soviet and Chinese influence in Somalia. In order to make sure that Somalia did not fall into the Soviet Union's camp, Western countries were willing to present themselves as important patrons.

However, the then Somali leadership knew that America and its Western allies were providing more substantial military assistance to both Ethiopia and Kenya than was on offer to them. Furthermore, the leadership of the Somali Republic was preoccupied with building a strong army so as to realise one day their dream of Pan-Somali unity, with this gradually driving them to align themselves with the Soviet Union as a powerful ally. This alliance finally culminated in a special Friendship Agreement, which guaranteed steady aid programmes, mostly arms and military equipment. Meanwhile, its arch enemy Ethiopia remained on the side of the USA-led bloc and from then on an arms race between the two countries took place. Somalia became a state controlled by a military regime. The military government in Somalia, with the support of the Soviet Union, built the fourth largest modern and sophisticated army in sub-Saharan Africa, after Nigeria, Ethiopia and Ghana (Marte 1994). Furthermore, the militarisation of the state has also militarised the body politic. In this respect, violent methods became the means for internal suppression of dissent and external strategies. The regime used violence to control the population, while opposition groups also resorted to similar tactics in retaliation. For almost twenty years, Somali society was organised along these vicious lines. Yet the military regime of Somalia remained in power with the political, military and economic support of its Cold War patrons, despite its naked human rights violations. The reason was very simple, namely that in terms of geopolitical significance, Somalia ranked high, and as long as this strategic position served the interests of foreign powers, the domestic brutality of the ruling regime remained unquestioned – as was the case with most African, Asian, Central and South American despots and dictators at the time. It is argued that the political, military and economic support of the foreign powers during the Cold War was what exacerbated the interstate or intrastate conflicts in many Third World countries (Ayoob 1995). Interestingly, in sub-Saharan Africa, the states which have now fragmented are the very ones which were once sustained by the military, technical and financial assistance of the superpowers during the Cold War. For example, it is unequivocally the case that three of the collapsed states in Africa in this decade, namely Liberia, Somalia and Zaire, were among the Cold War's leading foreign aid recipients (Lyons and Samatar 1995, Walle 1996). The simple fact is that the abrupt end of Cold War politics, which had enlisted the state in those countries as clients of foreign patrons, is what in part dismantled those states.

When the Cold War ended, Somalia was left awash with thousands of armaments, the tragic legacy inherited from the political game of ideological supremacy. According to one Somalia observer, 'today the prevalence of modern weapons, Somalia's most significant legacy of superpower involvement during the Cold War, has undermined the very foundation for order in Somalia's society ... the authority of clan elders' (Clark 1993:207–8). The departing superpowers left behind an enormous quantity of high-powered weaponry, which turned the entire land of Somalia into an arsenal and, as a result, when the international community intervened in Somalia, each household had more arms than food, and this is what kept the civil war going.

USA-dominated UN intervention forces came into Somalia in December 1992. This mission was dubbed 'Operation Restore Hope', because at the time Somali civilians were dying in large numbers due to the civil war raging and the armed bandits who prevented food from reaching them. However, the troops did not intervene as 'peacekeepers', because that would have required two preconditions – a peace to keep in the first place and an invitation from a host government. At the time, President Bush, addressing the American public just hours before the dispatch of US marines, said that the mission was 'purely humanitarian' but that statement reveals less than it obscures. Some experts interpret the USA-led intervention in Somalia as 'conducting an experiment in world order'. They further explain that if it succeeded, it might encourage further interventions in hot-spot areas in the region, namely southern Sudan. If this explanation was true then Somalia, a poor African country, had been chosen as a guinea pig for the testing of American military efficacy and that may explain why the military option became a top priority in 'resolving the conflict'. The second factor is the possibility of external influence, which has all along been suspected by those who are privy to internal Somali politics. Many have even argued that the underlying reason for the impulsive US intervention was not humanitarian but was to prevent Somalia from falling into the Iran–Sudan camp. Such an eventuality could directly threaten Western economic interests – in this case oil, given the strategic position of Somalia, lying at the back of the Arabian oilfields, across the Gulf of Aden (Mohamoud 1993a).

The USA-dominated military intervention in Somalia failed to bring peace and security, restore law and order, establish central authority and prevent regional involvements in the internal affairs of the country. In a broader global context, the intervention failed badly as an experiment in world order. Initially, the intervention looked a modest success, ending much of the starvation and reducing domestic armed conflicts, but as time went by the presence of foreign soldiers sparked renewed violence. One of the worst mistakes the USA-led UN intervention made in Somalia was the failure to tackle one of the primary tasks it set itself – notably, the disarming of the 'warlords' insofar as arms were the main threat to security in the country, both for Somalis as well as for the workers from humanitarian agencies. In New York, the then UN Secretary-General, Boutros Boutros-Ghali, said in a statement to the Somali people, shortly before the first troops landed, that the UN was acting 'in the cause of security, humanitarian relief and political reconciliation' (Mohamoud 1993a:684). Yet the commanders of the troops in the country disobeyed the mandate of the UN to ensure restoring security as their top priority and the disarming of the warring factions. Their contention was that disarmament was not part of the mandate they received from their respective countries and their task in Somalia was limited to the protection of humanitarian relief operations. This example clearly indicates how unplanned and hasty interventions, a lack of clear command structures and discrepancies between the statements and mandates of the UN and individual countries can completely derail the success of any humanitarian intervention mission. This is one of the lessons from the débâcle in Somalia which we must keep in mind, if military intervention in the form of peacemaking is to be used again elsewhere – a strategy that has been a deeply tarnished and discredited alternative.

Furthermore, we must also take into account the reported serious human rights violations carried out by the soldiers of several countries involved in the peacekeeping mission. Lately, international newspapers have published a series of revelations concerning racism, physical abuse, sadistic torture of children and adults, running of brothels, drug trafficking and black marketeering, all of which soldiers involved in the peacekeeping operation have been directly implicated with. However, these shocking violations have happened not only in Somalia but also in Mozambique, Angola and Bosnia. The soldiers involved are not from any particular country, with those reported so far coming from Belgium, Canada, Italy, the Netherlands and the Ukraine. These incidents are enough of a warning to those who may contemplate using military forces in peacekeeping operations – unless they are re-educated, restructured and transformed from their present organisation and orientation. Soldiers are trained to shoot people but not to care for them, therefore they have a different mentality and work ethic which are not suitable for such delicate missions as in Somalia. This problem has now been recognised by officials at the department of peacekeeping missions in the UN. Kofi Annan, the current Secretary-General of the UN, when he was head of peace missions previously, understood the problem of sending soldiers who are trained for warfare to handle such tasks. It is now suggested that police forces are better trained than the military in policing streets, managing conflicts and communicating with the people. The other ingredient would be the reinstating of a judicial system and the rule of law.

The presence of the UN in Somalia was a plague rather than a blessing in another way, for, as time went by, the intervening UN troops in Somalia gradually deteriorated into another clan faction especially after relationships with General Aideed became embittered. Hostilities between UN troops and fighters from the Aideed faction escalated the conflict and plunged the country into another civil war. Apart from this, the presence of the UN peacekeeping mission in Somalia perpetuated the conflict in Somalia in another fashion, given that the UN presence was turned into an industry of sorts. It generated revenue and wealth for rival factional leaders, and was therefore a valuable incentive for the warlords to keep on fighting. Michael Maren's article 'For Somalia's Sake, Get the UN Out' has made this point clear – 'In the most violently contested areas, the UN presence means job, contracts and money. The United Nations rents houses, hires trucks and issues millions of dollars in contracts and sub-contracts to businessmen with close ties to the warlords' (Maren in the *International Herald Tribune*, July 1994). A good example of this is Mohamed Sheikh Osman, former finance minister in Siyad Barre's regime, who has rented out several of his mansions to UN personnel. For one of the compounds, he received 70 000 US dollars per month in rent from the UN. Politically, Osman was aligned to the most powerful faction in the south led by Aideed. There were many former functionaries of the collapsed Barre regime like him who overnight turned themselves into rich businessmen through the services they provided for UN personnel in the country. For them, continuation of the conflict meant profit and financial backing, which thus lured the warlords into continued fighting. Thus, the UN not only failed to stabilise the situation in the ravaged south of Somalia but its presence also fuelled the continuation of armed conflicts.

Evidently, what the failure of the UN intervention in Somalia teaches us is the importance of diplomacy before considering military or policing options. In the case of Somalia, diplomacy was not considered seriously as a means of ending the conflict, prior to the military intervention. This is the point that Mohamed Sahnoun (UN special representative to Somalia in 1992) and other inside observers had argued all along (Omaar and De Waal 1994). According to Sahnoun, diplomacy came too late in resolving the conflicts in Somalia and was abruptly ended before it had time to work (Sahnoun 1994). Thus, before allowing diplomatic negotiation to take their course in Somalia, a hurried military intervention was undertaken. This is an important lesson for 'peace-keepers' to keep in mind in the future, before opting for military intervention elsewhere. In countries like Somalia, where all vestiges of formalised and institutionalised authority have disintegrated, military intervention is not a sensible alternative. Sending experienced and credible diplomats in order to mediate with the protagonists would have been the best, most rational, first-choice option. In the future, especially with regards to Africa, respected and credible leaders like Nelson Mandela, and others of his stature could serve as peace mediators when hot-spots flare up.

The Somali case differs with respect to other cases examined in this volume as follows:

- First, the intensity of the conflict not only fragmented central authority but the very state itself entirely ceased to exist. At present, the

absence of central government in the country is allowing the conflict to continue and causing the deterioration of domestic security.
- Second, although Cold War-related conflicts ended and the superpowers departed from the scene, external involvement in Somalia has not yet ceased. Given that central authority has collapsed, the country has now become prey to various radical groups, as well as regional powers.

Today, Somalia has become a 'free port' for radical Islamist groups from the region (much like Afghanistan in South-Central Asia), which have already established bases in certain pockets of the country in collaboration with their Somali counterparts. The presence of these radical groups in the country further escalates intra-Somali conflicts. Since the early 1990s, Somalis have fought each other along religious and secular lines on a number of occasions. Since May 1997, these radical Islamist groups have also been fighting the Ethiopian army and this unabated conflict is viewed with grave concern by observers in the Horn of Africa subregion.

Similarly, regional powers have been interfering in Somalia since it ceased to function as an independent and sovereign state. Neighbouring states, who are still playing a role as 'peace-brokers' in bringing about dialogue and reconciliation among rival Somali factions greatly impinge on Somali internal affairs. Those states currently interfering in Somalia do not have uniform national interests and these differences further exacerbate the role of external factors in the conflict. These states and others race to court one or another of the contending factional leaders, in order to find or create 'their man'. To give an example, in July 1997, I was in Addis Ababa when the second reconciliation conference of the National Salvation Council (NSC) of Somalia was taking place and the leaders of the Somali political factions were housed in the same hotel as myself. As the conference was closed, diplomats from Italy, Egypt, Yemen, Djibouti and several other countries were secretly visiting the hotel in the evenings in order to coax separately each of the five co-chairmen of the NSC. In this respect, each diplomat was conducting these secret meetings with the aim of ensuring that the political influence of his country would prevail in Somalia. Thus today, even if all the rival factions in Somalia agree to a reconciliation package and sign a peace accord, the extent of external involvement will not permit such a peace to last. That would eventually mean that, despite the end of the Cold War, the conflicts in Somalia could remain intractable. It will also ensure that Somalia remains for the foreseeable future a land of 'clan fiefdoms', in which each one is aligned subordinately to one of the regional states.

Conclusion

As political reconciliation and peace in Somalia now stand, very little has been achieved. The latest of the dozen or so political reconciliation and peace-related conferences which have taken place abroad since 1991, one after another, has been the closed conference held in Cairo on 20 December 1997. Among other things, it was agreed that the lack of central government in Somalia, which had been going on for the past seven years, should be ended. Furthermore, it was also agreed that a start should be made so that a period of peace and stability could prevail in a country ravaged by years of clan wars, brutal killings and non-productivity. Consequently, a further reconciliation peace conference was held inside Somalia, in the south-western town of Baidoa, on 15 February 1998.

Although on paper these agreements are precise and seem tenable, in practice their implementation is fraught with difficulties. The problems, as I discussed in the body of this chapter, are both historical and structural, as well as external in character. Both the deleterious effect of the historic and structural poverty of the pastoral economic existence and the perpetual external influence in Somali political affairs are an impediment to a genuine and serious peace. For example, rival political élites in Somalia often begin their negotiations by discussing how to apportion state power and positions in government. They never discuss or pay enough attention to how to first rebuild state structures and develop a viable domestic economic base, which was what was also not done initially at the time of independence in 1960. During that period, even when the Somali state was in its embryonic stage, the nationalist elites were contesting each other over who would get what position in the new government. They did not consider at all, how and where the newborn state would generate its revenues. It was as if they thought that the 'Humpty-Dumpty state', formed during the colonial era and abandoned by the departing colonialists, would make itself work. Indeed, their sole interests were how to appropriate the revenues accruing to the state, which came largely from foreign aid.

An interesting saga to note here is that the majority of Somalis likened the new state to a she-camel in a rich pasture land, which does not require much attention but is always ready with abundant milk. Due to their received nomadic mentality, Somalis of all generations consider a she-camel (the mother of all resources) as the rightful property of all men which should be milked, killed, eaten and even looted, while the looter remains scot-free and without any guilt. Unfortunately, this is the way that many Somalis view the state, from independence to the present day. A good example of this 'spoils politics' is the continued jockeying for power among the present batch of factional leaders in Somalia. Since the early 1990s when central authority collapsed in Somalia and the state literally withered away, only one issue has dominated the negotiating process. In each and every reconciliation conference, the crucial matter that the factional leaders are bargaining about is 'how to build a central government and appoint its higher echelons'. They have as yet neither asked nor addressed the question of how we establish a police force and concomitant courts of justice. Thus, to a considerable extent, it is the perpetuation of this log-jam mentality of spoils (that is, who gets what), prior to the establishment of a minimum basis of state structures, that is hampering current political progress in Somalia.

Another striking phenomenon in the political affairs of Somalia throughout these wasted years is that every time the Somali factional leaders meet, they begin the reconciliation dialogue anew – from scratch. Thus, their political mediation has no process, lacks structural procedures and is conducted instead on an *ad hoc* basis. This type of politics, which I am sure has been baffling many foreign observers for many years, is rooted in Somali history. For example, the political character of pre-colonial Somali nomads living in the pastoral wilderness was such that problems and conflicts were resolved on an *ad hoc* basis due to the absence of permanent political authority. The continuation of this age-old precolonial political practice is what we can observe today with respect to the peace dialogue between the Somali factional leaders. For outside parties, such as neighbouring states and subregional organisations, like the Inter-Governmental Authority and Development (IGAD), the Organisation of African Unity (OAU) and the United Nations (UN), this *ad hoc* basis of conflict reconciliation and political dialogue is not only unusual but also frustrating to say the least.

The factional leaders are, in a sense, not what they seem to be. They are not corporate groups but rather a collection of individuals representing different vested interests and contradictory political agendas. Thus they lack corporate class interests, commitments and determination. Much worse, each one of them keeps his own secret agenda hidden behind the camouflage of 'concern for broader national interests'. In public, they pay lip-service to overriding national issues, while in private they strategise their personal pursuits. As I mentioned earlier, I was in Addis Ababa in July 1997 at the same time as the second reconciliation conference of the NSC was taking place. After the meeting ended, a press conference was held, during which journalists questioned the co-chairmen, Ali Mahdi and Abdullahi Yusuf, about their differences. The two men simply could not provide an explanation and they simply replied that 'we have no differences'. When asked, 'If you have no disagreements why do you not work together?', once again they were unable to explain themselves.

The recently ended Cairo conference would have been much more fruitful if it could have helped the factional leaders to resolve their internal differences before attempting the difficult task of restoring central governmental rule in Somalia. I believe that a series of serious peace dialogues must be first conducted, the aim of which should be to sort out differences between the factional leaders, prior to the reestablishment of centralised political authority in Somalia. This is an urgent prerequisite that must be attended to before taking on any other initiative. After this 'little' problem is settled, the next responsibility of forming a government in Somalia will logically follow. By contrast, what the international community is now doing is hastily forcing the process of a political settlement in Somalia. Unfortunately, despite all the good intentions, this political strategy cannot produce results unless the leaders of the Somali factions first patch up their mundane private differences for the sake of the common national good.

Another problem often disregarded, which is making peace and national reconciliation accords difficult to abide by, is the absence of binding and codified written laws. A wise Somali I met recently in London said to me, 'The problem of Somalia is that the reconciling warlords are not using proper procedures. They should either negotiate through the rules and regulations of their [our] nomadic tradition, or that of modern constitutions. Otherwise, their reconciliation process will remain in a vicious circle.' I believe in these wise words, which go to the heart of the problem and provide a simple, yet profound answer to the question mark over peace in Somalia.

References

Africa Report 1964: January Issue.
Ayoob, M. 1995: *The Third World Security Predicament: State Making, Regional Conflict, and the International System,* Boulder, Colo: Lynne Rienner.
Clark, J. 1993: 'Debacle in Somalia: Failure of the Collective Response' in L.F. Damrosch (editor), *Enforcing Restraint: Collective Intervention in Internal Conflicts,* New York: Council on Foreign Relations Press.

Horn of Africa Bulletin 1995.
Lewis, I.M. 1961: *A Pastoral Democracy: A Study of Pastoralism and Politics Among the Northern Somali of the Horn of Africa*, Oxford: Oxford University Press.
Lewis, I.M. 1988: *A Modern History of Somalia: Nation and State in the Horn of Africa*, Boulder, Colo: Westview Press.
Lewis, I.M. 1993: *Understanding Somalia: Guide to Culture, History and Social Institutions*, London: Haans Associates.
Lewis, I.M. 1994a: *Blood and Bone: The Call of Kinship in Somali Society*, Lawrenceville, NJ: The Red Sea Press.
Lewis, I.M. 1994b: *Peoples of the Horn of Africa: Somali, Afar and Saho*, London: HAAN.
Lyons, T. and Samatar, Ahmed I. 1995: *Somalia: State Collapse, Multilateral Intervention, and Strategies for Political Reconstruction*, Washington, DC: The Brookings Institution.
Marte, F. 1994: *Political Cycles in International Relations: The Cold War and Africa 1945-1990*, Amsterdam: VU University Press.
Mohamoud, A.A. 1993a: 'Somalia: Towards Pacification' in *West Africa*, 26 April–2 May, pp. 684–5.
Mohamoud, A.A. 1993b: 'Somalia: Why Peace Eludes Mogadishu' in *West Africa*, 11–17 October, pp. 1818–19.
Omaar, R. and Waal, A. de 1994: 'Can Military Intervention Be "Humanitarian"?' in *Middle East Report*, March–June, pp. 3–8.
Omar, M.O. 1992: *The Road to Zero: Somalia's Self-Destruction*, London: Haans Associates.
Sahnoun, M. 1994: *Somalia: The Missed Opportunities*, Washington, DC: United States Institute of Peace Press.
Samatar, Abdi I. 1989: *The State and Rural Transformation in Northern Somalia, 1886–1986*, Madison, Wisconsin: University of Wisconsin Press.
Samatar, Abdi I. 1992a: 'Destruction of State and Society in Somalia: Beyond the Tribal Convention' in *The Journal of Modern African Studies*, vol. 30, no. 4, pp. 625–41.
Samatar, Abdi I. 1992b: 'Dictators and Warlords are a Modern Invention' in *Africa News*, 21 December, 1992–3 January 1993.
Samatar, Ahmed I. 1988: *Socialist Somalia: Rhetoric and Reality*, London: Zed Books Ltd.
Samatar, Ahmed I. 1989: 'Somali Studies: Towards an Alternative Epistemology' in *Northeast African Studies*, vol. 11, no. 1, pp. 3–17.
Samatar, Ahmed I. 1991: *Somalia: A Nation in Turmoil*, London: Minority Rights Group.
Samatar, Ahmed I. 1993: 'Under Siege: Blood, Power, and the Somali State' in P. Anyang'Nyong'o (editor), *Arms and Daggers in the Heart of Africa: Studies on Internal Conflicts*, Nairobi: Academy Science Publishers.
Samatar, Ahmed I. (editor) 1994: *The Somali Challenge: From Catastrophe to Renewal?*, Boulder, Colo and London: Lynne Rienner.
Samatar, S.S. 1982: *Oral Poetry and Somali Nationalism: The Case of Sayyid Mahammad 'Abdille Hasan'*, Cambridge: Cambridge University Press.
Walle, N. van de 1996: 'The Politics of Aid Effectiveness' in S. Ellis (editor), *Africa Now: People, Policies and Institutions*, London: Heinemann.

9
Sri Lankan Futures: Conflicts, Alternatives and Twenty-First Century Possibilities[1]

Purnaka L. de Silva

By the end of the Cold War and the fall of the Berlin Wall, which symbolised the so-called 'Iron Curtain' dividing Eastern and Western Europe, Sri Lankan society (far removed from the global geopolitical dynamics of the time) was in the throes of two major theatres of, albeit low-intensity, conflict and warfare.[2] I examine here the lineage of these related though dissimilar conflicts (in brief) and then move on to a (selective) narrative exposé of enduring problems, followed by a discussion of future alternatives and possibilities beyond conflict.

Centuries-old processes of assimilation, integration and blood ties – in combination with 443 years of Portuguese (1505–1658), Dutch (1658–1802) and British (1802–1948) colonial rule – have given rise to a number of heterogeneous and hybrid social formations in Sri Lanka. In the present day, however, these formations have been homogenised, categorised and constructed – for administrative, cultural, historical and (contemporary) political purposes – according to four major divisions or 'ethnic groups', namely, *Sinhalese, Sri Lankan Tamil, Indian Tamil* and *Sri Lankan Muslim*. At the dawn of the twentieth century, the 'ethnically' diverse peoples of this Indian ocean island (who share a common heritage) face a stark choice: to continue with prolonged warfare between (Sinhala-majority) *unitary-nationalist* and (Tamil-minority) *separatist-nationalist* forces or to shape alternative futures beyond conflict.

Looking back to the late 1940s – when Sri Lanka (then Ceylon) was granted independence by imperial Britain – budding politicians belonging to local traditional élites inherited the mantle of executive and legislative power, in accordance with the dictates of 'parliamentary democracy'. It was during this formative period that the first seeds of the coming ethnocide and fratricide were sown. The simplistic model of Westminster 'parliamentary democracy' – involving periodic one–person-one-vote general elections, leading to victory for the (party) first past the post – could not work adequately. The seeds of future ethnic conflict were to be found within the practice of this model of predominantly electoral democracy – a conflict that has been raging with increased intensity in Sri Lanka since the 1970s.

Many post-colonial political élites have, in fact, perpetuated the systems, policies and finer mechanics of politics exercised by colonial rulers under the Machiavellian maxim *divide et impera* – in opposition to regular, multi-party and above all non-violent, free and fair elections, involving alternation of government – through their official parties and organisational praxis. These practices can be observed very vividly in South Asia and are pertinent to the conduct of daily affairs of state and influence the lives of millions. Over the span of fifty years, since the end of colonial rule in South Asia, there have been various attempts to 'stay in power at all costs', by the likes of Shrimati Indira Gandhi, General Zia Ul Haq and Junius Richard Jayawardene, among a plethora of national and provincial level actors. This has led to a brand of less-than-democratic electoral politics – ranging from different shades of 'constitutional' authoritarianism, demagoguery and majoritarian (politico-religious, ethnic and/or identity-based) supremacism to thuggery, opportunism and crass populism.

In Sri Lanka, Sinhala and Tamil traditional political élites and upper castes (*Goyigama*, *Radala* and *Vellala*)[3] have historically engaged in a growing competition for power and resources through the 'ethnicisation' of electoral politics. For example, post-independence intra-Sinhala power struggles – between the United National Party (UNP) and the Sri Lanka Freedom Party (SLFP) – included the 'scapegoating' and marginalisation of minority Tamils, which in turn aggravated ethnic discord and led to periodic anti-Tamil riots, first unleashed in 1956 and 1958. In this volatile context, the politics of numbers and identities involved in seemingly innocuous census statistics (the antecedents of which hark back to British colonial times – see Cohn 1987) that categorise, highlight and enumerate diversities are troublesome to say the least. In Sri Lanka such practices have long been embedded in the 'rights and wrongs' of contemporary political and cultural discourse, and is a basis for the 'authority of conventional wisdom'[4] – particularly through the representation of numbers in nationalist discourse (Appadurai 1993). The unproblematic and widespread use of statistical enumeration as being infallible, rather than being contested – either on the basis of contextual reality or methodological clarity – and delineated accordingly, has inadvertently fuelled the stereotyping and reification of the peoples of this island. A whole host of statisticians, bureaucrats, technocrats, journalists, politicians and academics alike participate in this process and, knowingly or unknowingly, substantiate the conventional 'wisdom' pertaining to demarcations, designations, stereotypes and populist perceptions of 'Otherness' – whether it be in terms of race, ethnicity, language, religion, culture, history, caste, class, politics, majorities or minorities. Moreover, the imagined infallibility of these practices contributes to the discourse of maintaining differences and divisions in what is effectively today a deeply divided society in which the trappings of a (separate) mini-state are being actively constructed – in parts of the hinterland in the north-central and south-eastern provinces (and along the eastern seaboard) – by the exclusionary and separatist-nationalist Tamil paramilitaries of the Liberation Tigers of Tamil Eelam[5] (LTTE).[6] Today, the ground reality is that the charismatic *Karayar* paramilitary supremo Velupillai Prabhakaran and his separatist-nationalist cohorts have considerable financial resources, armaments, power, prestige and a transnational logistical network – which amounts to *de facto* control over territory and the lives of untold numbers of people living in the eastern, north-central, north-western and northern provinces of Sri Lanka, not to mention the overseas Tamil diaspora.

Not so long ago, Sri Lanka was stereotypically portrayed as a stable, model democracy inhabited by friendly and fun-loving natives; a place in the sun reserved for enjoyment; an oasis in the so-called (poverty- and disease-ridden) 'Third World'; a virtual paradise for tourists and natives alike. According to this romantic mytho-history (see Bailey 1953), the prevalent stability and democracy were seen as attributes of the Westminster parliamentary system[7] (for more details see Wilson 1980). Echoes of this discourse can be heard even today, as in contemporary Britain during the July 1997 handover of Hong Kong to the People's Republic of China. From an indigenous perspective, the first (abortive) insurrection, mounted islandwide in April 1971 by the youthful Janatha Vimukthi Peramuna (JVP or the People's Liberation Front),[8] and its brutal suppression, cast the first doubts on the accuracy of this idyllic representation. These misgivings resurfaced around 1972 and thereafter, when politicised elements within the Tamil social formation also embarked upon a struggle – that is still ongoing – for a greater share of power and resources. This counter-hegemonic activism became more vocal and radical (especially among sections of militant youth) during and after the Sri Lankan army's initial occupation of the principal Tamil city of Jaffna in the northern peninsula, and following successive bouts of anti-Tamil rioting in 1971, 1977, 1979, 1981 and 1983. The JVP's second failed insurrection (August 1987 to mid-1990), was much 'closer to home' for many Sinhalese, in comparison to the relatively 'faraway war' being fought against 'the Tamils' (despite heavy casualties and infrastructural damage caused by occasional bombings and attacks in the capital city Colombo). It also brought a rude halt to any illusions *vis-à-vis* the notion of *dharmishta aanduwa* (just government). The only exceptions to those rudely awakened were possibly overseas tourists enjoying the experience of 'sun, sea and sand' along the southern and western coast, oblivious to daily extra-judicial executions and other death squad-related activities that were being conducted in the same region. In other words, paramilitary challenges were set in motion by politico-military groups within the Tamil and (in the recent past) Sinhala social formations, countering state power and hegemony. New technologies of war have created centres of power which (logistically overstretched) traditional structures of authority are unable to control, making the state's conventional monopoly of violence no longer absolute but an actively contested space.

Hegemony over state power, traditionally exercised by upper echelons within the Sinhalese social formation, has also eroded somewhat with time. An example of a new breed of politician who has emerged centre stage was the late President Ranasinghe Premadasa[9] – the first Sri Lankan head of state who was, class-wise and caste-wise, *not* from the traditional ruling political élite. With these changes, however, have come other unwelcome shifts in contemporary political culture and practice, with dire implications for the future, for example, the tendency by some newcomers to treat a career in politics and parliament (generally for life, unless assassinated in mid-stream) as a veritable business venture, which goes hand in hand with (high-level) bribery, corruption and (a new-look) gangsterism. The self-interest motives of such parliamentarians and their (high-living) cronies – in government bureaucracy (including influential elements within the armed services) and private sector big business – is to capitalise on the frustrations, ignorance, naivety and/or gullibility of respective constituencies during election time, in order to further their eventual profit-driven objectives. Ironically, such high-level corruption simply disregards ethnicity and the professed 'national interests' of the players. Last but not least, among militaristic decision-makers across the Sinhalese–Tamil divide, the favoured *modus operandi* is the assassination of political opponents and internal dissenters, which is fuelled by a tremendous intolerance of oppositional points of view, together with a total disregard for the rule of law and the tenets of the Geneva Convention.

Since the early 1970s then, Sri Lanka has seen the burgeoning of revolutionary struggles and nationalist fervour, from *putschist* attempts to capture state power to liberation and self-determination movements. In spite of all these complexities and obstacles, Tamil nationalism has endured in a variety of forms. From collaborationist-nationalisms (practised in the 1990s by the EPDP,[10] EPRLF,[11] PLOTE,[12] TELO[13] and breakaway factions – like the former EPRLF 'Rasik group' in the east and former PLOTE 'Mohan group' in the Jaffna peninsula, that operate as auxiliary units of the Sri Lankan armed services)[14] to chauvinist-separatism (typified by the Eelamist LTTE), it has come to be recognised as a force to be reckoned with, in the Sri Lankan politics of the 1990s and beyond. Underlying this phenomenon are structural changes to the constitution in 1978, which, combined with an authoritarian style of government, ensured the continued marginalisation of minority (Tamil and Muslim) aspirations. It is this phenomenon more than any other – that is, the potentially dangerous cocktail of narrow nationalist and parochial agendas, within a redefined electoral democracy that is commanded by an omnipotent executive presidency – which laid the seeds of exacerbated political conflicts and violence, the bitter fruits of which are being harvested today. In such circumstances, the task of shaping alternative futures beyond ethnic violence and armed conflicts is genuinely formidable. At the very least, working out a more viable future for Sri Lanka requires accommodating the aspirations of all ethnic groups, as well as facing the stark reality of the Sri Lankan predicament honestly.

Conflict and beyond: narrative perspectives

Highlighted in this section are certain experiential insights of Tamil paramilitaries-in-exile. These are presented in the form of selected verbatim narratives which deal with conflict-related issues viewed from the (at times emotion-laden) perspectives of former agents of political violence, which conclude with perceptions of how to establish a peaceful, multicultural and multiracial society in Sri Lanka. I have deliberately chosen paramilitaries from outside the hegemonic Jaffna-centric, pro-LTTE milieu, so that hitherto underepresented contradictions and nuances within Tamil paramilitary nationalism will become apparent. Three of these men[15] belong to a generation of paramilitaries born and bred in the eastern province districts of Ampara (Amparai) and

Batticaloa; they were active as field operatives (from the late 1970s to the early 1990s) and belonged to the middle-level leadership of the EPRLF. The fourth paramilitary belongs to a more recent generation, also from the east, who saw active service as a member of the LTTE. The ethnic, caste and class compositions of these particular Tamil paramilitaries provide clues as to some of the nuances alluded to above.

Uncommon for a nationalist Tamil paramilitary, *Thambi* (Premanatha) comes from a mixed Tamil–Sinhalese, lower-middle-class, professional cum land-owning family from the village of Karativu. His father is Batticaloa *Vellala*,[16] while his mother is Sinhalese *Goyigama* from the Matara district (located in the deep south and considered by Sinhala chauvinists to be their heartland). *Thambi* – like many other 'Tamil' paramilitaries of mixed lineage (predominantly from the eastern, north-central and north-western provinces) – is a 'nuanced' character, who defies any neat representation or facile Tamil nationalist generalisation which fits into a black and white image of 'the Sri Lankan ethnic conflict' (that is, between Sinhalese and Tamils). At the age of 15 he was arrested as a suspected Tamil paramilitary, tortured and imprisoned, and survived the prison massacres of July 1983 (where Tamil political prisoners were brutally murdered by Sinhalese inmates), subsequently escaping captivity in the legendary Batticaloa jail-break.

Of the other three former paramilitaries, *Raghu* (Archchunan) has a rural (peasant) working-class background and is from the village of Veeramunai. He belongs to the *Mukkuvar* matriclan, exogamous social formation, traditionally regarded as one of the lowest-ranking fishing castes among Batticaloa Tamils with a warrior ancestry, who originated from Malabar. Considering that *Raghu* has survived serious injuries sustained in an assassination attempt by the LTTE, his lack of malice and positive outlook are remarkable. *Bhaskaran* (Udayan) comes from a middle-class, land-owning family from Karativu, with Batticaloa *Vellala* antecedents. His dilemma is rather unique, with his fiancée having been killed by the LTTE, his father shot dead by Sri Lankan police commandos and his current wife's family having a history of supporting the LTTE. *Aravindan* (Ahilen), who belonged to the LTTE, comes from a mixed-caste, non-land-owning, lower-middle-class family of professionals. Relatives on his father's side are Batticaloa *Vellala* from Valaichchenai and include very senior LTTE field commanders in current service (1998). His mother's family are *Karayar* from the village of Araipattai and given the prevalent matriclan, exogamous family structure of Batticaloa, he is also considered to be *Karayar*. Ironically, his Sinhalese wife has an upper-middle-class, *Radala* family background and is reported to be a close relative of the current (hawkish) Sri Lankan Minister of Defence, Anuruddha Ratwatte.[17] Let me now allow these four former Tamil paramilitaries to speak for themselves.

Understanding the vexed question of revenge versus counter-revenge killings and underlying personal feelings and emotions – experienced by many paramilitaries and other agents of political violence – is an invaluable first step to conflict resolution and beyond. Here are some insights;

> (*Thambi*): Every step we took against them [LTTE] I was very happy. For how many of our cadres they killed? Just for nothing. So many clever, bright and committed young people. Bastards [LTTE]. They are innocent, they tried to do something [his comrades-in-arms]. That is the truth because that is the feeling we gave them. I don't know how many of them realised this, but we believed and they believe us. After the LTTE's attacks from December 1986, the first thing we thought to complete is revenge. That is the way we can go through this struggle. Somehow we must finish LTTE, only then we can do the struggle. But the party's line is not that. Because I thought *machang*,[18] they are killing the civilians and there are no possibilities to stop that without finishing them. We cannot put a full stop to that ... What I believe is over, once we went into this third class [electoral] politics ... Thereafter, I was with the party because I need to take revenge. Somehow, I like the party have to carry [*sic*] something forward, the party has to live ... Because they have to do something for our dead cadres, they lost their lives for something they believe.
>
> I don't believe this struggle is going to end in the Eelam, but I would like to see a peaceful democratic situation established by whoever comes to power; including the Tigers. I don't want any more the arms culture, arms in the hands of future children. What about revenge? That might die with us. If they [LTTE] come in a good line and if we excuse them; what is the difference between them and us? But I will never forget them till I die. I know that I am not going back till LTTE is there. Even if they come to the democratic level, because they spoil my identity. They give the picture to the people that we are very bad, we did everything wrong, we did and sacrificed our lives for ourselves. That's all *vera enna* [what else]? People are looking at us like that *machang*. If I go to my village, how many of them are going to respect me? Because I am in the party. I lost my studies, I lost my family,[19] I lost everything ... I might go one day but not for living. It is not easy *machang*, life. Everything I

have to do on my own, you see. You can't satisfy both ways *machang*. I can't satisfy my family and myself. They gave me a hand to come here finally, when I made up my mind to leave. That is the last favour I asked my father. But they are not expecting anything from me but they want me to do better in life. But I am still living in my memories. I don't even write to them *machang*. I have a few friends and I am happy. I did everything my own. I don't think that I am going to contribute in a direct manner again. Can't be a part of EPRLF any more. But I like EPRLF to survive. My identity is this, I don't know afterwards what will happen.

The next narrative involves some practice-oriented reflections, which includes an impression of the psycho-social dimension of post-conflict situations. If long-term problems posed by agents of political violence are to be adequately addressed, then it must involve a multidisciplinary response that is sensitive, flexible, holistic and honest.

(*Bhaskaran*) With all the changes taking place in the Eelam national liberation struggle, such as the attacks by the LTTE on the TELO and EPRLF in 1986 and the killings of our own Lebanon-trained comrades prior to these events, as well as the regional problems [Jaffna-centrism] within the running of the EPRLF, I felt very sad. Because at that time we haven't got enough arms as a result of the regional problem caused by Douglas [former head of the the EPRLF's military wing, and currently MP for Jaffna and leader of the EPDP], we could not resist the attacks by the Tigers. I began to hate the Tigers, along with all the others who had suffered at their hands. After 1986 we stopped fighting against the government because we couldn't do that and we began to eventually fight the Tigers who became the main enemy.

When I was first involved in operations and there were human casualties, I had no sympathy because they were our enemies and had to be destroyed. Now when I think back upon those events, I feel sad, that people had to lose their lives in vain, whether they be comrades or enemies. In wartime there is no good or bad. There is only bad. As far as the cadres of the Tigers who have been involved in acts of mass murder (stabbing and hacking to death of villagers) are concerned, they have been taught that through the killing of people they can achieve their objectives. Even we were taught when we got Indian training [provided clandestinely by the government of India], that if one of our comrades were killed that we should kill five people from the enemy side. However, in our party, it was politics that determined our actions and we were told not to kill innocent people. In the LTTE the killing of enemies has long been their driving force. I think however, that if these LTTE cadres get to live as long as we have, some of them too will regret their actions. They will be able to do so, only once they have been able to escape from the grip of the LTTE's ideology and look back at their past actions from without. I also think that these mass-murderer types need help, if and when peace comes. I hope that there will be some organisations who will help them. I think that if they do not get help, such people may get into the business of killing whenever they become angry.

For example, when I came to England from Sri Lanka, the anger I felt at the beginning is not the same as what I feel now. In the beginning when I went to work in a restaurant, there was very hard work and I couldn't speak English very well. There was far too much work, because we did not know English very well [sic]. So we had no choice but to stick it out despite the hard conditions. I was told immediately after finishing a job to get onto the next and so on. Therefore I used to get angry very much [sic] because our employers were cheating us and at these moments, I wanted to do something violently. The reason being, in Sri Lanka, we came out of a violent situation, and in our minds we had a high opinion of ourselves as former liberation fighters. Being in a violent situation back home, it was always easy to resort to violent action, to sort out our frustrations.

Now, I have cooled down a lot because the living situation has changed and we are thinking in a different way. Therefore, in order to sort out the frustrations and traumas of the mass murderers from the LTTE, their living situations must also change so that they can have the opportunity to cool down. And given the nature of their organisation and the type of struggle they waged, they will definitely need professional help too. A change in the living situation involves financial help to set up their own livelihoods, as well as a conducive environment that will help them cool down. In other words, their contact with the violent policies and tactics of the LTTE must come to an end. Without this of course, these young persons will continue to do violent actions, that they would in different circumstances, live to regret.

You know *machang*, I wanted to forget because I hate the fighting and other things. *Poratam verndaam* [no more struggle]. Especially *machang* because of killing each other. Internal problems. But you never let us forget. You come back to us every year and remind us.

I think *machang*, the Tamil people must be given powers equal to that enjoyed by Sinhalese. Nothing more or less. And also, the north and east should be made one province. Otherwise, all the liberation activities that have gone on for so long are pointless. [Question: *But aren't they pointless in a way after the internecine fighting among the Tamil liberation fighters?*] That is true. Our identities did change from the ideas we held at the beginning of the struggle. My idea is that if you give more power, the Tigers will come to a settlement. I think *machang*, the army cannot finish the Tigers. If they don't give more power, the fight continues for another ten years or more. It will continue. So, it is better to settle with the Tigers. There is no other choice because there are no alternative Tamil groups that can control the Tigers. If the Tigers got the power, maybe after two or three years there could be an election and maybe then the Tamil people will reject them. However, I don't think that the Tigers will allow ex-paramilitaries from other opposing groups to come and settle if they have power over the north-east of Sri Lanka. Personally I think that I am affected by both sides, by the government and the LTTE. But if I think about the Tamil people, they should get a solution. So, even if I cannot go back personally, a solution to the problem is what the Tamil people need. I think that most of the Tamil people are supporting the LTTE. In my eyes there are no regional differences. If the LTTE hands over its arms and there is a general demilitarisation, then maybe there is a possibility for the hundreds of exiled paramilitaries from other groups to come back. If they don't have arms and they come to a peace accord the LTTE cannot do anything. I think that the government has not done enough in the [Peace] Package that they have offered. They can't give Eelam but they can give more powers and maybe this can be the basis for a future settlement. Furthermore, as far as the behaviour of the Sri Lankan military personnel are concerned, they think more along the lines of Sinhala-ness and Tamil-ness, than a fight between say, the army and the Tigers. They have not changed their racist attitudes much, even under the Chandrika [Kumaratunga] government. If they want to separate the people and the Tigers, the army must support the Tamil people. If there are army casualties, then they must not take [sic] revenge from innocent people. If they do so continuously, then the people [sic] give their support to the Tigers. For example, the Tigers were in my village, Karativu. When they [LTTE] were withdrawing from the village on June 22, 1990, they threw a grenade at the Karativu junction. Nobody was injured, the Tigers were only making a brave show by making noise before withdrawing. However the army entered the village soon after and killed 160 people, one of them being my father. [Much of *Bhaskaran's* bitterness is, directed primarily against the Sri Lankan military and the STF in particular, and stems from this personal tragedy.]

As far as rehabilitation and reconstruction are concerned, financial support as well as education and training opportunities for employment, will help to change attitudes among paramilitaries from the LTTE. It is a problem however, though [sic] for other ex-paramilitaries from other organisations. Even whether the Tigers have or don't have power under a peace accord, their character is to destroy members of other paramilitary groups. How this kind of culture can be changed, I don't know. I hope that it will change over time. If Prabhakaran is dead, then maybe there is a better chance.

I still feel guilty about some of the things that I did in the movement. In that time, whatever we do, we think that we are doing for the Tamil people or for their betterment. But if we think now, whatever we did then was a waste. So sometimes, I think about those times and then worry, about those things, I ... did for nothing. *Pirosanayam ille* [no use] *machang*. When I went for operations, what was most important for me was my *iyyakkam* [movement/organisation], that we have to fight, we have to win, we have to do more operations, we have to win the war, including that against the Tigers. At that time, we want more arms, more powerful arms, more ammunition, more uniforms, more camouflage, etc. Because we believe in the armed struggle, so this was our priority (*mukyamana vishayam*). At that time *machang*, I am not believing in God. I am not going to temple, I am not praying. Now *machang*, we completely changed to another culture here [in Europe], back to normal. We are not fully normal but we pretend to be coming back to normal by following Hindu rituals. We go to the temple in Wales, observe religious festivities and rituals, make *pukkai* [milk rice] during *pongal* [*Thaipongal*, a Hindu festival], etc. But there is a difference between other civilian believers and myself, and it has to do with a question of morality. I think that what it means to be a human being depends on the situation where that person is. If they live in a war situation, they are fully involved with that situation. But even if these persons leave the war situation, the past concerning the war touches them. There is no escape. It is a question of morality, something that even cadres of the LTTE have to deal with. You cannot forget the past, it is something that we have to learn to live with. I have dreams *machang*, always, that the army comes and catches me or that the Tigers come and shoot me. Different, different dreams, in different locations. Sometimes, my friends are killed or I kill or am killed myself, and wake up to find myself lying on my bed. I have seen *Nabha, Kirupa, Muhundan*, [the EPRLF leader and two senior comrades who were assassinated by the LTTE] everybody. Because *machang*, because we didn't see the body [*sic*], we think in our dreams that they are alive. Shooting and shooting and not killing, running, running, running but can't escape. I think that ex-paramilitaries like ourselves need to learn how to cope with these traumas.

For politico-military conflicts in Sri Lanka to be overcome comprehensively, then as pointed out below, underlying politico-religious considerations also need to be addressed, honestly and earnestly, leading to societal/national reconciliation, and the accommodation of difference and 'Otherness'.

(*Raghu*) There can be no peace in Sri Lanka unless it originates from the *Mahanayaka Theros* [chief priests, held in the highest veneration by the majority Sinhalese Buddhists] residing in the *Dalada Maligawa* [Temple of the Tooth Relic in Kandy, one of the holiest sites of Sri Lankan Theravada Buddhism] as well as other key decision-makers. Peace must be based upon the justice of the Three Jewels of the Buddhist religion, namely, the Buddha, the *Dhamma* and the *Sangha*.[20] The reason is that from the time that Sri Lanka achieved its independence till 1996, the loss of lives and material damage caused so far are the responsibility of the *Mahanayake Theros* and Sinhala and Tamil politicians. When teaching school children geography, they should not be taught from maps on walls. There must be compulsory efforts to encourage Sinhala school children to travel to places like Jaffna, Batticaloa, Vavuniya, Mannar, Trincomalee, etc. [towns or cities of political, religious or economic significance in regions where a greater proportion of the local population are Tamils]. And for Tamil and Muslim children to travel to places like Galle, Kandy, Ratnapura, Anuradhapura, Kurunegala, etc. [towns or cities of political, religious or economic significance in regions where the Sinhalese are predominant]. And this must not be restricted only to children, there must a friendly atmosphere of exchange, cooperation and understanding that stimulates travel and communication between all Sri Lankan peoples, from all regions and walks of life. We must bring an end to mistrust, suspicion, racist prejudice and stereotyping. The dead and injured, belong to all sides. And to stop this, there is nobody on the Tamil side. Because of the parochial politics of Tamil politicians, *kutti arasiyalvaadihal* [small-time politicians]. As long as they remain in positions of power nothing is going to change in the short term. Therefore it is up to the majority people [Sinhalese] to make the peace. And this peace must originate from the steps of the *Dalada Maligawa*. It is only with a decision and support made there and handed over to the Sinhala politicians, that stands a chance of long-term success. The *Mahanayakas* must take responsibility for all the peoples of Sri Lanka and present an equitable proposal, based upon the full backing of Sri Lanka's Buddhist establishment, with a view to resolving the conflict. This decision must include all the virtues stipulated in the *Buddha Dhamma* [Buddhist Doctrine].

I end this set of verbatim narratives with some rather pointed opinions voiced by a member of a younger generation of Tamils, who today form the bulk of those paramilitaries currently engaged in the combat zones of Sri Lanka.

(*Aravindan*) And now, I am 23, I am in London, I had some education, I read a lot and I have some idea about the international community and most importantly, I know about the value of humanity. I do worry about the boys [paramilitaries] and army who are still fighting. I do really worry about them. For nothing, they lose their valuable lives, because of funny political games. We are Sri Lankans, I am very proud to say that, rather than to say we are refugees. Unfortunately, in the foreign countries, Sri Lankans are refugees, cheap labourers and housemaids, and they are killers. I started to think positively nowadays, which is that we are fighting for nothing. Our country is very small, it is a small island. The people who live there have the same colour, similar religion and language. Of course the politicians from both sides play the game for their own profit and they use the youngsters towards these ends, in a death game. I believe the civilians on both sides started to think about the peace.

Now the problem is only between the Tigers (which is a very strong weapons group) and the army and government. I think that nowadays it is a prestige problem as to who will win. Nobody care about the civilians and about who will lose their lives. Both sides never trust each other because there are strong grounds for mistrust. But for this dirty game, why we have to give these young boy's [sic] lives from both sides? How many politicians and how many rebel leaders are willing to send their children to the battlefield? From this Tamil side, all the poor boys and the boys who live without safety, go to battle, and from the Sinhalese side, the boys who are unemployed and the poor people from the villages go and die. So what is the end? How can we end this problem now?

I really don't want to talk about the past. I want to talk about the future. How can we sort things out? When I was sixteen, I feel that I must kill all the Sinhalese. Six years later, now, my wife is Sinhalese. I have got seven Sinhalese brothers and two sisters.[21] And my mother-in-law is Sinhalese. And my wife is also the other way around. She got brothers-in-law who are Tamil. So in this six years if I can change all the way around, then why can't the other people change? What we have to do for them? Let them understand each other's problems, their life standards in Sri Lanka, multiculturalism in other countries (like Singapore) and how happily they live. I don't believe any political parties or revolutionary organisations. I believe the ordinary [folk] who know the value of humanity, they can take the job to enable people to understand. It is a very hard job. You have to suffer a lot. Maybe you can be killed or hurt a lot. But rather than just sit there and talk about the revolution it is better to do something. Don't take any weapons, don't talk about any political solution now. Just try and introduce them [civilians] to each other and try and make them to see one another and talk to each other. For example, the main questions have to be why, when, what and how. Try and find positive answers. Try and introduce the people who live together from both communities. Try and start from the schools, from the low education. Go to the villages, talk to the boy's [sic] mothers. Tell them what is going on. And tell them what is the value of our country and what we can do without this country and where we can go. Tell them about countries like Japan, after the second world war of how they managed to get back to normal. Tell them about Singapore, Malaysia, Mauritius. That is only the first step.

The second step is that with that understanding, whether any party or group likes it or not, we must tell that there must be respect for all communities, languages, religions and peoples. Don't talk about separate country, but we can do as like the other countries did (Malaysia), to give self rule to all [9] provinces. If we need it, we can ask international observers to help our schools and if we want to pass the [secondary school] O/L exam, we must pass both languages, Sinhala and Tamil. Support mixed marriages, exchange of peoples living in different regions. It is a long task, but it can be done. We got a very long, nice history, we follow some of the best religions in the world, Hinduism and Buddhism. Back to our history all these people love each other and fight together against colonialism and they have lived together. I believe, 75 per cent of people who live in Sri Lanka, like to live together without any problems. All they need is a guarantee of peace and stability. We people, who love humanity and the people come join together and work for the peace. Not work together with any groups, parties. We work alone and go and meet the ordinary people, through TV, newspapers, radios and public meetings and tell them, that we believe from our experience it is possible to bring peace. I believe the boys who live with me now and whom I know, most of them are Tamil, they are ready to work for it. Can anyone from Sri Lanka? Now I am 23 and I am ashamed for the things I did before and now I want to do something for my country. I no longer want to live like a refugee.

The non-LTTE paramilitary perspectives represented above will at the very least provide food for thought, to politicians, power-brokers, policy-makers and bureaucrats (local and international), currently involved in one way or another with the problematic of the ongoing conflict between the government and the LTTE. A wider examination of the Western European Tamil diaspora, might very well present pro-LTTE, Jaffna-centric perspectives as well. Nevertheless, what is clear is that in any deeply divided society, which has to contend with exigencies of political violence and conflict, there is much war-related psycho-social trauma, hatred along with revenge, and counter-revenge mentalities that have become 'normal' due to the effects of brutalisation (de Silva 1995,1997a,b,c).[22] These problems need to be researched, understood and taken note of in detail, a daunting but necessary task in contemporary post-Cold War global political culture, where the media magic of sound bites, slogans and other rhetorical devices rule. If such problems are understood through a long-term perspective and in all their complexity, as illustrated in part by the above narratives, then it would be clear that long-term counter-measures are not only logical but financially sound practice.

The basis for alternative futures

In a so-called 'era of post-nationalism', conflicts between competing nationalisms have endured and new identity-based conflicts have also emerged, as in countries of the former Soviet Union. And in Sri Lanka, contemporary militarisation of the body politic and bloody hegemonic versus counter-hegemonic conflicts, along with war-related kickbacks and commission-taking (the government of Sri Lanka spends an average of 50 billion rupees a year on military procurements), have led to the continuation of politics by other means and incalculable costs. However unpalatable it might be for nationalists of the majoritarian variety (which includes majority Sinhala Buddhists *and* minority Sinhala Christians) or their collaborationist-nationalist Tamil paramilitary allies, the reality on the ground is that the separatist-nationalist LTTE has *de facto* control over land and resources (both human and material). Moreover, substantial popularity and sustenance from among a largely chauvinist (Jaffna-centric) Tamil diaspora that is plugged into an efficient global support network helps the LTTE to solve logistical problems, resupply its arsenal and access new technologies of warfare. Thus far, the logic of militarism, continuing conditions of political antagonism and their relational practices have served the LTTE in good stead. Nevertheless, the ongoing stalemate has been costly for both sides, in terms of daily depletion of resources (human and material) through combat and drastic reduction of (much-needed) volunteer recruits. The bulk of the LTTE's paramilitary fighters now live in malaria-infested jungles – south of Elephant Pass, north of Trincomalee and Vavuniya and east of Mannar, as well as in the eastern districts (down to the Yala game sanctuary in the south-east) – with lack of access to conventional medical and surgical facilities. The morale of the (predominantly Sinhalese) Sri Lankan armed services has also been seriously dented, signified by literally thousands of desertions. For a graphic display of the background to the present military stalemate, see Figure 9.1.

On the humanitarian side, there is a desperate need for a political settlement, to bring about a lasting cease-fire and resolve the ongoing conflict, in order to end needless loss of life and horrific injuries (both physical and psychological) inflicted on combatants and civilians alike.[23] In other words, there is a dire need to support all efforts at demilitarisation, disarmament, decommissioning of weapons stockpiles, demobilisation, reintegration, rehabilitation and reconstruction. The Sri Lankan crisis has been nominally ameliorated, with the elec-

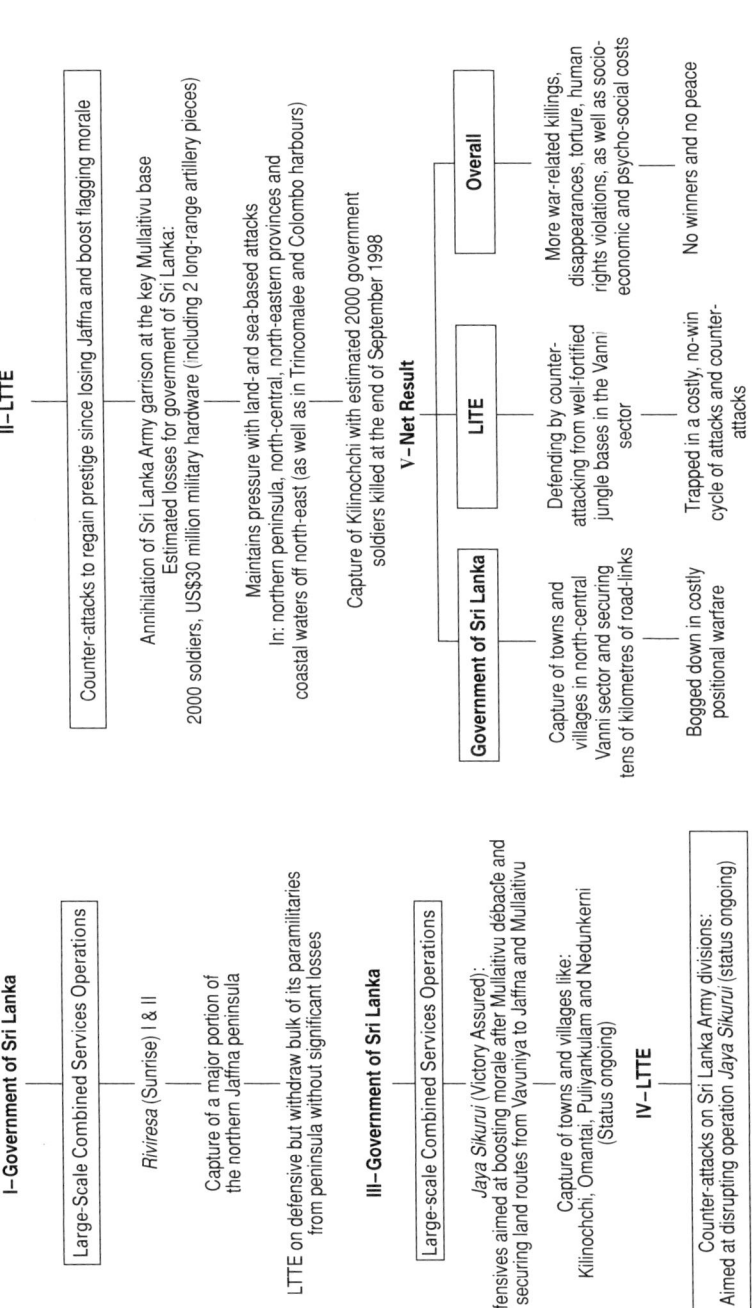

Figure 9.1 Background to Military Statement, September 1998

tion of an eleven-party, centre-left, People's Alliance (PA) coalition government in 1994, which was elected to office on a peace and reform platform. Moving towards overcoming the crises at hand will however require a great many changes to be implemented (not only in practice but also in approach) – in contrast to well-worn paths of authoritarianism, lack of consultation, arbitrary policy decisions, intrigue, corruption and eventual political insecurity, that cumulatively lead to and nurture the corrosive hatreds of the recent past. Alternative and more positive processes of democratic change, responsible government and conflict resolution (as advanced in the PA's election manifesto) must involve not only aspects of dialogue, mediation and negotiation, but also a long-term perspective geared towards reasonably equitable peace, reconciliation and justice.

The terms of what constitutes 'reasonable equity' over the long term is of course open to interpretation and negotiation, and is therefore relational to the outcome of talks between the protagonists, not to mention the skill of mediators. The process of long-term peace, reconciliation and justice, initiated in post-apartheid South Africa and given expression through the Truth and Reconciliation Commission (TRC), is a perfect illustration of what was considered by the protagonists to be reasonably equitable at the time, for that country. There the Commission can grant amnesty to perpetrators, if it decides that confessions divulge the complete story (including roles of accomplices) and crimes (of commission or omission) were politically motivated (on behalf of a recognised political organisation). However, there is no single blueprint that can be applied *carte blanche* to engineer the short, medium- or long-term resolution of every conflict, without considering diverse and complex factors, ranging from differences in political, historical and cultural contexts to the personalities and idiosyncrasies of key players. Statesmanship is a rare commodity in contemporary politics the world over and not everyone can be as wise, broad-minded, accommodating, long-sighted, skilled in the arts of government, charismatic and therefore as successful as Nelson Mandela or Mahatma Gandhi. Nevertheless, if human social formations are to evolve to a higher plane of civilisational existence and humane governance in the twenty-first century, then all (positive) efforts, even by those less than ideal, can point the way towards progress and fulfilment of such an ambition.

While the above is a noble ideal of global proportions, it needs to be fleshed out by getting down to the nitty-gritty of the Sri Lankan context. First and foremost, a multi-partisan consensual approach on the side of the political parties represented in the Sri Lankan parliament is essential from the inception of such a venture – so that a united negotiating position can be garnered, in order to cope with the problem posed by the separatist-nationalist LTTE and to reach a reasonably equitable settlement to 'the Tamil question'. And a basis for achieving such an accord over the long term *vis-à-vis* peace, reconciliation and justice must involve not only legalities but also the spirit of reconciliation, amnesty and generosity on the part of most, if not all, parties to the conflict. It definitely must not be part of cynical attempts to gain strategic advantages on the military playing field – which has in any case never offered constructive hope to the beleaguered islanders who are championed, only years of blood-letting, violent struggle and sacrifice. The process of gaining and reciprocating trust is an integral component of reconciliation. For long-term peace to be a viable option in Sri Lanka (or Eelam for that matter), special attention and care must be given to resolving problems of demilitarisation, disarmament, decommissioning of weapons stockpiles, clearing landmines, demobilisation and reintegration of agents of political violence, as well as catering to the psycho-social needs of erstwhile combatants and non-combatant civilians (war-affected women, men, teenagers, children, the elderly and the disabled), together with post-conflict rehabilitation and infrastructural reconstruction. These activities also need new practical perspectives of democracy, which can only take effect in a permissive environment that is created through a politics of conscience, humane understanding, negotiated compromise, accommodation of difference and above all, good faith. It must involve all parties and political groupings, to ensure that political violence and conflict, as a means to an end, has no mandate. In other words, practical democracy entails a new ethical politics that overcomes petty, short-term manoeuvrings of narrowly defined 'electoral democracy' (a legacy of the Westminster model).

The recent bipartisan protocol signed on 3 April 1997 (reportedly after prodding by British Foreign Service emissaries from the outgoing Tory administration of John Major) between the PA coalition government's leader President Kumaratunga and the UNP's Ranil Wickremasinghe (leader of the parliamentary opposition) seems to point in the right direction. On 9 August 1997 Professor G.L. Peiris (Minister of Justice, Constitutional Affairs, Ethnic Affairs and National Integration) was quoted in the *Daily News*, stating that 'the government would talk to the LTTE only after the Tigers agreed to discuss a political solution *within a set time limit and a basis for such talks was worked out with the UNP'* (emphasis added). These efforts at generating a common negotiating position, though unsuccessful so far due to the parochial character of Sri Lankan politics, must not dishearten those involved, whose activities should also be extended so as to encompass all the partners of the eleven-party PA coalition government. The evolution of such a broad-based consensus must tend to the mechanics of what each party wants, as well as understand how far each one is willing to extend and accommodate oppositional or contentious points of view. This must also involve a clear assessment of the capabilities and limitations of the personalities chosen to represent the Sri Lankan parliamentary perspective, together with the development of close, professional working ties between them. It is only after a thorough understanding and review of such issues – worked out in some sort of binding fashion – that parties to such an agreement can begin to cope with the LTTE's negotiating position, in a convincing and empowered fashion.

Understanding the LTTE

In the process of drawing up a flexible equation capable of satisfying some, if not all, aspirations of the protagonists – while taking into consideration macro-level realities, costs of protracted warfare and local actualities on the ground – other factors that need to be studied in serious fashion include the future of the unitary state. To do this, a comprehensive understanding of the character and make-up of the LTTE is *sine qua non*. Here, mediators and negotiators must comprehend a crucial factor, that Prabhakaran *is* the Chief Executive Officer (CEO) of his organisation. There is no second-tier leadership within the LTTE that is empowered to negotiate, except either by name or in order to rubber-stamp the supremo's orders. The brutal 'removal' of *Mahattaya* and many other charismatic figures within the LTTE's original second-tier hierarchy (through executions and 'missions impossible' over the years) is a grim reminder of the operational character of Prabhakaran, who is an almost Macbethian figure, with blood on his hands and ghosts looking over his shoulder. None of the young teenage cadres of today, who die willingly at the behest of their near-godlike leader, nor most of their older field commanders, have either the stature or background to countermand or contest Prabhakaran's grand narrative – of establishing a separate, sovereign state of Eelam. In other words, the LTTE's negotiating position is indistinguishable from the wants and needs of its leader. Therefore, without directly engaging the LTTE's CEO in the dialogic, mediatory or negotiating process – and ultimately getting him to participate as a signatory to a legally binding document under national or international law – progress and a positive outcome would be minimal if not worthless.

A related factor of equal significance is that the LTTE's CEO controls an awesome income or profit-generating capacity that easily runs into millions of US dollars every month. Not surprisingly, the LTTE has a huge portfolio of investments not just in Sri Lanka, but also in India, South East Asia, Europe, North America and Australasia, as well as venture capital in offshore facilities, with access to money-laundering facilities. The organisation's main sources of income involve:

- monthly or weekly collection of 'donations' and 'taxes' from the Tamil diaspora (made up of refugees, business entrepreneurs, professionals and blue-collar workers);
- monthly or weekly collection of 'donations' and 'taxes' from nationwide or provincial Tamil business houses, wealthy merchants, professionals, landowners, agriculturalists and general citizenry in Sri Lanka;
- smuggling of people of Sri Lankan/South Asian origin (predominantly Tamil) by air, sea and overland to countries in the European Union (EU), Australasia and North America, as well as to countries in East Asia, the former Soviet bloc, the Middle East, North and West Africa or any other location on the globe that can serve as a staging post to an asylum-granting 'developed country';
- general smuggling of contraband (defined as per international excise and customs regulations) and other banned substances, including narcotics (primarily heroin and derivatives) and black-market weaponry;
- sales of propaganda-related material (videos, compact discs, music cassettes, wrist watches, publications, periodicals, newspapers);
- collections made during Tamil cultural events, religious festivals, commemorative happenings or showing of video footage at places of worship, schools, mini-cinemas and other public spaces (mostly outside Sri Lanka).

Given Prabhakaran's secure organisational position, considering the resources at hand, including his cadres' prowess on and off the battlefield and his historical intransigence to any reasonable alternative to an 'all or nothing' option, the future looks set for a long-drawn, protracted conflict that will slowly but surely bleed the

Sinhalese and Tamil social formations, not to mention the Muslims, over the long term and on all fronts. The LTTE supremo's relatively young age, good health and penchant for personal security implies a scenario where he will survive the exigencies of warfare over a long term, unless his enemies get lucky. Therefore, his presence and continued existence, as a key source to establishing peace, is a position from which negotiators or mediators must begin their considerations. Thereafter, for a viable agreement to be accepted and implemented, a second vital step is to understand the self-interest motives of key players. I perceive three major blocs, along with a number of ancillary players of varying importance, who also need to be accommodated,[24] including non-governmental actors with a proven track record and popular mandate:[25]

1. the position of the representatives of the Sri Lankan parliament (and their Tamil nationalist collaborators);
2. the position of Prabhakaran and the LTTE;
3. the position of host governments, where the predominantly Tamil Sri Lankan diaspora reside, particularly in the EU, Canada, the United States of America, Norway, Switzerland, Australia and New Zealand on the one hand (henceforth referred to as bloc 3a); and India, Malaysia, Singapore and Thailand on the other (henceforth referred to as bloc 3b).

A cross-section of (at times contradictory) self-interested motives are discernible in relation to the first category of key players, in a marriage of convenience between (moderate) Sinhala unitary-nationalist and Tamil collaborationist-nationalist forces. Within this more or less amicable union there are two extremes or tendencies:

- advocates of an *inviolate unitary state* that is organised and managed in the greater interest of the majority of Sri Lankans (that is, Sinhalese Buddhists), but simultaneously accommodative of some of the wants and needs of the Tamil polity (within a single Sri Lankan entity);
- anti-LTTE Tamil nationalists, who advocate an *undivided northeastern province or traditional Tamil homeland* – a politico-geographical entity that must be recognised constitutionally (albeit within the boundaries of the Sri Lankan nation state) under a multifaceted package of reforms involving the actual devolution of powers and resources.

Despite apparent contradictions and rhetorics of discord in the above positions (interparty as well as intraparty), it is quite possible – with a little give and take on all sides – for forces loyal to this primary bloc to reach some sort of reasonably equitable settlement. Such an agreement could possibly be fashioned within a 'federated' system of provincial government, particularly when considering this matter from the light of the pragmatic political, military and intelligence cooperation that continues to exist (from the late 1980s on) between successive governments and anti-LTTE collaborationist-nationalist Tamil paramilitaries. An interim settlement along these lines could be made more successful and stable, with the help, cooperation and generosity of influential sections of civil society – not least the *Mahanayake Theros* and respected non-governmental actors. Reaching such a consensus, however 'difficult' it might be in practice, is the 'easy' part. Most of the parties within this bloc would welcome demilitarisation, disarmament, decommissioning of weapons stockpiles and demobilisation, together with a reintegration, rehabilitation and reconstruction package and an end to political violence, in exchange for peace, security and possible future socio-economic prosperity. However, for long-term peace to take effect, this bloc must also successfully negotiate and reach a reasonably equitable accord with Prabhakaran and his exclusionary, separatist-nationalist paramilitaries.

For the LTTE's CEO – whatever the outcome of his organisation's war efforts and professed intentions of setting up an exclusively Tamil, sovereign separate state of 'Tamil Eelam' – the first priority would be to secure his own position and safety at the helm of the postwar Tamil polity. Therefore, any deal that might ensue from dialogue, mediation or negotiations with Prabhakaran and the LTTE must cater to this requirement in good faith (however unpalatable for those opponents who seek retribution and punitive justice). If the South African case is to be taken as an example, it is quite similar to the accommodation of the Inkatha Freedom Party's (IFP's) Chief Mangosuthu G. Buthelezi of the Zulu royal house, within the folds of the first post-apartheid regime. This is in spite of all the terrible blood-letting, massacres and revenge/counter-revenge mentalities which had existed between Mandela's ANC and Buthelezi's IFP. The second priority for Prabhakaran would be to maximise the LTTE's claim towards separate statehood. I cannot predict what the outcome to this demand will be, considering the LTTE's legendary intransigence over the issue and particularly since previously rejected proposals had all but granted the LTTE 'limited control' of the north and east on a silver platter. One matter though is more or less certain here; Prabhakaran and the LTTE are not open to power-sharing or pluralism. Considering this, the Tamil population at large seem most likely to be the recipients of an authoritarian/puritanical one-party state – that is, if the secondary aspirations of the LTTE and its CEO come to fruition. Whether or not the LTTE's CEO will accept any alternative proposition in exchange for long-term peace, reconciliation and justice depends wholly on what there is on offer.

By way of contrast, in similar situations elsewhere in the Indian sub-continent, as in the cases of Kashmir in the north, and Assam, Manipur, Nagaland and Tripura in the east of India, small-scale initiatives and cheap palliatives aimed at weaning insurgents away from political violence and confrontation with the state and into gainful, economically viable occupations have been mooted. Such proposals cater to local economic needs and the sustenance of rebels (and would-be rebels) through the establishment of self-employment enterprises with private and state sector help (for example, the supply of sewing machines to set up tailoring outlets) and provision of other work opportunities in the public sector, corporations and state police, together with initiatives such as the supply of medical vans for first-aid purposes and scholarships for educational and prevocational training.

Such small-scale efforts would probably fail in north and east Sri Lanka. The first of two primary stumbling blocks here is the LTTE's economic self-sufficiency and phenomenal income-generating capacity. The second is Prabhakaran's negative stance towards all attempts or schemes perceived to dilute his primacy, authority and hegemony. This position applies not only to the LTTE's fighting cadre and the Tamil people at large, but also to non-LTTE or anti-LTTE paramilitaries and all political opponents – who are actively barred from access and freedom to participate in Tamil socio-economic and politico-cultural life – through threats, coercion, press-ganging[26] or worse. Therefore any government-sponsored measure to provide economic sustenance to former combatants or rejuvenate the defunct civilian administration in areas inhabited predominantly by Tamils is bound to be resisted. As in previous attempts at demobilisation, voluntary or otherwise induced, Prabhakaran has revoked 'agreements' to which his organisation was a signatory (for example, the failed Indo-Sri Lanka Peace Accord or in less formal agreements, as with the late Sri Lankan President Premadasa).

The LTTE's considerable economic strength, relative self-sufficiency and military sophistication (in comparison with rebels from Kashmir,

Assam, Manipur, Nagaland or Tripura) means that any direct or third-party attempt to win Prabhakaran over to the side of negotiation, conciliation, accommodation and compromise must involve the wider issues of a comprehensive peace settlement. While ironing out the terms of such a large-scale initiative, a compromise, half-way solution could be to position small-scale palliatives aimed at individual or small groups of Tamil paramilitaries within the framework of an integrated rural development programme (IRDP). Such programmes aimed at creating post-conflict socio-economic realities should be administered and funded by overseas donor/lending agencies, development-oriented non-governmental organisations belonging to countries from bloc 3a and/or South East Asia, and/or multilateral institutions such as the World Bank, IMF, UN, ADB and Soros (Open Society) Foundation. Since the LTTE leadership would not overtly want to risk antagonising or terrorising non-Sri Lankan IRDP managers and/or politicians in the bloc 3a and South East Asian countries, an interim strategy like this would be somewhat protected – primarily because the LTTE uses these countries as staging posts in its strategic global network. This rule of thumb would not necessarily apply to the case of initiatives put forward by the government of either Sri Lanka or India, considering their role as protagonists (past or present), unless and until there are cast-iron guarantees made by the LTTE's CEO to convince them otherwise. Whatever the merits of such an interim approach, the thorny issue of progressing towards a comprehensive peace package remains, however, a vexed question – an interminable 'chicken and egg' situation. For without a comprehensive settlement, acceptable to all parties within the bounds of reasoned choice and made in an environment free of coercion or intimidation, short-term, piecemeal palliatives will not resolve the conflict. They can at best alleviate difficulties of but a portion of society. A future alternative to the dialogic and military impasse in Sri Lanka is for an altogether new approach and it is here that key movers belonging to bloc 3a can come into play, possibly limiting their role to one of underwriting or simply bank-rolling post-conflict scenarios, if they so wish.

There are also a couple of other local specificities and regional considerations (that is, the role of India, Malaysia, Singapore and Thailand) that need attention. First of all a potentially explosive local issue is that the borders and status of the eastern province have to be clearly defined and demarcated, taking into account the aspirations of its Sinhalese and Muslim inhabitants, who make up more than 50 per cent of the local population on average and who have no wish to be governed by an LTTE-led administration (provincial or otherwise). Depending on how negotiations develop, it might be possible to defuse this issue by adopting a strategy similar to that of the American-sponsored Dayton Peace Accord, which carved up Bosnia–Hercegovina (somewhat unsatisfactorily) between bitterly divided Serbs, Croats and Muslims. Other options might include demilitarised mini-buffer-zones between three social formations (Sinhalese, Tamil and Muslim) and peacekeeping by (non-Indian or Pakistani)[27] South Asian or South East Asian regional forces – the costs of which need to be covered, possibly over the long term, through assistance from the developed countries identified in bloc 3a and multilateral agencies. Success of such operations depend on ground realities, such as the ability to contain ceasefire violations through dialogue and maintain law and order in spaces where there is considerable tension and overlap in the day-to-day activities of all three social formations.

Foremost among bloc 3b regional considerations are Indian security interests. A great fear among Indian policy-wallahs is the possibility of separatism, as in north and east Sri Lanka, catching on in the mainland – which could, in a hypothetical worst-case scenario, spark off the beginning of the end for the unitary character of the Republic of India given its extremely heterogeneous composition.[28] Furthermore, the LTTE (allegedly) assassinated a possible Indian head of state, former Prime Minister Rajiv Gandhi (then head of Congress-I and leader of the opposition), and even trained and supplied weapons to a number of anti-Indian, separatist insurgent groups – particularly after the induction of the Indian Peace Keeping Force (IPKF) in 1987 to supervise the Indo-Sri Lanka Peace Accord, and subsequent fighting between the Indian peacekeepers and LTTE paramilitaries. Insurgent groups (allegedly) patronised by the LTTE include:

1. In Tamil Nadu: Viduthalai Kulihal (a literal translation would be the 'Liberation Cuckoos', a group headed by Suba Veerapandian – in spoken Tamil, 'Kulihal' rhymes with 'Pulihal', a reference to 'the Tigers', the feared *nom de guerre* of the LTTE); Thamilar Pasarai (or Tamilian Camp, a group linked to P. Nedumaran, leader of the Tamil Nadu Kamaraj Congress, a long-standing supporter and personal friend of Prabhakaran); '*Thileepan*[29] *Mandram*' (or Thileepan Foundation, a group led by 'Thiagu'); and *Thamil Theseeya Meedpu Padai* (Tamil National Retrieval Troops or TNRT);
2. In Andhra Pradesh: a faction of the People's War Group (PWG) led by Kondapalliseetharaman;

3. In Assam and Nagaland: the United Liberation Front of Assam (ULFA) and National Socialist Council of Nagaland.

The LTTE also has substantial commercial interests, both legal and illegal, in each of the bloc 3b countries, often in collaboration with local partners, who are prominent business personalities – a number of whom are sympathetic or at least not-antagonistic to Prabhakaran's separatist-nationalist cause. Any long-term peace and reform package must therefore envisage not only a negotiated end to the LTTE's alleged illegal activities in the region, but also consider possibilities of tapping into private capital sources to fund part of the rehabilitation and reconstruction effort. In contrast to other South East Asian countries, India and Thailand also need to link the question of repatriating Tamil refugees to such an agreement. Coming to terms with the possibility of Prabhakaran's future leadership of a post-war Tamil polity and coping with its impact is a factor that Sri Lanka's bloc 3b neighbours need to consider thoroughly.

Foundations for a viable future

It is an imperative for shaping viable futures in Sri Lanka that a new ethics and moral conduct of good governance – which includes transparency in government and politics – be initiated. As an initial measure of taking up this ethical and political challenge in what will prove to be a long-term, future-oriented process, custodians of state power must, at the very minimum, implement the following propositions. Such steps will illustrate in no uncertain terms to the peoples of Sri Lanka and the wider diaspora of Sri Lankans in Europe and elsewhere, as well as global onlookers and multilateral institutions – such as the EU, the World Bank, Amnesty International, Human Rights Watch, Transparency International[30] – that meaningful and positive change has been initiated for the benefit and long-term peace of future generations.

1. *Bringing to account members of death squads*, particularly those who were affiliated with the Sri Lankan armed services (some of whom are still in operational units), either through the judicial system (punitively) or via a scheme of truth and reconciliation (as in post-apartheid South Africa). In any future peace agreement with the LTTE this aspect of accountability – in relation to war crimes, crimes against humanity and violations of human rights, perpetrated by all agents of

political violence (including members of that organisation) – must also be brought before full public view. Such a mechanism or 'ritual' of serious accounting of atrocities is part and parcel of national reconciliation (at all levels – including the psycho-social dimension, where victims and perpetrators need to be involved in a healing process of reconciliation, forgiveness, remorse and generosity);

2. *Creation of a more cosmopolitan and inclusive Sri Lankan armed services recruitment policy*, along with compulsory national service, particularly in order to educate the country's middle- and upper-class armchair warmongers of the actualities and pains in situations of warfare and mortal combat;

3. *Implementing the right to free media and other forms of public expression*, particularly in the realm of politics, which is in accordance with internationally accepted standards of democracy to which Sri Lanka is a signatory. Censorship or distortion of information and news concerning actualities pertaining to war-related misdemeanours and crimes (including those of omission and commission), not made public knowledge, is unhealthy for the evolution of any democracy, and therefore the media, unhindered, must play their designated societal role in fashioning transparency, professionally and responsibly – provided that they do not transgress boundaries of individual freedoms, such as the right to privacy;

4. *Eradication of corruption and ethical malpractice* within all levels of government – including the armed services and police – as well as within national and local trading cum commercial circles in relation to bribery, commission-taking and misuse of authority (such as political favouritism and nepotism in appointments and promotions, including politically or personally motivated demotions and punishment transfers);

5. *Increased transparency and fiscal scrutiny* where all senior government officials and private sector moguls are obliged by law to declare convertible and non-convertible assets, and are liable to stringent independent external audits. Here, an amnesty procedure along the lines of the South African Truth and Reconciliation Commission, which leads to the recovery of public funds in exchange for non-prosecution, might prove helpful;

6. *Reducing chances for abuse of executive power*, for example, dismantling the omnipotent powers of the executive presidency (an election promise of the current regime) – thereby making president and party more accountable to parliament and the vagaries of proportional representation, and providing parliamentary select commit-

tees or a non-political national ombudsman, with enough authority to initiate judicial inquiries, as a check on the abuse of power and privilege.

Without these basic changes, it is difficult to conceive a viable, violence-free alternative future for Sri Lanka.

Notes

1. The author gratefully acknowledges comments made by Cedric T. de Silva and Dr Azza Karam on earlier versions of this chapter, and the technical wizardry of Mohammed Karam.
2. In strict military terms, the warfare in Sri Lanka (particularly from the mid-1980s onwards) could be classified logistically as low-intensity conflicts or described as skirmishes. Nevertheless, in the twentieth century, such 'small-scale' conflicts or 'skirmishes' have accounted for more than their fair share of dead, injured, disabled, brutalised and traumatised humans (the majority of whom are invariably civilian women, men, children and the elderly).
3. *Goyigama* is the highest-ranking cultivator or farmer's caste among Sinhalese, while *Radala* is a collective term of reference for members of the Kandyan *Goyigama* nobility from the central highlands. *Vellala* is the highest-ranking cultivator or farmer's caste among Tamils.
4. Examples of 'authoritative' writing (including politics of numbers and party preference) are displayed by the conventional historian Kingsley M. de Silva (1981, 1986, 1995, 1997).
5. Interestingly, the word *Eelam* in Tamil is a reference to Ceylon. However, in its contemporary, post-Indo-Sri Lanka Peace Accord usage (post-1987), it refers to an independent, sovereign and exclusively *Tamil* state of Eelam, that separatist-nationalist paramilitaries from the LTTE and their supporters want to establish in north and east Sri Lanka. While the LTTE continues to maintain its separatist stance, other erstwhile Eelamists from rival paramilitary groups have softened their hard-line position, in order to pursue more 'Federalist' options of coexistence and accommodation *vis-à-vis* the hegemonic (majority) Sinhalese social formation.
6. Samuel James Velupillai Chelvanayakam (an élite Jaffna–Tamil–Christian), is undoubtedly the father of modern Tamil nationalism and his separatist-nationalist legacy was collectively hijacked (around the mid-1970s) by a spectrum of Tamil paramilitary groups. The leadership of these organisations, though non-traditional elite, remained predominantly Jaffna-centric. *Thanthai* (Father) Chelva's bequest was later modified and cornered (in the late-1980s), by the predominantly *Karayar* (low-ranking coastal people's caste) new politico-military élite – belonging to the inner circle of Velupillai Prabhakaran's LTTE. And in order to do so, they unleashed fratricidal warfare, leaving them at the helm of the Tamil polity and destroying any real chance for a united, separatist-nationalist paramilitary position. Much Tamil blood was spilt by Tamils (from the mid-1980s on) in these power struggles and internecine warfare, between (and within) paramilitary groups, which demonstrates very clearly that 'the Tamil rebellion' is not a

homogeneous challenge to Sinhala (Buddhist) hegemony – contrary to popular (mis)perceptions. The five major paramilitary groups that came into prominence (including LTTE) were the Eelam People's Revolutionary Liberation Front (EPRLF), the People's Liberation Organisation of Tamil Eelam (PLOTE), the Tamil Eelam Liberation Organisation (TELO) and the Eelam Revolutionary Organisation (EROS).

7. The Westminster system of government was first amended in 1972, when Sri Lanka adopted a Republican Constitution that, among other things, did away with the British monarchy's ceremonial role as 'head of state', along with the office of its representative, the 'Governor-General', and changed the (colonial) name of 'Ceylon'. In 1978, under a new constitution (that was approved by the UNP's two-thirds majority), state power was removed from parliament and placed in the hands of a Gaullist (French Fifth Republic) cum American-style, omnipotent executive presidency, together with the introduction of a proportional system of representation.

8 During the 1956 general elections, due to intra-UNP wrangling, a breakaway section of the traditional Sinhala political élite – led by the (soon-to-be-assassinated Prime Minister) S.W.R.D. Bandaranaike – wooed the majority Sinhala–Buddhist constituency (outside the avenues of social advancement) by promising them a greater share of power and resources. The non-materialisation of these promises added to the discontent of these politicised but marginalised sections, particularly the (non-*Goyigama*) youth, culminating in the emergence of the JVP a decade later. Membership was largely constituted by unemployed youth (many with degrees owing to free higher education) from the Sinhalese majority rural hinterland – who adhered to the rhetoric of 'Maoist' revolutionary ideology, backed by nativist putsch. The first JVP insurrection of April 1971 was swiftly crushed (with external assistance) by the ill-prepared Sri Lankan armed services and the leaders jailed (from 1971 to 1977). They were subsequently executed (extra-judicially) in 1989, following a second failed attempt (1987–9) to capture state power.

9. Premadasa was assassinated by a Tamil paramilitary suicide-bomber from the LTTE, with the *nom de guerre* 'Babu', on 1 May 1993.

10. The Eelam People's Democratic Party (EPDP), a breakaway faction of EPRLF, is led by Douglas Devananda – currently MP for Jaffna and a key Tamil paramilitary ally of the ruling PA coalition government. EPDP, along with six other Tamil organisations – namely, TULF, EPRLF, ENDLF, ACTC, EDF (Eelam Democratic Front the political party of EROS) and DPLF (Democratic People's Liberation Front the political party of PLOTE) – has been party to recent political negotiations with President Kumaratunga and other Sinhalese power-brokers. An objective here, is meaningful devolution of power and resources, reflected by constitutional change – with transition from a unitary state to a more accommodative 'federalist' option – as an interim solution to the ongoing crisis in the north and east.

11. The EPRLF broke away from EROS and was instituted in 1982 by the late Kandiah Pathmanaba, who was murdered in Madras by an LTTE hit-squad on 19 June 1990, along with twelve of his comrades (including the then MP for Jaffna, V. Yogasankery and Finance Minister of the first North-East Provincial Council, P. Kirupakaran). EPRLF is currently led by

K. Premachandran (alias *Suresh*), a former MP for Jaffna, though its influence has waned under his leadership.
12. The former chairman of the LTTE, Uma Maheswaran, founded the PLOTE around 1981 (following an acrimonious break with Prabhakaran). He was later killed on 16 July 1989 due to an internal feud (one of the assassins, a former bodyguard, was later murdered in Zurich by Maheswaran loyalists). PLOTE is now led by a duumvirate made up of the MP for Jaffna, Dharmalingam Sidharthan (political wing) and *Manikkadasan* (military wing).
13. TELO was founded in 1977 by the late Thangadurai *Mama* (uncle), who was eventually murdered by Sinhalese prisoners while in state custody, during the Welikada prison massacres of 1983. Sri Sabaratnam, who took over the leadership, was also killed (by the LTTE) on 6 May 1986, leading to the decline of TELO as a significant politico-military force.
14. The minimalist negotiating position maintained by these Tamil paramilitary collaborationist-nationalists is that the PA coalition government should (1) formally create a Tamil brigade or division (made up predominantly of their cadres), as part of the Sri Lankan armed services (which are currently made up of over 90 per cent Sinhalese); and (2) facilitate the formation of an interim council for the governance of the north and east, in order to create an alternative power base and institutionalised structure to counter the LTTE's politico-military hegemony.
15. I am unable to discuss gender aspects of Tamil paramilitarism in detail, due to lack of access. A significant development arising out of civil war, however, is that there are far more female-headed families in north and east Sri Lanka than, say, in the 1930s – which has given rise to a more socially and politically visible role for Sri Lankan Tamil women (in what is a patriarchally dominated social formation, where gender discrimination is self-evident). Due to a 'manpower shortage', around a third of the LTTE's paramilitary forces are made up of teenage and young women. For a critical examination of the role of 'woman' in contemporary Tamil nationalist experience, see Sitralega Maunaguru (1995), and from a more general Sri Lankan perspective, see Malathi de Alwis (1998).
16. While *Vellala* is the highest-ranking cultivator or farmer's caste among Sri Lankan Tamils, Jaffna *Vellala* are considered to be the highest-ranking caste and in comparison, Batticaloa *Vellala* are in a subordinate position.
17. The self-styled 'General' Ratwatte (originally a retired second lieutenant of the Sri Lanka Army Volunteers) is himself related to the ruling Bandaranaike clan, which includes the current Prime Minister Sirimavo Ratwatte Dias Bandaranaike and her daughter, Sri Lanka's chief executive, President Chandrika Kumaratunga.
18. The term *machang* is used in these narratives to denote close friendship. In its literal meaning, it refers to brother-in-law or, more specifically, husband-of-my-sister.
19. Leaving home is not easy *machang*. After all it is a part of you. It is very difficult to leave. I know ... A big thing why I don't like to see them [parents] *machang*, is whenever they see me, they think about my brother. They blame me for his death. I explained to them that it is not because of me but they still blame me. [*Thambi's* second brother, a schoolboy,

'disappeared' almost two decades ago after being picked up from home in a Special Task Force Police Commando 'round-up' of Karativu, never to be seen again.] Therefore I don't like them to see me, I would like them to forget me.'
20. For more details concerning Theravada Buddhist doctrine and practice, see the works of Kitsiri Malalgoda (1976), Richard F. Gombrich (1988), Richard F. Gombrich and Gananath Obeyesekere (1988) and Stanley Jeyaraja Tambiah (1992).
21. Given extended family relations in Sri Lanka, Aravindan refers to his brothers-in-law and sisters-in-law, quite literally, as 'brothers and sisters'.
22. For comparative examples, see the articles in the edited volume by Kay Warren (1993) and the excellent work by Usha Welaratna (1993).
23. Prohibition of access for journalists or human rights monitors to active combat zones by successive governments has created a situation where independent verification of human rights violations and war crimes has been virtually impossible.
24. Sensitivity to all perspectives is of particular importance when considering a detailed settlement (on the ground) to unitary and separatist aspirations, in areas of mixed population where Sinhalese, Tamils and Muslims live and work cheek by jowl. And it would be a mistake to overlook such realities in the consociational appeasement (*à la* Arend Lijphardt) of binary opposites.
25. To safeguard the common interests of civil society (locally or nationally) and uphold democratic freedoms, human rights, respect of minorities and fundamental rights, and the rule of law.
26. A tactic still adopted by LTTE, due to acute human-power shortages of combat-trained and combat-age paramilitaries (of all ages and both sexes) given the relatively high casualty figures in current battles.
27. It is alleged in certain quarters that anti-Indian actions carried out by the LTTE after 1987 were secretly aided and abetted by the Pakistani Inter-Services Intelligence Agency (ISI). In return, the LTTE was apparently provided with unhindered access to Pakistani-based arms markets (of Afghan origin) in Peshawar and the North West Frontier province. Considering this allegation and India's own politico-military débâcle in Sri Lanka, it is wiser not to involve either Pakistan or India in any future peacekeeping role.
28. The Indian federal union is made up of 25 states (including Tamil Nadu) and seven centrally administered union territories, which accommodate literally hundreds of ethnic, linguistic, religious and social formations, groups and subgroups.
29. Amirthalingam Thileepan is the Bobby Sands of the LTTE and fasted to death in September 1987, in accordance with the orders of his leader Prabhakaran.
30. Transparency International or TI is a Berlin-based NGO with national chapters in 38 countries, national contacts in 16 countries and a further 19 national chapters in formation (by April 1997). Though it has used and released warped statistical indexing (*sic*, ratings) – made up on the basis of sample interviews with Western businessmen, regarding their perceptions and observations of the levels of corruption in developing countries, while at the same time not taking into account their roles and complicity as bribe-givers – the basic idea of attempting to turn the tide against the global

phenomenon of corruption is a sound one. For more details, see the report by Transparency International (1997).

References

Appadurai, A. 1993: 'Number in the Colonial Imagination' in C.A. Breckenridge and P. van der Veer (editors), *Orientalism and the Postcolonial Predicament: Perspectives on South Asia*, Philadelphia: University of Pennsylvania Press.

Bailey, S.D. 1953: *Parliamentary Government in Southern Asia*, New York: International Secretariat, Institute of Pacific Relations.

Cohn, B. 1987: 'The Census, Social Structure and Objectification in South Asia' in *An Anthropologist Among the Historians and Other Essays*, Oxford and Delhi: Oxford University Press.

de Alwis, M. 1998: 'Moral Mothers and Stalwart Sons: Reading Binaries in a Time of War' in L.A. Lorentzen and J.A. Turpin (editors), *The Women and War Reader*, New York and London: New York University Press.

de Silva, K.M. 1981: *A History of Sri Lanka*, London: C. Hurst & Co.

de Silva, K.M. 1986: *Managing Ethnic Tensions in a Multi-Ethnic Society: Sri Lanka, 1880–1985*, Lanham, Md: University Press of America.

de Silva, K.M. 1995: *Regional Powers and Small State Security: India and Sri Lanka, 1977–1990*, Washington, DC: Woodrow Wilson Center Press and Baltimore, Md: Johns Hopkins University Press.

de Silva, K.M. 1997: 'Sri Lanka: Surviving Ethnic Conflict' in *Journal of Democracy*, vol. 8, no. 1, January, pp. 97–111.

de Silva, P.L. 1995: 'The Efficacy of 'Combat Mode': Organisation, Political Violence. Effect and Cognition in the Case of the Liberation Tigers of Tamil Eelam' in P. Jeganathan and Q. Ismail (editors), *Unmaking the Nation: The Politics of Identity and History in Modern Sri Lanka*, Colombo: Social Scientists' Association.

de Silva, P.L. 1997a: 'The Growth of Tamil Paramilitary Nationalisms: Sinhala Chauvinism and Tamil Responses' in *South Asia: Journal of South Asian Studies*, vol. XX, Special Issue, edited by S. Gamage and I.B. Watson, 'Conflict and Community in Contemporary Sri Lanka', pp. 97–118. Forthcoming in the book version (London: Sage).

de Silva, P.L. 1997b: 'Sri Lanka: Futures Beyond Conflict' in *Futures – The Journal of Forecasting, Planning and Policy*, vol. 29, no. 10, Special Issue, 'South Asia: Fifty Years On' (published by Elsevier Science), pp. 971–84.

de Silva, P.L. 1997c: 'Hatred and Revenge Killings: Constructions of Political Violence in Sri Lanka' in J. Uyangoda and J. Biyanwila (editors), *Matters of Violence: Reflections on Social and Political Violence in Sri Lanka*, Colombo: Social Scientists' Association.

Gombrich, R.F. 1988: *Theravada Buddhism: A Social History from Ancient Benares to Modern Colombo*, London and New York: Routledge.

Gombrich, R.F. and Obeyesekere, G. 1988: *Buddhism Reformed: Religious Change in Sri Lanka*, Princeton, NJ: Princeton University Press.

Malalgoda, K. 1976: *Buddhism in Sinhalese Society 1750–1900: A Study of Religious Revival and Change*, Berkeley: University of California Press.

Maunaguru, S. 1995: 'Gendering Tamil Nationalism: The Construction of "Woman" in Projects of Protest and Control' in P. Jeganathan and Q. Ismail (editors), *Unmaking the Nation: The Politics of Identity and History in Modern Sri Lanka*, Colombo: Social Scientists' Association.

Tambiah, S.J. 1992: *Buddhism Betrayed? Religion, Politics, and Violence in Sri Lanka*, Chicago, ILL: University of Chicago Press.

Transparency International 1997: *The Fight Against Corruption: Is the Tide Turning?*, Berlin: TI.

Warren, K.B. (editor) 1993: *The Violence Within: Cultural and Political Opposition in Divided Nations*, Boulder, Colo: Westview Press.

Welaratna, U. 1993: *Beyond the Killing Fields: Voices of Nine Cambodian Survivors in America*, Stanford, Calif.: Stanford University Press.

Wilson, A.J. 1980: *The Gaullist System in Asia: The Constitution of Sri Lanka (1978)*, London: Macmillan.

10
Women, War and Peace: Engendering Conflict in Post-Structuralist Perspective

Honor Fagan

While this book seeks to examine political identity formation in conflict situations with a view to developing a post-structuralist perspective, I would argue that an analysis of the relationship between gender and war is essential to a post-structuralist perspective. Thus some chapters have referred, in brief, to women's involvement in political processes, but the intersection between gender and identity formation has not been explored in any depth. Ignoring the all-pervasive role of women in war, historically and in current practice, simply produces poor analysis. This chapter thus seeks to highlight the importance of an engendered analysis of political processes and identity formation in the context of wars. I start with a broad overview of women's roles in war and possible changing trends pointing towards the growing importance of women's involvement in political processes. I then turn to the post-structuralist debate on gender and war in order to explore key issues that arise in analysing the intersections between the cultural formations of gender and war and their associated narratives. The negotiation of gender identities in a context of war leads us to some critical insights into the formation of political identities in contemporary war situations. We explore what happens to the constructs of 'masculinity' and 'femininity' in postmodern warfare and how they are manipulated.

I also introduce a specific site of political activity to portray the complexity and diversity of negotiations currently taking place when gender identity and the formation of political identities intersect. The activities of the Mothers of Plaza de Mayo in Argentina are seen internationally to be of great significance in terms of providing a glimpse of the possibilities of women's resistance to state militarism and torture. It is useful to turn to this well-investigated site since there is copious analysis of political agency and the gendering of political identities available. In contrast, the use of women in the United States army and their role in the war against Iraq also affords us an opportunity to unravel gendering and warring as cultural formations constructed in contexts of the militarisation of women, and has also attracted plenty of academic attention. Finally, though I use the tools of post-structuralism to investigate the gendering of political identity formation, I will conclude with a critical look at the transformative politics espoused by particular theorists embracing this framework.

Women and war

Stiehm in 1983 edited a collection titled *Women and Men's Wars* (Stiehm 1983) a title which played on the common assumption that wars were men's business. Writing in 1996 Pettman easily dismisses the common assumption of women's exclusion from war, showing that talking of war as if it is simply about men is a nonsense:

> In World War 1, 80% of casualties were soldiers; in World War 2, only 50%. In the Vietnam War some 80 per cent of casualties were civilian, and in current conflicts the estimate is 90 per cent – mainly women and children.
>
> (Pettman 1996:96)

She further argues that women have everything to do with war, that war would not be possible without women's co-operation at all practical levels. At the symbolic level women 'force' men to fight. At the level of citizenship women as taxpayers, voters and citizens are necessary for warring. At the practical level, the number of women joining state militaries is on the increase. Pettman asks what effect this will have on both the military and the women themselves.

Georgina Waylen provides a useful summary of the role of women in revolutionary and liberation struggles, though she focuses on selected examples which exclude fundamentalist revolutions and only looks at socialist revolutions with a capital 'S' and a capital 'R'. She, too, points to the increase in women's participation in socialist revolutionary movements and, in particular, the change in the form women's participation has taken in the twentieth century:

> with few women being organised or organising themselves in any sustained way in revolutionary movements in the first half of the

century and culminat[ing] in much more active roles played by
women in revolutionary movements of the 1970s.
(Waylen 1996:72)

Alongside this practical increase in involvement, the portrayal of women fighters at the symbolic level has increased. The potential of apparently 'weak' and 'powerless' people (such as women) to fight back was of huge symbolic value to revolutionary socialist movements (ibid.:74) The oppositional politics of the 1960s was discursively dominated by the heroism of Che Guevara, the revolutionary who chose violent confrontation with death, but later the movements generally changed towards urban revolution, and notions of a 'prolonged people's war' came into operation. In different national struggles this involved gaining the support of large numbers of women as activists, combatants and supporters. Mass mobilisation and mass participation involved the inclusion of women, and a revolutionary agenda for women's emancipation was put forward.

Waylen points to a huge contrast in women's participation between the early 1960s and the late 1970s as the change in tactics took hold. She compares the Cuban revolution with the Nicaraguan revolution: in the latter the FSLN had a high female membership, women making up between 20 and 30 per cent of the fighting force, with some women as leading commanders. In the 1970s the Tupamaros in Uruguay had an estimated figure of around 28 per cent female membership (ibid.:73).

Both Molyneux and Waylen describe this increased participation of women in political practices as positive advancement. At the symbolic level, in the first phase of revolutionary activity, women as victims were seen to be able to fight back. In the second phase, women as revolutionaries were seen to be able to mobilise. These are seen as crucial developments, but from a feminist point of view these authors are disappointed with the gains made by women through this involvement (Molyneux 1981; Waylen 1996:89–90). Their evaluation of change in women's involvement in revolutionary activity rests at an evaluation of the success or failure of a feminist agenda at the level of social policy and conventional political representation. The involvement of women in socialist revolution is looked on as having given women material practice in political activity and a degree of political empowerment that they can build on to mobilise as women for improvements for women.

The effect of women's involvement in socialist revolutionary politics, including war, is analysed in these texts for its effects on gender within a political rather than a cultural remit. It is perceived as emancipatory for the female gender because it achieved better living conditions for women in specific countries at specific times. While I generally share this political viewpoint, the question of what happens to the formation of gender remains somewhat unanswered. What happened as women formed their revolutionary political identity and how did that act on their identities as women? Was it simply positive, were they unambiguously emancipated or were further demands placed on their resources as women? On the other hand, did the construction of war change with women being actively included wholesale in warring processes? Did this new form of gendering – women's increased participation – limit or increase the power of the war machine? There is a tendency here not only to read the inclusion of women in war as simplistically positive, but also to under-investigate the interconnections between narratives of war and gender. The impact of women's increased involvement also influences the narratives of warring and this inter-relationship is not fully investigated in this literature.

Irene Matthews, analysing the war in Guatemala, makes some interesting points in relation to changing processes of war and women's inclusion in war. She argues that in the first half of the twentieth century, civil war still involved codes of practice that distinguished between 'belligerents' and 'non-combatants', but in the second half civil war took on a different perspective: 'no longer of "socially sanctioned" open conflict but of a diffuse and generalised violence pitting unequal forces against each other' (in Cooke and Woollacott 1993:160). The classic structure of interstate war – where men are recruited to protect women and children who are left at home to weep – changed to the direct confrontation of the weak and the civilian against the strong and the militarised. In low-intensity warfare 'immune space is entirely eroded', including the space of the feminine and of the domestic (ibid.:160–2). Whether or not there ever was immune space for women in war is questionable – since I suspect the immune space was entirely in the hands of the more powerful and 'winning' contingent – but the fact is indisputable that war now includes women at every level. Unlike Molyneux and Waylen, Matthews does not stress the emancipatory political potential of this involvement, rather the contrary. She reads this involvement of women in resistance/revolutionary/defensive activity in Guatemala as having punishing effects on women, where women share the costs of repression with men, but as women. In this sense we see the cost on women of engendering conflict:

> In a country where colonial identity is still self-perceived through sexual and ethnic superiority, women are now punished not (only) because of their chasteness, nor (only) to intimidate or humiliate

their menfolk, but for the public nature of their own actions: for the assumption of a voice – unprecedented and unwelcome and insistent 'noise' from a normally 'discreet' source. The *mother's* body is punished for daring to stray away from her silent subaltern identity and her home.

(ibid.:162)

Women are increasingly going to war, and war is increasingly coming to women, so as Pettman points out, the choice to say no to war is simply unavailable in most situations (Pettman 1996:131). Women have been at war, and are at war, in revolutionary and nationalist struggles (Jayawardena 1986) and in state armies (Enloe 1989), and they have been there as feminists too. In a war situation, where organisations have been explicitly set up to campaign on a feminist agenda, where violence rapidly increases against women in families, these organisations have repeatedly had to freeze their activities as the conflict and violence takes over and the women cannot override the effects to the extent of even maintaining their group activities (Pettman 1996:130).

Women's experiences of war are so extensive and all-embracing in the global context that the two issues – women's rights and achieving an end to warring – are now being totally collapsed into each other. Jeanne Vickers discusses the main issues surrounding the question of women and war in a double context of armed conflict and structural violence, and suggests that:

> It is now generally accepted that ending discrimination against women and achieving a non-violent world are mutually interdependent, inseparable goals. It is also generally recognised that effective development and an end to structural violence require the full participation of women. The relationship between women's rights, social and economic justice, and non-violent conflict resolution has not only become clearer over the years, but it is now seen as of the greatest importance to all, not only to women.

(Vickers 1993:149)

While this understanding is crucial to building a radically democratic political strategy toward justice and peace, collapsing the two together creates as many theoretical difficulties at it does closures on the debate. A political strategy might readily incorporate just, solemn and sanctimonious aspirations and objectives and address these to the global 'collective' of feminist women and achieve political advancement.

However, the intellectual task of critically analysing the relationship of women to war cannot be furthered without an analysis of the social construction of gender and its relationship to political processes and the advent of war. This intellectual task demands a post-structuralist theoretical framework and its associated tools of deconstruction. The post-structuralist turn allows us to look at narratives of war and their intersection with narratives of gender; narratives of masculinity, femininity, and heterosexuality as they are being produced, reproduced and constructed, not as fixed, immovable, indestructible and inevitable social facts. It is to this field of debate that I now turn.

Gendering and political identity formation

To point to the inclusion of women in war and in political processes, and to explore the nature of their inclusion, serves as a critique of accounts that ignore the gender dimension to political identity formation, but this is not enough. However, if we switch from the concept of women to the concept of gender – the social construction of sexual difference – we can tackle the analysis of women's relationship to warring processes in a non-essentialist way and this also allows us to examine the impact of women's involvement on discourses of war and on warring processes. In other words we can analyse the intersections of narratives of war and narratives of gender (for a recent comparative study along these lines see Cockburn 1998). Furthermore, this switch from focusing on women to focusing on gender allows us to take a non-essentialist approach to identity formation, where identity is seen as more unstable, always under construction and fragmented through multiple discourses. The nature of women's inclusion in warring is taken up from a deconstructionist perspective when we turn to the analysis of engendering political identity formation. It is within this field of debate that we can gain some insights into women's and men's political identity formation in contexts of warring, in particular in postmodern warfare, and the processes of gendering that occur in the formation of these political identities.

The post-structuralist approach rejects the unitary category of 'women' but, rather argues that there are individuals who take up a variety of subject positions and that these subjects positions are constituted through discursive practices within different discourses. Individuals are multiply-constituted subjects, they can and do take up multiple subject positions which can be in conflict with each other. The internally differentiated subject constituted in and through discourse is the subject of post-structuralist theorising (Moore, 1994).

Gender discourses position men and women in different ways and individuals constitute their self-representations as engendered subjects through the selection of, or imposition of, different and hierarchically constituted subject positions on gender.

The post-structuralist perspective on the discursive construction of the subject allows us to view the everyday practices of gendering and warring, the formation of political identities, and the intersection of gender processes and war/insurgency/military processes as being culturally constituted. They are inherently contingent and thus open to transformation. The key insight resulting from this perspective is that, at the level of cultural and discursive construction, war is gendered and that gendering impacts warring (Cooke and Woollacott, 1993). While this insight can frustrate at the level of feminist political practice (since it fails to absolve the female sex from the responsibility of the brutality of war), it has implications for the analysis of the formation of political identities since it indicates that a gendered analysis is always necessary. It points to the fact that where narratives of gender and war intersect, increasingly complex negotiations take place in the formation of political identities. Constructs of masculinity, femininity and heterosexuality are being negotiated and reformulated in contemporary warfare, and political agency arises out of these negotiations. Insurgents and military personnel form their political identities through gendered revolutionary and/or gendered military discourses, whatever side they fight on.

Following this theoretical trajectory I move to a particular site, a much-discussed site of political identity formation in a warring context, to examine how an engendered post-structuralist reading can be applied to the analysis of political agency. Moving from the theoretical to the concrete and particular, we look at the intersection of cultural formations of gender and war in the particular instance of Plaza de Mayo in Buenos Aires. If we turn to this site we can see an instance of the formation of political identities writ large in gendered identities and gendered political agency, but we can also see the complexity at play in the intersection between gendering and warring processes.

In 1976, Amnesty International found evidence of serious human rights violations in Argentina, such as illegal detention, execution, torture and disappearance. This came after nine months of what has been termed the 'dirty war', a war waged on the people by the military government. The dictatorship lasted until 1983 when it was brought down after the military's defeat in the Malvinas/Falklands War. In 1977, mothers began to walk around the square of Plaza de Mayo in the centre of Buenos Aires desperate to hear word of their children who had been 'disappeared' by the state. They walked in a circle, in silence, wearing white head scarves with the words '*Aparición con vida*' (Return our Children Alive) or the names of their children embroided on their scarves. In time they were joined by up to a thousand women. They became a social movement for human rights and democracy, symbolically and practically. Their narrative strategy was so simple, straightforward and potent that it received international attention and it became incredibly vocal in its opposition to the dictatorship and its parallel violence.

How did this come about? Jo Fisher interviewed several of the women who initially participated in the 'protest' and who still protest every Thursday. Jo Fisher records the words of María Del Rosario whose son was kidnapped from her home in May 1976:

> 'It's very difficult to explain how you feel when they take a child from you and you don't know what's happened to that child. It's like a terrible emptiness, like something's been wrenched away from inside of you and there's nothing you can do about it. No one would help us. At the police stations and the barracks we stood in queues for hours and they turned us away, they played games with us, they laughed at us. They insulted us and called us the 'mothers of terrorists'. As we began to recognise in the faces of other women the same despair and desperation we felt, we began to realise that we weren't alone, that there were hundreds of mothers like us, searching for their children.
>
> A few of us thought that if we all signed a letter together – which is how we started – we might make more progress. Then we found that if we all went to the courts they paid more attention to us. Then we all stood in lines outside the Ministry of Interior or an army barracks to drive the military mad. Working together was a very important step for us. At first we cried a lot, but together we began to find the strength to fight.'
>
> (Fisher 1993:105)

Another woman, Hebe, describes how the marching began:

> 'When the police saw there were a lot of us in the square, sixty or seventy sitting on the benches, they said "you can't sit here, there's a state of siege, this is a meeting; you'll have to move on." They began to hit us with their hands and with sticks. So we began walking. It was the police that forced us to march around the monument.'
>
> (ibid.:107)

The mothers' and grandmothers' protest continues as 213 children are still unaccounted for, despite a change in government. Maria Del Rosario tells Fisher that:

> 'The square is our citadel. We'll only stop going to the square the day we're all dead, and not even then, because now Mothers are dying and they ask for their ashes to be scattered there.'
>
> (ibid.:137)

Hebe tells her how:

> 'Our struggle is forever. In Argentina torturers and murderers walk the streets freely. I've met two of the torturers of my younger son, Raul. I know where they are. But they know we are fighting so that one day we'll have a government that will condemn all those who have forced us to live through horror for all these years.'
>
> (ibid.:137)

How has this particular incident, the case of the *Madres*, impacted on the discourse of war? We see a clear of intersection between the two. The *Madres* use their gendered role of motherhood as a symbolic form and as a practical basis to contest the military oppression. Indeed, they designed their discourse to reflect their traditional domestic roles: theirs was a struggle on behalf of motherhood and in defence of children.

In human rights circles, the mothers symbolise resistance to oppression and they are lauded for the innovative form their protest took. It was initially a silent one and only when they were asked later on in the campaign why they did not speak did they begin to shout for their children. From a gender perspective we can see that they used their female gender, in this case their role as mothers, as the pivotal point of their protest. This, of course, fitted in with and overlapped the military's discourse on gender, which indicated that the traditional role of motherhood should be lauded, and in a sense left this discourse of oppression ruptured momentarily by countering it with the discourse of motherhood (Hollander 1997:140).

At the level of material practice these women used their gender to stand up publicly to the military. There was no show of military strength, in fact their weakness was their strength, for how could a military maintain its masculinity by beating up grandmothers *in public*? We know they could use overt force in private, but to use it in public under the gaze of Amnesty International would have negatively impacted on the pediment of masculinity on which their status as military personnel depended. These women, because of their public action, achieved the attention of the press, and at the level of narrative strategy their silence under international cameras was the strongest narrative strategy possible at that time. Here we see in this site the cultural formations of gender and war intersecting at the level of material practices, symbolic forms and narrative strategies. Was this gendering resistance – the protest was particular in its femininity, silent, caring, maternal and passive – to militarism successful?

There was a modicum of success at the material level, though this was not immediate. Information on bodies and on some kidnapped grandchildren was recovered, but the military's torture and murder of their children at some 340 torture camps was not blocked. At the symbolic level they were hugely successful, in that once the military were removed from power, they symbolised what had been wrong with militarism in the constructive post-military polity. At the level of narrative strategy this discourse, established at the height of repression, had its impact later, when the democratic political process came into play and held the leaders responsible for their action. For the first time in the history of Latin America a civilian government made the military force accountable and jailed them.

Georgina Waylen draws our attention to the feminist debate on these activities (Waylen 1996:110). Are these activities regressive to a feminist cause because they involve women entering the public sphere on the basis of a traditional role, or are they transformative in that they challenge the dominant discourses of motherhood as passive? Those who see this type of activity as transformative tend to argue that this gendering of political identities is a foundation for doing politics in a new way. The logic of this is that mothers become revolutionary and motherhood is revolutionised. On the other hand, what is worrying is that in a discourse where motherhood and sacrifice go hand in hand, the celebration of the actions of these women can be construed as a celebration of femininity under torture from 'assaultive masculinity', to borrow a phrase from Sara Ruddick (1993).

Let us place this site in its wider context where we see other patterns, other constructions and deconstructions of gender in place. We can see at the level of practicality that the appearance of the mothers on the streets of Buenos Aires was a result of a defensive reaction to military invasion of the home. At the discursive level we can see it as resulting from the feminine being under attack in the first place. The home, the private, the civilian, the peaceful were in fact undergoing annihilation by their binary opposites – front line, state, combatant and war – and the public centre became the only possibly safe place for the women. Here we have a situation where the grossness of war and the discourse of authoritarianism took control. Of the 30 000 (human rights figure estimate) disappeared, over 30 per cent were women and an estimated 3 per cent of these had been pregnant at the time of their 'disappearance' (Fisher 1993:105). In the camps these women were tortured, brutalised and murdered in the same way as the men were. There was also gender – specific and sexualised torture. Bunster-Burotto (1985) describes family torture, where women were raped in front of their children and vice versa, where sexual assault on women was enacted by a man, men or animals. Here women's babies were taken from them before they were murdered and the babies 'disappeared' into homes approved by the military. Many women were active participants in the resistance and at the practical level their involvement gave strength to the movement. However, it also afforded the military the opportunity to go to new lengths of torture and oppression to annihilate so-called 'safe spaces'.

Desperation, the mother of protest, brought the mothers themselves out in search of answers on the 30 000 '*desaparecidos*'. In the face of the dirtiest of wars, where the governor of the province of Buenos Aires stated clearly that 'First we will kill all the subversives, then we'll kill their collaborators, then ... their sympathisers, then ... those who remained indifferent and, finally, we will kill the weak' (cited in Fisher 1993:104), these women felt compelled to make public protest. First the military called them mad, then they called them mothers of terrorists, then they moved on them, kidnapping and intimidating them. Meanwhile, newspapers and the international press had taken up the story. The protest was well established and the activities of Plaza de Mayo are well remembered at the symbolic level.

Whatever site we view, whether it is the almost passive resistance of the Plaza de Mayo or the militarisation of the revolutionary women, we can go through this process of unravelling and warring as cultural formations insofar as they are constructed in tandem. Leaving this site, we can turn to a contrasting site, one almost the opposite in its politics. The instance of women in the United States army and their role in the war against Iraq affords us an opportunity to examine a very different construction of gender and its intersection with war processes. While the Gulf War was brought by others to many women, it is also correct to say that many women brought that war to themselves. Some 32 340 US service women were active combatants in the Gulf War (Pettman 1996:148) and for the first time the media focused on service women and on service mothers: women were included in a new way as fighters.

What happened to the narratives of gender here, and are women empowered through playing an active military role? Was warring any less violent or any more peaceful as a result of this inclusion of militarised women? Was the feminine eradicated through the use of women soldiers and can women be as masculinised as men? Was there an incorporation of the feminine into the representations of warfare? Were the resulting new representations of gender positioning the feminine in new positive ways and were female gender identity formations strengthened? Was this empowering from a feminist political perspective? Some American women and Saudi Arabian women felt it was! Saudi Arabian women dismissed their chauffeurs and drove their own cars in a one-day demonstration during the Gulf War, according to Jeanne Vickers (1993:63), in an effort to force a reform of women's political representation, having watched US women driving army jeeps and enjoying equal status with their male colleagues. The post-structuralist framework allows us to investigate gendered political identity formations in extensive detail. The details emerging from this form of analysis of the intersection of gendering and warring is very useful at the analytical level, though perhaps less so at the level of transformative strategies.

Negotiation and/or assimilation?

Taking up the question of engendering political identity formation from a deconstructionist point of view has certain political drawbacks when it comes to developing transformative strategies as many feminists, particularly those writing on women and war, tend to want to do. Cooke and Woollacott, most recently and most coherently, have taken up the question of women and war from a deconstructionist perspective. They start from a position where they see war as central to gendering: 'after biological reproduction, war is perhaps the arena where division of labour along gender lines has been the most obvious, and thus where sexual difference has seemed the most absolute and natural' (Cooke and Woollacott 1993:ix). They move to a position where they argue that 'war is beginning to undo the binary structures that it originally put in place: peace and war; home (female space) and front (male space); combatant and civilian. Women as participants in wars of this century have blurred distinctions between gender roles in peace and in war. They argue that war has become a terrain in which gender is negotiated (ibid.:xi).

Despite the lack of historical depth such an approach entails (the book is concerned with twentieth-century wars only) we can accept their central point, namely that war is a terrain in which gender is negotiated, and that cultural conceptions of gender reshape the experience and meaning of war. However, they move on to the corollary that warfaring depends on gendering to develop possibilities of transformation. Several authors writing within a post-structuralist perspective in the Cooke Woollacott collection see this as the point where feminist politics can now make a difference (Cooke and Woollacott, 1993). Enloe, writing on international relations in her book *Bananas, Beaches and Bases* (Enloe, 1989), also sees the fact that international relations depends on gendering as the point where feminist politics can begin to make a difference. For her, focusing on women's involvement in international relationships will offer revelations from which 'may come fresh proposals for making countries less violent, more just and ultimately more rewarding for women as well as men' (ibid. 1989:xii). In the 1980s the hope had been for women's values and maternal thinking to stem the construction of militarism and war (Elshtain 1983; Ruddick 1983); now Cooke and Woollacott argue that the deconstruction of the war machine will in fact rely on deconstructing gendering:

> As we reinterpret and redefine gender roles and identities in war, it becomes clear that war has also become negotiable. The certainties constructed by binary thinking are revealed to be subject to question.
> (Cooke and Woollacott 1993:xi)

Again, a more historical and comparative view of war would find that war has always been optional or negotiable. We can also see that the discursive construction of war is not possible without gender relations in place and that the object of war, in the current hierarchical configuration of male as powerful and female as passive, is often at the discursive level about the elimination of the feminine. See, for example, the discursive space allocated to the feminine in militarism as represented in the latest Hollywood text on militarism, *G.I. Jane*. However, Cooke and Woollacott develop their transformative politics on the following basis:

> we believe that breaking the nexus (real or assumed) between military service and masculinity on the one hand and pacifism and femininity will weaken the social pediments on which militarism rests.
> (Cooke and Woollacott 1993:321)

Unlike in Enloe's work, where she repeatedly refers to women's collective action and women's political networking as important to the development of feminised international relationships, Cooke and Woollacott focus on deconstructing gender. Therein they see our hope for the future! Deconstructing war, they say, will in fact rely on deconstructing gendering, because the basis of war is the construction of the enemy as the binary opposite and that is why war talk, as it is narrated, is so gendered. It is difficult to put faith in this politics. This poststructuralist approach to identity formation sets up the theoretical framework for us to explore how a negotiation of violence has been put in place, but I argue that it is also possible that the deconstruction of gender can help hegemonise militarism. In fact, contrary to what Woollacott and Cooke argue, the spread of militarism could benefit from breaking the nexus between 'military service and masculinity' and 'pacifism and femininity' at the discursive level in order further to assimilate women into warring, and femininity into discourses of warring. Women's increasing involvement in militarism is occurring within particularly powerful ideological formations, with the 'hegemonic masculinity' (Connell 1987) associated with global capitalism deconstructing the feminine side at a more rapid pace than the masculine side. It seems to me that symbolic representations of passivity and femininity are on the decrease, whereas symbolic representations of strength and femininity are on the increase (for example, the Spice Girls, Xena the Warrior Princess, GI Jane in the media world, and representations of women as armed soldiers and armed revolutionaries in actual wars). Are not the construction of identities around strength and femininity as readily incorporated into warring discourses as those of passivity and femininity? Has the discourse of war dominated to such an extent that we are brought to the point where women's incorporation into warring processes has been about the assimilation of the feminine into the discourse of war? Woollacott and Cooke argue that 'war is a terrain in which gender is negotiated', but what form does this negotiation take? It is arguable that the only negotiation that takes place, looking (in the context of twentieth-century warring) at the resistance of women to militarisation and processes of militarising women, is one on the foreclosure of the feminine. The inclusion of women in war, in the 'dirty war' of Argentina and those other 'dirty wars' which mark twentieth-century warring, can be readily read as being about the foreclosing of the feminine. In a postmodern global cultural context we can see changing signs and symbols of war, but is there really a basis to read these positively?

If we look back to our example of the resistance of women in Argentina it is ironic that, at the material level, it was not the international public outcry in defence of these women and their children that brought down the military dictatorship. Rather, it was the militarisation of the UK, under Maggie Thatcher, that was the force which finally brought down the regime. Another irony in terms of gender politics is that the military regime was brought down by another military might led by a woman. Can we read the site of the Plaza de Mayo as signifying the final breakdown of the private, the feminine, where the weakest resist by showing their vulnerability, not their strength? The last symbol of the feminine exposes itself to be finished off publicly and yet it cannot be done publicly. Is this not as close to total defeat of the feminine as one can get? Is it not central to the picture of the defeat of the feminine that the military power that defeats the regime that grinds its heels into the feminine is led by a woman who lays no claim to the feminine? On the other hand, there is no such thing as total defeat and the subaltern feminine discourse of the grandmothers that was laughed at by the military regime could reassert itself in times of peace. Therefore would engendering peace processes, rather than narratives of war, not be a more likely source of political transformation? Can you engender peace processes without engendering conflict? While in a context of warring gender is negotiated, appropriation is but another form of negotiation. Discourses of war can certainly accommodate the notion of femininity and strength without necessarily weakening the pediments on which war rests. I believe that discourses of war are increasingly hegemonic to the extent that they incorporate notions of strength and femininity combined with notions of femininity and passivity in their narrative of late twentieth-century postmodern warfare.

In conclusion, women are being included in more ways and in increasing numbers in wars and in peace processes. Whereas up until now it has been argued that war was men's business, or women were not included in war 'as women', there are changes on this front too. Given the involvement of women in war, insurgency and peace processes it is easy to identify change, but far less easy to identify progressive change. Where women have been included and empowered through inclusion in both resistance to military regimes and through inclusion in militarisation, this can be read as extremely problematic if our vision of transformation includes notions of the world as a more peaceful place for all to live in. A turn towards a post-structuralist analysis allows us to understand better the intersections between gendering and warring, to perceive the pervasiveness of the interrelationships between the two, and to see the manipulation of concepts of 'masculinity' and 'femininity' in warring processes. However, at the level of democratic political strategy it is also clear that post-structuralism as presented by Cooke and Woollacott promises us much, but requires no engagement of the polity whatever.

References

Bunster-Burotto, x. 1985: 'Surviving beyond fear: Women and Torture in Latin America', in J. Nash and U. Safe (eds), *Women and Change in Latin America* South Hodley, MA: Bergin & Garvey.

Cockburn, C. 1998: *The Space Between Us. Negotiating Gender and National Identities in Conflict*, London: Zed Book.

Connell, R.W. 1987: *Gender and Power: Society, the Person and Sexual Politics*, Cambridge: Polity Press.

Cooke, M. and Woollacott, A. (editors) 1993: *Gendering War Talk*, New Jersey: Princeton University Press.

Elshtain, J.B. 1983: 'On Beautiful Souls, Just Warriors and Feminist Consciousness' in J. Steinhem (editor), *Women and Men's Wars*, Oxford: Pergamon Press.

Elshtain, J.B. 1987: *Women and War*, New York: Basic Books.

Enloe, C. 1989: *Bananas, Beaches and Bases*, Berkeley: University of California Press.

Fisher, J. 1993: *Out of the Shadows: Women, Resistance and Politics in South America*, London: Latin American Bureau.

Hollander, N.C. 1997: *Love in a Time of Hate, Liberation Psychology in Latin America*, New Brunswick: Rutgers University.

Isaksson, E. 1988: *Women and the Military System*, New York: Harvester Wheatsheaf.

Matthews, I. 1993: 'Daughtering in War: Two "Case Studies" from Mexico and Guatemala' in Cooke M. and A. Woollacott, *Gendering War Talk*, New Jersey: Princeton University Press.

Molyneux, M. 1981: 'Socialist Societies Old and New: Progress Toward Women's Emancipation, *Feminist Review*, 8, pp. 1–34.

Moore, H. 1994: 'The Problem of Explaining Violence in the Social Sciences' in P. Harvey and P. Gow (editors), *Sex and Violence: Issues in Representation and Experience*, London: Routledge.

Pettman, J.J. 1996: *Worlding Women: A Feminist International Politics*, London: Routledge.

Ruddick, S. 1983: 'Drafting Women in the Interests of Peace', *Signs*, vol. 8, no. 3.

Ruddick, S. 1993: 'Notes Towards a Feminist Peace Politics' in Cooke M. and A.

Stiehm, J. (ed.) 1983: *Women and Men's Wars*, Philadelphia: Temple University Press.

Waylen, G. 1996: *Gender in Third World Politics*, Buckingham: Open University press

Vickers, J. 1993: *Women and War*, London: Zed Books.

11
Islamisms: Globalisation, Religion and Power

Azza M. Karam

On 19 November, 1997, the Temple of Hatshepsut, one of the longest-standing witnesses to ancient Egyptian history and one of the oldest symbols of power of a woman queen in history, was the scene of a bloody massacre of more than 60 overseas tourists and Egyptians. The slaughter was allegedly carried out by six individuals, all Islamists, and thereby constituted the second time that Egyptian Islamists had attracted large-scale world media attention in the recent past – the first time being the assassination of Egyptian president and first Arab architect of peace with Israel, Anwar Sadat. The theme of enquiries, on CNN in particular, centred on the possibility of a conspiracy involving Iraq, the 'newest' hero-cast-as-villain in US and Western 'show', due to the recent global tension over Iraq's repeated recalcitrance to allow UN arms and weapons inspection to proceed as 'the International Community' thought it should.

Speculation in Western media was rife as to what other forms of 'outside interference' were implicated and news reports reverted back to the rhetoric of 'Islamic fundamentalism' – in general linking it to Islam and Islamic communities all over the world and to the character of Middle Eastern conflicts in particular. In short, here was another grand opportunity for Islamophobia to flourish and become a new entry in the English dictionary. Islam as a 'worldwide threat' is once again firmly on the map, with 'global connections' ranging from Afghanistan, the former Soviet Republics and the Philippines to the Middle East, North Africa, Europe and North America. Of course news-worthiness is fickle and, for example, Iraq's Saddam Hussein has on occasion been displaced by the Saudi multimillionaire-turned-'terrorist,' Osama Bin Ladin,[1] following his alleged role as the mastermind behind the almost simultaneous US Embassy bombings of 7 August, 1998 in

Kenya and Tanzania. Nevertheless, it is fair to say that politicians, policy-makers and analysts in 'think-tanks' are all scratching their heads wondering how to neutralise this latest 'threat' and the likes of Bin Ladin and Saddam Hussein.

Ironically, only a short time before this global preoccupation, there was an emerging belief among some Arab intellectuals and even international journalists that Islamism or political Islam was on the wane. The evidence cited for this statement was the performance of Islamist candidates in various elections which had been held in Lebanon, Palestine, Jordan and Pakistan among other countries. Also cited was the fact that some of the leaders of the Islamist radical fringe in Egypt (including the blind Sheikh jailed in the United States, Omar Abdel Rahman) had called for a truce in their violent confrontation with the government and that their 'terrorist' activities seemed to have been brought under control by the Mubarak regime's draconian anti-terrorist measures.

It is interesting to note that according to the above opinion, 'elections' were seemingly used as an adequate measure of public opinion. Not only that, but apparently there seems to be a bewildering confidence in the elections carried out – that is, being free and fair opportunities for people to express their choices, *and* that political space is such that articulations of political opinions avail these choices. The other point made to strengthen this argument was that Islamism, is after all, but a political fashion and like all fads, it gains in momentum, peaks, and then eventually peters out as people find other more exciting and/or attractive ideas. Yet another argument, one characterised above all by its economic reductionism, but popular nonetheless, is that since the economies of the respective countries are improving, relatively speaking, then the need for Islamist creativity and refuge diminishes accordingly.

In this chapter, I seek to explore the simultaneity of these events and this particular belief, particularly in light of globalised societies and politics, and to examine why some Arab and Muslim intellectuals, as well as others, are eager to see the end of Islamism as a political ideology and predict its downfall. Undoubtedly, there is more than an element of truth in the assertion that the appeal of Islamism is not as strong overall as it used to be. Violent events in Algeria, Afghanistan and Sudan must have left many disillusioned. But is the disillusion of some with certain specific groups – for example, with the Armed Islamic Group or GIA in Algeria, the Taliban in Afghanistan and the ruling regime in Sudan – to be equated with a general decline? More pertinently, why is it convenient to dismiss these groups from the political arena? Finally, what consequences are there when 'Islamic fundamentalism' is perceived as a global threat – as illustrated by the Clinton administration's recent (unilateral) moves?

Islamisms: diversity in motion

Part of any discussion on this topic involves the stating of some facts. First, Islamisms are not a homogenous phenomenon but encompass a variety of movements, which are diverse in their demands, their *modes d'emploi* and many of their goals. Yet, in the manner in which it is portrayed, Islamisms tend to be seen as synonymous with 'terrorism' and with the most radical or extremist fringes thereby conveniently ignoring the fact that moderate Islamism has its own distinct characteristics. These include benefiting from the big furore around the radical elements, and stressing how free and fair and politically sound, and indeed, what a much-needed and appreciated 'real' alternative the moderate main stream is.

Second, Islamisms, in their diversity and multi-facetedness, are not only a feature of the Muslim world, but in fact are manifested within pockets of some Muslim communities located as far afield as Europe and the USA – for more details see Karam (1997), Vertovec and Peach (1997) – thereby making it more difficult to conveniently dismiss their varied impact and nuances, whether in terms of the aims and strategies adopted or in terms of the manner of manifestation and appearance.

Third, Islamism – as embodied by the moderate mainstream – was not merely a feature of a particular political era, but has been around since 1928 with the first such movement being the Muslim Brotherhood (*al-Ikhwan al-Muslimin*) set up by Hasan al-Banna in Egypt and later replicated in many Muslim countries, such as the Sudan, Palestine and Indonesia. In other words, there has been ample opportunity for this tendency to develop politically, ideologically and strategically within various establishments. Indeed, moderate Islamism can justifiably be characterised as having a long political history in opposing colonialism and, later other forms of state repression. In other words, moderate Islamism is no stranger to the forum of organised social and political opposition, and the provision of long-term and sustainable alternatives to the status quo. The varied political discourses adopted and the strategies espoused since the inception of such thought, and their spread in and accommodation of different political, social and cultural conditions (whether in Asia, Africa or even in

Europe or North America) makes it important to respect the subtleties of this political formation.

Fourth, too many studies and portrayals of Islamism have tended to build on and feed existing stereotypes and negative imagery of Islam and anything associated with it as threatening, violent, backward, and basically something akin to a curse. These also play a part in conveniently ignoring the intentions, credibility and political ingenuity of the far more popular than credited moderate mainstream. In any event, even when not portrayed as such, it is an irony that those academic studies which have portrayed these movements in their diversity, pragmatic contours and non-violent discourse often tend to be marginalised as 'defensive' and/or 'apologetic' in character at worst and as 'few and far between' at best. Moreover, it is also the case that the more positive portrayals tend to lack the glamour and intrigue value of the more 'nasty' cases, which does not count in their favour, nor does it render them more appealing to a wider audience. In other words, the predominant notions on Islamism tend to get confused with the more radical fringes, so that references to Islamist movements[2] or 'fundamentalism' generally lump together and erroneously homogenise a wide diversity of social, economic and political tendencies and groupings from across the globe into a single entity.

A new class of studies, however, claims to acknowledge these differences while homogenising the movements nevertheless. One edited study by the theologian Martin Marty and the historian Scott Appleby – grandiosely named 'The Fundamentalism Project' – put together five mammoth volumes and presented a (mis)construction of 'fundamentalism' in almost every known religious denomination and their derivatives from across the globe, and thus created a *de facto* canon (see Marty and Appleby 1991, 1993a, 1993b, 1994, 1995). The case studies in this overambitious endeavour range from Hinduism, Buddhism, Sikhism, Confucianism, the so-called 'new religions' of Japan, Judaism, Christianity (covering Catholicism in North America and derivatives of Protestantism in North and South America) to Islamism in Egypt, Sudan, Iran, Iraq, Lebanon, India, Pakistan, Malaysia and Indonesia – with the notable exception of Algeria and other countries belonging to the *Maghreb* in North Africa, as well as from the Arabian peninsula. Marty and Appleby (the coordinators of The Fundamentalism Project at the University of Chicago) also compiled a companion volume, sensationally titled *The Glory and the Power: The Fundamentalist Challenge to the Modern World* (1992), focusing on three groups, namely, American Protestant Fundamentalism, the Gush Emunim (ultra right-wing fundamentalist militants operating in the territories occupied by Israel) and the ubiquitous 'Islamic fundamentalism' – a generic term that erroneously homogenises a whole range of disparate phenomena and politico-religious activisms. Other studies follow up this concerted effort and even attempt to provide guidelines for global conflict management, by lumping Islamisms with Serb nationalism and with the protagonists of the civil war in Sri Lanka – all under the heading of 'religious militancy' (see Little 1996). Whereas these studies doubtless offer important information and analyses, it remains wise to err on the side of caution when assessing such representations, which purportedly take on the world while claiming to recognise differences.

Fifth and following from the last point, as far as relationships to states and global arenas of power are concerned, Islamisms tend to be seen in homogenised, unilinear terms – that is, as rather narrow in their aims and intentions and, as such, inflexible and stringent. It is not unheard of that Islam in general is seen as a 'threatening religion', so that its politicisation is but a step nearer to catastrophe – according to the world-view of Islamophobes and other ill-informed populists who are deeply concerned about the alleged spread of the 'green menace'. This is a point of view supported by Willy Claas, the former Secretary-General of NATO, who was reported to have stated that following the disintegration of the Soviet Union, NATO's new enemy was 'Islamic fundamentalism'. At a loss to find future enemies and with a mass of weapons fit to destroy the world many times over, NATO has found another hunting ground. These views were no doubt vindicated when some Algerian 'elements' (as yet unclear as to whom or what entity they actually represented) saw fit to cause explosions in a number of subways in Paris; when foreign tourists were killed in Egypt; when the World Trade Centre was bombed in New York; when the al-Turabi and al-Bashir regime in Sudan allegedly provided training for Islamist 'terrorists' of all hues; and when the American embassies in Kenya and Tanzania were bombed, purportedly by terrorists backed by the exiled Saudi 'Islamist crusader' Bin Ladin, with assistance from elements within the Islamist regime in Khartoum.

Bin Ladin for his part denies any involvement in these attacks and has instead 'vowed retaliation against the United States after missile strikes on his operations in Afghanistan', according to an 22 August, 1998 Reuters report from Islamabad, Pakistan, which quoted a local English-language daily, *The News* as its source. In the original Pakistani version, it is reported that Bin Ladin, in a message read by his Egyptian ally Ayman al-Zawahiri over satellite telephone, had said: 'The war has just started and the Americans should wait for an answer.' Al-Zawahiri, the alleged head of 'an Islamic *jihad* organisation and wanted by the Egyptian government', is reported to have said that Bin Ladin had escaped the American attacks and was safe in Afghanistan, and to

> Tell the Americans that we aren't afraid of bombardment, threats and acts of aggression. We suffered and survived Soviet bombings for 10 years in Afghanistan and we are ready for more sacrifices ... [And that] The whole Muslim (community) must change its attitude and fight the challenges posed by America and its agents. We should strengthen in Ladin's hands in his struggle.

Reuters goes on to report that on 21 August, 1998, Abdel-Bari Atwan, editor of the London-based *al-Quds al-Arabi* newspaper, also reported a statement from Bin Ladin's spokesperson saying: 'The battle has not started yet. The response will be with action and not words.' Needless to say, this war of words and related actions versus counter-actions provides ample 'evidence' to fuel already entrenched Islamophobia on a larger scale on the global stage.

Certainly what the Taliban are doing in Afghanistan must also be somewhat disturbing to the Western powers, particularly when women are the butt of the distorted 'carrying out of rules' of this allegedly Pakistani-backed group of Islamist zealots. The unpleasant treatment meted out to European Union Commissioner Emma Bonino during her fact-finding mission to Afghanistan in October 1997 would have done little to counter allegations of the mistreatment of women and other abuses of human rights in that part of the world. It is notable, though, that the international community was almost 'instinctively' enraged by the plight of women in Afghanistan and yet in other instances, for example when Bosnian women suffered systematic mass rape, human rights activists seemed to have to go to great lengths to elicit parallel disgust and attention.

What is conveniently ignored in these somewhat unqualified statements by spokespersons for the international community is that *any* political ideology (for example, Islamism or nationalism) creates a dynamic stream or current of its own, which does not abruptly die out, particularly when some of the socio-political and symbolic conditions that nurtured it (both internally and externally) remain in place, which in fact may make it grow stronger. In this regard, the crisis of legitimacy faced by most regimes in the Muslim world, from Indonesia to Morocco, coupled with global power inequalities, the negative effects of market forces and their resulting insecurity, are not about to disappear or diminish in importance. Moreover, as long as the ideology – that is, a particular Islamist derivative in a given country – is an untested political alternative and an alternative to it has yet to manifest itself, then it becomes something of a generalisation to assume that this ideology would conveniently self-deconstruct and vanish into thin air.

After stating these hard truths, the following sections examine the theoretical underpinnings behind the local and global dynamics that are involved, together with a reassessment of the activism of Islamist streams, in light of contemporary incidents from around the international arena.

Local and global: theoretical underpinnings and current dynamics

The underlying reasons behind the rise of contemporary Islamisms are many and fall beyond the scope of this chapter, particularly in light of the fact that numerous studies have explored and analysed them at length – for more details see, among others, Kepel (1985), Halliday and Alavi (1988) and Ruedy (1996). Nevertheless, it is worthwhile to note that Islamisms can be delineated into two interrelated categories:

- issues of legitimacy related to Arab states in particular and to Muslim states in general;
- issues of citizenship.

As far as the former is concerned, it is not a coincidence that Islamists form the strongest opposition force in precisely those countries where democracy is more lip-service than reality, and where most of the leaders have yet to be elected in free and fair context. Issues of citizenship are also important, because they underline the resentment felt by many – not least of which are immigrants in many European and North American countries – that their rights and status as equal citizens are being consistently denied. This denial can take place via certain 'policies of integration' envisaged primarily from the point of view of dominant (non-Islamic) host societies *or* via random arrest and imprisonment of those who have dared to voice opposition to the status quo in the name of a particular credo/ideology elsewhere in the Muslim world.

In many respects, Islamism can be seen as a strategy of resistance to power (for example, that of the state), but also as a power in and of itself – in so far as it provides the tools necessary for countering hegemony and providing an alternative way of existing in a social and political context. Thus the power of Islamists and that of the state or the larger ideology they are attempting to replace are interdependent. Michel Foucault's arguments come to mind here, as the interplay of antagonistic interdependencies which highlights the power–resistance paradigms evident in the assertion that 'as soon as there's a relation of power there's a possibility of resistance' (Foucault 1980:13).

In many instances ruling élites manipulate public discourse and media via the structure of the state, and especially in the Muslim world, so as to insist that they are the 'better Muslims', while simultaneously using their repressive apparatuses of power and authority (police and armed forces) to clamp down on all forms of Islamist and other opposition. The latter is the scenario particularly in countries such as Egypt, Algeria, Morocco, Tunisia, Malaysia and Indonesia. Yet, these are instances where the state's self-defeating devices are underscored – for in the ensuing power struggles, Islamists are merely furthering the discourses they are themselves inventing and hence masters of. The latter are *discourses of resistance vis-à-vis state power*, which per Foucauldian definition is *productive power*. The attempts of some states to manipulate these discourses themselves trigger a self-defeating mechanism, in so far as the discourse of the state is centred around maintaining repressive and thus *unproductive power*. The net result, as the situation in certain Arab countries indicate, is a cycle where unproductive power de-legitimises itself and the discourse of Islam *per se* dominates almost all political, social and cultural interaction. Other Muslim countries, however, choose to coopt their Islamist streams and thereby attempt to neutralise this form of opposition through the creation of certain controllable democratic frameworks.

An examination of certain theoretical underpinnings behind many of the terms used throughout this chapter now follows – namely, the interaction between and impact of globalisation and localised dynamics. Looking at authors who have best captured the moments of Islamist activism and their resultant responses and respondents, I argue that much of the discussion on Islamism, not to mention its inception and characterisation, is a function and consequence of globalisation and postmodern dynamics – both of which in turn impact upon the manner in which Islamism is understood by its practitioners and perceived by those who study it.

'Globalisation', to follow Roland Robertson (1990:19), has become a commonly used term in different circles (intellectual, business, media and so on). In each context, the term is employed to indicate a wide range of meanings with varying degrees of precision – for example, the strengthening of a Westernised global culture, or the internationalisation of economic, social and political methods of interaction, norms and values. For Jan Nederveen Pieterse, globalisation implies an *'increase in the available modes of organisation*: global, transnational, international, micro-regional, municipal, local, institutional. Globalization increases the range of organizational options, all of which are operational simultaneously' (Nederveen Pieterse 1995:50). Meanwhile, Mike Featherstone states that the most important aspect of globalisation is the centrality of culture, or the extension of global cultural interrelatedness (Featherstone 1990:6). Featherstone argues that a globalised culture admits a continuous flow of ideas, information and values. These flows engender situations where previously homogeneous cultural niches are forced to face each other and relativise themselves *vis-à-vis* each other. This process of relativisation may entail what I consider twin oppositional processes of globalisation: on the one hand, certain cultural values are incorporated; and on the other hand, a self-reflexive process takes place wherein fundamental values are restated and redesigned in the face of perceived threats of cultural 'absorption' and/or 'inauthenticity'. Elaborating along these lines, Arjun Appadurai conceptualises five dimensions of global cultural flows which move in non-linear paths: ethnoscapes, finanscapes, technoscapes, mediascapes and ideascapes, the latter pointing to the flow of images and ideologies which are associated with state or counter-state movements 'explicitly oriented towards capturing state power or a piece of it' (Appadurai 1990:296–9). Appadurai emphasises that the ideologies are associated with the appropriation of certain 'key words' within Western Enlightenment world-views (for example, democracy, human rights).

Malcolm Waters follows Appadurai's idea of cultural flows and 'scapes' and develops what he terms a 'sacriscape', or the distribution of religious ideas and practices (Waters 1995:126). Waters argues that postmodernism is congruent with the universalistic tendencies of the major world religions, with its displacement of the certainties offered by modernisation, and hence it 'accelerates the search for a single, often mythologised truth that can reference all social mores and practices' (ibid.:130). In Robertson's terms, religious systems are obliged to relativize themselves in relation to global postmodernising trends. This is done, as referred to above, in the context of other processes of globalisation, either by appropriating a postmodernist abstract ecumenism, or by taking the form of a 'rejectionist' search for original traditions.

Hence postmodernism, in the context of global culture, is seen in terms of a symptom and a powerful cultural image of the move away from conceptualisations of global culture as simply homogenising processes (for example, 'Macdonaldisation') towards an understanding of the diversity and hybridity of local discourses, codes and practices, or, in Robertson's terms, a situation where particularity is a global value and what is taking place is the 'universalization of particularism' (Robertson 1992:130). Postmodernities in the plural have become a symptom and a result of the 'glocalisation' of culture, wherein simple dichotomies between unity/diversity, East/West, integration/disintegration no longer sufficiently explain the dynamism and plurivocality characterising the economic and cultural spatial compression that is an aspect of globalisation processes and postmodernism (see Harvey 1990). The persistence of certain ways of thinking in dichotomies or binary opposites, however, renders postmodern critique of this aspect of Enlightenment thinking extremely valid. The latter is especially the case when referring to the argument as to the supposedly diminishing impact of Islamisms. It is clear that Islamisms are perceived as either 'alive and kicking' – with terrorist incidents highlighting this – or they are 'dying/diminishing/receding'. Other ways of perceiving Islamisms are notable by their absence.

I maintain here that Appadurai's ideascapes and Water's sacriscapes converge to refer to the flow of counter-state movements, as well as movements which are opposed to what they perceive as dominant and oppressive identities. These movements are exemplified by moderate ideologies of political Islam, which seek to capture state power, or counter certain state policies (as in Europe), while being opposed to Western world-views. However the latter is carried out nevertheless by selective reappropriation of certain key words or concepts of Enlightenment-related thinking (for example, democracy, which is seen as equivalent to an intrinsically Islamic ideal of *shura* or consultation). Islamisms, then, can be seen as an example of the restructuring processes of globalised cultures, while benefiting from the postmodern 'cultural chaos' that is also an aspect of both postmodernity and globalisation. In that respect, Islamisms are a feature of contemporary life, which select the ideas and modes of action relevant to their respective enterprises. This is a very different interpretation from that of Islamisms as simple reaction, a harking back to some distant and undeveloped past. If Islamisms are a process and a feature of the times, then perhaps we can reorient ourselves and realise that the symbiosis with events happening all over the globe also entails a certain capacity for dynamism and change that is difficult to capture in static and prejudiced terms.

As mentioned above, the first Islamist movement was the Muslim Brotherhood of Egypt, set up early in the twentieth century. One of the Brotherhood's main motives included resistance to British colonialism and particularly its cultural and political hegemony. This was later developed over the Brotherhood's many years of activism to include an intricate and popular socio-economic network aimed at those least well-off in society. The Brotherhood played a key role in mobilising support for and solidarity with the Free Officers movement, which carried out a 'revolution' against the King and the British in 1952. Yet, once the Free Officers were holding the reigns of government, interpretations at the time as to the Free Officers' non-involvement in rule tend to differ. Some accounts claim that the Brotherhood felt that the posts they were offered were not influential and powerful enough, while others maintain that the Free Officers themselves were careful to exclude the Brotherhood from power. Yet another explanation is that members of the Brotherhood did not want to sully themselves with governmental authority and power politics in general. Nasser's regime in the 1950s subsequently cracked down heavily on the Brotherhood, notably because they were seen as an effective opposition. Yet, even though these are referred to in Brotherhood memoirs as 'the black days' of the movement and the Egyptian regime then (and even now) sincerely attempted to totally eliminate the organisation, the Brotherhood has survived and is continuing to flourish. The point is that the politics of mobilising popular support, creating alternative socio-economic and political structures, and working from within existing state structures is not new to the Brotherhood. Eventually the Muslim Brotherhood, whose ideology of an Islamic *umma* (community) was integral to much of their thinking, spread to the Sudan, Jordan, Palestine and many other Arab and Muslim countries.

Today, the cry of *Allahu Akbar* (God is Great), which has become almost a tautology for 'terrorist-speak', can still be heard across many parts of the Islamic world. This will probably continue to be the case until such time as certain basic issues, local in nature but global in character, receive some form of just resolution. Among these issues is what Edward Said, nearly 20 years ago, termed 'the question of Palestine', for indeed it is a question which has yet to receive a justifiable answer according to the tenets of international law. It is worthwhile to note that despite the many issues on which Islamists (of all hues and forms) disagree – that is from the manner of government to the purpose and shape of that rule and consequently its socio-political and cultural-religious organisation – they agree on two specific issues, namely:

- the need to implement the *shari'a* (Islamic law), though how and which aspects is still, thankfully, open to debate;
- the need for a resolution to the Palestinian problem.

The latter structures their thinking and activism to a large extent, for after all pre-Zionist Palestine was Arab–Muslim land and Jerusalem continues to be a place of significance and veneration, the second most holy site for all Muslims, thus a source of collective identity and pride, which has been lost for 50 years to Israel – a repressive, foreign nation state that conquered this land through war and which is supported by a militarily, politically, economically and culturally dominant foreign power, namely the USA (and its allies). Not only that, Palestine is also the cauldron of the Middle East, where the local and the global are constantly interacting, and where an almost permanent multilevel contestation of power is taking place.

The same can be said of other disparate Muslim territories and lands, as far afield as Bosnia–Hercegovina, Afghanistan, Chechnya and the former Eastern Turkestan in north-east China,[3] during their respective territorial wars and rebellions against foreign aggressors and occupiers – be they Serbs, Croats, Russians or Han-Chinese. This is a key factor not taken into the equation or given adequate significance when US President Bill Clinton ordered cruise missile strikes against alleged Islamist terrorist targets in Sudan and Afghanistan, or when his predecessor authorised the permanent presence of (non-Muslim) US troops in order to defend American interests in Saudi Arabia – considered sacrilegious acts by Islamists of the ilk of Bin Ladin. To quote Bin Ladin on this and other points of contention:

> We declared *jihad* against the US government, because the US government is unjust, criminal and tyrannical. It has committed acts that are extremely unjust, hideous and criminal whether directly or through its support of the Israeli occupation of the Prophet's Night Travel Land [Palestine]. And we believe the US is directly responsible for those who were killed in Palestine, Lebanon and Iraq. The mention of the US reminds us before everything else of those inno-

cent children who were dismembered, their heads and arms cut off in the recent explosion that took place in Qana [in Lebanon]. This US government abandoned even humanitarian feelings by these hideous crimes. It transgressed all bounds and behaved in a way not witnessed before by any power or any imperialist power in the world. They should have been considerate that the *qibla* [Mecca] of the Muslims upheaves the emotion of the entire Muslim World. Due to its subordination to the Jews, the arrogance and haughtiness of the US regime has reached to the extent that they occupied the *qibla* of the Muslims [Arabia] who are more than a billion in the world today. For this and other acts of aggression and injustice, we have declared *jihad* against the US, because in our religion it is our duty to make *jihad* so that God's word is the one exalted to the heights and so that we drive the Americans away from all Muslim countries. As for what you asked whether *jihad* is directed against US soldiers, the civilians in the land of the Two Holy Places [in Saudi Arabia, Mecca and Medina] or against the civilians in America, we have focused our declaration on striking at the soldiers in the country of The Two Holy Places. The country of the Two Holy Places has in our religion a peculiarity of its own over the other Muslim countries. In our religion, it is not permissible for any non-Muslim to stay in our country. Therefore, even though American civilians are not targeted in our plan, they must leave. We do not guarantee their safety, because we are in a society of more than a billion Muslims. A reaction might take place as a result of US government's hitting Muslim civilians and executing more than 600 thousand Muslim children in Iraq by preventing food and medicine from reaching them. So, the US is responsible for any reaction, because it extended its war against troops to civilians. This is what we say. As for what you asked regarding the American people, they are not exonerated from responsibility, because they chose this government and voted for it despite their knowledge of its crimes in Palestine, Lebanon, Iraq and in other places and its support of its agent regimes who filled our prisons with our best children and scholars. We ask that may God release them.[4]

Yet, despite the 'circumstantial evidence' in Bin Ladin's statements and all the intelligence-related rhetoric and anti-terrorist 'logic' of the Washington sound-bite show, the careful timing of Clinton's military strikes on suspected Islamist terrorist targets in Sudan and Afghanistan on 20 August, 1998, however, points more towards a diversionary tactic to boost his popularity ratings. In other words, it was a meticulously stage-managed manoeuvre aimed at offsetting his domestic predicament as a result of the Monica Lewinsky 'scandal' – as in the Hollywood movie *'Wag the Dog'*, but maybe for real (that is, real life imitating art). What is certain, of course, is that he has succeeded in stirring up a veritable hornet's nest and given the disparate Islamist groups another good reason to unify, this time against 'naked American aggression' – an unfolding scenario celebrated only by out-of-work Cold War warriors and to the detriment of those US citizens at large who might happen to be at the wrong place at the wrong time. In fact, what the Clinton administration has inadvertently done is to construct Bin Ladin into the role of a headline-grabbing, 'crusading Islamist folk hero', thereby making him a far more potent symbol and greater threat to US interests than had he been just another nondescript 'Anti-American terrorist'.

It will certainly take more than lip-service to bring about damage limitation – for as the saying goes, 'actions speak louder than words'. A case in point is President Clinton's post-East African Embassy bombings address to the UN on 21 September, 1998, which focused on the 'fight against global terrorism' and where he stressed that fighting terrorism did not mean fighting Muslims: 'There is no inherent clash between Islam and America ... Americans respect and honour Islam. As I talk to Muslim leaders in my country and around the world, I see again that we share the same hopes and aspirations.' What is clear here is that in order to bring about a qualitative improvement, there are no short cuts to long-term processes of constructive engagement and not just with not-so-democratic 'Muslim statesmen'. Failure to do so with any sincerity, understanding and long-term commitment, will only add to the current popular climate of acrimony, misunderstandings, misconceptions and tension.

One of the major differences between Islamist groups as a whole exists between the moderates as exemplified by the Muslim Brotherhood and other Islamists. Whereas the former believe that the proper Muslim state will come about gradually through preaching to the masses and via existing structures of state and civil society, the latter usually believe that organised violent action (whether in isolation from the rest of society or through some form of *jihad*) has to be carried out in order to arrive at an Islamic state. This distinction has direct implications for the manner in which political discourse is articulated, since the moderates make a point of working within existing state and societal structures domestically, regionally and globally (for example, international Islamist conferences are held in the world's nerve centres such as London and though most are permitted in theory by the local authorities, some are cancelled at the last minute).

Moreover, the *raison d'être* of Islamists is based upon religion and religious symbolism, namely Islam, or their particular interpretation of it, to be more precise – which is their ideological creed, sense of identity and purpose in life, if not livelihood. Their whole structure, internal or external, is based upon if not derived from 'Islam'. The Brotherhood's motto in Egypt, for example, was 'Islam is the solution'. Indeed, their main political demand (and that of other Islamist groups) is the implementation of the *shari'a*, or Islamic law, as the constitutional law of the countries in which they operate. Events in the Paris subways have indicated that unwelcome and less-than-genuine interventions, such as those of France after the Algerian military cancelled the 1992 elections following the victory of the Front Islamique du Salut (FIS), can bring the Algerian civil war to bear on internal French politics.

It is undeniable that these groups have formed at one time or another, by their mere existence and function, a very noticeable 'power constellation'. Furthermore, their mode of operation makes it very clear that the working out of strategies and tactics to overcome opposition, is an integral aspect of their planning. Hence their political alliances, populist social policies and micro-economic alternatives (aimed at filling gaps in the service sector left by an overstretched state apparatus). The phenomenon of the Islamic Investment Companies in Egypt, which proliferated in the 1980s and were rumoured to be financing Brotherhood activities, is a good example (for more details, see Zaalouk 1989).

Within many of the Islamist groups, both mainstream and extremist, a body of knowledge has been created, based on some form of 'Islamic teachings', which was thereafter used as a disciplinary practice (in the sense employed by Foucault) to elicit control – that is, obedience – from individuals. The latter feel empowered because 'Islam is the solution', while at the same time becoming more docile because they are not questioning the teachings as such but using them. This body of knowledge serves in its diversity the purpose of creating divisions between individuals, labelling them as Muslims/Copts, believers/non-believers, Muslims/Westerners, us/them, and so on. Some moderate Islamists and many of those who lean towards the extreme end of the continuum take this aspect to an excessive level through their policy of *takfir* (to render a non-believer), which is used to totally delegitimise the discourse of their ideological opponents. Since they claim to be speaking on behalf of God, those who oppose them are cast in the role of being opposed to God and thus non-believers. Particularly in a context where religion forms an important part of the identity and legitimacy of both the people and state, this tactic can be extremely alienating. These disciplinary practices, based on dichotomous and polarised thinking, and enshrined in the chaos of global events, form part of the power base which moderate Islamists possess.

Other elements of such bases of power are, ironically and as indicated above, dependent on 'external' interactions *vis-à-vis* moderate Islamism – where the dimensions of legitimacy and citizenship, the lack of a credible ideological alternative to Islamism, along with the larger dynamic of international relations between states, all feature in these interactions. Acknowledging these power bases is important in any attempt to understand why it is then perceived as necessary to overestimate the impact and role of Islamisms, or conversely to wish them away and pretend they did not exist. Moreover, the latest killings of tourists in Luxor, Egypt, also indicate that six Islamists – even when representing an extremist fringe movement that is hardly well-organised – can cause a great deal of damage to a country of 60 million and a religion with billions of adherents.

Futurescapes

The above representation explores the interconnectedness between global dynamics and Islamisms in an attempt to dispel the simplified notions that Islamisms are either an internal matter inherent to 'the nature of Islam', or some enemy totally dependent on external political dynamics and particularly opposed to all things Western. These notions are not only claimed by some Islamists, but are also propagated by those who oppose Islamisms. Negative media images in much Western media coverage of events surrounding or relating to Islamist phenomena, coupled with the international mobilisation of intelligence services to prevent the spread of Islamist activism (in the West as well as elsewhere), will do nothing to dispel the misperceptions and stereotypes that predominate, and which further compound an already difficult situation.

The repressive power of states and intelligence services in the Muslim world is only likely to constantly provide Islamists with further fuel for their *raison d'être*. Moreover, it is important to realise that Islamists – moderates and extremists alike – are further encouraged partly by the fact that they perceive their philosophy as a yet untried political alternative. The experiences in Shi'a Iran and Sunni Sudan are dismissed as 'not the real thing' or sincere endeavours gone awry as a result of concerted Western efforts against these countries. Another factor of encouragement for Islamist activism is the mere threat of or actual politico-military action by the Western world – which is an incentive that would unite rather than defeat. Examples of this abound: from recent 'Clintonesque' blunders on the anti-Islamist terrorist scene to Palestinian politics, where the political behaviour of Netanyahu and his American allies (for example, the non-exertion of pressure by the so-called peace-brokers on the recalcitrant Likud regime to honour Israel's commitments under the Oslo declaration of principles) only vindicates rather than refutes the arguments of the Hamas and all other Islamists, within and without the region. Egyptian Islamist extremists from the Jihad and Gama'a Islamiyya first decided to call a truce with the Egyptian government earlier in 1997, using the necessity of a united stance against Israel and the United States for the sake of salvaging a credible Palestinian position. Radical Islamist attacks against tourists in Egypt (apart from other civil unrest) tend to occur just after a particularly frustrating experience or series of experiences relating to the Palestinians. These examples indicate that as long as there is a common external enemy to unite against and to resist, Islamisms and their adherents (including those on the extremist fringe) are not about to 'go with the wind' but will instead enhance their power.

Interestingly, however, the same thesis or rationale can be applied to the Western world. A common external enemy, coupled with the power of resistance, seems also to be the order of the day, if one reads into NATO's search for a role and rationale after the collapse of the Soviet bloc. The Oklahoma bombing of a US Federal building remains an important incident, not only because of its catastrophic human consequences, but precisely because of the socio-political reactions it evoked. Until today, the immediate predictions publicly made by some 'top experts' on 'terrorism', that the bombing was the action of 'Islamic terrorists', remain telling. Why was there a rush to look anywhere but at home? Why was it so convenient and so 'logical' to assume that the terror came from outside? These are questions which once again are tied to issues of power. For to admit that the 'enemy' is 'one of us' is to admit a certain defeat and weakness, whereas to assume it is external is to maintain some form of strength of unity, which can then be harnessed to achieve power for resistance.

So in this dynamic of interaction, should we then be asking who has the most power for resistance, or who has the most powerful tools of repression at their disposal? Neither, since it is clear that at some stage resistive power leads to escalation and may well lead to a vicious cycle that can spin out of control and create a dynamic of its own. It is argued here that some form of accommodation will have to be sought at the end of the day, if Western and moderate Islamist worldviews are to reach a non-acrimonious accord. The next issue of course is what forms this accommodation will take. A highly credible and realistic arrangement can be found through common economic interests. The history of interactions between Muslim countries and Western ones is littered with events where economic interests have predominated over ethical, moral or political issues. The Gulf War was an excellent example of the motivation for consensus that economics can provide to stimulate political will for involvement – not just for Western countries, but also for them to convince other countries to take part. The continuous issue in the USA of according China 'Most Favoured Nation' status as a trading partner, and the general political attitude of turning a blind eye to a multitude of human rights violations, suitably dubbed as the 'internal affairs' of a sovereign nation state, are but a few examples of such accommodation. As long as certain economic interests are looked after, the world can turn peacefully in its orbit.

It is further contended that Islamists will also be tempered from their side by the exigencies of the economics of *realpolitik* once they capture state power and have to rule, no longer as opposition, but as officials of the state. They too will be forced to make economic deals with the Western world and once the repressive power of the state and the armed forces are in their hands, they will do what they see as right to safeguard their power. The price of the interactions involved will be instrumental in forming the socio-political fabric of society (see Karam 1998) and by impacting 'glocally', they will create another feature of postmodernity. Religion is an alternative mobilising ideology as long as its political manifestation stands in opposition to some other socio-political regime and remains an untried political alternative. However, once this *alternative* is seen to be and is itself the ruling power, then the element of 'being-in-opposition' is significantly weakened and with it their strength. In fact, Islamisms in power as evidenced in Iran, Sudan and Afghanistan, themselves generate other contesting forces, be they local, regional or global.

Notes

1. Bin Ladin has been described by the former US Secret Service Chief for Foreign Intelligence and ex-CIA man, David Breset, as 'a radical Saudi financier of terrorist organizations. This is an individual that was drawn in again like Arab Afghans, as I mentioned earlier, into the Afghan conflict early on, and rose to a position of prominence. And now a lot of people consider him the godfather of the so-called Arab Afghan movement. I believe he's the heart and soul of that movement' (quoted from *The Newshour with Jim Lehrer* transcript, 17 August 1998).
2. See for example, the article 'Islamism in Egypt' in *The Economist*, 27 July – 1 August 1997.
3. The Muslim Uygurs are the native (majority) community in this territory, referred to by the Chinese authorities as Xinjiang or the Xinjiang Uygur Autonomous Region. A recent Chinese census estimated the present population of the Uygurs at 7.2 million (with the fastest birth rate in comparison with other ethnic groups). And it is reported that there are 500 000 Uygurs in Kazakhstan, Uzbekistan, Kyrgyzstan, Turkmenistan and Tajikistan (all formerly part of the now defunct Western Turkestan), as well as 75 000 in Pakistan, Afghanistan, Saudi Arabia, Turkey, Europe and the USA respectively.
4. Excerpt from the first-ever television interview with Osama Bin Ladin, which was conducted by Peter Arnett in eastern Afghanistan in late March 1997. The questions posed to him were submitted in advance and Bin Ladin responded to almost all of them. CNN was not allowed to ask follow-up questions and the interview lasted just over an hour.

References

Appadurai, A. 1990: 'Disjunction and Difference in the Global Cultural Economy' in M. Featherstone (editor), *Global Culture: Nationalism, Globalization and Modernity*, London: Sage.

Featherstone, M. (editor) 1990: *Global Culture: Nationalism, Globalization, and Modernity*, London: Sage.

Foucault, M. 1980: *Power/Knowledge: Selected Interviews and Other Writings 1972–1977* (edited by C. Gordon and translated by C. Gordon *et al.*), New York: Pantheon Books.

Halliday, F. and Alavi, H. (editors) 1988: *State and Ideology in the Middle East and Pakistan*, London: Macmillan.

Harvey, D. 1990: *The Condition of Postmodernity*, Oxford: Basil Blackwell.

Karam, A.M. 1997: 'Islamisms There and Here' in *MERA Journal*, vol. 1, no. 1, Amsterdam: Middle East Research Associates.

Karam, A.M. 1998: *Women, Islamisms, and the State: Contemporary Feminisms in Egypt*. London: Macmillan and New York: St Martin's Press.

Kepel, G. 1985: *The Prophet and Pharaoh: Muslim Extremism in Egypt* (translated by Jon Rothschild), London: Al Saqi Books and distributed by Zed Books.

Little, D. 1996: 'Religious Militancy' in C. Crocker, F.O. Hampson and P. Aall (editors), *Managing Global Chaos: Sources of and Responses to International Conflict*, Washington, DC: United States Institute of Peace.

Marty, M.E. and Appleby, R.S. (editors) 1991: *Fundamentalisms Observed*, Chicago, IU. and London: University of Chicago Press.
Marty, M.E. and Appleby, R.S. 1992: *The Glory and the Power: The Fundamentalist Challenge to the Modern World*, Boston, Mass.: Beacon Press.
Marty, M.E. and Appleby, R.S. (editors) 1993a: *Fundamentalism and Society: Reclaiming the Sciences, the Family and Education*, Chicago, IU. and London: University of Chicago Press.
Marty, M.E. and Appleby, R.S. (editors) 1993b: *Fundamentalisms and the State: Remaking Politics, Economics and Militance*, Chicago, IU. and London: University of Chicago Press.
Marty, M.E. and Appleby, R.S. (editors) 1994: *Accounting for Fundamentalisms: The Dynamic Character of Movements*, Chicago, IU. and London: University of Chicago Press.
Marty, M.E. and Appleby, R.S. (editors) 1995: *Fundamentalisms Comprehended*, Chicago, IU. and London: University of Chicago Press.
Nederveen Pieterse, J.P. 1995: 'Globalization as Hybridization' in M. Featherstone, S. Lash and R. Robertson (editors), *Global Modernities*, London: Sage.
Robertson, R. 1990: 'Mapping the Global Condition: Globalization as the Central Concept' in M. Featherstone (editor), *Global Culture*, London: Sage.
Robertson, R. 1992: *Globalization: Social Theory and Global Culture*, London: Sage.
Ruedy, J. (editor) 1996: *Islamism and Secularism in North Africa*, London: Macmillan.
Shaw, M. 1994: *Global Society and International Relations*, Cambridge: Polity Press.
Vertovec, S. and Peach, C. (editors) 1997: *Islam in Europe: The Politics of Religion and Community*, London: Macmillan.
Waters, M. 1995: *Globalization*, London and New York: Routledge.
Zaalouk, M. 1989: *Power, Class and Foreign Capital in Egypt: The Rise of the New Bourgeoisie*, London and Atlantic Highlands, New Jersey: Zed Books.

12
Post-Cold War Futures: Peacemaking, Conflict Management and Humanitarian Action

Purnaka L. de Silva[1]

The future is always informed by the past and genocide has been inflicted over centuries of human existence, across the globe and without exception. In a unique study of the history and sociology of genocide, Frank Chalk and Kurt Jonassohn argue that:

[The] coarseness and brutality of human existence throughout much of history was a subject that hardly ever appeared in the curricula of our schools ... The great massacres of the past lay beyond the range of the telescopes designed to focus upon evidence that justice always triumphed. In high school and university textbooks, Athens flourished, but the massacre of the men of Melos was rarely mentioned. The Romans destroyed Carthage and Corinth, but the fate of their people was not discussed. The authors of history textbooks hardly ever reported what the razing of an ancient city meant for its inhabitants. In other words, the fate of millions of human beings who died unnatural deaths as defenseless civilians was invisible ... Many factors entered into this process of collective denial. *Throughout most of recorded time, it was the victors who wrote the history of their conquests*, and even the victims of mass exterminations accepted their fate as a natural outcome of defeat. The idea of human rights is relatively new in Western society; even today, many parts of the world still emphasize duties more than rights. The Enlightenment tradition of viewing human beings as inherently good and rational also played a part in the denial, as did the rise of nationalism and fear of stirring up ethnic enmity. The slaughter of people of *other* races, religions, and nationalities barely offended anyone's sensibilities. (Chalk and Jonassohn 1990:7–8, emphasis added).

Included in the catalogue of terrible injustices committed against *other* peoples is the racism, bigotry, white-supremacism, Eurocentrism, exploitation, cruelty and inhumane practices – including the killings of thousands of 'rebels', 'insurgents' and other 'undesirables' in order to maintain the 'law and order' of the day – which were perpetrated on millions of non-European indigenous peoples and selected European outcasts, from the age of slavery to that of empire-building, colonial expansion and beyond. This sorry saga of human history also involves the arbitrary carving-up of territories and resources, both human and material, in all five continents and needs no elaborate introduction.[2]

Examination of political violence in the twentieth century illustrates in no uncertain terms the barbarism and brutal excesses of conflicts over power – whether in terms of ideological supremacy or control over resources – which have been conducted at global, regional, national or local levels. The volume edited by Totten, Parsons and Charny (1995) goes into some of the horrific details of this phenomenon in *Century of Genocide: Eyewitness Accounts and Critical Views* and covers, Armenia (1915–23), Bangladesh (1971), Burundi (1972), Cambodia (1975–9), East Timor (1975–9), the holocausts of the Jews, the Gypsies and the disabled (1933–45), Indonesia (1965–6), South West Africa (1904) and the Ukraine (1932–3), as well as the physical and cultural genocide of various indigenous peoples. While this list is certainly not comprehensive, which speaks volumes in itself, it records the extent to which humans have exterminated other humans during the past 100 years. Relying on the opinion of former US President Jimmy Carter's National Security Advisor, Zbigniew Brzezinski, Herbert Hirsch argues in this context that:

> genocides ... have plagued human history in general and our troubled century in particular. Estimates of the toll taken in the twentieth century are astounding; Brzezinski (1993) claims that '167 000 000 to 175 000 000 lives have been deliberately extinguished through politically motivated carnage' (p. 17). (Hirsch 1995:xi–xii).

Bearing in mind the accelerated blood-letting in various parts of the globe since Brzezinski's observations of 1993,[3] such thought-provoking and quite literally shocking statistics (however generalised they may be) motivate the following evaluation of the future of peacemaking, conflict management and humanitarian action in the late twentieth century and beyond.

Political violence and the civilisational process

All governments, as well as many insurrectionary forces, exercise varying degrees of power through institutionalised forms of violence. 'Law and order' is maintained by nation states, through the police, judiciary, prison services and other branches of the military. This type of legalised structural violence goes almost unnoticed, given its everyday character and constitutional justification, unless of course the normative boundaries of such legalities are contravened and thereafter contested, as in the case of the much publicised Rodney King beating in 1992 and the ensuing race riots.[4] Likewise, insurgent forces also maintain 'rough justice', albeit through the barrel of the gun, without many of the legal niceties or accountability.

While acknowledging that a major methodological problem in research on violence is that of inconsistent definitions – that is, 'in the distinction between the behaviour and the influences and evaluation of its observers' (Drinkwater and Gudjonsson 1992:289–90) – my focus here is not so much on everyday aspects of violence (such as policing or domestic abuse) as on violence as an explicit political tool in situations of armed conflict. Political violence is a process where the deliberate use and/or threat of force is carried out to the detriment of perceived enemies, competitors or inferiors, with an intention to cause death and/or injury, and/or destruction of person(s), property and interests, by organised groups or members of such entities, which belong to government or insurrectionary forces. The aims of political violence are political – in so far as they pertain to policies and intrigues of state or insurgent actors – and are continuations of power struggles by means other than dialogue, debate, discussion, accommodation, compromise and tolerance. Ethnic and/or race riots and the specificities of political rape, as in Bosnia–Hercegovina and Pakistan,[5] also fall within the ambit of this definition.

Political violence, like its institutionalised variant, which is exercised under the label of 'law and order', is justified and used frequently in many, if not all societies – with the only difference being its scale, degree and intensity. Such action and the lack of humane morals (whether of a universalistic or relativistic character) are specific to prevalent conditions of contemporary ethics, killing and war. According to the moral philosopher Richard Norman:

> Insofar as there is a moral consensus within our culture, and beyond it, its most deep-rooted feature is the recognition of the wrongness

of killing another human being. When it comes to the killing of thousands and even millions of people in war, however, this is widely accepted as a necessary and inevitable part of our way of life ... Nevertheless, for most people it is beyond question that nations have to pursue their interests or defend themselves by war if necessary, with the recognition that this will normally involve killing on a massive scale. Those who perpetrate the killing will be treated by their fellow countrymen [sic] not as moral outcasts but as heroes.

(Norman 1995:1)

My argument here is the rather obvious one, that dependence on violence as a strategic and tactical means to settle conflicts and power struggles betrays *a serious deficiency in the civilisational development* of human socio-political formations – despite the manifold technological developments of the space age and the information age. No amount of theorising about strategic thinking, 'just wars' and 'future wars' can take away from the barbarism and brutality of situated practices of political violence. In fact, such efforts only underline the underdeveloped character of contemporary moralities and the *uncivilised* aspects of contemporary human politico-economic culture and praxis. The need to redress the civilisational imbalance away from the celebration and romanticisation of violence is a priority and a creative director such as Steven Spielberg deserves full credit for trying his best to depict the horrors of war as graphically and honestly as possible in the critically acclaimed film *Saving Private Ryan* (1998). This film is a first on celluloid and a welcome change in popular cultural production. Nevertheless, such commendable efforts have to be sustained, become more widespread and be taken up by leading lights in all types of human endeavour if they are to make a qualitative difference and help redress the civilisational imbalance.

Boom or Bust?

In the late twentieth century, while there are a plethora of ongoing 'low-intensity' conflicts and civil wars in a number of 'less-developed' countries from the south, advanced or late capitalist societies are posited as pinnacles of human civilisation, development and culture. Consumption is the name of the game in these societies, where globalisation and economic well-being – in the form of market forces, economic efficiency and upward mobility – are represented as the be-all and end-all of what is meaningful and significant. Anthony Richmond comments from a more down-to-earth perspective that:

> Notwithstanding the economic trend towards a 'borderless world', globalization is far from complete. A substantial portion of the world's population is still excluded from the more affluent regions and some are in danger of being perpetually exiled.
> (Richmond 1994:233)

In the post-Cold War world, despite the uneven spread and lack of uniformity of the capitalist global economic system, it has tremendous influence and impact on the running of the day-to-day affairs of billions of humans. Moreover, this information-age global economy, which was ushered in by the digital revolution, is also *cultural* and *political*, and goes hand in hand with technological development and innovation. If we are to agree with the likes of Samuel P. Huntington (1989, 1991, 1996), Robert Kaplan (1996), Alvin and Heidi Toffler (1995), Francis Fukuyama (1989) and Alvin Toffler (1990), the battle lines of post-Cold War cultural and political conflict are now drawn between a homogenised 'liberal and democratic Western civilisation and its allies' and 'alien civilisations' and 'Third Wave' enemies of 'Western interests, values and power', who must be confronted and defeated, particularly in the realms of economics and politics. Fukuyama even makes the optimistic claim that liberal democracy (as the high point of modern Western civilisation) represents the 'end of history'. Commenting on common reactions against and resistance to post-Cold War secular liberal capitalism and echoing conventional thinking in international relations, Joseph S. Nye, argues in somewhat contrary fashion that:

> The end of the Cold War suggests that liberal capitalism has prevailed, and there is no longer one single competitor to liberal capitalism as an overarching ideology. For authors like Francis Fukuyama who believe that ideas drive history, then history might well seem to be over. But rather than the 'end of history,' the post-Cold War world could be described as the *return* of history ... Liberal capitalism has many competitors, albeit fragmented ones. China allows for capitalism in its southwestern provinces, particularly Guangdong and Hong Kong. Yet, China in its politics and ideology is neither liberal nor fully capitalist. In other areas, religious fundamentalism [sic] challenges the norms and practices of liberal capitalism ... The major

response and competitor to liberal capitalism after the Cold War is ethnic nationalism.

(Nye 1997:184)

While many observers would agree with most of what Nye has to say, I would contest his claim that 'ethnic nationalism is a major response and competitor to post-Cold War liberal capitalism', simply by looking at case examples. In fact, many leaders who participate in ethnic fratricide do look towards the global power-brokers to help bail them out in the difficult task of post-conflict reconstruction, which necessarily entails playing by the rules of market-led economics. Huntington, on the other hand, continues to persist in his erroneous conservative line and uses a stereotypical argument against his critics that is somewhat reminiscent of the *blut und boden* (blood and soil) theme, and concludes his 'defence' thus:

> What ultimately counts for people is not political ideology or economic interest. Faith and family, blood and belief, are what people identify with and what they will fight and die for. And that is why the clash of civilizations is replacing the Cold War as the central phenomenon of global politics, and why a civilizational paradigm provides, better than any alternative, a useful starting point for understanding and coping with the changes going on in the world.
>
> (Huntington *et al.* 1996:67)

More recently and in a similar liberal democratic tone, Kaplan (1997) and Fareed Zakaria (1997) present rather pessimistic arguments concerning the merits of electoral democracy. The first-past-the-post system of electoral democracy might indeed spawn negative spin-offs that result in discrimination of minority rights through petty political praxis. However, it is *not* the only factor that has led to 'the threat to freedom' by regimes which Kaplan and Zakaria label as 'illiberally democratic'. Moreover, 'liberal non-democratic' authoritarianism is most certainly not the remedy, as the authors suggest, to solving the problems of electoral democracy. By contrast, Daniel Pick presents an excellent analysis of Western perceptions of war in the nineteenth century and after, traces the origins of modern philosophies pertaining to the character of war and conflict, in particular the rationalisation of slaughter. Gleaning ideas from the writings of a plethora of novelists, anthropologists, psychiatrists, poets, natural scientists and journalists, Pick argues that:

> The 'unstoppable engine of war' has become something of a modern truism. As though in answer to the question 'Why War?', the answer

finally might turn on the insatiable and irresistible drive of the 'military–industrial complex' – that ambiguous phrase crucially begging the question of human agency and responsibility. Or as though war today might not only involve the deployment of new technologies, but be *essentially* redefined by them: satellites, television, computers and video games after all have occupied centre stage in the representation and military news management of the Gulf War. Are we not so often caught in the fascination and massive distortion of this 'high-tech' image of conflict today – as though war is both decreed and exclusively played out by high-precision automata? But how new are such perceptions of war's own technological triumph and irresistible momentum? (Pick 1996:11)

Despite all their sophistication, erudition and high profile as great thinkers, the point that the information age gurus of the 'liberal' and not-so-liberal democratic sort miss or tend to overlook is that their 'futuristic' thinking is, in fact, quite archaic. Despite catchy sound bites and triumphant acclaim of their work among Western foreign policy-makers, they display an inability or unwillingness to understand difference and acknowledge the tremendous *positive* impact that the mixing of peoples, civilisations and cultures has had over centuries of human existence – evidence of which can be seen in a whole range of contributions from advancements in the sciences, medicine and technology[6] to arts, crafts and music. Post-Second World War global economic reconstruction and market-led successes have benefited tremendously from the cheap labour and hard work of millions of unsung heroes from several labour diasporas, in particular Mexicans in the USA, North Africans in France and Turks in Germany, as well as emergent Asian diasporas in Japan and the USA (Esman 1994:176–215), a trend that is highlighted in no uncertain terms by recent migrants from Hong Kong to Canada, whose business activities and acumen have stimulated a phenomenal economic upturn in their new country of domicile – much to the amazement and envy of conservative British civil servants who had earlier rejected these would-be migrants from entering the UK. Similarly, the new turn to the far right in German politics forgets or totally rejects the contribution of generations of migrant labourers, particularly Turkish, in rebuilding a war-ravaged infrastructure and economy in their insane search for homogeneous 'Germanic purity' based on bloodlines. Therefore, rather than regurgitating and feeding on age-old phobias based on religious, racial, cultural or pseudo-civilisational differences, the challenge of the twenty-first century is for open, flexible and alternative thinking, combined with the development of an advanced and constantly evolving set of moralities, ethics and values, the cumulative impact of which must be the capability of bridging 'civilisational' divisions between and within human social formations – be they religious, historical, racial, ethnic, linguistic, traditional, cultural or political differences – and thereby usher in a new age beyond conflict. The alternative would be to descend to the barbarity of the former Yugoslavia, Rwanda, Liberia, Sierra Leone and many other violent places. One of the first steps that must be taken is to pay attention to detail and depth, and to move away from the homogenising, generalising and stereotyping methods of contemporary sound-bite discourse, – which more often than not lead to brutalisation and/or indifference, apathy and socio-political inaction.

The context

Since the end of the Cold War, the range of 'complex emergencies' and scope for peacemaking, conflict management and humanitarian action have expanded exponentially. However, the political will, leadership, ability, motivation and financial backing to deal with these situations has *not* kept pace. In late capitalist societies, where postmodern and post-industrial lifestyles ostensibly mingle with advanced forms of democratic government and political correctness, legislators nevertheless tend to demonstrate a lack of moral substance and integrity, particularly when confronted by the exigencies of *realpolitik*. For example, in a detailed study aimed at strengthening the human rights movement in the United Kingdom, Conor Foley with Liberty (National Council for Civil Liberties) presents a comprehensive catalogue of human rights abuses in England, Wales and Northern Ireland (from 1989 to 1994)[7] which provides alternative testimony to that which was presented to the UN Human Rights Committee by the previous Tory administration led by John Major, in its 'official record' (Foley with Liberty 1995). I am in no way suggesting that this lack of morality and ethics is the privilege of advanced capitalist societies, as any scrutiny of current affairs and recent histories – such as those made by the contributors to this volume – will testify. Rather, my criticism is of moral postulations and lip-service made to 'the greater good of humanity' and in 'defence of freedom' by the leading lights of the international community, *with little or no follow-up action* – whether it be in terms of resource allocations or political will for positive change – particularly during armed conflicts and related humanitarian disasters.

Given the plethora of conflicts that have emerged or continue to fester in the aftermath of the Cold War, government officials, policy-makers, non-governmental actors, researchers and concerned persons alike must come to terms with the growing problems of political violence and armed conflicts. The old and new media-interactive public in many countries is being constantly bombarded with snippets of information about conflicts and political violence here, there and everywhere (Minear, Scott and Weiss 1996). It is almost impossible for 'lay-persons' and even so-called 'experts' to keep track of events and obtain an in-depth understanding of what appear to be 'wars' that seem to proliferate, and take place in remote regions of the globe. In fact, the use of mechanisms of media control and media abuse (for example, distortion, disinformation and propaganda) – as in the former Yugoslavia (Article 19 1994) and in the use of extremist Hutu radio broadcasts in the Rwandan genocide – leads this medium of mass communication to become an instrument of war more often than not.

As an exercise in countering sound-bite discourse, we can examine a random checklist that illustrates certain exigencies of *realpolitik* by the governments of advanced capitalist nations:

- the genocide in the Great Lakes region encompassing Rwanda, Burundi and Eastern Democratic Congo (formerly Zaire) and along the border with Tanzania;
- the Balkans (particularly Bosnia–Hercegovina);
- the annexation and occupation of East Timor by Indonesia;
- the war in the Falklands (Malvinas);
- the bombing of Pan Am flight 103;
- the high-tech, 'mother of all wars' in the Gulf region.

Beginning with Rwanda, the moral ambiguities and ethical questions raised by the involvement of France, particularly under the helm of the late socialist President François Mitterrand, in actively supporting the extremist Hutu-led regime at the height of the genocide of the minority Tutsi population and opposition Hutus, are hard to match. As an example of the mind-set of the French power-brokers at the time and their complicity in the Rwandan genocide,[8] *Le Figaro* published a document in January 1998 which acknowledged an US$8 million order for the supply of heavy machine gun and mortar rounds from the French state-run armaments supplier Sofremas to the Hutu authorities in Rwanda, *after the genocidal massacres*. The last delivery of this consignment was flown to the Great Lakes region on 18 July 1994 – that is, *after* France had dispatched a UN-mandated peacekeeping force (*Guardian Weekly*, 18 January 1998, p. 3). Notwithstanding the gross violations of human rights, and the untold hardships and indignities suffered by millions of Rwandans across the board during the genocide, member states of the Western alliance (Anglophone and Francophone), as well as NGOs which provide humanitarian assistance, have continued to make matters worse through their indecisiveness in dealing with the manifold post-genocide problems of Rwanda. Even more alarmingly, a number of NGOs, through naivety and a degree of arrogance, have overplayed their own importance in terms of what they can contribute and have become partisan, thereby tainting all NGOs in the process.[9] (For a comprehensive critical evaluation of an international NGO engaged in the arena of conflict management, mediation, fieldwork and advocacy, see Sørbø, Macrae and Wohlgemuth (1997), and for a critical evaluation of the aid and development policies of the world's richest nations and an exposé of the gap between rhetoric and reality, see the most recent edition of *Earthscan*, 1997).

Former US Republican President George Bush's 48-hour ultimatum to 'the Arab world', to find an 'Arab solution' to the complex diplomatic crisis caused by Iraq's invasion of the oil-rich sheikhdom of Kuwait, is another case in point. US military, political, diplomatic and economic power, combined with information-age technological superiority and war-making capabilities was demonstrated during the Gulf War and translated into global power. It was this long-term geopolitical consideration and ambition to remain the hegemonic superpower which overdetermined other non-military initiatives aimed at pressuring Saddam Hussein to withdraw Iraqi forces and amicably resolve a deep-rooted conflict – created historically by arbitrary colonial border demarcation by short sighted imperialist bureaucrats (a widespread problem in the post-colonial era). Undoubtedly shuttle-diplomacy would have been more time-consuming and tedious, but at the end of the day a far less costly option, in terms of both financial and human expenditure. The irony of the Gulf War is that the USA and its allies portray their post-Cold War military intervention as upholding international jurisprudence, but had the world's richest oilfields not been located in the Gulf, the story would have been rather different, as has been demonstrated time and again in other cases, such as in Bosnia–Hercegovina, Rwanda, Burundi, Liberia, Sierra Leone and Algeria.

Even more insidious, however have been the many silences, inaction and proxy wars which accompanied the Cold War:

- Indonesia's annexation of East Timor and the repression of its majority Roman Catholic population, along with a number of other rebellious indigenous peoples (for example, in Irian Jaya, Aceh) and political opponents of the (now-deposed) Suharto-led military dictatorship inhabiting the sprawling archipelago, not to mention the long-term ecological disaster with implications of truly global proportions, brought about by alleged presidential cronyism and mismanaged development policies, particularly in the timber, agricultural and forestry sectors.
- China's bloody annexation of Tibet and unjust suppression of indigenous cultural and politico-religious expression;
- the overthrow of the democratically elected socialist regime of Salvador Allende by a CIA-backed coup headed by the (recently arrested) military dictator General Pinochet;
- the 'humanitarian intervention' in Grenada by US troops;
- the bloody and cruel proxy wars in Angola, Mozambique, Guatemala, El Salvador, Nicaragua and Afghanistan;
- the unfinished saga of the disparate and long-suffering Kurdish peoples who are spread over the territory of six countries, namely, eastern Turkey, north-western Iran, northern Iraq, north-eastern Syria, south-west Armenia and Lebanon – involving persecution at the hands of the Turks and Iraqis in particular and the armed resistance of a number of Kurdish nationalist organisations.

The priorities of the Cold War, among Western, right-wing, liberal, Christian democratic and social democratic forces on the one hand, and pro-Communist, pro-Soviet forces on the other, were ideological and geopolitical hegemony at whatever cost. Incredible cruelties and gross violations of human rights were not only tolerated, but justified and promoted by key decision-making bodies and policy-oriented think-tanks – a fact that epitomised a bipolar and an apparently 'civilised' world order. The dictates of geopolitics, the safety of intercontinental (submarine and other) linkages and the defeat of communist forces in South East Asia were deemed to be strategically more important than, for example, the human rights and political freedom of native East Timorese. The post-Cold War era has also spawned a number of civil wars connected with the break-up of what was once the Union of Soviet Socialist Republics (USSR) and its empire:

- the war for independence waged by outnumbered, out-gunned and disparate nationalists in Chechnya versus their former Russian imperial overlords and Ingushetian opponents;
- the colossal blood-letting in the former Yugoslavia between Serb, Croat and Muslim nationalists in Bosnia–Hercegovina, Croatia and Slovenia, and in Kosovo between Serb and native Albanian nationalists;
- the now dormant armed conflicts in Abkhazia and Ossetia, between Georgian government troops and Abkhaz separatist rebels, and in the Georgian region of South Ossetia, between Georgian government forces and Ossetian rebels (demanding unification between North and South Ossetia), and in North Ossetia between North Ossetian forces and Ingushetian forces;
- the battles in Azerbaijan involving the breakaway Armenian enclave of Nagorniy Karabakh between Armenian and Azeri government forces;
- the simmering cross-border conflict in Tajikistan between Russian-backed Tajik government forces and Tajik rebels supported by Afghan *mujahideen* on the one hand, and, on the other, sporadic fighting between feuding Tajik political factions in and around the capital Dushanbe, involving former communists and Islamic Renaissance Party (IRP) supporters.

Collective human memories and attention spans tend to be quite ephemeral, and as news coverage flits from one crisis to another, processes of forgetting take place almost unconsciously. In other words, a silent brutalisation of majority of media-watchers from among the public at large is taking place on a daily basis. While it is not possible to examine in detail all the cases listed above, a *remembering* of some of the post-Cold War human horrors of a forgotten proxy war in Angola illustrates the effectiveness of this process of forgetting (for more details see Brittain 1998). On the BBC World Service radio programme 'The World Today' (16 September 1993), correspondent Michael Cochrane remarked that in Angola 'horrific atrocities take place very casually every day'. In the same context, Margaret Amstead, the UN Special Envoy to Angola, who was in charge of overseeing a peace settlement and cessation of hostilities between the MPLA government and UNITA rebels, said that in September 1993 more than 'a thousand people were dying every day', and that Angola was 'a humanitarian tragedy of incalculable proportions'. A further BBC World Service radio report broadcast on 'News Hour' (27 September 1993) called the conflict in Angola as 'the world's worst war' and 'a war without witnesses'. The reporter on that occasion also stated that 'Indeed conditions in the besieged town of Kuito are said to be so bad that survivors are eating the dead.' The internal conflicts in Angola are yet to be fully resolved and yet the majority of the international community has already forgotten the past horrors of this deeply divided society.

The human tragedy of all this carnage in the twentieth century is that while the psycho-social recovery from the brutalities of such warfare is always a slow, painful and long-term process, similar atrocities are repeated in one form or another, ranging from ideologically-based power struggles to conflicts over lucrative mineral rights. In a recent throwback to imperialist colonial times, British forces fought their Argentine counterparts, apparently for the control of a wind-blown chain of islands referred to respectively as the Falklands or Malvinas. It has only recently become evident that there are possibly lucrative petrochemical deposits in waters off these islands but, at the time of the war, much ado was made about the rescue of an intrinsically 'British' territory and its community of sheep farmers from the clutches of the 'Argies', a jingoistic manoeuvre to secure Britain's place in the global order.

The prolongation of the wars in the Balkans, particularly in Bosnia–Hercegovina, and the loss of more than a quarter of a million lives, is due to a large extent to the inaction of leaders of the so-called 'civilised' world. They simply witnessed crimes against humanity on an almost daily basis for a couple of years and did nothing until the US State Department got involved somewhat late in the day. It is simply *not* morality, ethics, human rights and justice according to international standards and jurisprudence that count in the global scheme of things. Rather, as in the case of Kuwait, it is profit and the unhampered access to valuable resources that is significant in the post-Cold War world order, with ideologically-based conflicts on the wane.

The tragic case of the Pan Am flight 103 bombing on 21 December 1988 over Lockerbie in Scotland presents the global audience with a special dilemma in view of accusations (thus far unfounded in a court of law) that the upholders of democracy, justice, freedom, morality and ethical values are willing to compromise these principles by 'wrongly' prosecuting two Libyan agents as the chief culprits. According to a Washington-based report by CNN filed on 4 November 1995:

> Some relatives of victims of the 1988 Pan Am jetliner bombing over Scotland boycotted Friday's dedication of a memorial to the 270 dead, saying the U.S. government is covering up information on the

case ... One relative accused the U.S. government of 'giving lip service' to U.S.–British investigations that blamed the bombing on two Libyan agents of Col. Moammar Gadhafi, while ignoring alleged Iranian, Syrian and Palestinian connections. She said those alleged connections were covered up to promote the anti-Iraq coalition in the Persian Gulf War and later, the Arab–Israeli peace process.

It has been further alleged in current affairs programmes, that despite strenuous efforts to the contrary by involved governments, there is circumstantial evidence pointing to a Syrian-backed terrorist network behind this bombing. While all this may sound like conjecture, the 'truth' of the matter will be eventually decided in the International Court of Justice (World Court) in The Hague, probably according to the tenets of the Scottish justice system. Such an outcome ought to be welcomed by all concerned but if there is evidence which points to intrigue at the highest levels of the international community, then the question that needs to be asked is why Libya is in the dock instead of Syria. The answer to this may lie in the 'strategic thinking' behind the motley alliance built up during the Gulf War in opposition to Iraqi aggression and in Syria's continuing importance as a key player in guaranteeing the fashioning of a long-term peace arrangement in the Middle East – and thereby securing the interests of the global superpower and its allies in the Middle East and North Africa region.

Weapons overproduction and its effects

Geopolitical considerations aside, the continued proliferation of the global arms trade – particularly that of conventional weapons – poses not only moral and ethical questions but also the problem of long-term insecurity. Short-term economic benefits by industrialised, arms-producing nations are seen as vital for the growth of local manufacturing industry. The same countries that postulate liberal, democratic values and the virtues of post-Cold War freedom are, ironically, among the world's leading arms exporters. According to the annual report on military balance published by the International Institute for Strategic Studies (IISS), despite a 'significant drop' in real terms since the Cold War, there were US$40 billion worth of arms sales in 1996 – that is, an 8 per cent increase over 1995 (which recorded a 13 per cent increase over 1994). These facts run contrary to the commonly-held perception that 'Military expenditure has, globally, diminished continuously since 1985' (Swedish Ministry of Foreign Affairs 1997a:12). Despite arguments to the contrary by arms-producing nations, the world has definitely *not* become a safer place in the aftermath of the Cold War. The powder keg in the Middle East in particular keeps getting more and more conventional weaponry, and accounts for more than US$15 billion worth of weapons purchases in 1996 alone, or 40 per cent of total global arms sales. There is also a significant arms build-up in East Asia where there are disputes:

- over the control of the mineral-rich Spratly Islands group (including the Paracel Islands) and reportedly vast seabed resources in the South China Sea between China, the Philippines, Vietnam, Malaysia and Brunei (Hindley and Bridge 1994:109, Valencia 1995);
- between China and Taiwan;
- between North and South Korea, China and Japan, Japan and Russia, and more recently between Iran and Taliban-controlled Afghanistan (allegedly backed by Pakistan's Inter-Services Intelligence agency or ISI)

All these have the *potential* to spark off international conflicts of varying degrees of regional or global proportions. Apart from all the potential land and sea based conflicts that might occur in the twenty-first century, such as between Greece and Turkey over ownership of uninhabited islands off the Turkish coast, oil rights in the Aegean Sea and Cyprus, there is one more factor that can lead to local, national and regional warfare, namely conflicts over the refusal to share the increasingly scarce resource of fresh water (both above and underground) – a scarcity due to pollution, desertification, increased salinity, and other environmental changes such as global warming and deforestation.

It is unconscionable at the dawn of the twenty-first century, that war-making capacities continue to be stimulated and supported by profit-oriented weapons manufacturers and arms dealers across the globe. Furthermore, it highlights a schizophrenic attitude among legislators who, on the one hand, bemoan the fact that due to the wide-range of ongoing conflicts and warfare across the globe, the United Nations (UN), European Union (EU), Organisation for Security and Cooperation in Europe (OSCE), North Atlantic Treaty Organisation (NATO) and other multilateral agencies face escalating costs when providing humanitarian assistance, conflict management expertise and/or peacekeeping forces, while, on the other hand they do not curb or halt their national arms-producing and trading practices, but in fact promote and stimulate them at every opportunity, on the grounds of short-term economic gains. John Tirman (1997), executive director of the Winston Foundation for World Peace based in Washington, presents a well-documented exposé of the US arms trade (which has the largest market share of sales) and related foreign policy.[10] In reviewing this book, Colman McCarthy argues that:

> In *Spoils of War* John Tirman examines with dispassionate resolve and clarity the mechanics of cold violence – *the speciality of arms lobbyists, corporate weapons-exporters, pro-military politicians, Washington policymakers and think-tank rationalizers who are removed from the gore and madness* that can result from America's technology of death – fighter jets, attack helicopters, missiles, land mines, tanks, guns – is profitably sold to client states. Tirman's reporting which is rich with historical allusions and fair-minded analysis of what he calls 'the ingrained habits and shibboleths of the arms business,' ... [Tirman goes on to note that] '*In a country now in the grip of a debate over 'values,' it is astounding that so little heed is given to the values underlying the promiscuous provision of lethal weaponry'*.
> (McCarthy 1998, emphasis added)

The outcome of such market-driven logic without moral and ethical checks in the 'politically correct West' is that countries like China, Russia and the Ukraine, along with a host of other major and minor arms-manufacturing nations across the globe, continue the scramble to sell more and more weapons of greater sophistication (some with capacities for mass destruction) – unimpeded by foreign policy implications or concerns for restraint. Needless to say, this money-making ignores the logical outcome of such sales and technological development, which ultimately involve the killing, maiming and traumatising of humans by other humans.

Andrew J. Pierre argues that the near-total preoccupation with weapons of mass destruction masks the risks and dangers resulting from the *spread of advanced conventional arms and post-Cold War overcapacity in weapons production*. For Pierre, the most serious threat to post-Cold War peace and the greatest diversion from economic and social development is posed by conventional weapons proliferation, given that such hardware will most likely to be used in contemporary and future conflicts (Pierre 1997:1–6). He argues for the establishment of an international regime for conventional arms sales, as a means towards managing, restraining and bringing order to a hitherto unfettered global arms trade. Pierre's call is made in spite of the numerous and often conflicting strategic, political, economic and bureaucratic interests involved, not least of all, the lack of initiative for the achievement of multilateral arms restraint by the world's largest producer and exporter of arms, the USA and the other five major arms exporters, Russia, France, the United Kingdom, Germany and China. In global terms, the 'big six' *'made 86 percent of the $190.8 billion (in constant 1995 U.S. dollars) in arms deliveries to the world in 1990–95'*. (Ibid.:5, emphasis added).

Peacemaking, conflict management and humanitarian action

Humanitarian action during armed conflict, is conducted in contexts where multilateral agencies (for example, the UN, EU and OSCE), donor agencies, aid organisations, international development cooperation bodies and concerned NGOs have to determine the most appropriate response in situations where political, legal, diplomatic and even moral clarity is lacking. As Adam Roberts argues:

> Humanitarian action as a response to war, and to violent crises within states, has been tried in the 1990s as never before ... [taking] many forms – provision of food and shelter for refugees; airlifts of supplies to besieged populations; proclamations of 'safe areas'; attempts to ensure implementation of the laws of war; monitoring of detention conditions; the use of outside armed forces for 'humanitarian intervention' in situations of chaos, warlordism, massive atrocities and tyrannical government; mine-clearance; and post-war (even sometimes intra-war) reconstruction ... The fact remains that alongside the growth of humanitarian action there has been a policy vacuum. Major powers and international organisations have lacked long-term policies addressing the substantive issues raised by the conflicts of the 1990s. The vacuum increases the demand for humanitarian responses but reduces their effectiveness.
>
> (Roberts 1996:7, 9)

Therefore, agencies which seek a more accountable and professional role for humanitarianism and conflict management, despite criticism from certain quarters, need to have a thorough political understanding of emergency situations. Only by fully understanding a given situation in all its complexity and nuances can such agencies ensure that a non-partisan approach is retained and avoid some of the serious blunders of the recent past in Somalia, Bosnia, Rwanda and Sierra Leone among other cases. Apart from hands-on knowledge and operational criteria, policy-makers must also acknowledge the occupational hazard of peacekeeping, namely, that peacekeepers run the risk of being killed or injured. Planning field operations from the relative safety of New York or Geneva can lead a strategist to paint an unrealistic assessment of the situation on the ground. Similarly, struggles for democratic freedoms also entail varying degrees of suffering, loss of life and pain, often overlooked by a majority of 'practitioners' and policy-makers who operate largely at the level of semantics and on short-term 'flying-in/flying-out' agendas.

The questions of neutrality and impartiality are key issues that need to be addressed. The chief predicament faced here is whether it is possible to supply humanitarian assistance in locations under the control of authorities – whether government or rebel armies – which are ignoring basic human rights, without providing even tacit support to those authorities and thereby, in principle, doing disservice to the people designated for relief. In the world of life-and-death situations where humanitarian action is warranted, relatively inexperienced project managers and bureaucrats take on-the-spot decisions in locations far removed from the realities of their superiors. The immediacy of such decisions can lead to the making of unacceptable compromises (for example, sharing the cargo space of a relief plane with weapons, provision of supplies to one side or the other in an ongoing armed conflict) and entail long-term negative consequences for a particular programme of action or for all NGOs operating in a particular area or region.

A way out of this dilemma would be to create a more accurate system of forecasting situations that warrant humanitarian action and to conduct in-depth research *before* an intervention phase is initiated. Of course humanitarian action during natural disasters like earthquakes, floods, land-slides and so on does not provide agencies with the luxury of time, but even in these situations advances in environmental and climate studies can provide accurate forecasts. This 'lack of time' scenario is simply not the case in situations of political violence, civil war and armed conflict, given that many specialist researchers can and do understand a number of the trajectories of a particular 'complex emergency'. What needs to be done is for agencies engaged in the manifold tasks of humanitarian action, to tap into as many of these primary sources of understanding as possible, to preempt the escalation of conflict through concerted external pressure. Failing this, they can prepare a well-thought-out and planned intervention *with the cooperation and participation of local authorities and peoples*. Such a measured course of action, backed by sufficient funding and the creation of a knowledgeable permanent cadre of senior, middle- and lower-level project managers, would undoubtedly lead to more effective responses to the increased demand for humanitarian action *and* compensate somewhat for the current policy vacuum.

There have been, of course, attempts in the 1990s by a number of policy-making bodies, academic institutions and think-tanks across the globe to examine armed conflicts, identify problem areas and come up with specific recommendations for positive change. One such initiative is the influential Carnegie Commission on Preventing Deadly Conflict, established in 1994 to address threats to world peace as a result of intergroup violence, and to advance new ideas for conflict prevention and resolution. After publishing a number of reports (Holl 1996, Hamburg 1993), some of which examined *enforcement as a means of prevention* (Stremlau 1996, Goodpaster 1996), the Carnegie Commission produced a final report (1997). Like similar initiatives however, the recommendations made by the Carnegie Corporation lack a vital perspective, namely, a comprehensive *reassessment* of post-Cold War policy-making in the arena of conflict management and humanitarian action. Such a perspective must necessarily involve an honest appraisal and acknowledgement of *double standards* in the diplomatic and political praxis of the international community. Excuses and justifications for the operation of double standards can only lead to a lack of confidence in the post-Cold War world order, and in the recommendations aimed at conflict management made by representatives of such a system – particularly on the part of protagonists engaged in armed conflict. Even-handedness and non-preferential treatment of countries like Israel and Kuwait is essential, and will prove to be a decisive factor in resolving the bitter conflicts in that troubled region and in promoting greater global stability over the long term.

As for the international legal system, which is charged with responsibility for administering punitive justice against persons who are found to be guilty of directing or committing crimes against humanity and genocide, it is simply too unwieldy, lacks adequate funding, permanent courts and staff, and the means to apprehend suspects. On top of that, it is operationally slow and unable to cope with the sheer volume of cases in situations as diverse as Bosnia–Hercegovina and Rwanda. Another anomaly is the basis of determining what constitutes genocide and war crimes, where the killings in Rwanda are only the second 'recognised' act of genocide after that of the Jews killed by the Nazis during the second World War. Also the lack of clear legal precedents and policy guidelines from the political bosses of the international community results in many cases not being tried at all. In the cases of Augusto Pinochet and Erik Priebke, legal action had to be initiated by an interested third country (that is, Spain and Italy respectively). More often than not, such judicial exceptions to the norm of non-action is brought about by a country that is reasonably well-placed within the international power hierarchy and which wants to exorcise past national guilt or complicity. Most, if not all, such international showpieces, starting with the Nuremberg War Trials, are a mix of punitive justice according to the tenets of international law and populist spectacles sanctioned by politicians and reported by the media. Realistically, it is impossible for all those guilty of crimes against humanity committed, for example, against the Jews, gypsies, disabled, communists, socialists, Russians, Poles and many other so-called 'misfits' or 'enemies' during the Nazi era, or in Bosnia–Hercegovina or Rwanda, to be processed even under the most efficient or largest legal system. According to a February 1998 report filed by CNN correspondent Catherine Bond from Gisenyi, Rwanda, in 1997, the Rwandan courts tried only 300 genocide suspects and she notes that if the legal proceedings went on at this rate, it will take Rwanda's judicial authorities an estimated 400 years to hear the 120 000 or more cases – out of which 1946 are of those persons suspected of orchestrating genocide – not to mention any appeals or the colossal financial cost of conducting such an exercise.[11]

Future agendas for change

Transformation of international relations and jurisprudence will not occur, unless radical reform is initiated so as to ensure that transitional justice in post-conflict situations is swift, legally binding and exacting, irrespective of the political or military clout, prestige and position of perpetrators. From a macro-perspective, such change also necessitates a different policy from the US Congress and Senate, which has in the recent past promoted foreign policy directives that are obstructionist and at times even isolationist. Examples of such obstruction range from the refusal to pay the US$1 billion owed in arrears to the UN, the blocking of large-scale UN peacekeeping operations and subverting the treaty aimed at a global ban on landmines, to defeating consensus on the substantial reduction of greenhouse gas emissions at the Kyoto summit in 1997. These isolationist US foreign policy measures, as well as the use of trade sanctions, have the potential for alienating its allies, for example, the heated controversy that has taken place between the USA, and Western Europe and Canada over the retaliatory procedures in trade relations called for by the Helms–Burton law.

If the USA is to play a pivotal and valuable leading role in fashioning a new global order based on fair play, freedom and equitable justice for all, then the provincialism and parochialism of Congress and the Senate must be replaced by an *outward-looking, dynamic and caring* new generation of legislators. For credible change to take place, these stateswomen and statesmen must also have sizeable electoral support from better-educated[12] and less populist voters in order to supersede the status quo. From an alternative eco-developmental perspective, the authors of the report of the Independent Commission on Population and Quality of Life argue that:

> Care is the antithesis of competition ... and its reinforcement now will necessitate a dramatic change in mind-set. The transactional concepts of the past, excessive competition and the philosophy of ever more may destroy us. We need, therefore, to explore if and how the reservoirs of caring capacity can sustain us, and lift at the same time at least 1 billion people mired in poverty – and growing – from the level of eking out their survival and on to the path of sustainable improvement in the quality of life. This will require nothing short than *another kind of development* than hitherto pursued. Humankind faces challenges of a civilizational change. Its survival and existence in dignity requires a transition to a fundamentally new type of development – ecodevelopment – which should govern all forms of human activities and all interactions of people with nature. (Report of the Independent Commission on Population and Quality of Life 1996:287)

Such a strategy would be in marked contrast to the individualistic and consumerist values currently being marketed globally through the mass media and via advertising among consumers of all ages. It represents a long-term investment towards a more humane, equitable global order *and* the attainment of environmentally sustainable consumption patterns.

Failure to change existing attitudes and lack of political will, meagre funding, medieval foreign policy objectives and double standards for rich and poor will only fuel opposition to the wide-spread acceptance of universalist values. Chandra Muzaffar, a Malaysian contributor to the 'Asian values' debate in South East Asia, argues that human rights (and humanitarianism) is the epitome of contemporary, advanced Western imperialism (Muzaffar 1996). Zia Sardar notes that 'Like Muzaffar, many non-Western intellectuals favour a discourse of human dignity based on the right to food, housing, basic sanitation and the preservation of one's own identity and culture' (Sardar and Van Loon 1997:166). A more equitable distribution of income and resources can make a tremendous difference towards defusing a wide range of armed conflicts and political violence – the success of which can be enhanced if such a long-term, development-oriented objective is extended to also encompass the welfare of former combatants. However, this measure alone will not be a panacea, without a comprehensive overhaul of all the out dated strategies of the Cold War warriors, which were based to a large extent on an irrational fear of the 'other' and of the unknown, and driven by neo-imperialist geopolitical considerations.

One example would be the transformation of the United Nations:

> The history of the United Nations to date has been marked by the ability of a few powerful countries in the North to exercise an overriding influence on its institutional framework and policy direction, in particular by using the 'financial whip.' With the ending of the Cold War, the resulting lopsided balance of power in the Organization has opened the way for some major powers to embark on more vigorous and systematic efforts to shape the United Nations and specialized agencies even more in line with their own interests, priorities and political preferences.[13]
>
> (South Centre 1997:xv)

The bureaucrats who pursue these hegemonic, unipolar geopolitical aspirations and the narrow agendas of the major powers alluded to by South Centre do not understand that their well-worn formula of 'might is right' *cannot* be the basis for civilised outcomes to disputes and conflicts in the twenty-first century, let alone within the UN system. This was demonstrated through the diplomatic settlement over the Iraqi arms inspection issue brokered by the Secretary-General of the UN, Kofi Annan, in February 1998, reportedly achieved despite substantial impediments (including the arrogant and deliberately provocative behaviour of certain members of the Unscom team of inspectors).[14] Secretary-General Annan's efforts and diplomatic skill circumvented, at least over the short term, planned US-led military strikes against Iraq, which was the *only* option consistently put forward in public by the world's remaining superpower.

The end of the Cold War calls for redundancies in relation to the old order and there is a need for new kinds of investments – which will ensure long-term peace, stability and coexistence – based upon humane value systems, equitable justice and sustainable management of the global environment and its finite resources. Furthermore, these humanitarian values, justice systems and sustainable management need not necessarily be either homogeneous or universal. Instead, they can be built upon respect for difference and otherness, and reflect the aspirations of as many of the world's 6 billion people as possible.

While more relativist interpretations of identity and cultural rights might help generate support for a greater commitment towards internationalist ventures in the future, the moral authority of the UN also needs to be bolstered, in tandem with the allocation of adequate means and resources, to fulfil its mandates *for long-term peace, the rule of international law, the promotion of better standards of life and systems of care, and freedom for all to become everyday actualities across the globe*. The UN is undeniably the only truly global organisation in existence today and it has a crucial role to play. However, there are significant problems associated with reforming the UN:

> The central dilemma to be faced in reforming the United Nations is that it is an institution with a highly unequal and diverse membership, operating in a global economic and political system which many would like to see changed in major respects, while others are determined to maintain the *status quo* at all costs ... The voices mostly heard on the subject of United Nations reform reflect a 'reductionist' view, following the current Northern fashion of trying to 'roll back' government and public institutions. With the declared purpose of rationalizing the Organization, modernizing management, cutting costs, reducing waste and 'adapting the United Nations to the changing world', the United Nations is being sorely impaired. In the process, the Organization is being tailored in ways favoured by major Northern powers, eliminating activities they like least. At particular risk are those activities which often give rise to dissent or which challenge the dominant economic system. And it is likely that such reforms would thwart efforts to achieve greater cooperation and participation in the management of the world economy through the United Nations System. In that event, the

United Nations would see its influence over the world economy virtually end.

(South Centre 1997: xv–xvi)

Reforming the UN system and its politico-economic control *in a more equitable and representative fashion, that does credit to its multinational membership*, is an important if not vital task to its survival as the key global institution of the future.[15] Similarly, specialised departments, such as the newly set-up Department for Disarmament Affairs and existing bodies such as the UN High Commission for Human Rights and the UN High Commission for Refugees, need to reach the highest possible levels of professionalism and ethical standards. The time has come to implement far-reaching changes for a more efficient management, streamlined fiscal policy and moral order. The political will, along with concomitant financial and other resources, which is necessary to bring about UN reform, is part and parcel of more responsible governance of the international community. As highlighted in the report of the Independent Commission on Population and Quality of Life:

> Developed nations must contribute, actively and credibly, to the demilitarization of life – for no State that profits from war can convincingly argue for peace. It is not enough to admonish developing countries that their military expenditures must be reduced – as they indeed should be – or to introduce forms of conditionality to aid-and-assistance programmes. Military assistance, often under the 'cover' of development assistance, must decline further and be phased out.
>
> We further propose that the concept of collective security be revisited accordingly. The Security Council of the United Nations, the body entrusted with the maintenance of international security and peace, should thus be enabled to address also threats to the socio-economic security of humankind.
>
> In pursuing a sustainable improvement of quality of life, highest priority must be given to meeting the population's minimum survival needs. In order to make these needs operational, they should be related to *rights* – striking a balance between civil–political rights and economic–social rights.
>
> (Report of the Independent Commission on Population and Quality of Life 1996:288–9)

Furthermore, no situation or 'complex emergency' can be deemed unworthy of dedicated attention and people do *not* have to be killed or maimed in their hundreds of thousands – as in today's Algeria and as was the case in Rwanda and Bosnia–Hercegovina – for concerted action and pressure to be applied by the international community, to bring about a balanced outcome and to oversee the ascension of moral order and the rule of law.

Accompanying the immediacy of such reforms in global organisational praxis and in order to democratise the international policy-making process, a sea change in human moralities, ethics and values is called for. This is the bedrock upon which such changes can be preserved and developed over the long term by future generations. In order to move away from the negative effects of established patterns, norms and relations of *acquiring and maintaining power and control over resources at all costs* and from the 'coarseness and brutality of human existence' (Chalk and Jonassohn 1990:7), a number of difficult questions have to be raised and answered philosophically and pragmatically *vis-à-vis* the human condition.

The formation of identities is crucial in the human condition and its relational practices. Very often, perceived or actual external threats and fear of the unknown/other lead towards stereotyping, exclusionary practices, silencing, polarisation, 'black and white' imagery and other such negative phenomena. This, together with naked ambition and greed, is accompanied by varying levels and degrees of conflict. If humans can see change taking place in advance and from a secure politico-economic location there is a good chance that they will not be so fearful or hateful. Control over group and personal phobias/identities is vital for positive change. Such processes take place in contexts of *changing values*, where the mixing of peoples as a result of societal transformation and increased globalisation is evident. The long-term cumulative effects of such phenomena can prevent organisations and individuals from lashing out – as can be observed in today's eastern Germany by racist sections of unemployed and undereducated youth – and provide a chance for more positive outcomes.

Acknowledging that there are serious societal problems and acting upon them – for instance, through poverty alleviation programmes and significant job creation to bring down unemployment – is the productive way forward, rather than pandering to intangible, unreal and at times speculative 'market forces' *at the expense of sustainable human and ecological development, and the quality of life.* These are necessary steps for political, economic, social, religious and cultural leaders to take, without which all the policy recommendations aimed at conflict management and the bridging of political, cultural, historical, social, class and economic differences will come to nought. In a recent interview, EU Commissioner Emma Bonino notes:

> Europe is more than a bank. Europe is about solidarity. To make people enthusiastic you must have a dream. If we don't put greater value back into politics we'll have no dream for young people. The need for values represents our spiritual side, and that goes also for an old non-believer like myself.
>
> (Sjogren 1998:28)

At the psycho-social level it is well-documented by human rights-oriented organisations, such as Amnesty International, Human Rights Watch and Physicians for Human Rights, that physical and psychological torture of human beings by other humans and other related practices of inhumanity, cruelty, interrogation, captivity, depraved brutality and killing takes place on a *daily basis* in many parts of the globe, even in the 'civilised West'.[16] At the psycho-social level, sensibilities of control, satisfaction and even pleasure are often intertwined with events like torture, bullying and cruelty for persons engaged in this 'profession'. For example, torturers work a well-worn routine and have been reported to eat biscuits nonchalantly amidst the screams, blood and gore (as narrated to me by a former Tamil paramilitary political prisoner). How much old traumas, both psychological and social, including experiences of warfare, state repression and other forms of bullying, or due to extreme poverty feature in such behaviour is relatively unclear and differs from case to case.

Similarly, the cultivation of hatred and revenge mentalities and sensibilities is involved in most politically motivated killings and genocide. The common denominator here is the frightening ordinariness of such phenomena, which has even led to slaughter among neighbours, as in Rwanda and Bosnia (Human Rights Watch 1995). The human condition may contain seeds of self-destruction, and killings continue to be an integral part of that experience, involving histories of peasant wars, rebellions, revolts, coups, revolutions and genocide, and more recent scenarios like gang wars, drive-by shootings, teenage violence and gun culture in large urban centres. Needless to say, identity formation, peer pressure and petty jealousies are crucial in the generation of 'Us versus Them' stereotypes, which in turn lead to the build-up of hatred and concomitant brutalities. It is easy to appeal to a sense of identity (for example, race, nationality, ethnicity or organisational affiliation), due to an emotive instinct of group belonging and bonding, as a greater extension of one's self. Bonding together as a form of protection against perceived external enemies or an unknown quantity (for example, strangers/strangeness) is a common human reaction.

Conclusion

Serious alternatives to redress the negative aspects of the human condition necessitate a sea change in structures that promote aggressive, competitive attitudes and naked ambition and their replacement by more caring, humane consciousness and values. The time is ripe for concerted action across the globe to articulate a new humanitarian agenda, in an era where 'complex emergencies' still continue to take place, while the international community appears to be almost paralysed in its engagement. While no single agency or authority can claim to possess the perfect politico-economic solution, the art of the possible is to bolster the political will for engagement through understanding and acceptance of parameters of humanitarian action and assistance. 'Experts' who lack analysis but who claim to have the solutions are simply dangerous. While it is quite fair to call for donor nations, aid agencies and concerned NGOs to clean up their act and take full responsibility for their actions, it must also be noted that they cannot be held accountable for the inaction of other authorities and agencies.

Responsible institutions and bodies *answerable to civil society* must be created to help shoulder the manifold burdens of coping with the exigencies of 'complex emergencies' through concerted programmes to promote a 'human rights culture' at the global, regional, national and local levels. Semantics aside, there is an urgent need to counter public apathy and promote awareness of, and access to, the opportunities provided by such a culture among civil society. This will be an important foundation for other building blocks such as a Bill of Rights with stronger and more specific statutory bulwarks against the abuse of power by legislative, public and corporate authorities. A comprehensive Bill of Rights, that unifies civil and political rights with social and economic rights, must safeguard human dignity based on the right to food, housing, basic sanitation and the preservation of identities and cultures. Similarly, a code of fundamental human rights must not only be enshrined within the tenets of international law, it must also be made *enforceable* through a series of practical mechanisms, including monitoring, evaluation, consultative pressure and sanctions and be *affordable*, so that plaintiffs can seek redress without hesitation or hindrance. These measures should be combined with the establishment of a permanent International Criminal Court geared towards the swift processing of cases pertaining to genocide and crimes against humanity. Concerted efforts like these can have a profound impact on global political culture, not only as a deterrent, but also in promoting new practices, for example, when legislators are required by law to conduct comprehensive explorations of the implications for human rights, prior to the enactment of any new legislation, or through the adoption of a model such as Truth Commissions – which has had varying results in Argentina, El Salvador, Chile, Uruguay, Uganda and most recently in South Africa.[17] Furthermore, in post-conflict situations, *tangible support* from the international justice system, as well as related agencies and institutions, can make a significant difference in situations where *transitional justice* is operative in emerging democracies which have to cope with the criminal legacies of previous regimes (Kritz 1995a,b,c), for example, in Rwanda, where approximately 120 000 cases of alleged genocide need some form of legal redress urgently. Whether or not punitive justice is viable where there are massive violations of human rights is questionable, not from a moral or ethical standpoint, but rather from the more practical perspective of *how* equitable justice can be meted out in conditions where there is an excessive volume of cases to be heard. Developing viable new mechanisms to cope with such problems is the way forward and the international justice system needs to obtain the necessary resources to tackle such critical issues, rather than engaging in interminable legal arguments that remain largely bogged down at the levels of semantics and minutiae.

The tracing of post-Cold War futures has been an arduous and painful task. Only *practical solutions* will see humanity safely through to the next epoch away from the evil of genocide, politicised rhetoric and the sheer waste of scarce planetary resources by an unthinking, rapacious global politico-economic system.[18] We are all responsible in one way or another for future outcomes. Needless to say, successes cannot be achieved either by organisations or individuals that work in isolation or at cross-purposes, therefore, good coordination, networking, flexible management, sustainable funding (which overcomes 'funding fatigue') and improved, real-time communication – along with the evolution of new systems of knowledge, morality and politico-economic survival techniques (that avert the dissipation of energies and resources) – is indispensable. Such shared processes of global, regional, national and local cooperation must be based upon the identification and recognition of individual entitlements and rights

– *civil, political, social and economic* – that are clearly linked to those of other fellow human beings inhabiting this planet.

Notes

1. The author thanks Dr Kennedy Graham, Dr Azza Karam and Dr Rohan L. de Silva for lending assistance during a time of intense pressure.
2. However, for those who would like more details, see for example Nederveen Pieterse (1990, 1992), Breman (1990), Taussig (1991), Donald and Rattansi (1993), Sardar, Nandy and Davies (1993), Rattansi and Westwood (1994), among others.
3. For example, Ruth Leger Sivard estimates that in the past 50 years in around 159 wars more than 25 000 000 human lives have been lost (Sivard 1996:18–19).
4. For further details of the problems and recommendations for positive change – which include greater police accountability and civilian monitoring of police departments to avoid future police misconduct and racism, as well as more training programmes to create greater cultural sensitivity – see the study commissioned by the National Association for the Advancement of Colored People (NAACP) by Ogletree (1995) and Gooding-Williams (1993). For a discussion of structural violence and related issues see Burton (1997).
5. The *systematic* rape and torture of allegedly more than 20 000 Muslim women in camps by Serbian soldiers and irregulars in Bosnia–Hercegovina (up to 1993) is unprecedented, even by the gory standards of modern warfare. For a convincing argument concerning gender as an ethno-marker, see Meznaric (1994). For a well-documented exposé of political rape during the Balkan wars see Allen (1996) and Bassiouni (1996), and for personal testimonies of women from three refugee camps in Slovenia, all victims of war crimes in Bosnia–Hercegovina, see Beç and Dragulj (1997). Another infamous example from recent history is the indiscriminate rape of thousands of women by soldiers and other combatants during the Indo-Pakistani wars – particularly during the 'liberation' of Bangladesh in 1971. And in Pakistan, the selective rape of female family members of perceived political opponents continues to be reported, even in the 1990s.
6. For more details, refer to Helaine Selin (1992, 1997).
7. These human rights abuses involve violations of the rights of specific groups – for example, Afro-Caribbeans, Asians, women, lesbians, gays, bisexuals, disabled persons, mentally ill persons, migrants, refugees and asylum-seekers – as well as broader issues involving censorship, and failures of democracy and the criminal justice system.
8. 'Although Mitterrand ordered a reinforcement of links with the Hutu majority in Rwanda from 1990, it was Edouard Balladur's Gaullist-led government that was in power when the massacres began ... France's refusal to inquire publicly into the political background has shocked human rights organisations. [And] *Le Figaro* said Mitterrand's initiative was incomprehensible because France was a "co-belligerent" in the civil war' (*Guardian Weekly*, 18 January 1998, p. 3).

9. See the letter to the editor submitted by Angela Penrose, Save the Children (London) in the *Guardian Weekly*, 26 October 1997.
10. For more information and independent analyses, concerning facets and details of the US arms trade, see the work of Fitzgerald (1972, 1989), Melman (1985), Burrow and Windrem (1994), Hartung (1995), Gottlieb (1997) and Pierre (1997), and annual reports of *World Military and Social Expenditures* by Ruth Leger Sivard, among others.
11. It is also reported that there are around 9000 suspects who are represented by only sixteen defence lawyers, further illustrating that the Rwandan justice system is hugely overstretched and structurally less able to cope.
12. In this text, I use the term 'better-educated' to mean persons – voters *and* legislators – who have considerable intellectual capital, a strong perception of civilised behaviour and a humane conscience, garnered through critical, analytical capabilities that are based on experiential knowledge and/or multidisciplinary or cross-disciplinary academic training, and/or multicultural exposure.
13. The South Centre is an intergovernmental organisation of developing countries. It has a close working relationship with the Non-Aligned Movement and the Group of 77 developing countries. And its objectives are the promotion of South solidarity, South–South cooperation, and coordinated participation by developing countries in international forums. The South Centre enjoys full intellectual independence, and it prepares, publishes and distributes information, strategic analyses and recommendations on international economic, social and political matters of concern to the South.
14. For more details, see the translation of Afsané Bassir Pour's article 'No Love Lost Between UN Groups in Iraq' for *Le Monde* in the *Guardian Weekly*, 8 March 1998, p. 19.
15. For a more detailed discussion of the key issues at stake as well as the implications of the character and direction of UN reform, and for an overview and main policy conclusions, see Chapters 4–8 and 10–11 of South Centre (1997).
16. For example, see Foley with Liberty (1995) for a thorough examination of the United Kingdom's record of human rights abuses in England, Wales and Northern Ireland; as well as the Lawyers' Committee for Human Rights (1997), which assesses the United Kingdom's record in Hong Kong and Northern Ireland (albeit through the review of the US Department of State's somewhat biased Country Reports on Human Rights Practices).
17. For an interesting, if brief, comparative assessment of Truth Commissions, see Harvard Law School Human Rights Program (1997).
18. For discussion of 'planetary interests' by a multinational collection of senior politicians and diplomats see Graham (1998).

References

Allen, B. 1996: *Rape Warfare: The Hidden Genocide in Bosnia–Herzegovina and Croatia*, Minneapolis: University of Minnesota Press.

Amnesty International 1997: *Amnesty International Report 1997*, London: AI Publications.

Article 19 (International Centre Against Censorship) 1994: *Forging War: The Media in Serbia, Croatia and Bosnia–Hercegovina* (authored by M. Thompson and edited by A. Naughton), London: Article 19.

Bassiouni, M.C. 1996: *The Law of the International Criminal Tribunal for the Former Yugoslavia* (written with the collaboration of P. Manikas), Irvington-on-Hudson, New York: Transnational Publishers.

Beç, J. and Dragulj, E. 1997: *The Shattering of the Soul*, Ljubljana: Helsinki Committee for Human Rights in Serbia and Radio B92.

Breman, J. (editor) 1990. *Imperial Monkey Business: Racial Supremacy in Social Darwinist Theory and Practice*, Amsterdam: VU University Press.

Brittain, V. 1998: *Death of Dignity: Angola's Civil War*, London: Pluto Press.

Brzezinski, Z. 1993: *Out of Control*, New York: Charles Scribner's Sons.

Burrow, W.E. and Windrem, R. 1994: *Critical Mass: The Dangerous Race for Superweapons in a Fragmented World*, New York: Simon & Schuster.

Burton, J.W. 1997: *Violence Explained: The Sources of Conflict, Violence and Crime and their Prevention*, Manchester and New York: Manchester University Press.

Carnegie Commission on Preventing Deadly Conflict 1997: *Preventing Deadly Conflict* (Final Report with Executive Summary), New York: Carnegie Corporation.

Chalk, F. and Jonassohn, K. 1990.: *The History and Sociology of Genolide: Analyses and Case Studies*, New Haven, Conn. and London: Yale University Press.

Donald, J. and Rattansi, A. (editors) 1993: *'Race', Culture and Difference*, London: Sage Publications in association with The Open University.

Drinkwater, J. and Gudjonsson, G. 1992: 'The Nature of Violence in Psychiatric Hospital? in K. Howells and C.R. Hollin (editors) *Clinical Approaches to Violence*, New York: John Wiley & Sons.

Earthscan 1997: *The Reality of Aid: An Independent Review of Development Cooperation* (edited by J. Randel and T. German, Development Initiatives), London: Earthscan Publications Ltd.

Esman, M.J. 1994: *Ethnic Politics*, Ithaca , NY and London: Cornell University Press.

Fitzgerald, A.E. 1972: *The High Priests of Waste*, New York: Norton.

Fitzgerald, A.E. 1989: *The Pentagonists: An Insider's View of Waste, Mismanagement, and Fraud in Defense Spending*, Boston, Mass.: Houghton Mifflin.

Foley, C. with Liberty (National Council for Civil Liberties) 1995: *Human Rights, Human Wrongs: The Alternative Report to the United Nations Human Rights Committee*, London: Rivers Oram Press.

Fukuyama, F. 1989: 'The End of History' in *The National Interest*, no. 16, Summer, pp. 3–18.

Gooding-Williams, R. (editor) 1993: *Reading Rodney King, Reading Urban Uprising*, New York and London: Routledge.

Goodpaster, A.J. 1996: *When Diplomacy is Not Enough: Managing Multinational Military Interventions* (a report of the Carnegie Commission on Preventing Deadly Conflict), New York: Carnegie Corporation.

Gottlieb, S. 1997: *Defense Addiction: Can America Kick the Habit?*, Boulder, Colo: Westview Press.

Graham, K. (editor) 1998: *The Planetary Interest*, London: University College London Press.

Hamburg, D.A. 1993: *Preventing Contemporary Intergroup Violence*, New York: Carnegie Corporation.
Hartung, W.D. 1995: *And Weapons for All*, New York: HarperCollins.
Harvard Law School Human Rights Program 1997: *Truth Commissions: A Comparative Assessment*, Cambridge, Mass.: Harvard Law School.
Hindley, M. and Bridge, J. 1994: 'South China Sea: The Spratly and Paracel Islands Dispute' in *The World Today*, June, vol. 50, no. 6, pp. 109–10.
Hirsch, H. 1995: *Genocide and the Politics of Memory: Studying Death to Preserve Life*, Chapel Hill and London: University of North Carolina Press.
Holl, J.E. 1996: *Carnegie Commission on Preventing Deadly Conflict: Second Progress Report* (a report of the Carnegie Commission on Preventing Deadly Conflict), New York: Carnegie Corporation.
Human Rights Watch 1995: *Slaughter Among Neighbours: The Political Origins of Communal Violence*, New Haven, Conn. and London: Yale University Press.
Huntington, S.P. 1989: 'No Exit: The Errors of Endism' in *The National Interest*, no. 17, Fall, pp. 3–11.
Huntington, S.P. 1991: *The Third Wave: Democratization in the Late Twentieth Century*, Norman: University of Oklahoma Press.
Huntington, S.P., Ajami, F., Bartley, R.L., Binyan, L., Kirkpatrick, J., Mahbubani, K., Piel, G. and Weeks, A.L. 1996: *Samuel P. Huntington's The Clash of Civilizations? The Debate*, New York: *Foreign Affairs* (Special Issue).
Independent Commission on Population and Quality of Life 1996: *Caring for the Future: Making the Next Decades Provide a Life Worth Living*, Oxford: Oxford University Press.
Kaplan, R.D. 1996: *The Ends of the Earth: A Journey at the Dawn of the 21st Century*, New York: Random House.
Kaplan, R.D. 1997: 'Was Democracy Just a Moment? in *Atlantic Monthly*, December, Vol. 280, no. 6, p. 55.
Kritz, N.J. (editor) 1995a: *Transnational Justice: How Emerging Democracies Reckon with Former Regimes – Volume I General Considerations*, Washington, DC: United States Institute of Peace Press.
Kritz, N.J. (editor) 1995b: *Transnational Justice: How Emerging Democracies Reckon with Former Regimes – Volume II Country Studies*, Washington, DC: United States Institute of Peace Press.
Kritz, N.J. (editor) 1995c: *Transnational Justice: How Emerging Democracies Reckon with Former Regimes – Volume III Laws, Rulings, and Reports*, Washington, DC: United States Institute of Peace Press.
Lawyers' Committee for Human Rights 1997: *Critique: Review of the U.S. Department of State's Country Reports on Human Rights Practices for 1996*, New York and Washington, DC: Lawyers' Committee for Human Rights.
McCarthy, C. 1998: 'Peddlers of Violence and Death,' Review Article: Tirman, John 1997: *Spoils of War: The Human Cost of America's Arms Trade*, New York: Free Press, in *The Washington Post*, reprinted in the *Guardian Weekly*, 15 February, p. 20.
Melman, S. 1985: *The Permanent War Economy: American Capitalism in Decline*, New York: Simon & Schuster.
Meznaric, S. 1994: 'Gender as an Ethno-Marker: Rape, War, and Identity Politics in the Former Yugoslavia' in V.M. Moghadam (editor) *Identity Politics and*

Women: Cultural Reassertions and Feminisms in International Perspective, Boulder, Colo: Westview Press.
Minear, L, Scott, C. and Weiss, T.G. 1996: *The News Media, Civil War, and Humanitarian Action*, Boulder, Colo and London: Lynne Rienner.
Muzaffar, C. in Just World Trust 1996: *Human Wrongs: Reflections on Western Global Dominance and Its Impact Upon Human Rights*, Penang: Just World Trust
Nederveen Pieterse, J.P. 1990: *Empire and Emancipation: Power and Liberation on a World Scale*, London: Pluto Press.
Nederveen Pieterse, J.P. 1992: *White on Black: Images of Africa and Blacks in Western Popular Culture*, New Haven, Conn.: Yale University Press.
Norman, R. 1995: *Ethics, Killing and War*, Cambridge: Cambridge University Press.
Nye, J.S. Jr 1997: *Understanding International Conflicts: An Introduction to Theory and History* (2nd edn), New York: Longman.
Ogletree, C.J. (editor) 1995: *Beyond the Rodney King Story: An Investigation of Police Conduct in Minority Communities*, Boston, Mass.: Northeastern University press.
Pick, D. 1996: *War Machine: The Rationalisation of Slaughter in the Modern Age*, New Haven, Conn.: Yale University Press.
Pierre, A.J. (editor) 1997: *Cascade of Arms: Managing Conventional Weapons Proliferation*, Washington, DC: Brookings Institution Press and Cambridge, Mass.: The World Peace Foundation.
Rattansi, A. and Westwood, S. (editors) 1994: *Racism, Modernity and Identity: On the Western Front*, Cambridge: Polity Press.
Report of the Independent Commission on Population and Quality of Life 1996: *Caring for the Future: Making the Next Decades Provide a Life Worth Living*, Oxford: Oxford University Press.
Richmond, A.H. 1994: *Global Apartheid: Refugees, and the New World Order*, Oxford: Oxford University Press.
Roberts, A. 1996: *Humanitarian Action in War: Aid, Protection and Impartiality in a Policy Vacuum*, Oxford: Oxford University Press for the IISS.
Sardar, Z. and Van Loon, B. 1997: *Cultural Studies for Beginners*, Cambridge: Icon Books.
Sardar, Z., Nandy, A. and Davies, M.W. 1993: *Barbaric Others: A Manifesto on Western Racism*, London: Pluto Press.
Selin, H. 1992: *Science Across Cultures: An Annotated Bibliography of Books on Non-Western Sciences, Technology and Medicine*, Garland Reference Library.
Selin, H. 1997: *Encyclopedia of the History of Science, Technology and Medicine in Non-Western Cultures*, Norwell, Mass.: Kluwer Academic Publishers.
Sivard, R.L. Annual Reports 1996: *World Military and Social Expenditures*, Washington, DC: World Priorities.
Sjogren, E. 1998: 'In the Line of Fire' in *Scanorama*, February, vol. 28, no. 2, pp. 24–8.
Sørbø, G.M., Macrae, J. and Wohlgemuth, L. 1997: *NGOs in Conflict: An Evaluation of International Alert*, Fantoft-Bergen: Chr. Michelsen Institute.
South Centre 1997: *For a Strong and Democratic United Nations: A South Perspective on UN Reform*, London: Zed Books in association with South Centre, Geneva.
Stremlau, J. 1996: *Sharpening International Sanctions: Towards A Stronger Role for the United Nations* (a report of the Carnegie Commission on Preventing Deadly Conflict), New York: Carnegie Corporation.

Swedish Ministry of Foreign Affairs 1997a: *Preventing Violent Conflict: A Study*, Stockholm: Ministry of Foreign Affairs.
Swedish Ministry of Foreign Affairs 1997b: *Preventing Violent Conflict: Thematic Reports* (Volumes I and II), Stockholm: Ministry of Foreign Affairs.
Taussig, M. 1991: *Shamanism, Colonialism, and the Wild Man: A Study in Terror and Healing*, Chicago, Ill.: University of Chicago Press.
Tirman, J. 1997: *Spoils of War: The Human Cost of America's Arms Trade*, New York: Free Press.
Toffler, A. 1990: *The Third Wave*, New York: Bantam Books.
Toffler, A. and H. 1995: *War and Anti-War: Survival at the Dawn of the 21st Century*, London: Warner Books.
Totten, S., Parsons, W.S. and Charny, I.W. (editors) 1995: *Century of Genocide: Eyewitness Accounts and Critical Views*, Garland Reference Library of Social Science, vol. 772.
Valencia, M.J. 1995: *China and the South China Sea Disputes: Conflicting Claims and Potential Solutions in the South China Sea*, Oxford: Oxford University Press for the International Institute for Strategic Studies (IISS).
Zakaria, F. 1997: 'The Rise of Illiberal Democracy' in *Foreign Affairs*, November/December, vol. 76, no. 6, pp. 22–43.

Index

AAPO 105
Abd-al-Salam, Amin 134
Abe, Abera Yemane 108
Abkhazia 248
Abreha, Seye 120
'abstentionism' 79, 80, 82
Abu-Jabr, Haj Ismai'il 139
Adam, H. 58, 59
Adams, G. 80, 89, 90, 91
Aden, Gulf of 155, 159
Adhana, Haile A. 113–14
Afars 99, 110, 111, 113
Afewerki, Isayas 119, 121
Afghanistan 162, 218, 221, 222, 228, 229, 234, 247
 mujahideen 248
 Taliban 218, 222, 251
Africa 158, 161, 219
 see also North Africa; sub-Saharan Africa; West Africa; South West
Africa, Horn of 102, 149, 155, 162
Africa Watch 115
 External Mission 61
Aideed, General 160–1
al-'Alami, Mahir 134
Alavi, H. 223
Albania 104, 248
ALF 100
Alfonsín 17
Algeria 113, 218, 220, 221, 224, 231, 246, 261
All Amhara People's Organisation 103
Allende, Salvador 17, 39, 40, 48, 247
Alter, P. 111
Althusser, L. 74
America *see* Central; Latin; North; South
Amhara ethnic group 98, 99, 112

Amnesty International 105, 115, 120, 193, 207, 209, 262
Amstead, Margaret 247
ANC 55, 59, 60–1, 62, 63, 68, 72, 189
Andhra Pradesh 192
ANDM 112
Angola 160, 247, 248–9
Annan, Kofi 160, 258
anti-apartheid 61, 63, 66
anti-imperialism 6
anti-Tamil 170
apartheid 55, 56, 58, 59, 60, 61, 62, 66, 67, 68
Appadurai, A. 168, 225, 226
Appiah, K.A. 4
Appleby, R.S. 220–1
Arabian peninsula 220
'Arafat, Yasir 125, 126, 127, 131, 133–9 *passim*
Aravindan (Ahilen) 172–3, 179–81
Araya, M. 112
ARDF 103, 106
ARDV 96, 108, 114
ARENA 44, 47, 48
Aretxaga, B. 73
Argentina 14–36, 217, 249
 'dirty war' 6–8, 18, 207, 214–15
 human rights violations 207
 macro-political context 16–20
 political sphere 21–6
 private sphere 30–4
 public sphere 26–30
 transition from revolutionary political identity 20–1
 Truth Commissions 264
 see also Mothers of Plaza de Mayo
Argentinian Revolutionary Left 14
Arias, Oscar 44

Armed Forces   40
armed services recruitment policy   194
Armenia   238, 247, 248
Asheron, A.   56
'Ashrawi, Hanan   134, 135
Asia   158, 219
  see also East Asia; South Asia; South East Asia
Asian Development Bank   191
Asmal, K.   59, 61, 62
Assam   190, 191, 193
Atwan, Abdel-Bari   222
Aubenas, florence   121
Australia   187, 188
authoritarianism   11, 15, 24, 25, 26, 27, 31
Avellaneda, A.   28
Ayoob, M.   158
Azerbaijan   248

Baas, Marc   102–3
Bahman, Omar Abdel   218
Bailey, S.D.   169
Balbín, R.   17, 18
Baloyra, E.   39
Bangladesh   238
Banna, Hasan al-   219
Barre, Sayad   148, 155, 156, 161
Barrell, H.   62
Baskin, J.   65
Begin, Benny   137
Belgium   160
Bell, J.   73
Beni Shangulis   111
Berhe, A.   96–123
Bermeo, N.   28
Bhaskaran (Udayan)   172, 174–8
Bill of Rights   59, 263
Bin Ladin, Osama   217–18, 221–2, 228–9, 230
bipartisan protocol (1997)   185
Bishop, P.   73
Bittel, E.   17, 18
'black' politics   54, 60–7
Black Sash   66
Bobbio, N.   14
Bond, Catherine   256
Boniface, D.   38–52

Bonino, Emma   222, 262
Border Campaign (1956–62)   72
border issues   120–2
Bosnia   160, 222, 254, 262
Bosnia-Hercegovina   192, 228, 239, 245, 246, 249, 255, 256, 261
Botha, P.W.   57
Boutros-Ghali, Boutros   159
Brady, Jack   76, 77
Brazil   47
Brewer, J.   56
Bridge, J.   251
Britain   71, 167, 169, 215, 244, 246, 249, 253
  colonialism   227
  and Northern Ireland   72, 75, 78, 80, 81, 82, 86, 87, 88, 89, 90, 92
  and Somalia   153, 154, 155
British Royal Air Force   98, 100
Brysk, A.   19
Brzezinski, Zbigniew   238
Buddhism   182, 188, 220
Bunster-Burotto, J.   211
Burrows, D.   62
Burton, F.   9, 73, 76, 86
Burundi   238, 245, 246
Bush, George   44, 158, 246
Buthelezi, Chief Mangosuthu G.   189

CARPDE   108
Cairo conference   165
'Call to Whites' campaign   64, 65
Cambodia   238
Campbell, B.   81
Canada   160, 188, 243, 257
Canary Wharf bombing   91
capitalism   241, 242
Carnegie Commission on Preventing Deadly Conflict   255
Carpio, Salvador Cayetano (alias 'Marcial')   43
Carter, G.   55
Carter Peace Centre Conference (1994)   112

Cash, J.   8, 9, 84
Castañeda, J.G.   43
Castro, fidel   42
Catholicism   5, 72, 75, 76, 77, 84, 86, 87, 220, 247
CD   45
CEDES   27
censorship   28, 30
Central America   44, 48, 72, 158
Centre for Conflict Resolution   66
Chalk, F.   237–66
Chandrika (Kumaratunga) government   176
Charny, I.W.   238
chauvinism   115
chauvinist-separatism   171
Chechnya   228, 248
Chile   39, 40, 45, 47, 48, 264
China   2, 40, 157, 169, 234, 241, 247, 252, 253
Christian Democrats   39
Christian Institute   60
Christian Party   17
Christianity   122, 155, 182, 220
churches   60
CISEA   27
citizenship   223
civic associations   63, 66
civil disobedience   114
civil rights campaign   72
civil society   15, 17
Claas, Willy   221
clan factors   151
Clark, J.   158
CLASCSO   27
class factors   57, 151
Clinton, B.   219, 228–30, 233
Cochrane, Michael   247
Cockburn, C.   206
COEDF   108, 114
Cohen, Herman   102
Cohn, B.   168
Cold War   149, 247
   Somalia   156–63
Collinge, J.   66
colonialism   149, 152, 153–6, 167, 227
Communism   27, 72, 256

Conference for Peace and Reconciliation   108
Confucianism   220
Connell, R.W.   214
consent principle   92
Constituent Assembly   107, 108–9
Constitution 1983   57, 58, 63
Constitution 1995   97
Constitution Articles 2 and 3   92
Constitution Drafting Commission by Proclamation No. 24/1992   107
constitutions   107, 109
Coogan, T.P.   73
Cooke, M.   204, 207, 212–13, 214, 216
Cooper, D.   65
Corradi, J.   11
corruption eradication   194
COSATU   65, 66
Council of Europe   2–3
counter-insurgency   9, 11
coup d'état   21, 40
covert security services   85
CP   57, 67
CPJ   115
CR   106
Crankshaw, O.   57
Crick, B.   10
Cristiani, Alfredo   44
CRM   43
Croats   192, 228, 248
Cronin, J.   61
CTT   18
Cuba   40, 203
cultural identity   2
currency   120
Cyprus   251

Dalton, Roque   43
D'Aubuisson, Roberto   44
Dayton Peace Accord   192
de Klerk, F.W.   57, 59
de Klerk, W.J.   59
de Silva, P.L.   167–99, 237–66
death squads   193–4
deconstruction   74

Defiance Campaign 66
Degenaar, Johan 59
Del Rosario, Maria 208–9
Delmas Treason Trial 63
democracy 242
  Argentina 17, 18, 19, 24–6, 34
  El Salvador 44–6
  Ethiopia 104–6
democratisation 14, 15, 68, 97
DEPDU 103
Derg regime 96, 101, 102, 105, 115, 117, 118, 119
Derrida, J. 74
desaparecidos (disappeared ones) 6–7, 11, 17
detenidos (detained ones) 7
dharmishta aanduwa (just government) 170
Dillon, M. 85
Disabled 238, 256
discontinuity 73
discourse of terrorism 4
Djibouti 153, 162
DMLE 117
DOP 125–8, 130, 132, 136–7, 139–43, 145, 233
Dowd, C. 81
Downing Street Declaration 90
Drinkwater, J. 239
Drumcree 91, 93
Duarte, José Napoleón 39
Dutch Reformed Church 59

Eagleton, T. 74
East Asia 187, 251
East Timor 238, 245, 247
Easter uprising (1916) 72
Eastern Europe 45, 104
EDU 96, 108, 117
education 28
Egal, Premier 154
Egypt 103, 113, 162
  and Islam/Muslims 217, 218, 219, 220, 221, 222, 224, 232, 233
EHRCO 105, 115
Eitan, Rafael 137

El Salvador 38–52, 88, 247
  democratic left dilemmas: socialism in a neo-liberal age 46–8
  negotiating peace: from revolution to democracy 44–6
  socialism, end of through peaceful means 39–43
  Truth Commissions 264
electoral democracy 242
electoralism 87
ELF 117, 118
ELF-RC 120
Ellis, S. 62, 113
Elshtain, J.B. 213
Emery, A. 54–68
End Conscription Campaign 60
Enloe, C. 205, 213, 214
EPDP 171
EPDM 96, 101, 108, 110, 112
EPLF 102, 106, 116, 117, 119, 120
EPRDF 96–7, 101, 103–19 *passim*
EPRLF 171, 172, 174, 178
EPRP 96, 100, 103, 105–6, 108, 111–12, 117
Eritrea 97, 99, 103, 119, 120, 121, 122
ERP 40, 42, 43, 46, 47
Esman, M.J. 56, 243
Esquipulas II accord 45
Esquivel, Adolfo Perez 18
Esterhuyse, Willie 59
ETA 3
ethical malpractice eradication 194
Ethiopia 96–123, 153, 155, 157, 162
  crisis, unfolding of 101–4
  cycles of conflict, breaking of 113–16
  democracy 104–6
  Ethiopian–Eritrean crisis (1998) 116–22
  ethnic polarisation 109–13
  transitional government formation and new constitution 106–9
Ethiopian Church 98

Ethiopian Marxist Leninist Organisation 104
Ethiopian Orthodox Church 98
Ethiopian Teachers Association 105
Ethiopian–Eritrean crisis (1998) 116–22
ethnic and/or race riots 239
ethnic polarisation 109–13
ethno-nationalism 98
Europe 145, 238, 262
 and Ethiopia 97, 118
 and Islamism 217, 219, 220, 223, 226
 and Northern Ireland 81, 92
 and Sri Lanka 187, 193
 see also Eastern; European; Western
European Parliament 81, 105, 115
European Union 89, 133, 187, 188, 193, 251, 253
execution 7
executive power, abuse of 194–5

Fagan, H. 201–16
Falklands War *see* Malvinas/Falklands War
Faluji, 'Imad al- 134
family 30
Fanjul, J.M. 2
FATEH 136, 137, 138–9
FDR 43, 45
fear 11
Feathersone, M. 225
Federal Assembly 109
Federal Congress 58
Federation of South African Trade Unions 65
Feldman, A. 9, 10, 73, 78, 86
femininity/feminine 201, 206, 207, 210, 212, 214, 215, 216
feminism 205, 210, 212, 213, 216
FIS 231
Fiscal scrutiny 194
Fisher, Jo 208–9, 211
FLACSO 27

FMLN 42, 43, 45, 46, 47
'foco' strategy 40
Foley, C. 244
FOM 96, 227
Fontana, A. 19
former Soviet Union 44, 88, 104, 143, 187, 217, 221, 228, 233, 256
 peacemaking, conflict management and humanitarian action 247–8, 251, 252, 253
 and Somalia 154, 157
 and Sri Lanka 182
former Yugoslavia 82, 114, 244, 245, 248
Foucault, M. 3, 4, 7, 8, 9, 73, 78, 84, 86, 224, 231
FPL 40, 42, 43, 46, 47
France 153, 155, 231, 243, 245, 246, 253
Franco, J. 6
Frederikse, J. 61
Freedom Charter 61
Friedman, M. 66
'Friend versus Foe' paradigm 21
Friendship Agreement 157
FSLN 203
Fukuyama, F. 241
Fundamentalism Project 220
fundi (fundamentalist) 79, 80, 81, 90, 91, 93

Gadhafi, Colonel Moammar 250
Galtieri, General 18–19
Gama'a Islamiyya 233
Gandhi, Mahatma 184
Gandhi, Rajiv 192
Gandhi, Shrimati Indira 168
Gaza Strip 125, 126, 127, 130, 131, 136, 139, 140, 142
Gaza-Jericho 127
gender identity 201
Geneva Convention 171
Georgia 248
Germany 154, 243, 253, 261
 Green Party 79
Ghana 157

GIA 218
Giliomee, H. 56
Gillespie, R. 15
globalisation 224–5, 241
Gold, Dore 137
Goldring, M. 77
González Bombal, I. 18
Good Friday Agreement 92
Goodpaster, A.J. 255
Gorbachev, M. 44
'graveyard universities' 27
Graziano, E. 7–8
Greece 251
Green Party 79
Grenada 247
Guatemala 204, 247
Gudjonsson, G. 239
Guevara, Ernesto Che 203
Gulf War 88, 144, 211–12, 234, 243, 245, 246, 250
Gurey, Imam Ahmed 155
Gush Emunim 220–1
gypsies 238, 256

Habash, George 137
Hagos, T.W. 97
Haile Selassie 98, 100, 107, 109
Haile-Mariam Reda, Bellata 98
Halliday, F. 223
HAMAS 127, 136, 233
Hamburg, D.A. 25
Hamill, D. 85
Han-Chinese 228
Hanf, T. 55, 61
Harvey, D. 226
Hassan, Sayyid Mohamed Abille 155
Hebron Protocol 142
Helms–Burton law 257
Herman, E. 3
heterosexuality 206, 207
Hindley, M. 251
Hinduism 220
Hirsch, H. 238
Holl, J.E. 255
Hollander, N.C. 209
holocausts 238, 256
holy war *see* jihad
Hong Kong 169, 241, 243

human resources 115
human rights movement 262, 264
 Argentina 15–17, 18, 20
 Britain 244
 Ethiopia 107
 Israel 133
 Somalia 156–63
human rights violations 222, 246, 247
 Argentina 207
 Ethiopia 105, 113, 114–15
 Somalia 158, 160
Human Rights Watch 193, 262
Hume, John 90
hunger strikes 76, 87
Huntington, S.P. 241, 242
Hussein, Saddam 145, 217–18, 246
Hutu-led regime 245

Ibrahim, Mohamed Haji 154
identity 2, 4, 56, 57, 201
identity *see* political identity
ideology 8, 46, 73, 74
IFJ 115
IFP 189
IGAD 164
IISS 250
Immorality Amendments Act 1950 55
Independent Commission on Population and Quality of Life 257, 260
India 2, 187, 188, 190, 191, 193, 220
Indian Tamil 167
Indo–Sri Lanka Peace Accord 190, 192
Indonesia 219, 220, 224, 238, 245, 247
INLA 79, 91
Institute for a Democratic Alternative for South Africa 66
insurgency, repression and peace 1–12
 constructing insurgency 4–6
 discourse and terror 2–4

Index 277

making peace 10–12
reading insurgency 8–10
state and terror 6–8
integrated rural development programme 191
Inter-American Commission 18
Interim Agreement (Oslo II) (1995) 127, 128, 129, 131, 132, 138, 139, 140
International Court of Justice (World Court) 250
International Criminal Court 264
International Monetary Fund 191
Interpellation 74
intifada 126, 127, 136
Intransigent Party 17
Iran 24, 159, 220, 233, 234, 247, 250, 251
Iraq 202, 211, 217, 220, 228, 229, 246, 247
IPKF 192
IRA 3, 33, 71–3, 75, 79, 82–3, 85–8, 90, 93
  Continuity 79, 93
  hunger strikers 4
  Real 79, 91
IRP 248
ISI 251
Islam/Muslims 6, 217–35, 248
  diversity in motion 219–23
  Ethiopia 113, 122
  localisation and globalisation 223–32
  Somalia 155, 157, 162
  Sri Lanka 171, 178, 188, 191, 192
Islamic fundamentalism 102, 221
Islamic Investment Companies (Egypt) 231
Islamic Jihad 127
Israel 72, 97, 217, 221, 228, 233, 255
Israeli Labour Party 141
Italy 121–2, 153, 154, 155, 160, 162, 256

Jamal, M. 136
Janke, P. 4
Japan 220, 243
Jaster, R.S. 60
Jaster, S.K. 60
Jayawardene, J.R. 168, 205
Jews 238, 256
jihad 155–6, 222, 228, 229, 230, 233
Johnson, R.W. 55
Jonassohn, K. 237–66
Jordan 218, 227
Judaism 220
Justicialist Party 17, 20
JVP 169, 170

Kaplan, R.D. 241, 242
Karam, A.M. 217–35
Kasrils, R. 62
Keane, J. 111
Kenya 153, 154, 157, 218, 221
Kepel, G. 223
Khattab, 'Umar bin al- 134
Khreisheh, Hassan 136
kidnappings 11
King, Rodney 239
Kondapalliseetharaman 192
Korea 251
Kosovo 248
Kritz, N.J. 264
Kumaratunga, President 185
Kuper, L. 55
Kurdish peoples 247
Kuwait 246, 249, 255
Kyoto summit 257

Labour Party 143
Lacan, J. 75
Laclau, E. 5, 7
Lange, J.P. de 59
language 29
Laplanche, J. 75
Laqueur, W. 3
Latin America 6, 11, 38, 45, 47, 48, 210
Lazerson, J. 65
Leadership Council 46
League of Brothers 59

Lebanon   218, 220, 228, 229, 247
Lechner, N.   7, 11
Leclaire, S.   75
Legal Resources Centre   66
Legassick, M.   56
Legislative Assembly   47
legitimacy issues   223
Lekota, Patrick   63, 65
Lemon, A.   58
Lenin, V.I./Leninism   24, 72
  see also Marxism–Leninism
Lewinsky, Monica   230
Lewis, I.M.   150, 152
liberalisation   14, 15, 29, 34
liberation   171
Liberation Cuckoos   192
Liberia   158, 244, 246
Liberty (National Council for Civil Liberties)   244
Libya   249–50
Lijphardt, A.   56
Likud regime   233
Little, D.   221
Lodge, T.   61, 63
London agreement (1991)   106
London peace negotiations (1991)   118
Loyalists   84, 85, 86, 93
LTTE   3, 169, 171–9 passim, 181, 182, 185, 186–93
Lyons, T.   106, 158

McCann, E.   91
McCarthy, C.   252
McClelland, M.   81
Macdonell, D.   2
McGlade, Charlie   75
McGuinness, Martin   80
McIntyre, A.   83–4
McKittrick, D.   80, 88
McLaughlin, M.   82
Macrae, J.   246
McThomas, H.   81
Maghreb   220
Mahanyake Theros   189
Mahattaya   186
Mahdi, Ali   165
Major, John   185, 244

Malaysia   181, 188, 191, 220, 224
Mallie, E.   73, 80, 88
Malvinas/Falklands War   15, 19, 20, 25–6, 207, 245, 249
Mandela, Nelson   61, 68, 161, 184, 189
Manipur   190, 191
Maoism   24
Maren, Michael   160–1
Markakis, J.   99, 100, 114
Marte, F.   155, 157
Marty, M.E.   220–1
Marx, A.   65
Marxism   22, 23, 24, 25, 27, 40, 56
  Ethiopia   99
  Northern Ireland   78
Marxism–Leninism   40, 47, 100
masculinity   201, 206, 207, 209, 210, 213, 214, 216
Mass Democratic Movement   66
material resources   115
materiality regime   4
Matthews, I.   204–5
Mbeki, G.   62
Mecca   229
MEDHINE   103
media   60, 194
Medina   229
MEISON   96, 106, 108, 112
Menelik II   121
Mengistu, Haile Mariam   96, 99, 101–2, 103–4, 109–10, 116–18
Mexico   17, 45
Middle East   72, 102, 187, 217, 228, 250, 251
militarism/militarisation   82, 85, 87, 157–8, 214–15
Mills, G.   62
Minear, L.   245
Ministry of Education   28
Mitterrand, François   245
MK   61–2
MLLT   104, 117
MNO   17
MNCPE   108
MNR   43, 47

mobilisation process 100
modernisation 57
Mohamoud, A.A. 148–65
Mohan group 171
Molyneux, M. 203
Montes, Mélida Anaya (alias 'Ana Maria') 43
Montoneros 21, 24
Moore, H. 206
Morocco 224
Moss, D. 9
Mothers of Plaza de Mayo (Argentina) 201, 207–12, 215
Mouffe, C. 4
Mozambique 160, 247
MPLA government 248
MPSC 43
Mubarak, Hosni 218
Mufson, S. 63
mujahideen 248
Mulholland, Liam 75
Multipartidaria 19
Multiple Party Assembly 18
Munck, G.L. 38–52
Munck, R. 1–12, 71–93
Muslim Brotherhood 219, 227, 230, 231
Muzaffar, C. 258

nación (nation) 25, 26
Nagaland 190, 191, 193
Nasser, Gamal Abdel 227
Nasson, B. 63
nation state 150, 152
National Being 19
National Education Crisis Committee 66
National Socialist Council of Nagaland 193
National Union of Mineworkers 65
National Union of South African Students 60
national unity 116
nationalism 5, 73, 242
  Albanian 248
  Argentina 24, 26
  Ethiopia 99, 100, 111

Northern Ireland 75, 76, 77, 79, 89, 90, 92, 93
Serb 221
South Africa 54–5, 56, 57
Sri Lanka 171
Nationality 19
NATO 81, 221, 233, 251
Natshe, Mustafa 129
Nederveen Pieterse, J.P. 225
Nedumaran, P. 192
Netanyahu, Binhamin 125, 136, 137, 138, 139, 140, 141, 142–3, 233
Netherlands 160, 167
New Zealand 187, 188
Nicaragua 40, 44, 45, 203, 247
Nigeria 157
no-warning bombs 11
non governmental organisations 66, 246, 253, 254, 263
non-racialism 63, 66, 68
Norman, R. 239–40
North Africa 187, 217, 220, 250
North America 145, 187, 217, 220, 223
  see also Canada; United States
Northern Assembly 92
Northern Ireland 3, 9, 71–93
  endgame 92–3
  method 73–4
  Republican currents 78–83
  Republican discourse 75–8
  Republicanism and the British state 83–6
  Republicans and peace 86–91
Norton, A. 84
Norval, A. 63, 65
Norway 188
Norwegian Observer Group 108
NP 55, 58, 59, 60, 67, 68
NSC 162, 165
Nuremberg War Trials 256
Nye, J.S. Jr 241–2

OAU 153, 164
O Brádaigh, Ruairi 80
O'Brien, B. 73, 80, 88
O'Donnell, G. 15, 18
O'Donnell, Peadar 75

Ogaden war (1977)   155, 156
Ogadenis   99, 110, 111, 113
O'Halloran, C.   79
OLF   96, 100, 102, 103, 105, 106, 107–8, 114
Ollier, M.M.   14–36
Olmert, Ehud   129
Omaar, R.   161
Omagh bombing   91
O'Malley, P.   87
Omar, M.O.   156\
ONC   103
ONLF   103, 105, 106, 109, 114
OPDO   96, 101, 110
ORDEN   39
O'Meara, D.   57, 58
organisational unity   77
Oromos   99, 110, 111, 113
Orwell, George   80
OSCE   251, 253
Osman, Mohamed Sheikh   161
Ossetia   248
O'Sullivan, G.   3

PA   184, 185, 186
PAC   59, 61
Pakistan   218, 220, 221, 222, 239
Palestine   88, 218, 219, 227–8, 229, 233, 250
  Communist Party   136
Palestine Liberation Organisation   125, 126, 127, 128, 130, 132, 133, 140, 144
  Executive Committee   134
Palestinian Authority and Israeli rule   125–47
Palestinian Council   127, 134–5, 136
Palestinian Executive Authority   127
Palestinian Legislative Council   135
Palestinian People's Party   136
Palestinian Supreme Court   134
Pan Am flight 103 bombing   249–50
Pandor, N.   66
Paracel Islands   251

Paris Peace and Reconciliation Conference (1993)   112
Parsons, W.S.   238
Patterson, H.   77, 78
PCS   39, 40, 42, 47
PD   47, 48, 60
peace accord (1992)   44, 46
peace processes   10–12
  El Salvador   44–6
  Northern Ireland   71, 85, 86–91
  see also insurgency, repression and peace; peacemaking; reconciliation; women, war and peace
peacemaking, conflict management and humanitarian action   237–66
  boom or bust   240–4
  context   244–50
  future agendas for change   256–63
  political violence and civilisational process   239–40
  weapons overproduction   250–3
Peach, C.   219
Pêcheux, M.   2, 74
Peiris, G.L.   185
Peres, Shimon   127, 137, 138, 141, 143
Perón, María Estela Martínez de   6, 15, 17
Peronism   15, 17, 24
Pettman, J.J.   202, 205, 211
PFLP   136
PFP   60
Philippines   217
physical force ideology   5
Physicians for Human Rights   262
Pick, D.   242–3
Pierre, A.J.   252–3
Pinochet, General Augusto   247, 256
PKK   3
Plaza Libertad massacre   39, 40
PLOTE   171, 197
political groups   63

political identity   4, 5, 9, 201, 204, 212
  Argentina   15, 20–1
  women   206–12
political pluralism   30
political prisoners   17
political rape   239
political sphere   14, 21–6, 34
political terrorism   2
politics of difference   6
Population Registration Act 1950   55
Porteñazo   15, 18, 19, 25
Portugal   167
power   4, 7, 9, 224
Prabhakaran, Velupillai   169, 186–7, 189, 190–1, 192, 193
Premadasa, Ranasinghe   170, 190
Preventative Security Agency   134
Preventative Security Force   139
Price, R.   63
Priebke, Erik   256
Prisk, C.E.   42
private pursuit (spoils politics)   151–2
private sphere   14, 29, 30–4
productive power   224
professional associations   66
Prohibition of Mixed Marriages Act 1949   55
Protestant Fundamentalism   220
Protestantism   71, 82, 84, 89, 220
Protocol Concerning the Redeployment in Hebron   141
Provisionals (Provos)   72
PRT/ERP   21, 24
PRTC   24, 42, 47
psychotherapy   30–3
public expression   194
public pursuit   153
public sphere   14, 26–30, 34
pueblo (people)   25, 26
Purdie, B.   78
PWG   192

Rabah, J.   135, 136

Rabbani, M.   125–47
Rabin, Yitzhak   125, 127, 141, 143
Radical Party   17, 20
Raghu (Archchunan)   172, 178–9
ra'is   133
Rasik group   171
Ratwatte, Anuruddha   173
Reagan, R.   44
realos (realist)   79, 80, 81
reconciliation and peace-related conferences   163–4, 165
recruitment   78
religious fundamentalism   115, 241–2
religious groups/organisations   63, 66
repression   30, 99, 116
  see also insurgency, repression and peace
Republicans/Republicanism   4, 5, 72–3, 74, 75, 83, 92, 93
  see also Irish Republican Army (IRA)
Restoration Ecologists   3
revolutionary ideology   31
Richmond, A.H.   241
Rivera, Colonel   39
RN   40, 42, 47
Roberts, A.   253
Robertson, R.   224, 225–6
Rolston, B.   75, 76, 77
Roosens, E.   114–15
Ross, Dennis   145
Roy, S.   131
RUC   80
Ruddick, S.   210, 213
Ruedy, J.   223
Rwanda   114, 244, 245–6, 254, 255–6, 261, 262, 264
Ryan, M.   88, 89

SACP   59
Sadat, Anwar   217
SADF   60, 62
Sageme   117
Sahnoun, M.   148, 161
Said, Edward W.   133, 227
Salih, 'Abd-al-Jawad   134, 135

Samatar, Abdi, I. 150, 152
Samatar, Ahmed I. 150, 158
Samatar, S.S. 150
Sandinista 45
Sands, B. 76
Santucho, R. 21
Sardar, Z. 258
Sarraj, Iyad al- 133
Saudi Arabia 131, 212, 228, 229
Savir, Uri 145
Sayyid, B. 5–6
Schlemmer, L. 56
Schmitter, P. 18
Schrire, R. 58
Schutte, G. 59
Scott, A. 79
Scott, C. 245
SDLP 90
secession 110, 111
Sechaba, T. 62
Second International 77
self-determination 109, 110, 116, 117, 143, 145
  Somalia 153
  Sri Lanka 171
separatism 167, 171
SEPDU 108, 111–12
September 1996 rebellion 139
Serbs 192, 221, 228, 248
sexuality 30
shabiba movement 138–9
Shanahan, C. 133, 135, 136
Sharon, Ariel 125, 137
Shear, M. 60
Shi'a 233
Shingler, J. 58
Showa 98
Sidamas 99, 111
Sierra Leone 244, 246, 254
Sikhism 220
Singapore 188, 191
Sinhala Buddhists 182, 188
Sinhala Christians 182
Sinhalese 167–8, 170, 172, 176, 178–81, 188, 191–2
Sinn Féin 72, 77, 79, 82, 85, 87, 88, 90, 92
  European Parliament 81

Scenario for Peace 88
Towards a Lasting Peace 88–9
Sjogren, E. 262
Slovenia 248
Slovo, J. 62
SLPF 168
Smith, M.L.R. 6, 8, 73
Social Republicanism 83
Socialism 5, 24, 75, 77, 87, 88, 256
El Salvador 39–43, 46–9
Socialist Party 17, 45
Socialist revolutionary movements 202–4
Somalia 103, 111, 114, 115, 148–65, 254
  Cold war and 'humanitarian' intervention 156–63
  state fragmentation 150–6; colonialism, deleterious effects of 153–6
Sørbø G.M. 246
Soros (Open Society) Foundation 191
Sosnowski, S. 28
South Africa 11, 23, 54–68, 140, 145
  'black' politics 60–7
  and Northern Ireland 72, 80, 88
  and Sri Lanka 184, 189, 193
  Truth Commissions 264
  'white' politics 57–60
South African Council of Churches 60
South African Institute of Race Relations 60
South African Truth and Reconciliation Commission 194
South America 158, 220
South Asia 168, 192
South East Asia 187, 191, 192, 193, 247, 258
South West Africa 238
Southern African Catholic Bishops Conference 60
Southern Ethiopian Political Parties 105

Spain   3, 17, 256
Spielberg, Steven   240
Spratly Islands   251
Sri Lanka   167–99, 221
  alternative futures, basis for 182–6
  conflict and beyond: narrative perspectives   171–81
  viable future, foundations for 193–5
  see also Sinhalese; Tamil
Stalinist party   117
Stanley, W.   39
state fragmentation   150–6
State Security Courts   134
state and terror   6–8
STF   177
Stiehm, J.   202
Stremlau, J.   255
student movements and youth groups   60, 63, 66
sub-Saharan Africa   153, 154, 155, 157, 158
subjectivity   4, 33
Sudan   102–3, 117, 159, 218–21, 227–9, 233–4
Suharto, Thojib N.J.   247
Sunni   233
Suttner, R.   61
Sweden   17
Swilling, M.   80–1
Switzerland   188
Syria   247, 250

Taiwan   251
Tajikistan   248
Taliban   218, 222, 251
Tamil   168, 170, 172, 176, 178–9, 181–2, 185, 187–90, 192–3, 262
Tamil Nadu   192
Tamil Nadu Kamaraj Congress   192
Tamil nationalism   171
TAND   103
Tanzania   218, 221
Taylor, R.   54–68
TELO   171, 174, 197
terror   6–8

terror and discourse   2–4
terrorism   3, 5, 11
TGE   107, 108–9
Thailand   188, 191, 193
Thambi (Premanatha)   172, 173–4
Thamilar Pasarai (or Tamilian Camp)   192
Thatcher, Margaret   215
Theodorus, Archbishop   134
Thiagu   192
Thileepan Foundation   192
think-tanks   66
Tibet   247
Tigers   *see* Liberation Tigers of Tamil Eelam
Tigrayan peasant uprising (1943)   100
Tigrayans   99
Tirman, J.   252
TLF   100
TNO   100
TNRT   192
Toffler, A.   241
Toffler, H.   241
Tone, Wolfe   93
Toolis, K.   73, 76–7
Totten, S.   238
TPDM   106
TPLF   97–104 *passim*, 106, 109–13, 116–17, 119–20
TRC   184
traditionalist line of approach 150–1, 152
transformationist school of thought   150–1
transparency   194
Transparency International   193
Treurnicht, A.   67
Tripura   190, 191
Trotskyism   24
Truth Commissions   264
TTE   103, 108
Tunisia   224
Tupamaros   203
Turkestan, Eastern   228
Turkey   247, 251
Tutsi population   245

Ubaldini 17
UDF 63, 65, 66
Uganda 103, 264
Ukraine 160, 238, 252
Ul Haq, General Zia 168
ULFA 193
Ulster unionism 84
Unabomber 3
Ungo, Guillermo 45
Unionism 84, 89, 91, 92
Unionists 93
UNITA 248
United Nations 89, 191, 217
  Disarmament Affairs 260
  High Commission for Human Rights 260
  High Commission for Refugees 260
  Human Rights Committee 244
  peacemaking, conflict management and humanitarian action 246, 248, 251, 253, 256, 258, 259-60
  Security Council 260
  Security Council Resolution 242 143
  and Somalia 148, 149, 157, 158-9, 160-1, 164
United States 23, 44, 246, 250, 253
  arms trade 252
  Asian diasporas 243
  Congress and Senate 138, 256, 257
  and Ethiopia 97, 102, 103, 104, 106, 113, 118
  foreign policy 257
  gender issues 202, 211-12
  and Grenada 247
  and Iraq 258-9
  Islam/Muslims 217, 219, 221, 222, 228, 229, 230, 233, 234
  Israel and Palestinian Authority 132, 142, 143-4
  Mexicans 243
  and Northern Ireland 88, 92, 93
  and Somalia 148, 149, 154, 157, 158-9
  and Sri Lanka 188
  State Department 249
  Universities Security Agency 134
UNP 168, 185, 186
unproductive power 224
Urban, M. 85
Uruguay 264
  Tupamaros 203
Usher, G. 126, 134

Valencia, M.J. 251
Van Creveld, M. 1
van den Berghe, P. 55
van Diepen, M. 63
Van Loon, B. 258
vecinazos 20
Veerapandian, Suba 192
verkamptes (reactionary Afrikaner nationalists) 57, 67
verligtes (enlightened Afrikaner nationalists) 58
Vertovec, S. 219
Verwoerd, H.E. 55
Vickers, J. 205, 212
Videla, Jorge Rafhael 6
Vietnam 40
Villalobos, Joaquín 47
Viola, E. 15, 16, 18, 19
Visker, R. 3
voluntary organisations 66

Waal, A. de 161
Waldmeir, P. 57, 59
Walle, N. van de 158
war crimes 115
Ward, M. 73
Wardlaw, G. 2
Waters, M. 225, 226
Waylen, G. 202-3, 210
Wazir, Intisar al- 131
weapons overproduction 250-3
Weber, Max 80
Webster, D. 66
Weiss, T.G. 245
Weizmann, Ezer 138
West Africa 187

West Bank   125–31 *passim*, 135, 136, 138, 139, 142, 144
Western Europe   132, 153, 181, 257
'white' politics   54, 57–60
White, R.   73, 78
White Warriors Union (UGB)   39
Whitehead, L.   18
Wickremasinghe, Ranil   185
Wilkinson, P.   3
Wilson, A.J.   169
Winkler, R.   66
Winston Foundation for World Peace   252
Wohlgemuth, L.   246
women, war and peace   5, 73, 201–16
  gendering and political identity formation   206–12
  negotiation and/or assimilation   212–16
  women and war   202–6
women's organisations   5, 63, 66
Woollacott, A.   204, 207, 212–13, 214, 216
workers' groups   63
World Bank   191, 193
Woyane revolt   98–9

Yasin, Shaikh Ahmad   136
Yemen   162
Yusuf, Abdullahi   165

Zaalouk, M.   231
Zac, L.   7
Zaire   158, 245
Zakaria, F.   242
Zamora, Rubén   45
ZANU   61
Zartman, W.   10–11
Zawahin, Ayman al-   221
Zawahiri, A. al-   222
Zenawi, Meles   101–4, 106–7, 109, 112, 114–15, 117, 119–21